Advances in
LIBRARIANSHIP

Volume 12

Advances in
LIBRARIANSHIP

Edited by
WESLEY SIMONTON
University of Minnesota
Minneapolis, Minnesota

Volume 12

1982

ACADEMIC PRESS
A Subsidiary of Harcourt Brace Jovanovich, Publishers
New York   London
Paris   San Diego   San Francisco   São Paulo   Sydney   Tokyo   Toronto

COPYRIGHT © 1982, BY ACADEMIC PRESS, INC.
ALL RIGHTS RESERVED.
NO PART OF THIS PUBLICATION MAY BE REPRODUCED OR
TRANSMITTED IN ANY FORM OR BY ANY MEANS, ELECTRONIC
OR MECHANICAL, INCLUDING PHOTOCOPY, RECORDING, OR ANY
INFORMATION STORAGE AND RETRIEVAL SYSTEM, WITHOUT
PERMISSION IN WRITING FROM THE PUBLISHER.

ACADEMIC PRESS, INC.
111 Fifth Avenue, New York, New York 10003

United Kingdom Edition published by
ACADEMIC PRESS, INC. (LONDON) LTD.
24/28 Oval Road, London NW1 7DX

LIBRARY OF CONGRESS CATALOG CARD NUMBER: 79-88675

ISBN 0-12-024612-0

PRINTED IN THE UNITED STATES OF AMERICA

82 83 84 85   9 8 7 6 5 4 3 2 1

Contents

Contributors.. ix
Preface... xi
Contents of Previous Volumes.................................... xv

The Demographic and Economic Status of Librarians in the 1970s, with Special Reference to Women

KATHLEEN M. HEIM

I.	Introduction.....................................	2
II.	Broader Definitions of Library Work................	2
III.	The Library Work Universe.........................	4
IV.	Association Surveys...............................	13
V.	Type of Institution Studies.........................	26
VI.	Surveys of Information Professionals................	40
VII.	Conclusion.......................................	42
	References..	42

Personnel Planning, Job Analysis, and Job Evaluation, with Special Reference to Academic Libraries

SHEILA CRETH

I.	Personnel Planning and Utilization	48
II.	Job Analysis	56
III.	Job Evaluation	73
IV.	Conclusions	91
	References	94

The Role of Information in Governmental Planning

COLLEEN L. COGHLAN

I.	Introduction	99
II.	Governmental Deliberative Activities	100
III.	Health Planning and Resources Development (Public Law 96–79)	106
IV.	Deliberated Government Documents: A Bibliographic Chain	119
V.	Conclusion	125
	References	125

The Journal Literature of Librarianship

RICHARD D. JOHNSON

I.	Introduction	127
II.	The Journals	128
III.	Subjects and Methodologies	132
IV.	Authorship	134
V.	Critical Reception of the Literature	138
VI.	Editor and Author	140
VII.	Interest of the Profession in Writing	143
VIII.	Book Reviewing	145
IX.	Indexing and Abstracting Services	146

X.	Conclusion	147
	References	148

A Guide for Searching in Anglo-American Main Entry Catalogs

ELIZABETH L. TATE

I.	Catalogs and Catalog Codes	151
II.	Bibliographic Citations	152
III.	Changing Main Entry Patterns	153
IV.	Conclusion	171
	References	172

The Colonial Legacy in West African Libraries: A Comparative Analysis

MARY N. MAACK

I.	Methodology and Background	174
II.	The Colonial Era: 1890–1945	183
III.	Decolonization: 1945–1960	199
IV.	The Colonial Legacy: A Comparative Analysis	231
	References	240

Information Access by Blind and Physically Handicapped Persons

ALFRED D. HAGLE

I.	Introduction	248
II.	Frequency of Impairment	248
III.	Resources and Services	250
IV.	Bibliographic Control	271
V.	International Cooperation	272
VI.	Conclusion	273
	References	274

Beyond the Master's Program: Library Schools and Continuing Education of Library, Media, and Information Professionals

JOHN A. MCCROSSAN

I.	Introduction	278
II.	Definitions	279
III.	Amount and Types of Continuing Education Opportunities Offered by Library Schools	280
IV.	The Relationship of Other Agencies to Library School Continuing Education Activities	285
V.	Priority for Continuing Education	289
VI.	Conclusions	291
	References	291

Subject Index 295

Contributors

Numbers in parentheses indicate the pages on which the authors' contributions begin.

Colleen L. Coghlan[1] (99), Health Planning Unit, Minnesota Department of Energy, Planning and Development, St. Paul, Minnesota 55101

Sheila Creth[2] (47), University of Connecticut Library, Storrs, Connecticut 06268.

Alfred D. Hagle (247), Public Resources Officer, National Library Service for the Blind and Physically Handicapped, Library of Congress, Washington, D.C. 20540

Kathleen M. Heim (1), Graduate School of Library and Information Science, University of Illinois, Urbana, Illinois 61801

Richard D. Johnson (127), State University of New York, College at Oneonta, Oneonta, New York 13820

Mary N. Maack[3] (173), Library School, University of Minnesota, Minneapolis, Minnesota 55455

John A. McCrossan (277), Graduate Department of Library, Media, and Information Studies, University of South Florida, Tampa, Florida 33620

Elizabeth L. Tate (151), Rockville, Maryland 20852

---

[1]Present address: Metropolitan State University, St. Paul, Minnesota 55101.

[2]Present address: University of Michigan Library, Ann Arbor, Michigan 48109.

[3]Present address: Ecole Nationale Supérieure des Bibliothèques, 17–21, Bd du 11 Novembre 1918, 69100 Villeurbanne, France.

Preface

As with other volumes in this series, the present volume includes a number of contributions reflecting several dimensions of librarianship. Kathleen M. Heim reviews the major sources of information relating to the demographic characteristics and economic status of librarians and other information-handling professionals in an attempt to discover patterns of economic discrimination and intraoccupational segregation based on sex. Drawing data from a large number of surveys of associations, studies of specific types of institutions, and surveys of information professionals, she finds that the task is complicated by problems relating to the definition of the field, by the recent expansion of the limits of librarianship, and by the need for additional economic and demographic data. She concludes that "a decade of activism on the part of women librarians has resulted in no clear improvement of status."

Developments of recent years, including equal employment and affirmative action legislation, budgetary restraints, rapid social and technological change, and demands for pay equity and comparability, are discussed by Sheila Creth as background for the assertion of an increased need for personnel planning in academic libraries. She provides a detailed analysis of the procedures of job analysis and job evaluation as essential to the identification of planning strategies to be developed by library administrators.

Colleen L. Coghlan considers the role of information in governmental planning, focusing on deliberative activities and the documents generated in the process. Working within the context of the models of Havelock and

Lippitt, she seeks to rationalize the processes by which executive agency deliberations occur. Her description of the process established in the National Health Planning and Resources Development Act leads to the identification of a sequence of documents that is compared with the products or documents presented in two models of the scientific communication process by Garvey and Griffith and by Doyle and Grimes.

The journals of librarianship, constituting the major medium for prompt communication of professional information in the field, are reviewed by Richard D. Johnson. Concentrating on journals serving librarians, with some attention to related journals in information science, he provides information on the number and variety of journals, qualifications of authors, editorial procedures and acceptance–rejection rates, patterns of publication, and degrees of bibliographic control provided through indexing–abstracting services.

It is generally recognized that computerization has brought a basic change to the library catalog and that January 1981 may be viewed as the beginning of a new era—the era of the "online" catalog with increased access points as compared with the traditional card and book catalog. An ever-increasing number of libraries are providing online access to all or to major portions of their resources, but until the several million entries of the *National Union Catalog: Pre-1956 Imprints* are converted to machine-readable format, scholars and librarians must be familiar with a catalog that essentially provides only a single entry for each item listed, an entry chosen in conformity with the theory of "main entry" as set forth in the Anglo-American cataloging tradition. Elizabeth L. Tate has prepared a guide to this tradition, as embodied in the five catalog codes whose rules govern the choice and form of the entries in the *National Union Catalog* and similar catalogs.

The interest of *Advances in Librarianship* in international librarianship is continued by Mary N. Maack's analysis of the pattern of library service that has emerged in the recently independent states of West Africa. For four countries of the area, she has identified the relevant economic, social, political, and educational factors of the colonial periods and the period of decolonization that have resulted in markedly different approaches to national library planning based on the several national heritages, modified to serve the needs of rapidly changing societies.

In his consideration of information access by blind and physically handicapped persons, Alfred D. Hagle first defines the population of persons suffering from a "handicap" or an "impairment" and enumerates the major resources and services available, with special reference to the National Library Service for the Blind and Physically Handicapped of the Library of Congress. The major portion of his work is devoted to consideration of technological developments, particularly in braille production and tactile

Preface

technology, tangible graphic displays, and direct access reading aids. Attention is also given to bibliographic control and to international cooperation.

In recent years, the rapidity of technological change (*vide* the development of computerized bibliographic data bases) and the necessity for development of new managerial skills in a period of financial exigency have created an ever-growing demand for continuing education opportunities. Among the agencies responsible for providing such opportunities, the library school has traditionally been the most important. John A. McCrossan surveys the role of the library school in this activity, with consideration of the role of the basic curriculum and of special opportunities outside the basic curriculum. He relates the activities of the school to other providers of continuing education such as library associations and state library agencies and libraries, and he forecasts increasing attention to continuing education by the schools in a period of declining enrollment of new students.

Contents of Previous Volumes

Volume 1

The Machine and Cataloging
  George Piternick
Mechanization of Acquisitions Processes
  Connie R. Dunlap
Mechanization and Library Filing Rules
  Kelley L. Cartwright
Standards for Technical Service Cost Studies
  Helen Welch Tuttle
The Undergraduate Library Trend at Large Universities
  Robert H. Muller
The Changing School Library: An Instructional Media Center
  Chase Dane
Reference Service to Children—Past, Present, and Future
  Lillian K. Orsini
Progress in Bibliotherapy
  Ruth M. Tews
Effectiveness in Cooperation and Consolidation in Public Libraries
  Ralph Blasingame and Ernest R. DeProspo, Jr.
Library Planning: The Challenge of Change
  Robert E. Kemper
Acceleration of Library Development in Developing Countries
  Carl M. White
SUBJECT INDEX

Volume 2

Access to Information
  William S. Budington
Control and Dissemination of Information in Medicine
  David Bishop
The Computer in Serials Processing and Control
  Don L. Bosseau
Micropublication
  Allen B. Veaner
The Changing Role of the State Library
  Kenneth E. Beasley
Censorship, Intellectual Freedom, and Libraries
  Edwin Castagna

Reader Services to the Disadvantaged in Inner Cities
Margaret E. Monroe

Oral History: Problems and Prospects
Louis M. Starr

Armageddon in International Copyright: Review of the Berne Convention, the Universal Convention, and the Present Crisis in International Copyright
Dorothy M. Schrader

AUTHOR INDEX—SUBJECT INDEX

Volume 3

On Beyond 999Z—Patterns of Library Service to Children of the Poor
Binnie L. Tate

Youth as a Special Client Group
James W. Liesener and Margaret E. Chisholm

The Emergence of the Community College Library
Harriett Genung and James O. Wallace

Teaching Library Skills to College Students
Miriam Dudley

Academic Library Buildings in the United Kingdom
H. Faulkner Brown

Academic Library Buildings in the United States
Ralph E. Ellsworth

Federal Grants and Public Libraries
James G. Igoe

Anglo-American Code Implementation
Elizabeth L. Tate

Catalog Use Studies and Their Implications
James Krikelas

Converting Bibliographic Data to Machine Form
Don Sherman

Archive and Manuscript Collections
Robert L. Brubaker

AUTHOR INDEX—SUBJECT INDEX

Volume 4

MARC and Its Applications to Library Automation
Roy B. Torkington

Selective Dissemination of Information
Georg R. Mauerhoff

Circulation Automation
Hugh C. Atkinson

Social Responsibility and Libraries
Arthur Curley

Women in Librarianship
Anita R. Schiller

The Use of Resources in the Learning Experience
Johnnie Givens

Reading as Information Processing
John J. Geyer and Paul A. Kolers

SUBJECT INDEX

Volume 5

International Information Systems
Jacques Tocatlian

National Planning for Library and Information Services
Foster E. Mohrhardt and Carlos Victor Penna

Statistics that Describe Libraries and Library Service
Thomas Childers

Coordination of the Technical Services
Helen Welch Tuttle

Trends in Library Education—United States
Lester Asheim

The Technologies of Education and Communication
Gerald R. Brong

Audiovisual Services in Libraries
Irving Lieberman

Sound Recordings
Gordon Stevenson

Joint Academic Libraries
Richard D. Johnson

AUTHOR INDEX—SUBJECT INDEX

Volume 6

Performance Measures for School Librarians; Complexities and Potential
Evelyn H. Daniel

Productivity Measurement in Academic Libraries
Thomas J. Waldhart and Thomas P. Marcum

Relevance: A Review of the Literature and a Framework for Thinking on the Notion in Information Science
Tefko Saracevic

The Impact of Reading on Human Behavior: The Implications of Communications Research
Roger Haney, Michael H. Harris, and Leonard Tipton

Trends in Library Education—Europe
Donald Davinson

The Role of Middle Managers in Libraries
Beverly P. Lynch

AUTHOR INDEX—SUBJECT INDEX

Volume 7

Vocabulary Control in Information Retrieval Systems
F. W. Lancaster

Major Developments in Classification
Ingetraut Dahlberg

National Libraries in Developing Countries
Simeon B. Aje

The American Library Association and the Library Association: Retrospect, Problems, and Prospects
W. A. Munford

Popular Culture and the Public Library
Gordon Stevenson

Public Library Use, Users, Uses: Advances in Knowledge of the Characteristics and Needs of the Adult Clientele of American Public Libraries
Douglas Zweizig and Brenda Dervin

Personal Roles and Barriers in Information Transfer
Anne Wilkin

The Applications of Citation Analyses to Library Collection Building
Robert N. Broadus

AUTHOR INDEX—SUBJECT INDEX

Volume 8

Collection Development in Large University Libraries
Rose Mary Magrill and Mona East

The Library of Congress in American Life
John Y. Cole

Affirmative Action and American Librarianship
Elizabeth Dickinson and Margaret Myers

American Indian Library Service
Charles T. Townley

Advances in American Library History
David Kaser

Trends in Library Education—Canada
John P. Wilkinson

Continuing Education for Librarians in the United States
Elizabeth W. Stone

SUBJECT INDEX

Volume 9

Intellectual Freedom in Librarianship: Advances and Retreats
David K. Berninghausen

User Fees in Publicly Funded Libraries
Thomas J. Waldhart and Trudi Bellardo

The Evaluation of Paraprofessional Library Employees
Charles W. Evans

Measuring Library Effectiveness: A Review and an Assessment
Rosemary Ruhig Du Mont and Paul F. Du Mont

Operations Research in Libraries
Abraham Bookstein and Karl Kocher

Funding Support for Research in Librarianship
George W. Whitbeck, Jean Major, and Herbert S. White

Advances in Medical Librarianship
Donald D. Hendricks

Advances in Australian Library Services
Carmel Maguire

SUBJECT INDEX

Volume 10

AACR 2: Antecedents, Assumptions, Implementation
Wesley Simonton

Academic Library Management Studies: From Games to Leadership
H. William Axford

And Gladly Teach: Bibliographic Instruction and the Library
Arthur P. Young

Library Materials Budgeting in the Private University Library: Austerity and Action
Frederick C. Lynden

Individual Decision Theory: An Overview
James D. Sodt

Library Education in India, Pakistan, and Bangladesh
P. B. Mangla

SUBJECT INDEX

CUMULATIVE SUBJECT INDEX VOLUMES 1–10

Volume 11

The Cultural Role of the Public Library
Margaret E. Monroe

Extended Library Education Programs in the United States
Edward G. Holley

Networking and School Media Centers
Joann V. Rogers

Libraries, Users, and Librarians: Continuing Efforts to Define the Nature and Extent of Public Library Use
Michael H. Harris and James Sodt

Advances in Reference Services
Kay Murray

Music Librarianship in the United States
Gordon Stevenson

SUBJECT INDEX

The Demographic and Economic Status of Librarians in the 1970s, with Special Reference to Women

KATHLEEN M. HEIM

University of Illinois at Urbana–Champaign

I.	Introduction	2
II.	Broader Definitions of Library Work	2
III.	The Library Work Universe	4
	A. Comprehensive Census Analyses	4
	B. New Graduates	5
IV.	Association Surveys	13
	A. American Library Association	13
	B. American Society for Information Science	16
	C. Special Libraries Association	18
	D. Society of American Archivists	19
	E. American Association of Law Libraries	21
	F. Music Library Association	24
	G. Association for Educational Communications and Technology	25
V.	Type of Institution Studies	26
	A. Academic Libraries	26
	B. Public Libraries	30
	C. School Libraries	34
	D. State Libraries and Agencies	36
	E. Library of Congress	36
	F. Library Science Faculty	37
	G. Medical Libraries	39
VI.	Surveys of Information Professionals	40
VII.	Conclusion	42
	References	42

Copyright © 1982 by Academic Press, Inc.
All rights of reproduction in any form reserved.
ISBN 0-12-024612-0

I. INTRODUCTION

The status of women in libraries first came under serious scrutiny by library work-force analysts such as Anita Schiller (1969a, 1969b, 1969c, 1970, 1974) in the late 1960s. Library women had long been aware of their depressed status within the profession, but there was little information available to corroborate this impression. The requirements of affirmative action, demands that data include breakdowns by sex and race, and the work of a number of researchers—often with a feminist perspective—have converged during the 1970s to generate a body of statistical information concerning the economic and social status of women in the library work force. We still do not have a complete understanding of the composition of this work force, but we can now make many more valid statements regarding patterns of economic discrimination and intraoccupational segregation.

The term "intraoccupational segregation" characterizes a single occupation which exhibits different career tracks for men and women. In librarianship, the pattern is clear both for specialization by library type and job function. The percentage of men engaged in academic librarianship is much greater than the percentage of men in the total profession, and women clearly dominate in school and children's services positions. Major administrative posts in all types of libraries are held by men nearly three times as often as their proportion of the total work force would suggest, while women cluster in the lower levels of the organizational hierarchy. A dual career pattern for male and female librarians emerges as a central fact in any study of the library work force.

The absence of a single set of demographic indices to describe the library profession is a major obstacle to studies of the library work force. Each new scholar must piece together incompatible reports and surveys in order to begin to develop a research model for a particular problem. This essay is an attempt to summarize present knowledge of the demographic characteristics of librarians and information-related professionals, with special attention to the relative status of men and women in the profession. It is hoped that *lacunae* pointed out in this essay will draw attention to areas in which more current data are needed. The collection of data in certain sectors over time will provide a base from which longitudinal observations may be made.

II. BROADER DEFINITIONS OF LIBRARY WORK

The limits of librarianship expand continually. As new technological advancements require greater skills and techniques of the librarian and as the opportunities for nontraditional careers increase, the delineation of field-specific demographic data becomes more difficult. Just as the incorporation of nonprint media in the human record demanded that librarians develop visual as well as print literacy, so the incorporation of computer-assisted information operations requires that librarians become conversant with electronic information transfer. For the researcher of the library work force, the expansion of the field's responsibilities raises questions about the limits of the demographic data to be gathered.

At its broadest, the information profession has been estimated at 1.64 million individuals working in industry, in federal, state, and local governments, and in colleges and universities, in a survey by the University of Pittsburgh that collected facts on the organization and data on the specific institutional subunits in which information professionals were located, their occupational titles, and their primary work function (University of Pittsburgh, 1980). Although data were not gathered on the race or sex of information professionals, this is an important study because of the expansion of the work place for librarians inherent in the definitions.

The survey defined work fields for the information professional by aggregating job titles into nine categories: computer, education and training, financial, information services, library, management support, research, statistical, and technical publications. Those in the "library" work field accounted for 10% of the total number of information professionals (University of Pittsburgh, 1980, p. 35). However, other work fields described clearly include job functions which can be performed by those with library training. The blurring at the edges of carefully defined job categories for librarians is underscored, not only by this survey, but by recent discussions of expanding opportunities in business and industry for library school graduates ("Placements and Salaries," 1981) and of media graduates (Sink, 1980). Perhaps the most perspicacious observations on the expansion of job opportunities for those with library training are to be found in Sellen's *What Else You Can Do with a Library Degree,* which rests on the premise that librarians have many special and widely useful skills and should no longer define themselves in relation to a specific institution but rather in terms of their abilities. Sellen presents discussions by developers of independent information services, researchers for corporations, administrators, library suppliers, media consultants, publishers, indexers, and freelancers. The volume concludes with the observation by Albrecht and Redfield that the profession will be profoundly affected as there are a greater number of jobs available in nontraditional areas for students completing their training in library and information science (Sellen, 1980, pp. 330–331). The library work force analyst in the 1980s will be required to keep in mind the expanding limits of work for the library-science-trained professional. By all indications, this is the growth edge of library work and the one about which there is the least information. This paper presents available data concerning the less well-defined areas of work for which library training is a possible requisite, but focuses, in the main, on more traditional settings.

III. THE LIBRARY WORK UNIVERSE

A. Comprehensive Census Analyses

Until the 1980 census data are available, the baseline information used to discuss the broadest possible universe of library employment will remain the 1970 census data as analyzed in a U.S. Bureau of Labor Statistics (BLS) report (1975). Although these data are old, they remain the source of the most often quoted information for the universe of librarians and will become even more important for comparative studies as the 1980 data are released and analyzed. The report identifies and describes factors influencing personnel needs and develops projections of demands for library personnel. The biggest problem with the report relates to definition of "librarian." Since census data were self-reported, there was no requirement that only holders of the professional master's degree in library science respond. The study notes that no more than 40–50% in the universe held the professional degree (U.S. Bureau of Labor Statistics, 1975, p. 16). This limitation makes it difficult to compare the data with the findings of Learmont's studies of graduates from American Library Association (ALA) accredited master's programs, and underscores the profession's difficulty in defining "librarian." The high number of school personnel in the report (45%), most of whom are not required to hold the professional degree to practice in school settings, confounds the work force analyst whose research is made continually difficult by the various educational backgrounds by which one may achieve a position labeled "librarian." The BLS report describes the 1970 library work force as overwhelmingly (92%) white, 84% female, and the women as older than the men. Because these data are old, they will not be discussed in detail here but will be used in discussions of more discrete studies to make observations about these studies' relationship to the larger universe of librarians. It must be kept in mind that those unfamiliar with the complexities of the library work arena will use these data without recourse to the qualifications one familiar with the field might make. For many purposes, such as studies done by general labor analysts, the BLS report presents the library universe.

At present, an update to the BLS report is being developed by King Research. The conceptual paper that will undergird the update outlines reasons why library staffing must be reexamined. In addition to automation, tax-limitation measures, and declines in library school enrollments, the growth of women's labor force participation is cited as of major importance (DeWath and Cooper, 1980). The conceptual paper delineates the intended major products of the projected study:

1. projections of the supply and demand for librarians in 1990, in traditional library employment settings, by type of library
2. a discussion of the skills most in demand among librarians through 1990
3. an identification of the factors affecting supply and demand in librarianship
4. a discussion of nontraditional (nonlibrary) employment settings for librarians
5. information on employment trends, staffing patterns, hiring requirements, and the employment and training impacts of new procedures and services
6. a compilation of sources of data on employment in libraries
7. a methodology for projecting supply and demand for librarians (DeWath and Cooper, 1980, p. 2–3)

It is hoped that this study, scheduled to be released late in 1982, will provide new baseline data on which to build studies of librarians in the 1980s.

Used in combination the BLS study and the King Research study will enable researchers to consider changes which have taken place in the library work force over the past decade. Both will be central sources for a general understanding of the training and deployment of library personnel. However—even with the additional data King Research plans to gather through an employer survey and a library school survey—these studies can be greatly augmented by the examination of other surveys discussed below.

B. New Graduates

New graduate information is the most consistently documented data available to the library work force analyst. Two ongoing data gathering efforts, the *Library Journal* series prepared by Frarey *et al.* ("Placements and Salaries," 1973–1981) and the American Library Association reports on degrees and certificates (American Library Association, Office for Library Personnel Resources 1977, 1980) provide longitudinal data on new entrants to the library field.

The ALA reports constitute the only source of information for all levels of library training. The series reports on graduates from associate of arts, baccalaureate, unaccredited and accredited master's, sixth-year, and doctoral programs. There are problems in the reporting. The rate of response for accredited programs is much higher than that for other programs. However, the documentation of reporting–nonreporting institutions in separate tabulations in these reports has been consistent and permits the researcher to make observations based on an understanding that the universe is not totally represented. In spite of the less than total response the availability of these data over time allow some longitudinal observations to be made. Table 1 presents a summary of these data for the 6 years tallied to date, with figures for number and percentage of degrees by sex for each category of program. The observation, "the higher, the fewer," is well substantiated by the distribution of degrees over the reporting period. Women comprise the

TABLE 1
Degrees and Certificates Awarded by U.S. Library Education Programs, 1973–1979[a]

	Associate of arts							
	Degrees awarded					As % of all degrees		
	M		F		Total			
Year	(N)	%	(N)	%	(N)	M	F	T
1973–1974	(19)	4	(462)	96	(481)	.2	5.3	5.5
1974–1975	(19)	8	(222)	92	(241)	.2	2.7	2.9
1975–1976	(21)	6	(324)	94	(345)	.3	4.2	4.5
1976–1977	(12)	6.9	(163)	93.1	(175)	.2	2.5	2.7
1977–1978	(19)	13.5	(122)	86.5	(141)	.3	2.2	2.5
1978–1979	(18)	9.9	(164)	90.1	(182)	.3	3.1	3.4

	Baccalaureate							
	Degrees awarded					As % of all degrees		
	M		F		Total			
Year	(N)	%	(N)	%	(N)	M	F	T
1973–1974	(75)	9	(762)	91	(837)	.9	8.8	9.7
1974–1975	(73)	10	(658)	90	(731)	.9	8.1	9.0
1975–1976	(31)	7	(410)	93	(441)	.4	5.3	5.7
1976–1977	(21)	5.8	(342)	94.2	(363)	.3	5.2	5.6
1977–1978	(33)	9.6	(311)	90.4	(344)	.6	5.5	6.1
1978–1979	(18)	6.2	(272)	93.8	(290)	.3	5.1	5.4

(continued)

majority of degree recipients at all levels except the doctorate, but the percentage decreases as the amount of education required for the degree increases. Perhaps the most promising positive change over the years reported is the increase in doctorates earned by women. There has been a 15.8% increase in the number of doctorates awarded women since 1973. This fact has been observed and highlighted in Brown's report to the National Center for Educational Statistics on degree awards to women which noted that out of 23 fields the largest percentage gain at the doctoral level occurred in library science (Brown, 1979, p. 17).

These ALA reports are also the primary source of information on racial and ethnic data on new entrants. For each degree, the number and percentage of white, American Indian–Alaskan native, Asian–Pacific Islander, black, and Hispanic graduates are recorded—broken out by sex and by region. Bidlack (1979b) has found that among the probable recipients of

TABLE 1 *Continued*

	Nonaccredited master's							
	Degrees awarded					As % of all degrees		
	M		F		Total			
Year	(N)	%	(N)	%	(N)	M	F	T
1973–1974	(162)	18	(736)	82	(898)	1.9	8.5	10.4
1974–1975	(90)	13	(602)	87	(692)	1.1	7.4	8.5
1975–1976	(125)	17	(611)	83	(736)	1.6	7.9	9.6
1976–1977	(52)	15.0	(295)	85	(347)	.8	4.5	5.3
1977–1978	(56)	18.4	(249)	81.6	(305)	1.0	4.4	5.4
1978–1979	(65)	21.0	(245)	79.0	(310)	1.2	4.6	5.8

	ALA-accredited master's							
	Degrees awarded					As % of all degrees		
	M		F		Total			
Year	(N)	%	(N)	%	(N)	M	F	T
1973–1974	(1391)	22	(4932)	78	(6323)	16.0	57.0	73.0
1974–1975	(1390)	22	(4929)	78	(6319)	17.1	60.8	77.9
1975–1976	(1330)	22	(4715)	78	(6045)	17.3	61.3	78.6
1976–1977	(1094)	19.9	(4404)	80.1	(5498)	16.8	67.5	84.3
1977–1978	(975)	20.6	(3749)	79.4	(4724)	17.3	66.6	83.9
1978–1979	(854)	19.4	(3545)	80.6	(4399)	16.0	66.6	82.6

(continued)

TABLE 1 *Continued*

Sixth-year certificate

	Degrees awarded					As % of all degrees		
	M		F		Total			
Year	(N)	%	(N)	%	(N)	M	F	T
1973–1974	(21)	28	(54)	72	(75)	.2	.6	.9
1974–1975	(19)	38	(31)	62	(50)	.2	.4	.6
1975–1976	(22)	33	(44)	67	(66)	.3	.6	.9
1976–1977	(21)	23.9	(67)	76.1	(88)	.3	1.0	1.3
1977–1978	(16)	23.9	(51)	76.1	(67)	.3	.9	1.2
1978–1979	(19)	21.8	(68)	78.2	(87)	.4	1.3	1.6

Doctorates

	Degrees awarded					As % of all degrees		
	M		F		Total			
Year	(N)	%	(N)	%	(N)	M	F	T
1973–1974	(30)	64	(17)	36	(47)	.3	.2	.5
1974–1975	(49)	63	(29)	37	(78)	.6	.4	1.0
1975–1976	(30)	54	(25)	46	(55)	.4	.3	.7
1976–1977	(26)	49.1	(27)	50.9	(53)	.4	.4	.8
1977–1978	(24)	51.1	(23)	48.9	(47)	.4	.4	.8
1978–1979	(27)	48.2	(29)	51.8	(56)	.5	.5	1.1

Total

	M		F		Total
Year	(N)	%	(N)	%	(N)
1973–1974	(1698)	19.6	(6963)	80.4	(8661)
1974–1975	(1640)	20.2	(6471)	79.8	(8111)
1975–1976	(1559)	20.3	(6129)	79.7	(7688)
1976–1977	(1226)	18.8	(5298)	81.2	(6524)
1977–1978	(1123)	20.0	(4505)	80.0	(5628)
1978–1979	(1001)	18.8	(4323)	81.2	(5324)

[a]Sources: American Library Association, Office for Library Personnel Resources, 1977, 1980.

the doctoral degree for 1979–1981, 52% were female and 48% male. Of the total population 78.2% were white, 13.7% were black, 3.5% Hispanic, 3.8% Asian, and 0.8% Native American.

The ALA reports provide important information about the characteristics of new graduates. Although the picture is beginning to brighten a bit at the advanced degree level in terms of numbers of women obtaining that degree, the picture is still not promising for the minority woman in all categories.

One new source to be monitored for information about students enrolled in library education is Learmont's report, which includes ethnic and sexual data and is based on statistics collected by the Association of American Library Schools (AALS) (Learmont, 1980). The analysis includes age, highest degree, undergraduate majors, and financial assistance by sex and ethnic background. While the study focuses on ALA-accredited programs, data on 11 AALS Associate Member schools are included as well. This ongoing report promises to be a rich new source for the investigation of the backgrounds of new librarians.

The *Library Journal* series is limited in its focus—only placements of graduates of ALA accredited programs are reported—but comprehensive in its treatment of these graduates. The many variables analyzed provide a year-by-year account of subtle demographic shifts in new graudates, employment and, by extrapolation, changes in the larger employment context as well. Since the 1972 report, all data have been analyzed by sex. Racial breakdowns are not included, but the ALA reports and the AALS statistical survey discussed above do assemble nearly all information about minorities in library education programs, and, used with the *Library Journal* series, provide information for research on affirmative action and entry level positions.

Table 2 shows the distribution of new graduates from 1972–1980 by type of entry-level employment and sex as reported in the *Library Journal* series. Over the last decade, the percentage of male graduates choosing public, school, and academic work has declined while the number electing "other" categories (special and nontraditional areas) has increased substantially. Women graduates have maintained a fairly steady entry into public and academic library positions but have dropped sharply in the school library category. Women also exhibit an increase in the "other" category. Overall placements have shifted considerably in the past decade. There has been a general drop in school placements and an increase in the "other" category. This shift provides evidence of the changing job market for librarians.

Although the *Library Journal* series data have been analyzed by sex for nearly a decade, there has been surprisingly little longitudinal analysis done by researchers. In 1980, there were nearly 1000 fewer new entrants to the

TABLE 2
Placement of New Graduates, United States, 1972–1980 (%)[a]

Year	Public		School		College & univ.		Other[b]		Total		
	M	F	M	F	M	F	M	F	M (N)	F (N)	T (N)
1972	30	29	14	31	41	25	15	15	783	2733	3517
1973	34	29	13	30	37	24	16	17	857	2718	3633
1974	31	30	13	29	38	23	18	18	797	2631	3514
1975	29	29	10	29	39	21	21	21	735	2476	3211
1976	27	27	12	27	39	22	21	23	593	1974	2616
1977	30.8	27.7	10.8	27.3	36.9	22.3	21.5	22.7	595	2121	2716
1978	26.1	26.6	8.9	24.4	39.3	24.5	25.7	24.5	575	2046	2676
1979	25.3	28.0	8.6	21.5	37.6	22.3	28.5	28.2	487	2078	2565
1980	27.5	26.5	10.4	23.3	37.1	22.6	24.0	27.6	385	1782	2170

[a]Sources: "Placements and Salaries" (1973–1981).
[b]In 1980, this category was subdivided into "Special" and "Other," which are combined here for comparison.

profession than in 1972, and the percentage of men entering in 1980 was the lowest since these data have been available. Table 3 demonstrates the changing median salary for men and women for the period 1972–1980. With the exception of 1975 and 1976, each year has seen a closing of the gap between men and women's median starting salaries. In 1980, however, we return to a greater differential—a 4.3% advantage to new male professionals.

Other data analyzed by sex in the series are regional summaries, individual school placements and salaries, placements by type of library, a comparison of U.S. and Canadian placements, high and low salaries by type of library, and the effects of experience on salary. From these studies, researchers will be able to document the number of librarians moving into nontraditional areas over time. Further information on one of the larger categories, "audiovisual and media centers" in the 1980 survey, is provided by the similar salary surveys conducted for media graduates (Peterson, 1973–1977; Sink, 1978–1980).

The relationship between librarians and media graduates is, at best, hazy. But we have good indication that there is considerable overlap in the first employment of graduates of library and media programs. Media graduates of 1978–1979 were employed in a wide variety of contexts which included (a) administration of media programs, (b) distribution of book media, and (c) print–nonprint combination in elementary and secondary schools, universities, junior, and community colleges, and industry. Prostano and Prostano (1979, pp. 38–39) have addressed the question of overlap between library and media programs: "in general, library schools have focused on providing graduates with the knowledge and skills required to meet all information needs of library users. Consequently, there has been a significant effort in recent years to expand to a full range of courses in educational technology." Although they also observe that library schools do not offer majors or concentration in media technology, there is justification for comparison of new graduates of the two types of programs because of the overlap in new placements.

Table 4 presents data on degree distribution of media graduates 1971–1979, by degree and by sex and reveals a larger percentage of women at all levels in recent years except in the Ed.D. and Ph.D. categories. The ratio of male and female graduates nearly has been reversed since these data began to be reported. As with the ALA reports, there is the problem of nonresponse on the part of many programs.

A comparison of mean salaries of media and library graduates at the master's level in Table 5 demonstrates that although librarians were ahead of media graduates at the outset, the latter caught up in 1973 and have remained ahead ever since.

These data-gathering efforts provide much information on the salary and distribution of new entrants to the field. We see that women are beginning to acquire more advanced degrees and are moving closer to salary equity at the entry levels. However, the gap between men's and women's salaries begins to widen as more time is spent in the work force, as demonstrated in a variety of association surveys.

TABLE 3
Median Salaries for Entry-level Librarians, 1972–1980[a]

Year of graduation	Median salary for women	Median salary for men	Women's salary as % of men's
1972	$ 8,756	$ 9,163	95.5
1973	9,000	9,303	96.7
1974	9,600	10,184	96.7
1975	9,980	10,350	94.3
1976	10,500	10,900	96.3
1977	11,000	11,311	97.3
1978	11,700	12,000	97.5
1979	12,885	13,103	98.3
1980	13,500	14,112	95.7

[a]Sources: "Placements and Salaries" (1973–1981).

TABLE 4
Degree Distribution of Media Graduates, 1971–1979[a]

Year	B.S.			Masters						Two-year						Ed.D. and Ph.D.				
	Males (N) %	Females (N) %	T	Males (N) %		Females (N) %		T	Males (N) %		Females (N) %		T	Males (N) %		Females (N) %		T		
1971–1972			—					480					26							
1972–1973			20					558					60							
1973–1974			—	(334)	54.4	(280)	45.6	614	(21)	61.8	(13)	38.2	34	(69)	79.3	(18)	20.7	87		
1974–1975	(6) 100.0	(0) 0	6	(431)	50.1	(429)	49.9	860	(36)	64.3	(20)	35.7	56	(72)	77.4	(21)	25.6	93		
1975–1976	(1) 11.1	(8) 88.9	9	(326)	52.5	(295)	47.5	621	(36)	66.7	(18)	33.3	54	(51)	77.3	(15)	22.7	66		
1976–1977	(9) 52.9	(8) 47.1	17	(305)	46.1	(357)	53.9	662	(25)	58.1	(18)	41.9	43	(51)	73.9	(18)	26.1	69		
1977–1978	(16) 35.6	(29) 64.4	45	(284)	49.1	(294)	50.9	578	(35)	52.2	(32)	47.8	67	(66)	69.5	(29)	30.5	95		
1978–1979	(21) 28.4	(53) 71.6	74	(343)	40.2	(510)	59.8	853	(28)	43.6	(36)	56.3	64	(80)	65.0	(43)	35.0	123		

[a] Sources: Peterson, 1973–1977; Sink, 1978–1980.

TABLE 5
Mean Salaries of Library and Media Graduates Compared, 1972–1979[a]

Year	Media			Library		
	Mean salary	% W	% M	Mean salary	% W	% M
1972	$ 8,693	—	—	$ 9,248	80.2	19.2
1973	10,138	—	—	9,423	77.1	22.9
1974	11,194	45.6	54.4	10,040	78.4	21.6
1975	10,978	49.9	50.1	10,594	78.2	21.8
1976	11,600	47.5	52.5	11,149	78.2	21.8
1977	12,467	53.9	46.1	11,894	80.2	19.8
1978	13,986	50.0	49.1	12,527	78.7	21.3
1979	15,330	59.8	40.2	13,127	81.0	19.0

[a]Sources: "Placements and Salaries," 1973–1980; Peterson, 1973–1977; Sink, 1978–1980.

IV. ASSOCIATION SURVEYS

Another source of data for library personnel demographic data is the survey conducted by a professional association. There are several ongoing data-gathering studies executed by associations as well as some that are done at varying intervals. It would be ideal if these studies were compatible and carried out at regular intervals. With the exception of the Special Libraries Association survey and several smaller association surveys, this is not the case. The various surveys differ in their scope and depth of analysis. It was a matter of coincidence, rather than comprehensive planning, that four major association surveys were done in 1979. While different surveys considered different variables, there are some comparisons that may be made of the reports issued in 1980 by the American Library Association, the American Society for Information Science, the Special Libraries Association, and the Society of American Archivists.

A. American Library Association

The American Library Association (ALA) does not currently support an ongoing survey of its membership relating to demographic data or salaries. In recent years, two units of the Association have conducted studies which provide some information on these subjects: a study in 1970 by the Library Administration Division (LAD) (Manchak, 1971) and one in 1980 by the

Committee on the Status of Women in Librarianship (COWSL) (Estabrook and Heim, 1980), the latter undertaken primarily in order to explore differences in career patterns of male and female librarians.

The COWSL study found that in 1979 the membership of ALA was 76% female and 24% male, as compared with figures of 84 and 16% respectively in the Bureau of Labor Statistics study and that advanced degrees were held by 19.5% of the men and 4.2% of the women.

Table 6 presents data from the two ALA studies and the Bureau of Labor Statistics report relating to type of library employment. From it we can see how ALA membership has changed over the 1970s and how ALA members differ from the library personnel universe. According to the Bureau of Labor Statistics report, nearly half of all individuals reporting themselves employed as librarians worked in school settings. The ALA study for the same reporting year (1970) shows that only 20.8% of the membership held school positions. The COSWL study demonstrates that ALA has declined in its number of school librarian members—down to only 13.6% in 1979. The inducements for school librarians to join unions or quasiunions that represent the total school faculty, such as the American Federation of Teachers or the National Education Association, may be eroding librarian membership in ALA. However, the reasons are not clear and require new research.

Table 7 presents data on the racial and sexual composition of the library work force based on three reports: BLS, ALA figures on recent graduates, and COWSL. As indicated, the percentage of whites is slightly higher among ALA members (COWSL report) than among recent graduates or among the total profession (BLS study, recognizing that the date of this study, 1970, may be significant).

TABLE 6
The Library Work Force by Type of Library (%)[a]

Type	LAD study[b] (total only)	BLS report			COSWL study		
		M	F	T	M	F	T
School	20.8	20.0	49.9	45.2	3.5	17.0	13.6
Public	26.8	20.6	23.5	23.0	22.8	30.7	28.8
Academic	29.0	36.7	13.3	17.0	44.6	27.7	31.8
Special & Other	23.4	22.7	13.3	14.8	25.7	22.4	23.3
Nonlibrary	—	—	—	—	3.4	2.2	2.5

[a] Sources: Manchak, 1971; United States, Bureau of Labor Statistics, 1975; Estabrook and Heim, 1980.
[b] Figures for sex not available.

TABLE 7
Percentages of Librarians by Race and Sex[a]

	BLS			New graduates of ALA-accredited programs												COSWL		
				1976–1977			1977–1978			1978–1979								
Race	M	F	T	M	F	T	M	F	T	M	F	T	M	F	T	M	F	T
White	92.3%	91.8%	91.9%	92.1%	91.7%	91.8%	91.3%	90.9%	91.0%	90.1%	89.7%	89.7%	93.6%	93.7%	93.6%
Black	5.7	6.7	6.5	3.4	4.4	4.2	3.0	5.1	4.6	3.5	5.1	4.8	1.6	3.9	3.3
Asian–American	1.3	1.1	1.1	2.0	2.7	2.6	2.3	2.3	2.3	3.8	3.4	3.5	2.9	1.6	1.9
Hispanic	(2.3)	(1.4)	(1.6)	2.5	1.2	1.3	3.4	1.6	1.9	2.6	1.8	1.9	.5	.6	.5

[a]Sources: United States, Bureau of Labor Statistics, 1975; American Library Association, Office for Library Personnel Resources, 1980; Estabrook and Heim, 1980.

Salaries for male ALA members continue to be higher than for female members. There is an overall median salary differential in favor of men of 25% (men $19,500; women $14,700) compared to a 23% differential in 1970. The differential is greatest in academic libraries where women earn 27.7% less than men and least in school libraries where women earn 21.2% less than men. There are no comparable data in the 1970 LAD study.

An analysis of the type of position held by ALA members reinforces a perception of patterns of intraoccupational segregation within the profession: 28.9% of the men are directors, compared to 11.2% of the women; 10.2% of the men are associate or assistant directors compared to 3.7% of the women; 18.7% of the men are department heads, compared to 17.8% of the women. These top managerial categories account for 57.8% of the male membership but only 32.7% of the women. Other variables analyzed in the COSWL study are professional involvement, level in the organizational hierarchy, publication rate, and supervisory duties. The full report contains a more complete analysis of these data.

B. American Society for Information Science

Over one-third of the American Society for Information Science (ASIS) membership holds the professional library degree. Consequently, any study of the library work force must take into consideration data available for ASIS members. A recent survey shows 56% of the membership as female and 44% male (King et al., 1980). The median female salary for ASIS members is $23,600 compared to the median male salary of $29,700. Men are more likely than women to receive high salaries: of those earning more than $30,000, 69.3% are men and 30.7% women; of those earning more than $50,000, 79.1% are men and 20.9% women. At the lower end of the earning scale, 74% of those earning less than $19,999 are women and 26% are men. King et al. suggest possible reasons: fewer women hold doctorates; women are slightly younger and therefore newer to the field; the women in ASIS are in their childbearing years and tend to work "on behalf of others"—but no statistical analyses are done to validate these typical explanations for male–female salary differential regardless of the field examined.

Data are provided on the highest degree held by sex (Table 8). The professional library degree accounts for the largest single type of professional education for the ASIS membership (34%), and nearly half the women members (44.9%) hold this degree. Income by degree is not broken down by sex, but professional library degree holders have the lowest medi-

TABLE 8
Degrees Held by ASIS Members by Sex, 1979[a]

Degree	Males		Females		Total	
	N	%	N	%	N	%
Ph.D.	(260)	77	(78)	23	(338)	17
MD	(2)	100	(0)	0	(2)	.1
Joint masters	(60)	38	(99)	62	(159)	8
MS–MA	(188)	45	(229)	55	(417)	21
MLS	(183)	27	(493)	73	(676)	34
BS–BA	(142)	45	(174)	55	(316)	15.9
Other	(43)	55	(36)	45	(79)	4.0

[a]Source: King et al., 1980.

an income ($20,000). Since this degree is the background of most ASIS women and is the lowest salary category, it seems likely that there is a correlation. There is a need for further investigation on these variables.

ASIS members' positions are analyzed by their primary work function and by type of employer. It is difficult to gauge the relative prestige and status of these positions except by weighing them against income. Women tend to work for various types of employers in percentages roughly equivalent to their ASIS membership level of 56% except in industry where they account for 64% and university–college settings where they account for 45%. Primary work function, however, does seem to display some occupational segregation, for women are predominant in performing on behalf of others (p. 16).

To make observations about the relative status of the various primary work functions we need to integrate data on two tables: income by work function and sex by work function, which are not analyzed together in the report. Women fall short in their representation in the primary work areas paying the median salary or above: systems analysis (42%); management (50%); education (35%); research and development (31%); and marketing (54%). The less lucrative work areas earning below the median salary, however, are populated by women in excess of their representation in the membership at large: systems design (60%); preparation (67%); analysis (68%); searching (75%); and "other" (69%). The lowest paid work function, "searching," pays a median salary of $18,000 and is 75% female—the largest category for women. It is hard to make precise observations from these data, but the general conclusion—based on the available information—is that ASIS women, like women in other sectors of the library work force, are concentrated in the lower paying positions.

C. Special Libraries Association

The Special Libraries Association (SLA) triennial salary surveys provide good longitudinal data on persons employed in the special library sector (Special Libraries Association, 1970, 1973, 1976, 1979). These surveys are supplemented by yearly updates of a sample of the membership, but the updates are not analyzed by sex as are the triennial studies. Table 9 provides membership information for the 4 most recent reporting years.

The SLA surveys have continually expanded their analysis of variables by sex, but for the period 1970–1979, only salary statistics were consistently reported by sex. Table 10 provides median salary information. In the 1970 survey the narrative analysis noted:

> To test the compatability [sic] of data from the 1970 survey, certain high income categories were re-analyzed by sex of the respondents. In all instances (geographic, job function, subject, and highest academic degree) men's salaries clustered above the overall mean and women's salaries clustered below the mean. In spite of the perhaps independent effects of geographic location, library subject, academic degree and job title, there is evidence for a real male-oriented sex bias in salaries reported for all categories (p. 348).

Observations made in the 1979 survey (p. 562) reconfirm the fact that women are paid on a lower scale than men. In addition to data on census regions and SMSAs, the SLA survey provides information on salary by total persons supervised, by sex. Although nearly as many women as men supervised more than 20 individuals these women earned a median salary of $29,000 compared to the male median of $32,700. For every category of individuals supervised, the female median salary was lower than the male median (p. 580).

TABLE 9
SLA Membership by Sex[a]

	Males	Females	No response
1970	20%	61%	19
1973	22	76	2
1976	21	79	(less than 1)
1979	21	79	—

[a]Source: Special Libraries Association, 1970, 1973, 1976, 1979.

TABLE 10
SLA Median Salaries[a]

Year	Males	Females	Women's earnings as percentage of men's
1970	$13,000	$10,400	77.0
1973	16,500	12,500	75.8
1976	18,100	14,700	81.2
1979	21,100	17,400	82.5

[a]Source: Special Libraries Association, 1970, 1973, 1979, 1980.

TABLE 11
SLA Median Salary 1979 by Years of Experience by Sex[a]

Years of experience	Males	Females	Women's salaries as percentage of men's
1–5	$14,800	$14,300	96.6
6–10	19,000	16,500	86.8
11–15	20,400	18,700	91.7
16–20	24,000	20,500	85.5
21–25	25,000	21,000	84.0
26+	27,000	22,300	82.3

[a]Source: Special Libraries Association, 1979.

One other salary variable analyzed by sex in 1979 was that of total professional experience. Table 11 displays this information for the median salary in each category. While men and women are comparatively close in salaries at starting levels, the disparity increases as more time is spent in the profession.

The SLA surveys differ in the variables analyzed by sex from year to year. In the 1976 survey, salary by age was provided (p. 580), but this information did not appear in the 1979 survey. These surveys are a potentially rich source of data but few variables are analyzed by sex in the published reports.

D. Society of American Archivists

The disparity between the economic status of men and women archivists has been highlighted by a series of studies conducted by the Society of

American Archivists (SAA) of which only the 1979 survey is discussed here (Deutrich and DeWhitt, 1980). Because regional archival association members as well as those in the SAA were surveyed, the results are not as association-specific as those of the ASIS, SLA, and ALA studies, but they do provide general information about the archival profession. There are more men (54%) than women archivists (46%). Men earn a higher mean salary ($18,680) than women ($15,230) and there are salary differences in favor of men, regardless of experience or type of position in most cases. Table 12 presents data on mean salary for men and women by job category.

Of those archivists responding to the 1979 survey, 32.6% had a professional library degree. Women had fewer Ph.D. degrees than men: 29% compared to 9%—and fewer second master's degrees——87% compared to 74%. Regardless of educational level, men earn more than women. Men with Ph.D.'s earn 9% more than women and 12% more at the Bachelor's level.

Data are provided also that display mean salary by type of employer. In every category of employment except archivists working in public libraries, women earn less than men. The differential is greatest in museums where women earn 74.9% of the salary of men and least in the federal government (excluding NARS) and business where women earn 94.3 and 95.4%, respectively, of the salary of their male counterparts.

The release of the results of association surveys for ALA, ASIS, SLA, and SAA in 1979 is the single most important statistical event in the comparison of male and female library work force compensation analysis. Table 13 compares salaries for male and female members of these major library and information associations.

TABLE 12
Mean Salary of SAA Members by Job Category[a]

Category	Males	Females	Women's salaries as percentage of men's
Archivist	$17,787	$14,341	80.6
Manuscript curator	16,046	14,202	88.5
Supervisor	22,451	18,520	82.5
Librarian	15,170	14,477	95.4
Professor–teacher	22,908	18,125	79.1
Records manager	19,571	14,424	73.7
Nonteaching historian	18,745	18,831	100.4
Museum curator	13,500	14,864	110.1

[a]Source: Deutrich and DeWhitt (1980).

TABLE 13
Salaries and Percentage of Male–Female Membership in ALA, ASIS, SLA, SAA, 1979[a]

	ALA		ASIS		SLA		SAA	
	Percentage of members	Median salary	Percentage of members	Median salary	Percentage of members	Median salary	Percentage of members	Mean salary
Male	24.1	$19,500	44.0	$29,700	21.0	$21,100	54.2	$18,680
Female	75.8	$14,700	56.0	$23,600	79.0	$17,400	45.6	$15,230
%[b]		75.4		79.5		82.9		81.5

[a] Sources: Estabrook and Heim (1980); King et al. (1980); Special Libraries Association (1979, 1980); Deutrich and DeWhitt (1980).
[b] Women's salaries compared with men's.

Any attempt to draw conclusions from these statistics is difficult. ALA women members are the least well-paid group of all the association members surveyed. ALA men earn more than the women of any association except ASIS, but considerably less than their male ASIS or SLA counterparts. It is clear, however, that women continue to lag behind men in the various major library and information professions and that no rational justifications for this discrepancy have been presented.

In addition to these four recent major association surveys which provide a wide-ranging set of data on the relative status of men and women in the library work force, there are several other association-based studies which add to the demographic information on librarians.

E. American Association of Law Libraries

The American Association of Law Libraries (AALL) conducts an annual statistical survey which includes some salary data, but the data are not routinely analyzed by sex (King, 1980). Table 14 presents data on male and female members of AALL in 1970 (Frarey, 1970). The data are old and can be updated only on a few variables by several recent regional surveys; nevertheless, the study provides baseline information on law librarians at the outset of the 1970s.

In 1970, women working in law libraries had less legal education than men. Only 22% held an earned law degree as compared to 63% of the men. Women were more inclined to work in law firms than men, who predominated in law school settings. Nearly half the men (44%) worked in larger law libraries and over two-thirds of the women in smaller institutions. Fac-

TABLE 14
Comparison of Various Characteristics of Male and Female AALL Members 1970[a]

Characteristics	Sex[b]	
	Males	Females
Education[c]		
MLS	59%	57%
Law degree	63%	22%
MLS/law degree	38%	12%
Neither	15%	31%
Employment		
Type of library		
Law school	55%	45%
Bar association	3	5
Law firm	8	14
Other firms	6	6
City related	1	2
County related	11	11
State related	9	12
Federal related	7	5
International agency	0	<1
Size of library		
Less than 50,000 volumes	30%	46%
50,000–100,000 volumes	26%	21%
100,001–200,000 volumes	23%	21%
Over 200,000 volumes	21%	12%
Type of position		
Chief librarian	58%	50%
Chief assistant librarian	15%	12%
Other supervisor	8%	9%
Reader services	10%	9%
Technical services	7%	17%
Other	2%	3%
Faculty rank		
Professor	20%	7%
Associate professor	12%	4%
Assistant professor	14%	8%
Instructor	6%	13%
Lecturer and other	3%	2%
Status, no rank	3%	3%
No rank or status	36%	49%
No response	6%	4%
Salary		
Median	$13,750	$8,500
$ 8,000–10,000	27%	63%
$10,001–15,000	35%	30%
$15,001–20,000	25%	6%
$20,000 or above	13%	1%

[a] Source: Frarey, 1970.
[b] Membership 36% male, 53% female, 11% no response.
[c] Percent is based on total distribution. Categories are not mutually exclusive.

ulty rank of assistant professor or above was held by 46% of the men but only 19% of the women. Women earned only 61.8% of the salary of men: a median salary of $8500 compared to men's $13,750. In the higher salary ranks, men were clearly ahead: 38% earned more than $15,001 compared to only 6% of the women. The lowest salary ranges accounted for 63% of the women and only 27% of the men. At about the same time, Hughes (1971) developed a profile of women law librarians who were members of AALL and compared women head librarians with their male counterparts. Her general demographic data do not provide comparable information on men although she did make comparisons with heads of law libraries who were male and female and found that more men (83%) than women (43%) were married and that men had better training than women: 24% of the women had law degrees compared to 41% of the men.

Renshawe (1976) updated the Frarey salary study, finding a continued differential between men and women AALL members. The female law librarian earned 66.4% of the salary of her male counterpart—a slight increase from the 61.8% she earned in 1970. Women were concentrated in the lower salary ranges—80% of those earning less than $15,000 were women; men predominated in the higher ranges—62% of those earning more than over $20,000 were men. Table 15 displays a small portion of Renshawe's data.

There has been no AALL-wide survey of salaries since 1976, so we have no current information on the larger universe of law librarians. Several small regional studies, however, demonstrate continued male–female disparity. The Greater Philadelphia Law Library Association polled its membership in 1977 (Shediac, 1978) and 1979 (Leinbach and Beardwood, 1980). Although a number of variables are analyzed, only age (in 1977) and salary are compared by sex. In the 1979 survey, women earned a median salary of $14,994 compared to men's $16,100.

TABLE 15
Selected Comparative Data on Male and Female AALL Members, 1976[a]

	M	F
Percentage of membership	32	68
Median salary	$16,000	$10,620
Faculty rank[b]		
Professor	68%	32%
Associate professor	65%	35%
Assistant professor	53%	47%

[a]Source: Renshawe (1976).
[b]Pertains only to AALS Members employed by law schools.

TABLE 16
Median Private Law Library Salaries by Age and Sex, 1979[a]

Age	Males	Females
20–29	$18,900	$15,360
30–39	19,410	18,930
40–49	25,890	18,785

[a]Source: Shediac, 1980.

TABLE 17
Median Southern California Association of Law Libraries Salaries by Age and Sex, 1979[a]

Age	Males	Females
20–29	$17,250	$13,700
30–39	20,750	15,000
40–49	23,000	17,000
50+	31,200	17,000

[a]Source: Estes, 1979.

A 1979 salary survey by the Private Law Libraries Special Interest Section found men in every age category earned a higher median salary than women (Shediac, 1980). These data are displayed in Table 16.

A survey by the Southern California Association of Law Librarians (SCALL) also analyzed median salary by age and sex as shown in Table 17 (Estes, 1979). No category of female law librarian, even those over age 50, earned more than the median salary of the youngest males. The differential at the 50+ age level found women earning only 54.5% of the salary of men.

The data provided do not include analysis of most variables by sex. Consequently, it is difficult to see what other factors (e.g., education, years in the profession) contribute to continuing salary disparity although the narrative accompanying the SCALL Survey notes that fewer women have law degrees. More analysis of law librarian salaries are needed with cross-tabulation of variables by sex.

F. Music Library Association

Filter (1969) gathered data on the membership of the Music Library Association (MLA). Table 18 displays some of the characteristics which

TABLE 18
Selected Characteristics of Music Library Association Members, 1969[a]

Characteristics	Males	Females
Percent of membership	59%	41%
Education		
B.A.	11.7	12.4
M.A.	65.0	82.0
PhD.	23.3	5.6
Directors	51.4	48.6
Committee membership	69.4	30.6

[a]Source: Filter, 1969.

were analyzed by sex based on tables in Filter's paper. Salary data are not presented as total medians but by education and position. Men earned in the higher ranges: 32% more than $12,000 compared to only 6.7% of the women, regardless of education. Other data analyzed by sex include participation in other associations and attendance at meetings. A 1975 survey sent to the MLA membership to evaluate future directions gathered information on a similar set of data—including positions and association involvement—but did not analyze these data by sex (Music Library Association, 1975).

G. Association for Educational Communications and Technology

As indicated earlier, data on placement of media graduates may be valuable to the library work force analyst because of the employment of many media graduates in library positions. The Association for Educational Communications and Technology (AECT) does not conduct an ongoing association salary survey and the only demographic information relating to its membership derives from a series of questionnaires sent to members in 1975 (Molenda and Cambre, 1977a,b.) Similar data on the same sample had been gathered by Molenda in 1971 (Molenda, 1971).

The AECT researchers analyze very few variables by sex. Many of the broad categories, however, indicate that AECT is a major piece in the puzzle of developing library work force models. Twenty-five percent of the respondents worked as administrators of "Library and/or Joint Media Services." While degrees are broken out by level, they are not differentiated by subject so we cannot tell if a significant segment of the membership has library training. Ethnic composition is similar to that of ALA with 89% of the membership white, 5% black, 2% Asian, 1% Hispanic, 1% Native American and 3% "other."

The AECT membership is predominately male (73%) even though new entrants at the master's level averaged 47.6% female over the period 1973–1976 (see Table 4). Female members earn less than males, with a mean salary of $18,594 compared to $21,309 for males—87.3% of the male base. Women are concentrated in the lower-paying salary ranges: 48% earned less than $18,000 compared to 31% of the men; men are concentrated in the higher ranges: 31% of the men earned more than $23,500 while only 15% of the women did so. The authors do not display any other income variables cross-tabulated by sex but do indicate in their analysis that some of the disparity might arise because "40 percent of all female members are found in the library/joint media services administration role" (Molenda and Cambre, 1977b, p. 51)—an observation that seems to indicate that within the AECT membership library positions are perceived as less prestigious and are thus less well paid.

Further investigation of linkages between the library and media professions would seem in order. The mirror image of AECT versus ALA membership vis-a-vis males and females is interesting and seems to lend some substantiation to a long-perceived dichotomy between men and women in these two allied but very different fields for the provision of materials in the print and nonprint areas.

V. TYPE OF INSTITUTION STUDIES

It is far easier to study librarians who belong to associations than all librarians since the membership lists make such inquiries reasonably straightforward. The labor analyst must recognize, however, that the factor of associational affiliation is itself a confounding one in the study of the library work force. Those who ally themselves with associations are likely to be the most professionalized members of the library workforce and thus may earn higher salaries than their nonjoining counterparts. We turn now to those broad studies which have surveyed librarians by institutional type rather than by association membership. These studies fill in and complement the association studies.

A. Academic Libraries

The most recent overall examination of the academic work force is provided in *Racial, Ethnic, and Sexual Composition of Library Staff in Academic and Public Libraries,* a study conducted in 1980 for affirmative action purposes by the Office for Library Personnel Resources (OLPR) of the American Library Association to collect racial, sexual, and ethnic information on librarians employed in academic and public libraries (American Library Association, 1981). Table 19 provides a broad picture of the staff composition of the academic library.

Asian–Pacific Islanders account for the greatest portion of male minorities. For females the racial/ethnic composition is more varied. Nearly three-fourths of all academic directors are male and they earn a median salary of $32,999—24.2% more than the median female director salary of

TABLE 19
Racial, Ethnic, and Sexual Characteristics and Median Salaries of Academic Librarians, 1980[a]

Characteristics	Males			Females		
	%	(N)	Median salary ($)	%	(N)	Median salary ($)
Total staff	37.7	(3,320)		62.3	(5,490)	
American Indian/Alaskan Native	.2	(5)		.1	(7)	
Asian/Pacific Islander	5.2	(173)		4.9	(267)	
Black	2.6	(85)		4.8	(266)	
Hispanic	1.7	(56)		1.6	(91)	
White	90.4	(3,001)		88.5	(4,859)	
Director (all)	73.1	(285)	32,999	26.9	(105)	24,999
American Indian/Alaskan Native	0.0			1.9		
Asian/Pacific Islander	2.8			1.9		
Black	4.6	(22)	27,000	13.3	(22)	20,010
Hispanic	0.4			3.8		
White	92.3	(263)	33,875	79.0	(83)	25,899
Branch and department heads (all)	42.2	(1,115)	20,396	57.8	(1,527)	18,307
American Indian/Alaskan Native	0.4			0.3		
Asian/Pacific Islander	4.1			2.9		
Black	2.3	(81)	19,909	5.9	(149)	17,258
Hispanic	0.5			0.7		
White	92.7	(1,034)	20,990	90.2	(1,378)	18,424
Beginning professional (all)	29.1	(347)	13,221	70.9	(844)	13,253
American Indian/Alaskan Native	0.1			0.0		
Asian/Pacific Islander	5.1			2.6		
Black	4.0	(29)	13,000	3.7	(85)	13,423
Hispanic	0.8			2.0		
White	89.9	(318)	13,235	91.6	(759)	13,235

[a]Source: American Library Association, Office for Library Personnel Resources, 1981.

$24,999. White male directors earn more than any other category of directors—23.5% more than white females, and 40.9% more than minority females.

White male branch or department heads are also earning at the top of their category, though not by so much as directors. They earn 12.8% more than white females and 17.8% more than minority females. At starting levels, white males and females are even—minority males are slightly behind the median and minority females slightly ahead of all others, though only by 1%.

The OLPR study is the most current source on the composition of academic staffs. It is interesting to compare it to other studies of the academic library work force in order to determine changes and trends. A study of salary structures of librarians in higher education for 1975–1976 conducted by the Association of College and Research Libraries of the American Library Association provides a great deal of information on the comparative status of men and women academic librarians including distribution by position, salary comparisons at all levels, minority distribution, and comparisons among four types of academic libraries: universities, 5-year institutions, 4-year colleges, and 2-year colleges (Talbot and von der Lippe, 1976). The study is an extension and amplification of earlier Council on Library Resources sponsored studies (Cameron and Heim, 1970, 1972, 1974) and is linked to the AAUP faculty compensation survey (American Association of University Professors, 1975).

Continuing salary information on academic librarians who work in institutions which are members of the Association of Research Libraries (ARL) has been gathered and displayed for minorities and women in ARL's annual salary surveys since 1977 (Association of Research Libraries, 1977–1980). The 1980 survey shows that 85% of the directors of these largest academic libraries are male and 15% female. Of those earning more than $40,000 (at all levels), 80% are male and 20% female. The average male director's salary was $48,084 and the female's $44,871. With only minor exceptions, men earned higher salaries than women at all levels, including those with the same amount of experience.

The College and University Personnel Association (CUPA) gathers information annually on the 52 highest-level administrative positions in higher education and includes data on the library director position. The 1979–1980 survey cites the median library director salary for 1979–1980 as $28,909 compared to $21,753 for females ("Administrators' Salaries," 1981).

Table 20 presents several statistics from the various surveys of academic libraries. The most striking observation to be made is that there is great difficulty in identifying statistics which are comparable across all the sur-

TABLE 20
Selected Statistics of Academic Librarians[a]

Selected statistics	Males						Females					
	BLS 1970	ACRL 1976	COSWL 1980	OLPR 1980	ARL 1980	CUPA 1980	BLS 1970	ACRL 1976	COSWL 1980	OLPR 1980	ARL 1980	CUPA 1980
Total work force	33.9%	38.5%	33.9%	37.7%	38.2%	—	66.1%	61.5%	66.1%	62.3%	61.8%	—
Director's percentage salary	—	64.2%	—	73.1%	84.7%	—	—	35.%	—	26.9%	15.3%	—
Salary	—	$22,242[b]	—	$32,999[c]	—	$28,909[c]	—	$17,062[b]	—	$24,999[c]	—	$21,753[b]
Department or branch heads	—	—	—	42.2%	37.8%	—	—	—	—	57.8%	62.2%	—
Salary	—	$15,979[b]	—	$20,396[c]	—	—	—	$14,387[b]	—	$18,307[c]	—	—

[a] Sources: United States Bureau of Labor Statistics, 1980; Talbot and von der Lippe, 1976; Estabrook and Heim, 1980; American Library Association, Office for Library Personnel Resources, 1981; Association of Research Libraries, 1980; "Administrators' Salaries," 1981.
[b] Mean.
[c] Median.

veys. Salaries are aggregated differently; distribution rather than medians is often given; not all studies look at the male–female or white–minority differences.

Academic library statistics are also gathered at the state and regional levels by a variety of regional and state library associations. The work force analyst may wish to take these into account since the larger surveys often analyze regions of the nation, and a rich data set on academic library demographic factors is beginning to be developed.

B. Public Libraries

Salary and demographic information for public librarians has not been as consistently collected as for academic librarians. It is interesting to speculate on the reasons for this. Public librarianship is the only major sector of the profession where librarians practice independently of larger institutional affiliation. Academic and school librarians are often included in larger surveys which examine the status of all professionals within the larger institutions where there is interinstitutional pressure to attain status at least equal to those of comparable training and experience. The public librarian has no umbrella association such as the AAUP to collect data, and there has not been the tendency toward self-examination on the part of public librarians that occurs in the academic sector. Thus, the data on public librarians has tended to be less complete. Clearly, only the ALA can develop studies for the public library sector.

There are, however, scattered sources which begin to contribute to a basic understanding of the public library work force. In 1974, there were 36,135 public librarians, of whom 15% were male and 85% female. As noted in Table 21, when libraries increase in size and fiscal resources, the percentage of male professionals grows steadily (U.S. National Center for Educational Statistics, 1980).

Other statistical sources for information on public libraries include reports by the Urban Libraries Council (large urban libraries), the St. Charles City County Library (West–North–Central States), and the Public Library of Fort Wayne and Allen County, Indiana (libraries serving populations of 100,000 or more) (Myers, 1981). Wolfson has provided salary information on head librarians in 1979 by size of municipality, but not by sex, as shown in Table 22 (Wolfson, 1980).

The most recent information about the total public library work force comes from the ALA/OLPR study cited earlier. As indicated in Table 23, in 1980 the public library work force was 79% female and 21% male. At the director level, males held 46.9% of the top posts and earned a median

TABLE 21
Men and Women in Public Libraries by Size, 1974[a]

Population served	Males (N)	%	Females (N)	%	T
Under 10,000	195	3.4	5526	96.6	5721
10,000–24,999	456	9.6	4271	90.4	4727
25,000–49,999	772	16.2	3988	83.8	4760
50,000–99,999	886	17.1	4309	82.9	5195
100,000–249,999	812	17.6	3811	88.4	4623
250,000–499,999	622	20.3	2448	79.7	3070
500,000 and over	1756	21.8	6283	78.2	8039

[a]Source: U. S. National Center for Education Statistics, 1980, p. 219.

salary of $30,241, which is 34.2% more than the 53.1% female directors who earned a median salary of $19,908. The director statistics may seem peculiar on first examination. While minority and white males are quite close in compensation, there is a salary advantage of nearly 40% of minority women over white women and 5% over white men. This is not as much a move forward as it may seem. It may be explained by the fact that a very small number of minority women hold director posts and these tend to be in major metropolitan areas. Thus, two or three minority women in highly paid positions raise the median for all minority women. More telling is the median salary for all women directors—$19,908, which indicates that there are very few women in the minority category or the entire female median

TABLE 22
Median Salaries of Public Library Directors by Population Served, 1979[a]

1,000,000+	$48,200
500,000–999,999	35,124
250,000–499,999	30,909
100,000–249,999	28,052
50,000–99,999	24,091
25,000–49,999	19,800
10,000–24,999	15,361
5,000–9,999	10,966
2,500–4,999	8,150
2,500 and under	7,292

[a]Source: Wolfson, 1980.

TABLE 23
Public Library Work Force[a]

	Males			Females		
	%	(N)	Median salary ($)	%	(N)	Median salary ($)
Total staff	21.4	(2,801)		78.6	(10,285)	
American Indian/Alaskan Native	0.2	(6)		0.2	(23)	
Asian/Pacific Islander	3.6	(79)		2.8	(367)	
Black	7.4	(155)		5.5	(763)	
Hispanic	1.5	(85)		3.0	(156)	
White	87.3	(2,476)		88.4	(8,976)	
Directors	46.9	(263)	30,241	53.1	(298)	19,908
American Indian/Alaskan Native	0.0			0.3		
Asian/Pacific Islander	0.8	(6)	28,686	1.0	(16)	30,073
Black	1.5			3.4		
Hispanic	0.0			0.7		
White	97.7	(257)	28,489	94.6	(282)	18,000
Branch and department heads	21.3	(923)	19,495	78.7	(3,410)	17,139
American Indian/Alaskan Native	0.1			0.4		
Asian/Pacific Islander	1.8	(88)	17,818	2.0	(378)	16,667
Black	5.4			7.2		
Hispanic	2.2			1.5		
White	90.5	(835)	18,464	88.9	(3,032)	16,401
Beginning professional (all)	19.8	(713)	13,316	80.2	(2,881)	13,271
American Indian/Alaskan Native	0.0			0.4		
Asian/Pacific Islander	3.1	(163)	13,107	3.4	(607)	12,950
Black	14.2			14.5		
Hispanic	5.6			2.8		
White	77.1	(550)	13,458	78.9	(2,274)	13,379

[a]Source: American Library Association, Office for Library Personnel Resources 1981.

would be pulled up. Nevertheless, it is a bright spot that the talents of a few minority women are recognized and are compensated at the director level at rates equal to or comparable to those of men.

Women comprise over three-fourths of all branch or department heads but earn 12% less than men. Both minority women and white women are below the male median. At beginning levels, men and women are quite close in compensation, and whites are slightly ahead of minorities in salaries. The number of minority beginning-level librarians in the public library sector is perhaps the single most exciting piece of information elicited by the OLPR survey. Minorities in public libraries are beginning to approach affirmative action goals.

A longitudinal series of surveys of public library directors by the Public Library of Fort Wayne and Allen County, Indiana, provides information on director positions at large libraries (those serving populations of 100,000 or more) (Heim and Kacena, 1981). Table 24 displays the number of male and female directors for this period.

In libraries serving a population of 750,000 or more, 83% of the director positions were filled by men as compared to a figure of 60% for libraries serving a population of 100,000–199,999. These figures are important in interpreting the figure of 53.1% of female directors found in the OLPR survey (see Table 23). Women direct over half of the public libraries, but for the most part, they direct the smaller libraries. This is a longstanding problem in discussion of public library leadership. As early as 1938, Alvarez pointed out that women held the majority of public library posts (Alvarez, 1938), an observation that was refuted by Harvey (1957) who noted that though women predominate in numbers, they are not in director posts in proportion to their number in the work force and that the posts held are in smaller libraries. The salaries of male and female directors of large public libraries are also disparate, regardless of region or size. The median female director salary in 1981 was $29,220, compared to the male median of $34,505 (Heim and Kacena, 1981). Women directors also generated less support for their libraries ($7.21 per capita) than male directors ($9.16 per capita) and lower salaries for beginning professionals ($13,164) than their male counterparts ($13,814) (Heim and Kacena, 1981).

Table 25 compares data on public librarians from four studies. As in the comparison table for academic libraries, there are few variables that are comparable for all studies. Comparison of the Bureau of Labor Statistics data with the COSWL and OLPR studies seem to indicate that there is a higher percentage of men now in public libraries than there was a decade age.

TABLE 24
Large Public Library Directors by Sex 1973–1981[a]

Year	Males (%)	Females (%)
1973	66	34
1975	72	28
1977	69	31
1979	66	34
1981	66	34

[a]Source: Heim and Kacena, 1981.

TABLE 25
Selected Statistics on Public Librarians[a]

	Males				Females			
	BLS	Fort Wayne	COSWL	OLPR	BLS	Fort Wayne	COSWL	OLPR
Total work force	14	—	19.1	21.4	86	—	80.9	78.6
Salary (all)	—	—	$19,319	—	—	—	$14,236	—
Directors	—	66%	—	46.9	—	34%	—	53.1
Salary	—	$34,505	—	$30,241	—	$29,220	—	$19,908

[a] Sources: United States, Bureau of Labor Statistics, 1975; Heim and Kacena 1981; Estabrook and Heim, 1980; American Library Association, Office for Library Personnel Resources, 1981.

C. School Librarians

Data on school librarians have been the most elusive information for a library workforce analysis (Heim, 1981). The complexities of drawing a statistically meaningful sample for schools and school systems throughout the United States have prevented the development of comprehensive library-association-sponsored surveys of this sector of the library profession.

TABLE 26
Mean of Mean Salaries of Librarians and Classroom Teachers by Enrollment Group[a]

Year	25,000 or more	10,000–24,999	2,500–9,999	300–2,499	Total all reporting systems
Librarians					
1974–1975	$12,689	$13,116	$12,221	$10,931	$12,546
1975–1976	13,666	13,867	13,151	11,287	13,207
1976–1977	14,180	14,689	14,099	12,265	13,921
1977–1978	15,076	15,582	14,926	13,073	14,739
1978–1979	15,996	16,726	15,816	14,145	15,727
1979–1980	17,106	17,549	17,095	15,356	16,764
1980–1981	19,214	19,742	18,964	17,006	18,689
Classroom teachers					
1974–1975	11,964	12,187	11,325	10,156	11,507
1975–1976	12,902	12,966	12,424	10,848	12,437
1976–1977	13,621	13,660	13,304	11,799	13,119
1977–1978	14,290	14,664	14,147	12,549	13,941
1978–1979	15,178	15,732	15,014	13,593	14,899
1979–1980	16,119	16,624	16,281	14,683	15,913
1980–1981	17,954	18,474	18,008	16,340	17,678

[a] Source: Educational Research Services, 1975–1981 (Part 2; Table 1).

The best general information on salaries for school librarians is included in annual studies conducted by Educational Research Services (ERS) (1975–1981). The ERS surveys include information on scheduled and paid salaries of professionals and salaries paid support staff in public schools analyzed by four enrollment groups, five per-pupil expenditure ranges, and eight geographic regions. Although the ERS data are not broken down by sex, they are particularly important to any analysis of the library work force since librarians working in schools are usually women and many are trained in programs not reported in surveys such as the *Library Journal* placement series. Because data are not provided by ERS on the educational background of these librarians, we cannot make generalizations about their economic status in relationship to educational background.

Table 26 displays salaries paid to librarians and to classroom teachers for 1974–75 through 1980–81. From it we see that librarians are paid slightly more than their classroom colleagues no matter how the data are presented (the same relation holds by geographic region and per-pupil expenditure range, data for which are not presented here).

The ERS survey also reports salaries paid to full-time library clerks, which are compared in Table 27 to building-level secretaries–steno-

TABLE 27
Mean of Mean Salaries of Building Level Library Clerks and Secretaries–Stenographers by Enrollment Group[a]

Year	25,000 or more	10,000–24,999	2,500–9,999	300–2,499	Total all reporting systems
Library clerks					
1974–1975	$5,440	$5,532	$4,596	$4,027	$5,052
1975–1976	5,867	5,879	4,833	3,982	5,333
1976–1977	6,319	6,181	5,360	4,587	5,668
1977–1978	6,528	6,418	5,780	5,023	5,970
1978–1979	6,895	7,010	6,274	5,500	6,449
1979–1980	7,523	7,342	6,596	5,844	6,778
1980–1981	8,445	8,150	7,355	6,606	7,573
Secretaries– stenographers					
1974–1975	$ 6,613	$ 6,587	$5,689	$4,952	$6,046
1975–1976	7,370	6,886	6,162	5,318	6,521
1976–1977	7,446	7,405	6,652	5,941	6,849
1977–1978	7,972	7,899	7,168	6,383	7,328
1978–1979	8,701	8,249	7,628	6,868	7,772
1979–1980	9,328	8,990	8,214	7,435	8,348
1980–1981	10,411	10,065	9,174	8,398	9,357

[a] Source: Educational Research Services, 1975–1981 (Part 3; Table 1).

graphers. This group, which is certainly composed almost entirely of women, earned very low salaries.

The ERS data provide ongoing information on the largest component of the library work force and should be carefully monitored when assessing the economic status of the profession as a whole.

D. State Libraries and Agencies

Barratt Wilkins' *Survey of State Library Agencies, 1977*, prepared for the National Center for Education Statistics, is the only major current analysis of state-level library positions analyzed by sex (Wilkins, 1979). Wilkins found that two-thirds of the professional staff at state library agencies were women but that a greater proportion of management positions was held by men. Administrative posts accounted for 21.4% of the male employees and only 12.9% of the women (p. 83). Wilkins presents tables which report position, sex, and type of service of employees for each state and territory.

Other state-agency-related data, which do not differentiate by sex, include the U.S. Civil Service Commission *State Salary Survey* series, which reports range, median, and mean for librarians, senior librarians, and library services directors for each state (U.S. Office of Intergovernmental Personnel Program) and a report from the American Library Association, Association of Specialized and Cooperation Library Agencies (1980), which provides salary ranges for eight state library positions, including beginning librarian, for each state, but does not identify numbers or sex in each position.

E. Library of Congress

The Library of Congress (LC) Women's Program analyzes employment data annually to determine the status of women at the Library (U.S. Library of Congress). The 1980 report indicates that although women comprise 53% of the LC work force they hold only 14% of the top positions (grades 16–18). The term "grade gap" is used in these annual analyses to describe the difference between the average grades of men and women. In 1980, women's average grade was 8.32 to men's 9.97—a grade gap of 1.65.

While women have made slight increases in management positions since these data have been reported, they do not hold management posts in proportion to their numbers in the LC work force. In 1980, women accounted for 13% of the Department Head position, 25% of the Director of Departmental Functions, Assistant or Associate Head positions, 32% of the

Division Chief positions, 28% of the Assistant Division Chief, and 44% of the Section Head positions. One woman was in an executive officer position. Minority women comprised nearly half of the women in the library, but their average grade, 6.77, was 1.55 lower than that of other women in the library.

F. Library Science Faculty

Good longitudinal data on the composition and compensation of faculty members involved in formal library education, analyzed by sex, are provided by a series dating from 1976 (Bidlack 1979a, 1980). The most recent report in the series expanded coverage to include associate members of the Association of American Library Schools, as well as full members.

1. ALA-ACCREDITED PROGRAMS

In 1979–1980, 58.8% of the total faculty was male and 41.2% female—a ratio that Bidlack notes has remained constant during the 5 years the data have been analyzed by sex. Table 28 compares the percentage of males and females at different ranks for the base year 1975–1976, and for 1979–1980.

Women faculty have gained in percentage at the professor level but not at the associate level. The greater number of women in the assistant professor ranks may augur long-term changes. Male deans and directors with fiscal-year appointments earned a median salary of $40,000—15.5% more than

TABLE 28
Faculty Distribution by Rank and Sex in AALS Member Schools, 1979–1980 (%)[a]

Rank	Males		Females	
	1975–1976[b]	1979–1980[c]	1975–1976[b]	1979–1980[c]
Deans–directors	80.3	79.1	19.7	20.9
Professors	70.5	67.4	29.5	32.6
Associate professors	54.3	61.3	45.7	38.7
Assistant professors	54.0	48.6	46.0	51.4
Instructors	25.0	20.0	75.0	80.0
Lecturers	42.1	29.2	57.9	70.8

[a] Source: Bidlack, 1980, p. F–4.
[b] 62 Schools; 697 full-time faculty.
[c] 67 Schools; 714 full-time faculty.

TABLE 29
Average Salaries of Male and Female Faculty at AALS Member Schools, 1979–1980[a]

Rank[b]	Males		Females		Women's salaries as % of men's	
	Fiscal year	Academic year	Fiscal year	Academic year	Fiscal year	Academic year
Professor	$36,579	$30,215	$35,722	$27,194	97.7%	90.0%
Associate professor	30,761	22,991	30,211	22,975	98.2%	99.9%
Assistant professor	24,501	19,033	22,815	19,071	93.1%	100.2%
Instructor	—	15,500	—	15,644	—	100.9%
Lecturer	22,504	23,237	20,547	20,710	91.3%	89.1%

[a] Source: Bidlack, 1980, F–12.
[b] There are 117 individuals with fiscal-year appointments and 516 individuals with academic-year appointments.

the female median of $33,800. Table 29 displays average salaries of other male and female faculty in 1979–1980.

Women earn less at the professor rank for academic year appointments than do men but are virtually even in the lower ranks with the exception of lecturer. For the first time, racial and ethnic data were included in the library faculty survey. These are not broken down by sex. Whites comprise 92.8% of the faculties and minorities 7.2%. Earned doctorates are also analyzed by sex, but not tested against salary to discover if this has a causal effect. Over half the women (56.8%) had earned doctorates as compared to over three-fourths (76.7%) of the men.

2. AALS-ASSOCIATE MEMBER SCHOOLS

Bidlack's earlier studies (1979a) did not survey AALS–associate member schools, and their inclusion in the 1979–1980 survey expands our understanding of the demographic background of those who prepare library-science practitioners. Future studies are planned to include these data. In 1979–1980, associate member school faculty composition was quite similar to that of member schools, as shown in Table 30. Salaries of men and women are more alike than in AALS member schools, but the overall distribution puts more men in higher ranks.

3. FACULTY AVAILABILITY IN TERMS OF AFFIRMATIVE ACTION

Bidlack has also provided a profile of the faculty and doctoral students in those institutions that grant doctoral degrees (Bidlack, 1979b). The faculty

TABLE 30
Faculty Distribution by Rank and Sex and Average Salary for Academic-Year Appointments at AALS Associate Member Schools, 1979–1980[a]

	Male		Female		
	Distribution	Mean salary	Distribution	Mean salary	Women's earnings percentage of men's
Deans–directors	64.0%	—	36%	—	—
Professor	67.9%	$25,234	32.1%	$24,351	96.5
Associate professor	62.9%	20,449	37.1%	20,523	100.4
Assistant professor	42.0%	17,590	58.0%	17,876	101.6
Instructor	12.5%	—	87.5%	14,526	—

[a]Source: Bidlack, 1980, p. F–28.

of these schools was predominantly male (59.7%) and the number of women in doctoral programs was 51.6%. The faculty at these schools included 5.6% minorities; doctoral students were 21.8% minorities. Bidlack concludes that with the new faculty coming very largely from these programs, it seems reasonable to predict that the male–female ratio will gradually shift over the next decade to provide balance, and minority representation on library school faculties should increase rather dramatically.

G. Medical Libraries

Information on librarians in medical settings has not been consistently gathered. Goldstein and Hill (1975, 1980) surveyed large biomedical libraries in 1972 and 1977 and found a striking disproportion in the number of women in the overall health sciences librarian work force. They analyzed their data differently in the two studies. In the first, responding libraries were categorized by type (medical school, society, government, pharmaceutical, and hospital); in the second, by size of library. Thus, it is not easy to compare the two studies on specifics in all cases. Table 31 displays selected characteristics from their 1977 study.

There has been a decline in the number of women heading large health science libraries. For 1950, 1972, and 1977, the percentage of women directors were 83, 43.3, and 39%, respectively. Women, when they did hold the top post, did so in the smaller libraries. Men were filling vacancies at the top nearly three times as quickly as women and were more likely to have been promoted externally, a trend that Metz has also pointed out in his study of academic directorships (Metz, 1978, p. 363). Goldstein and Hill conclude (1980, p. 15):

TABLE 31
Selected Characteristics of Health Science Librarians in Large Biomedical Libraries, 1977[a]

Characteristics	Male	Female
Distribution (all)	22.7%	77.3%
25 largest by collection	25.0	75.0
25 smallest by collection	26.0	74.0
Medical school	24.6	75.4
Directors	61.0	39.0
25 largest by collection	69.6	30.4
25 smallest by collection	43.5	56.5
Medical school	65.6	34.4

[a] Source: Goldstein and Hill, 1980.

Neither affirmative action nor social awareness, nor even legislation itself during the period from 1972 to 1977 has increased the number of women in top administrative jobs in health science libraries. As a matter of fact, the trend continues in the opposite direction.

A survey of salaries in U.S. and Canadian medical schools for 1976–1977 conducted under the auspices of the Medical Library Association's Survey and Statistics Committee reveals that 30% of the directors of the libraries were female and 70% were male (Stangl and Hoke, 1977). The men earned a mean salary of $18,900 and the women $14,782—78% of the male figure. Stangl and Hoke do not discuss their findings extensively but present numerous tables including cross-tabulations of salary and sex by professional experience, selected positions and minority–nonminority status.

VI. SURVEYS OF INFORMATION PROFESSIONALS

We noted earlier that as the fields of work for the library trained professional expand it becomes more difficult to obtain clear demographic data for those in nontraditional fields. We do not know to what extent library science graduates work in the many categories defined in the University of Pittsburgh (1980) study. Salary and demographic data on the information professional in the larger sense are not yet consistently gathered. The ASIS membership study provides an indication of one small sector of the information profession, but we really do not yet have a clear idea of the total frame of reference of this growing sector of potential employment for the library graduate.

There are several information sources that provide additional background about those employed in the information sector. None of these are differentiated by sex. They include the annual salary and budget survey in *Online,* which provides ranges and average salaries for head librarians, experienced searchers, and beginning searchers in corporate scientific–technical business–finance, medical, legal, and academic settings. Table 32 displays some of these data, undifferentiated by sex, and demonstrates the difference in earning between corporate and academic settings.

The Associated Information Managers (AIM) has reported selected characteristics of its members ("AIM profiles," 1980). Again, no data are reported by sex, but the fact that 39% of the respondents in the commercial sector, 44% in the government sector, and 33% in the nonprofit sector (40% overall) possessed the professional library degree indicates that those responding come in significant numbers from library training. The editors of *Datamation* used 55 job categories to query data processing professionals about 1980 salaries and cross-tabulated these with installation size (determined by monthly hardware rental), by selected industry, and by major metropolitan areas (Shaw, 1980). Several job categories contain the word "librarian" in the job description: "programming team librarian," "program librarian," "magnetic media librarian," and "librarian for technical documentation." It is impossible to assess, without educational characteristics, to what degree these positions require library training.

Although male–female response was insufficient to make statistical inference, Shaw notes (1980, p. 110) that "it was far easier to find women in the categories of data entry, librarians, and production control clerks than as senior system analysts." There is only minimal information on the overall data processing and computer field. But the emergence of a new professional group, the Association of Women in Computing, to promote communication, to further the professional development and advancement, and to promote the education of women of all ages in the computing professions

TABLE 32
Average Salaries of Online Searching Personnel, 1979[a]

Field	Head librarian	Experienced searcher	Beginning searcher
Corporate Sci–Tech	$22,800	$18,200	$12,700
Business and finance	24,800	21,100	14,700
Medical	24,600	20,900	15,300
Legal	18,900	—	—
Academic	25,000	16,200	11,300

[a]Source: "Salary and Budget Survey" 1979.

attests to the perception of a growing number of women in the field of disparities in opportunity and remuneration in this section of the information work place (Heim, 1980, p. 321).

One other potential source of information on the information edge of the library profession is *Computer Career News,* which publishes features on professional development of computer personnel. A recent survey assessing "hot" careers noted, "women will rise up the management ladder at an accelerated pace ("Recruiter survey," 1981).

VII. CONCLUSION

Whether women are rising up the ladder of librarianship at an accelerated rate is still an open question. A decade of activism on the part of women librarians has resulted in no clear improvement of status. There have been some gains and some losses. A closure of the starting salary differential (up to 1979) is outweighed by a continuing divergence of salaries in relationship to time spent in library work. Further compilation and analysis of economic and demographic data are necessary before a clear picture of the patterns of remuneration and status between the sexes will be available.

REFERENCES

Administrators' salaries rise 8.7 pct.; Women's pay is lower in most fields (1981). *Chronicle of Higher Education* 22 (23 March), 8–10.

AIM profiles the information management professional (1980). *The Information Manager* 2 (Spring), 32–33.

Alvarez, R. S. (1938). Women's place in librarianship. *Wilson Bulletin for Libraries* 13, 175–178.

American Association of University Professors (1975). Two steps backward: Report on the economic status of the profession, 1974–75. *AAUP Bulletin* 61, 118–199.

American Library Association, Association of Specialized and Cooperative Library Agencies (1980). "Salary Data—State Library Agencies—December 1980." American Library Association, Chicago.

American Library Association, Office for Library Personnel Resources (1977). "Degrees and Certificates Awarded by U.S. Library Education Programs 1973–1976." American Library Association, Chicago.

American Library Association, Office for Library Personnel Resources (1980). "Degrees and Certificates Awarded by U.S. Library Education Programs 1976–1979." American Library Association, Chicago.

American Library Association, Office for Library Personnel Resources (1981). "The Racial, Ethnic, and Sexual Composition of Library Staff in Academic and Public Libraries." American Library Association, Chicago.

Association of Research Libraries (1977–1980). "ARL Annual Salary Survey 1976–77, 1977–78, 1978–79, 1979–80." The Association, Washington, D.C.
Bidlack, R. E. (1979a). A statistical survey of 67 library schools. *Journal of Education for Librarianship* 19, 318–336. Earlier reports appeared in the same journal 16 (1976), 258–270; 17 (1977), 199–213; 18 (1978), 251–267.
Bidlack, R. E. (1979b). "Faculty availability in terms of affirmative action." Unpublished paper, University of Michigan, School of Library Science, Ann Arbor.
Bidlack, R. (1980). Faculty. *In* "Library Education Statistical Report 1980" pp. F1–F98. Association of American Library Schools, State College, Pennsylvania.
Brown, G. H. (1979). "Degree Awards to Women: An Update." U.S. National Center for Educational Statistics, Washington, D.C.
Cameron, D. F., and Heim, P. (1970). "The Economics of Librarianship in College and University Libraries, 1969–70." Council on Library Resources, Washington, D.C.
Cameron, D. F., and Heim, P. (1972). "How Well Are They Paid?" Council on Library Resources, Washington, D.C.
Cameron, D. F., and Heim, P. (1974). "Librarians in Higher Education." Council on Library Resources, Washington, D.C.
Deutrich, M. E. (1973). Women in archives: Ms. versus Mr. archivist. *American Archivist* 36, 171–181.
Deutrich, M. E. (1975). Women in archives: A summary report of the Committee on the Status of Women in the Archival Profession. *American Archivist* 38, 43–46.
Deutrich, M. E. (1981). Ms. versus Mr. Archivist: An update. *SAA Women's Caucus Newsletter* 5 (March), 3–6.
Deutrich, M. E., and DeWhitt, B. (1980). Survey of the archival profession-1979. *American Archivist* 43, 527–535.
DeWath, N. V., and Cooper, M. D. (1980). "1981–82 Library Human Resources. A Study of Supply and Demand." Unpublished paper, King Research, Inc., Rockville, Maryland.
Educational Research Services, Inc. (1975–1981). "National Survey of Salaries and Wages in Public Schools, 1974/75—1980/81." Educational Research Services, Arlington, Virginia.
Estabrook, L. S., and Heim, K. M. (1980). A profile of ALA personal members. *American Libraries* 11, 654–659.
Estes, M. E. (1979). The Southern California Association of Law Libraries 1979 Salary Survey. *Law Library Journal* 72, 526–533.
Filter, N. H. (1969). "Selected Characteristics of Members of the Music Library Association." Unpublished paper, Kent State University Library School. (Portions of the data were published in MLA: A membership profile. *MLA Notes* 26 (1970), 487–490.)
Frarey, C. J. (1970). Law library salaries. *Law Library Journal* 63, 471–504.
Goldstein, R. K., and Hill, D. R. (1975). The status of women in the administration of health science libraries. *Bulletin of the Medical Library Association* 63, 386–395.
Goldstein, R. K., and Hill, D. R. (1980). The status of women in the administration of health science libraries: A five year follow up study. *Bulletin of the Medical Library Association* 68, 6–15.
Harvey, J. F. (1957) "The Librarian's Career: a Study of Mobility." ACRL Microcard Series, No. 85. University of Rochester Press, Rochester, New York.
Heim, K. M. (1980). Women in librarianship. *In* "ALA Yearbook 1980" (R. Wedgeworth, ed.), pp. 317–322. American Library Association, Chicago.
Heim, K. M. (1981). Toward a workforce analysis of the school library media professional. *School Media Quarterly* 9, 235–249.
Heim, K. M., and Kacena, C. (1981). Sex, salaries, & library support . . . 1981. *Library Journal*

106, 1692–1699. Earlier reports by Heim and Kacena appeared in same journal **105** (1980), 17–22; **104** (1979), 675–680. Reports by the series initiators, Carpenter, R. L. and Shearer, K. D. appeared in same journal **101** (1976), 777–783; **99** (1974), 101–107; **97** (1972), 3682–3685.

Hughes, M. (1971). Sex-based discrimination in law libraries. *Law Library Journal* **64**, 13–22.

King, D. A. (1980). 1979 statistical survey of law school libraries and librarians. *Law Library Journal* **73**, 451–497.

King, D. W., Krauser, C., and Sague, V. M. (1980). Profile of ASIS membership. *Bulletin of the American Society for Information Science* **6** (August), 9–17.

Learmont, C. L. (1980). Students. *In* "Library Education Statistical Report 1980," pp. S1–S83. Association of American Library Schools, State College, Pennsylvania.

Leinbach, A. E., and Beardwood, L. B. (1980). Greater Philadelphia Law Library Association 1979 survey. *Law Library Journal* **73**, 498–505.

Manchak, B. (1971). ALA salary survey: Personal members. *American Libraries* **2**, 409–417.

Metz, P. (1978). Administrative succession in the academic library. *College and Research Libraries* **39**, 358–364.

Molenda, M. (1971). "The Relationship of Sociodemographic Characteristics and Opinion to Political Participation in a Professional Association." Unpublished dissertation, Syracuse University.

Molenda, M., and Cambre, M. (1977a) The 1976 Member Opinion Survey. *Audiovisual Instruction* **22** (March), 65–69.

Molenda, M., and Cambre, M. (1977b). The AECT member opinion survey: Income comparisons. *Audiovisual Instruction* **22** (April), 47–51.

Music Library Association (1975). Report of the Committee on Goals and Objectives. *MLA Notes* **32**, 15–30.

Myers, M. (1981). Recent library personnel surveys. *In* "The Bowker Annual of Library and Book Trade Information" (26th ed.), pp. 223–231. R. R. Bowker, New York.

Peterson, G. T. (1977). Graduates of media programs 1975–76: An optomistic study. *Audiovisual Instruction* **22** (April), 19–21. Earlier reports in same journal **21** (April 1976), 9–11; **20** (April 1975), 46–49; **19** (March 1974) 26–28; **18** (May 1973), 41–43.

"Placements and Salaries" (1973–1981). An annual survey published in *Library Journal* successive years by Frarey, C. J., and Learmont, C. L. **98** (1973), 1880–1886; **99** (1974), 1767–1774; **100** (1975), 1767–1774; Learmont, C. L., and Darling, R. L. **101** (1976), 1487–1493; **102** (1977), 1345–1351; **103** (1978), 1339–1345; Learmont, C. L., and Troiano, R. **104** (1979), 1415–1422; Learmont, C. L. **105** (1980), 2271–2277; and Learmont, C. L., and Van Houton, S. **106** (1981), 1881–1887.

Prostano, J. S., and Prostano, E. T. (1979). Technology courses in library schools. *Audiovisual Instruction* **24** (September), 38–39.

Recruiter surveys: Computer pros are hottest. (1981). *Computer Career News* **2** (23 February), 7.

Renshawe, M. L. (1976). The condition of the law librarian in 1976. *Law Library Journal* **69**, 627–629.

Salary and budget survey (1979). *Online* **3**, 51–53.

Schiller, A. R. (1969a). "Characteristics of Professional Personnel in College and University Libraries." Illinois State Library Research Series no. 16, Springfield, Illinois. ERIC ED 020 766.

Schiller, A. R. (1969b). Academic librarians' salaries. *College and Research Libraries* **30**, 101–111.

Schiller, A. R. (1969c). The widening sex gap. *Library Journal* **94**, 1098–1100.

Schiller, A. R. (1970). The disadvantaged majority: Women employed in libraries *American Libraries* 1, 345–349.
Schiller, A. R. (1974). Women in librarianship. *In Advances in Librarianship* 4 (M. J. Voigt, ed.), pp. 103–147. Academic Press, New York.
Sellen, B. C. (1980). "What Else You Can Do with A Library Degree." Gaylord Professional Publications in association with Neal-Schuman Publishers, Syracuse, New York.
Shaw, L. C. (1980). 1980 salary survey. *Datamation* 26, 110–118.
Shediac, M. (1978). Greater Philadelphia Law Library Association 1977 survey. *Law Library Journal* 71, 170–176.
Shediac, M. (1980). Private law libraries special interest section 1979 salary survey. *Law Library Journal* 73, 218–226.
Sink, D. L. (1980). Employment trends for media graduates 1978–79. *In* "Educational Media Yearbook 1980" (J. W. Brown and S. N. Brown, eds.), pp. 69–72. Libraries Unlimited, Littleton, Colorado. Earlier reports appeared in *Audiovisual Instruction* 23 (September 1978), 44–45; 24 (September 1979), 36–37. See also G. T. Peterson in this list of references.
Special Libraries Association (1970–1979). SLA salary survey. Surveys for 1970, 1973, 1976, and 1979 were published in *Special Libraries* 61 (1970), 333–348; 64 (1973), 594–628; 67 (1976), 597–624; 70 (1979), 559–589; and amended in 71 (1980), 542.
Stangl, P., and Hoke, W. N. (1977). "A Survey of Salaries of Medical School Librarians in the United States and Canada, 1976–77." Stanford University, Stanford, California.
Talbot, R. J., and von der Lippe, A. (1976). "Salary Structure of Librarians in Higher Education for the Academic Year 1975–76." American Library Association, Chicago.
U.S. Bureau of Labor Statistics (1975). "Library Manpower: A Study of Demand and Supply." Bulletin 1852. U.S. Government Printing Office, Washington, D.C.
U.S. Library of Congress (1979–81). Women's program statistical update. *Library of Congress Information Bulletin* 38 (1979), 210–212; 39 (1980), 238–240; 40 (1981), 109–112.
U.S. National Center for Education Statistics (1980). "Digest of Education Statistics 1980." U.S. Government Printing Office, Washington, D.C.
U.S. Office of Intergovernmental Personnel Programs. (1973–) *State Salary Survey.* U.S. Government Printing Office, Washington, D.C., annual.
University of Pittsburgh (1980). "Manpower Requirements for Scientific and Technical Communication: An Occupational Survey of Information Professionals." Prepared in conjunction with King Research for the National Science Foundation, Project DSI-7727115. University of Pittsburgh, School of Library and Information Science, Pittsburgh, Pennsylvania.
Wilkins, B. (1979). "Survey of State Library Agencies, 1977." GSLS Occasional Paper No. 142. University of Illinois, Graduate School of Library Science, Urbana, Illinois.
Wolfson, S. M. (1980). Salaries of municipal officials of 1979. *In* "The Municipal Yearbook 1980," pp. 83–108. International City Management Association, Washington, D.C.

Personnel Planning, Job Analysis, and Job Evaluation with, Special Reference to Academic Libraries*

SHEILA CRETH[†]

University of Connecticut Library

I. Personnel Planning and Utilization	48
A. The Need for Planning	48
B. Information for Personnel Planning	51
1. Turnover Rates	51
2. Recruitment Data	51
3. Library Programs	52
4. New Library Programs	52
5. Budget Information	53
6. Employee Information	53
C. Summary	54
II. Job Analysis	56
A. Personnel Functions Dependent on Job Analysis	56
1. Recruitment and Selection	56
2. Training and Development	57
3. Personnel Utilization and Job Redesign	58
4. Classification and Compensation Plans	58
B. Job Analysis Methodology	60
1. Job Descriptions	61
2. Questionnaires	62

*This article is based on research sponsored by a Council on Library Resources (CLR) Fellowship, 1980. The data were obtained in three phases: a survey of the literature, a questionnaire completed by personnel administrators in academic research libraries, and site visits to a select number of these libraries as well as several private firms.

[†]Present address: University of Michigan Library, Ann Arbor, Michigan 48109.

		3.	Interviews	63
		4.	Job Observation or Audit	64
		5.	Task Analysis	65
		6.	Other Considerations in Job Analysis	69
	C.	Summary		72
III.	Job Evaluation			73
	A.	The Process of Job Evaluation		73
		1.	Factor-related Problems	73
		2.	Evaluator-related Problems	74
	B.	Job Evaluation Methodology		75
		1.	Ranking System	76
		2.	Classification System	77
		3.	Factor Comparison System	77
		4.	Point System	78
	C.	Job Factors		79
	D.	Job Evaluation in Libraries		81
	E.	Summary		91
IV.	Conclusions			91
	References			94

I. PERSONNEL PLANNING AND UTILIZATION

A. The Need for Planning

An integral part of any organization's administrative program is the ability to identify and forecast staffing needs as well as to assess the needs of the employees in relationship to their work and the work environment. This aspect of personnel is historically referred to as "manpower planning" which has been defined by James Walker (1968) as "the rather complex task of forecasting and planning for the *right* numbers and the *right* kinds of people at the *right* places and the *right* times to perform activities that will benefit both the organization and the individuals in it."[1] An increased interest in personnel planning and utilization in the public and private sector, in business and service organizations, has developed in large part as a result

---

[1] The term "manpower planning" is still the predominant one in the literature whereas the terms "personnel utilization," "personnel planning," and "human resources management" are beginning to appear more frequently. In this paper, the terms "personnel planning" and "personnel utilization" will be used except in the quotation of another author's material.

of forces external to organizations. Equal employment and affirmative action legislation have made it mandatory for libraries along with other organizations to develop more objective means for identifying job requirements and standards for recruitment and for establishing the basis for salary compensation. Another external force which prompts a greater interest in personnel utilization is the present economic climate which places a premium on sound planning in the use of all resources, including staff. This is particularly true in libraries which are faced with stable or reduced budgets and spiraling costs, creating an environment in which more must be done with less. Libraries, like most service organizations, are labor-intensive, and the largest portion of the library budget is allocated to personnel costs—salaries and related benefits such as medical and retirement programs. Therefore, as libraries continue to face rising salaries and stable or reduced budgets, managers will have to rely on the effective use of their human resources to maintain or improve efficiency and effectiveness.

Another factor which is contributing to a heightened interest in sound personnel planning in libraries is the rapid rate of change which impacts on staffing needs and requirements. Library personnel must be equipped to respond to current as well as future needs. Library administorators will need to give as much attention to projecting and anticipating personnel needs as is given to planning for other library resources such as the book budget, space, and technology.

While administrators are frequently faced with reducing or eliminating programs, demands from users for new and expanded activities also continue and must be considered when allocating personnel resources. In all cases, it is necessary to plan for the allocation of vacant positions as they occur and the redeployment and retraining of existing staff as situations warrant. The inability to forecast and to prepare for change within the library organization is costly both in salary dollars when employees work below their level and, more generally, in decreased effectiveness and efficiency when staff morale suffers because of insecurity related to job assignment and status in the organization. As Bryant *et al.* have stated (1973, p. 69) "costs related to recruiting, hiring, training and maintaining employees go up along with other costs in the economy. . . . [An organization] therefore, has an increasingly large financial investment tied up in its labor pool." A successful personnel planning program requires detailed information in several major categories: job requirements, work force or labor pool, and a profile of current employees' skills, abilities, and interests. Lee and Lee (1971, p. 21) indicate that the "effectiveness and quality of the manpower plan depends upon establishing communication with all aspects of the organization and integrating this communication into a plan." They state further that essential information for a personnel planning effort should consist of a comprehensive profile of existing skills, an assessment of the promotable individuals within the organization, training or retraining requirements and capabilities, detailed turnover statistics and analysis, knowledge of current and expected salary levels and pertinent information about the labor supply. . . . In the development of the manpower plan an organization must utilize not only the generalized data from within the organization but it must consider the data available from the broad field in which it operates.

Current information in all of these categories provides the basic data for both short- and long-range planning. As Burack and Gutteridge (1978, p. 3) state, "the emphasis in short-range manpower forecasting is on budgeting and controlling manpower costs as well as identifying human resource talent. Over a longer range (five or more years in the future) period manpower forecasts are used in planning corporate strategy, facilities planning, and identifying managerial replacements."

Academic libraries are not static organizations, but are faced with the constant need to assess and reassess programs and activities and thus the personnel needs and requirements of the organization. In order to plan effectively, library administrators—particularly personnel administrators—need to develop a more thorough and sophisticated understanding of personnel planning and utilization. Personnel planning should be formulated with information internal to the organization as well as information on external forces which will affect staffing directly and indirectly. Organizational information should include data on programs, functions, and activities; availability of resources; and evaluation of employees' skills, abilities, and interests. Information on external factors should include recruitment trends (e.g., the availability of candidates with specific knowledge and experience, economic conditions affecting recruitment) as well as legal changes which may impact staffing such as labor contracts, environmental or safety requirements, and guidelines on "protected" groups in employment. When planning for a specific library program (particularly a new activity), the scope of the planning should include the impact of the program on other library activities and resources both immediately and in the future.

A number of activities within academic libraries have already been identified as requiring expansion or upgrading in order to meet current and future library goals. These include automation, conservation and preservation, personnel, fund raising and, more generally, management—all of which are among priorities for the decade. Attention now needs to be directed to identifying the competencies required to implement successfully or expand these activities and to determining whether potential candidates exist in the library profession. If there is an absence of qualified people, then members of the profession will need to determine what can be done to assure qualified candidates within three to five years. Planning for these contingencies on a long-range basis is a major aspect of personnel planning and utilization, and requires cooperation and communication between members of library organizations and those in the educational programs that support the profession.

B. Information for Personnel Planning

The following section describes data which is basic to a comprehensive personnel planning program and recommends a process for review and analysis of the allocation and effectiveness of personnel resources.

1. TURNOVER RATES

Turnover rates can provide important information for projecting potential vacancies and analysis of these statistics may identify personnel or managerial problems which are contributing to the number of vacancies within a department. Information on turnover and position vacancies should include: (*a*) number and level of staff by library department; (*b*) time period when vacancy occurred; and (*c*) reason(s) for leaving. This data can be analyzed by department, by level of position, by time period, and by the reason for resignation.

All vacant positions should be reviewed by library administrators or managers at the time the vacancy occurs to determine if the position will remain in the department and at the same previously assigned level. Library managers can be requested to provide written justification for continuing the position in the department and thus establish an administrative review of assignments and priorities in relationship to authorizing the filling of a vacant position. The importance of reviewing vacancies and assigning positions to departments and activities becomes even more critical when budget reductions are faced on a temporary or permanent basis.

2. RECRUITMENT DATA

The following information related to recruitment is essential to planning: (*a*) successful and unsuccessful recruitment strategies—advertisements, mailings, etc.; (*b*) positions that are difficult to fill and/or specific experience and knowledge for which it is difficult to locate qualified candidates—subject fields, language skills, managerial experience; (*c*) current information on affirmative action goals; (*d*) current information on graduate library school programs and other educational and training programs which provide potential candidates; and (*e*) appropriate comparative salary data for all levels of staff and types of positions. This information, compiled and analyzed on an annual basis, will contribute to an understanding of the previous years' recruitment efforts and allow for projections about future recruitment activities.

3. LIBRARY PROGRAMS

All library programs and activities should be reviewed on a regular basis in order to assess the current level of the programs and to determine the continued commitment of resources. In order to conduct periodic reviews, information should be available on (*a*) statistics on materials processed and circulated and services used (*b*) problems with specific services such as backlogs, inadequate equipment and facilities, inability to meet increasing demands and (*c*) plans for expansion of services or facilities and changes in policy or procedures that might result in shifting workloads and staffing requirements.

A cycle for reviewing all library programs through the analysis of such data would allow administrators to determine whether library activities still meet the goals originally established or whether priorities have changed sufficiently to diminish the commitment. A periodic review also can identify whether productivity and standards are acceptable and whether staffing is adequate in number and range of skills and abilities to meet existing commitments. This review process should be approached on both a departmental level for example, reference and cataloging, and at the divisional level—public and technical services—in order to assess the interrelationships among the levels of the organization and its various departmental units. This type of review every three to five years will allow for an analysis of interdepartmental coordination and cooperation, work-flow problems as well as any duplication in activities, and a determination whether staff are properly distributed and assigned among the public and technical services departments based on current priorities and existing problems.

4. NEW LIBRARY PROGRAMS

New library programs and activities should not be initiated prior to presentation by the appropriate persons of justification for such a program since the allocation of library resources is implicit in all new activities. Written justification for a new program or major activity, (that is, a new subject library or a bibliographic instruction program) should provide (*a*) an explanation of the scope of the program, how it will contribute to the goals and services of the library, and its relationship to existing library and university programs; (*b*) resources necessary to support the program over three to five years including staff—permanent and hourly, equipment, supplies; and

(c) potential impact on other library activities by the generation of more work for other departments through an increased work load or changes in procedures or work patterns.

New programs always should be weighed against existing programs and a determination made as to whether any existing commitment will have to be diminished or eliminated to support the new activity. Staff morale problems may be generated when work loads continue to increase without additional staff. If this occurs as a result of new programs and activities, then the staff may feel that they are "paying" for poor planning on the part of administrators and managers.

5. BUDGET INFORMATION

Budget information is critical to long-range personnel planning and the following information should be available on a continuous basis but with a careful analysis at least once during each fiscal year: (a) status of salary accounts including permanent, temporary, and student staff, with identification of savings that accrue from vacancies (even if the library is not allowed to capture these savings directly, the information may be important in negotiating for additional support from the institution); (b) identification of "soft" money in the budget such as grant funds, CETA funds, and the potential impact of such funds on continuing library activities and commitment to library personnel; and (c) comparative salary data for library positions in order to assess compensation for library personnel and to identify potential recruitment problems because of the salary structure.

By necessity, the collection and analysis of budget data goes on throughout the fiscal year though a thorough review and analysis is often overlooked as a means to contribute to effective personnel planning. Even in reviewing specific budget proposals, the importance of considering the impact of a single budget proposal against already existing budget allocations is not necessarily recognized. For instance, when a grant proposal is submitted for a new or expanded library activity, it is important to determine what demands will be placed on those library resources for which the grant will not provide reimbursement. It is possible that the receipt of grant funds for a specific project can have a deterimental impact on already heavily committed resources and result in an otherwise undesired shift in priorities among library programs and activities.

6. EMPLOYEE INFORMATION

Information on both professional and support staff should be periodically obtained in order to assess adequately the present and potential capabilities of the library's human resources. Basic information includes: (*a*) assessment of job assignments to determine whether they still reflect the priorities and needs of the departments and the library (often, employees alter their jobs to suit their own needs, thus altering to some degree what is accomplished); (*b*) quality and quantity of performance, and whether acceptable performance goals and standards have been established and are being met; (*c*) employees' abilities, interests, and potential, and whether developmental needs of staff are being met.

The review of job assignments and performance should be accomplished through an annual performance evaluation system. This approach, which is individually focused, can be supplemented by an administrative review of all staff on a periodic basis to assess major shifts and changes in assignments, substantial contributions by staff, personnel problems, and the identification of staff with potential for other assignments. Such a review process could be established between the administrator of a major library division (public services) and the appropriate department heads (reference) every two to three years to provide a collective review of the library's human resources.

This outline for the collection and analysis of data basic to personnel planning is recommended as a means for providing a more systematic approach to effective planning and utilization of personnel. It requires a commitment of time and energy on the part of library administrators and managers, and a willingness to make changes in existing activities, policies, and procedures which may not receive favorable reaction from the staff or the public. The results, though, could be a more effective and dynamic use of the library's most costly and valuable resource.

C. Summary

Clearly, there is much that can be accomplished in getting better control of the planning and utilization of library personnel. As in the past, the future of academic library service will place heavy reliance on the quality of people who work in the libraries. Though there is no way to predict the specifics of the next decade or so in libraries, certainly general trends can be identified and can provide the background for effective personnel planning and utilization.

While there is much that can be accomplished in personnel planning, the results of this study indicate that this activity may not have yet gained prominence in library administration. The data was obtained primarily through a questionnaire consisting of 24 questions related to personnel or manpower planning; 23 personnel administrators responded.

The results indicate that few libraries have an established process for identifying and analyzing personnel needs for the library and those that do indicate that these needs are identified in the annual budget request. The personnel administrators indicated that certain information was gathered regarding personnel—primarily turnover rates, including retirement information. The other types of information that were considered, according to the respondents, were termination of special projects, building changes, affirmative action goals, patterns of library use, acquisitions rates, national and local labor pools, and recruitment trends. Apparently, though, this range of information is not reviewed on a regular basis but as a particular situation arises (for example, building changes), it is considered.

A majority of the respondents also indicated that personnel factors are considered by administrators and managers when planning for new programs or services (or the reduction of same) though these considerations appear to be focused on immediate rather than long-range projections. In addition, the analysis appears to focus almost exclusively on the program and activity under immediate consideration without review of the impact on other library activities and resources. None of the libraries indicated that it has a system for periodic review of library programs, activities, and priorities as part of a process of personnel planning. Indeed, one respondent may have been more honest when stating that the approach to forecasting staffing needs is based on a "gut feeling" or a "seat of the pants" approach.

In assessing the degree to which the libraries routinely obtained information on employees' skills, abilities, and interests, only one respondent indicated that they collect employee data annually through the distribution of a form. Unfortunately, even in this case, the information gathered appears to be more for the record than for personnel planning and utilization. Clearly, information on employees is not routinely updated and used in academic libraries for determining the need for developing staff in order to assure currency in skills and abilities, and to determine more appropriate utilization of staff through transfers, reassignments, and potential for future promotion.

While it appears that personnel planning and utilization in libraries is still *ad hoc* in nature, the concern for better personnel planning was obvious in the list of improvements the respondents felt were needed:

1. a consistent and comprehensive manpower planning system.
2. more formal planning and analysis.
3. comprehensive projection of long-term staffing needs.
4. "hard" information regarding staffing needs in relation to automated systems—costs, productivity, standards, etc.
5. managers' knowledge of classification systems.

6. skills inventory information.
7. job enrichment and job redesign plans.
8. staff development program.
9. system of rewards and incentives.

II. JOB ANALYSIS

A. Personnel Functions Dependent on Job Analysis

Job analysis may be defined as the process of systematically collecting, analyzing, and interpreting information about jobs or occupations. This information is basic to an organization for a variety of personnel functions, including recruitment and selection, training and development, personnel utilization, job redesign, classification, and compensation plans. Occupation and job data also provide an important planning tool for long-range personnel activities, including the identification of future job compentencies required by the organization, aspects of union negotiations, and budget preparation. Occupational data are usually gathered by professional associations or organizations whereas data at the job level are usually gathered and analyzed by organizations.

Recent developments in each of the personnel functions indicated require administrators to become more familiar with the techniques and methods of job analysis.

1. RECRUITMENT AND SELECTION

Two major factors have generated a more careful consideration of methods for defining job requirements for purposes of recruitment and selection:

1. the changing needs and increasing complexity of libraries, resulting in shifts in the types of knowledge and skills needed by librarians and support staff;
2. legal guidelines encompassing equal employment and affirmative action, requiring the establishment of a justifiable basis for job requirements, recruitment and selection procedures.

Federal legislation that affects recruitment and selection criteria most directly is Title VII of the Civil Rights Act of 1964, later amended by the U.S. Congress in 1972 to include public as well as private employers, and

Executive Order 11246. Title VII embodies legislation related to "equal employment" while the Executive Order speaks to "affirmative action." Broadly, this body of legislation asserts that selection criteria should be job-related and should not have an adverse impact on "protected" or "affected" classes in particular women and minorities.

In August 1978, the Equal Employment Opportunity Commission (EEOC), the Civil Service Commission, the Department of Justice, and the Department of Labor jointly issued the *Uniform Guidelines on Employee Selection Procedures,* including the following statement on selection: "Selection procedures include the full range of assessment techniques from traditional paper and pencil tests, performance tests, training programs, probationary periods and physical, educational, and work experience requirements through informal or casual interviews and unscored application forms." The revised *Guidelines* also provide criteria on the validation of selection procedures and specifically mention the importance of job analysis in this process. They state that "any method of job analysis may be used if it provides the information required for specific validation strategy used." Other sections of the *Guidelines* have implications for selection procedures established in libraries and, though they are complex and technical, they outline important principles for employers. In particular, the *Guidelines* point to a need for library administrators to establish an effective method for analyzing library work and jobs specifically to allow for reasonable selection requirements to be identified. Although the *Guidelines* do not have the force of law, the expectation is that the courts will use them in evaluating the activities of any organization that finds itself in a lawsuit involving selection criteria and procedures.

2. TRAINING AND DEVELOPMENT

Although there has been increasing concern with staff training and development in libraries in the past decade (Stone, 1969; Mitchell, 1973; Sheldon, 1973; Breiting, Dorey, and Sockbeson, 1976; Snyder and Saunders, 1978; Martell and Dougherty, 1978; Conroy, 1978; Zweizig, 1979), libraries continue to lag behind other organizations in addressing the training and development needs of staff (librarians, specialists, support staff). This aspect of personnel administration is becoming increasingly critical to effective library service because of the rapidly changing nature of library activities, which requires that staff continually upgrade their skills and abilities. Library administrators need to identify the educational preparation which is required for staff prior to employment; they also need to look to their own responsibilities for training and development of their personnel.

Job analysis can provide detailed information on both training and development needs as well as the broader educational needs of library staff by focusing on the functions and activities within the library organization.

3. PERSONNEL UTILIZATION AND JOB REDESIGN

Administrators will want to know that they utilize personnel appropriate to their knowledge and abilities, that job requirements are appropriate to the demands of the assignments, and that staff salaries reflect the level of responsibilities and tasks assigned to the job. As the nature of library work has altered over the years, the perspective of what tasks are appropriate to professionals and nonprofessionals has also shifted. The allocation of duties between professionals and support staff have not always kept pace with the changes occurring in the library organization; as a result, there is often confusion regarding appropriate tasks as well as concern regarding fair compensation.

Recent studies (Rothenberg, et al., 1971; Ricking and Booth, 1974; Gerczak, 1977; Lee and Lee, 1971; Sergean, 1977; Ferguson and Taylor, 1980; Cottom, 1980; Benedict and Gherman, 1980) indicate an increasing concern within libraries for properly identifying job tasks, levels, and requirements through job analysis. Job analysis provides the detailed information on what currently exists and therefore makes it possible to determine what change is called for and where. Accurate information on jobs will also aid in identifying career ladders that exist (or their absence) for library staff. The identification of career ladders should be based on the similarities and relationships among jobs through an analysis of skills, ability, knowledge, and experience requirements within job families and between them.

4. CLASSIFICATION AND COMPENSATION PLANS

Classification plans are not new to libraries. Professional staff are usually included in a classification plan or system developed by the library while support staff are more likely to be part of the university or state classification system. Classification systems are used as a basis for establishing a hierarchy of jobs to determine a compensation plan or salary structure. A compensation plan that is based on a classification system usually has an established minimum, median, and maximum salary for each step in the plan. This plan may be established, by use of internal factors, salary comparisons, or developed from market salary surveys. It is this latter method that is often used to establish salaries for academic librarians. For example, information made available by the Association of Research Libraries Salary Survey provides the data for library administrators to analyze their compensation plan in relationship to other academic research libraries. Whatever method is used to determine a salary structure, classification and compensation systems should be built on thorough job data in order to insure a fair and equitable system.

As reflected in the literature (Tompkins, 1966; Wilkinson, et al., 1975; Sergean and McKay, 1974; Crowe, 1977; Position Classification at Michigan, 1979; Duda, 1980), the issue of classification increasingly demands the attention of library administrators and staff. In many cases, libraries have revised and restructured their classification systems over a number of years, and, for some professional staff, the issue of faculty status has altered the concept and approach to classifying positions.

Compensation plans also command a great deal of time and attention as library administrators attempt to stay competitive one with the other as well as the general status of salaries for library employees—professional and support staff. An important issue in salary compensation which faces all organizations in the 1980s is the issue of comparable worth. The concept of comparable worth is based on establishing that jobs of equal value pay equal wages. This differs from the "equal pay for equal work" concept in that the jobs compared need not be identical to each other and can, in fact, be entirely different. A mailing from the National Committee on Pay Equity to its members in August 1981 describes recent developments on the comparable worth issues:

1. The Supreme Court on June 8, 1981, declared in *Gunther v. County of Washington, Oregon* that sex-based wage discrimination cases could be brought under Title VII of the 1964 Civil Rights Act, even if women and men are not performing "equal work."
2. On July 5, 1981, men and women city employees of San Jose, California, represented by AFSCME Local 101 walked out in protest over the low wages paid to secretaries, librarians, and other female workers. Settling on July 14, the city and the union agreed to substantial wage increases for these workers in addition to across-the-board wage increases.

In the past several years, Norman D. Willis and Associates (1974, 1976, 1980) have conducted studies of the classification systems of the states of Connecticut and Washington, focused on identifying inequities within these systems based on female- and male-dominated positions. The conclusions of the Connecticut study (1980, p. 34), which compared a series of professional (including librarians), clerical, and laborer positions, indicates that "jobs staffed predominantly by men tend to be paid more at comparable levels of evaluated worth than jobs staffed predominantly by women." The study recommended that these inequities be corrected through the development of a salary structure that would reflect the "comparable worth of all positions within State service" (1980, p. 35). The results of the comparable worth study conducted in Washington State provided library employees at the Seattle Public Library with a tool during contract negotiations to achieve a 5% "catch-up" raise.

The issue of comparable worth will continue to be one of particular concern to members of the library profession in which 75–80% of the professionals are females as are an equal number of support staff. Recently, Eleanor Holmes Norton (1980, p. 7), chair of EEOC, identified comparable worth as one of "two rapidly emerging frontier issues in equal employment." While the comparable worth issue continues to be sorted out and clarified in the courts, through legislation, and across the bargaining table, administrators must still insure that the equal pay for equal work requirement is not overlooked in establishing compensation plans. The Equal Pay Act makes it illegal to pay men and women different wages for the same job. Title VII of the Civil Rights Act of 1964 further broadened this mandate by making it illegal to discriminate on the basis of hiring, firing, wages, or fringe benefits; classifying, referring, assignment, or promoting employees; extending or assigning facilities; training, retraining, or apprenticeships; or any other terms, conditions, or privileges of employment—not just pay. It is clear, therefore, that library employers have a responsibility to establish compensation systems which are not discriminatory, at least in the well-established definition of equal pay for equal work. And they must be increasingly concerned with the issue of comparable worth.

Any one—or all—of these personnel functions (recruitment and selection, training and development, personnel utilization and job redesign, classification and compensation) may generate the need for a job analysis. In some organizations, the desire to establish an integrated personnel system which includes these functions has provided the initiative for implementing a comprehensive job analysis. Whatever the purpose of job analysis, the data must be accurate, inclusive, and presented in a format that allows study and analysis.

B. Job Analysis Methodology

There are a number of different methods for obtaining job information, and no one method is likely to be suitable for all purposes or under all circumstances. Therefore, before beginning a job analysis, the objectives of the study should be clearly identified and consideration given to whether more than one method of data collection should be used in order to expand the usefulness of the study. Before examining the standard methods for gathering job information, it is first necessary to understand the two distinct ways in which job analysis information is categorized: job-oriented or worker-oriented. Van Rijn (1979, p. 2) states that a "job oriented analysis focuses on the job, the tasks performed, the tools used, or the work products. The worker oriented approach, on the other hand, focuses on the worker and the knowledges, skills, abilities, and other characteristics he or she needs, and at what level, to perform the job." These two different orientations to job analysis will generate different results; therefore, both should be considered when determining the job analysis method(s) to be used. For instance, van Rijn indicates that the job-oriented approach typically requires "direct observation and reports of what is done, while worker oriented analyses require a more indirect level of observation that goes beyond visible behaviors to their physical and psychological requirements. This latter level of observation makes greater use of inferences and judgments about the job than direct observation" (1979, p. 2).

When possible, the job-analysis methodology should combine the job and worker orientation in order to obtain a more comprehensive understanding of jobs. It is important also to clarify the meaning of the terms "job" and "position" and how each will be dealt with in the context of job analysis. According to Flippo (1966, p. 115) job refers to a "group of positions that are similar as to kind and level of work" (reference librarians, catalogers, secretaries). Flippo defines a position as "a group of tasks assigned to one individual. There are as many positions in a firm as there are personnel. The term is used in this narrow technical sense to facilitate more precise analysis of the job analysis technique." Job analysis is focused on both jobs and positons in order to obtain the most thorough information about the work employees are performing and the requirements of this work.

The standard methods for gathering information about jobs are job descriptions, questionnaires, observation, job audits, and task analysis.

1. JOB DESCRIPTIONS

One of the most frequently used methods for obtaining job information is through a job description, completed either by the employee, the supervisor, a member of the library or university personnel office, an outside consultant, or a combination of these. Typically, job descriptions provide a summary of job responsibilities as well as brief statements on major duties or activities. Traditionally, job descriptions have been standardized to describe activities performed within a number of positions with additional information provided on duties unique to individual employees. So a generic job description for reference librarians may be developed but with a separate section to provide information about distinctly different responsibilities among the reference librarians. Though job descriptions are a major method for acquiring job information there are shortcomings which include: (*a*) lack of specificity of duties and responsibilities; (*b*) insufficient data to provide an understanding of the complexity and authority of jobs; (*c*) inadequate information on priorities among job duties and the percentage of time allocated to the various duties; and (*d*) inadequate information on materials, equipment, and resources used in performance of duties.

Job information acquired through a job description can be easily inflated by the incumbent or supervisor; in addition, the method assumes that the person writing the description has adequate writing skills to describe the job in an articulate manner. If people do not have good writing skills and do not understand how to describe a job, the result can be a complete misunderstanding of the level and complexity of the particular job. The reverse may also occur when a job is made to sound more complex than it actually is because of a person's ability to articulate job information in a sophisticated way. In order for job descriptions to be valuable tools in job analysis, personnel staff should develop general requirements which would provide assistance to those completing the descriptions. For instance, they might provide a glossary of terms to encourage standardized language, provide directions and examples on describing job duties, and the degree of authority and decision making in the job, and require that percentages of time be indicated as well as information on tools and resources used to perform the job. Even with comprehensive job descriptions, a job analysis that relies entirely on this method for obtaining job information is weak. The inclusion of follow-up interviews should be considered when designing a study.

2. QUESTIONNAIRES

After job descriptions, questionnaires constitute the most widely used tool for obtaining job information. A variety of sources for developing questionnaires have been used in libraries, including university personnel, consultants, commercial agencies, and, occasionally, library personnel. When libraries have developed job-analysis questionnaires, they have usually received assistance from university personnel—particularly when support staff have been involved. The major advantage of the questionnaire is that it allows for a timely and cost-effective means for acquiring job data, particularly if a large number of jobs are to be included in the study. Also, it is possible to design a questionnaire which allows the data to be easily stored in machine-readable form, thus improving the accessibility to the data and the ease with which results can be analyzed, using a number of variables. These advantages to questionnaires can be offset, though, by some considerable disadvantages. A major problem with questionnaires, according to Flippo (1966, p. 116) is that the "technique places great faith in the job holder and his ability to organize the reporting of his job. It has not been found that this ability is very widespread, even among holders of managerial jobs. . . . The information received is often found to be incomplete, unorganized, and sometimes incoherent." Another problem is that job questionnaires developed by consultants or agencies may have both a focus as well as specific questions which are inappropriate to the library setting. In addition, questionnaires are often designed with only one orientation—either job or worker—and seldom include questions which will allow for information to be obtained on both *what* occurs and *how* it occurs. As with job descriptions, a job or duties questionnaire provides background information and will be most effective when combined with a follow-up interview.

3. INTERVIEWS

Interviews in job analysis are a common means for supplementing job information obtained from either the questionnaire or job description. In a few cases, the interview is the basic technique used to gather job information from which a job description is then developed. Flippo (1966, p. 117) comments that "the interview will provide information not readily observable plus the verification of information obtained by means of other techniques." A consideration in establishing interviews as the primary or secondary method for collecting job data is whether interviews will be conducted with every incumbent and/or supervisor or only a sampling of staff. If it is assumed that all jobs have differences to a degree because of variations in departmental assignments, then the most comprehensive information will be obtained if everyone is interviewed. For some libraries, though, this approach may not be feasible in terms of time and/or the personnel available to conduct a large number of interviews. In these cases, interviewing a representative group of staff may provide adequate job information in combination with a well-structured job description or questionnaire. When a large number of interviews are to be conducted, it is reasonable to use group interviews with employees who perform the same functions under the supervision of one person. For instance, all bibliographic searchers may be interviewed as a group, as may catalogers, reference librarians, and so forth. The use of group interviews will reduce the total time spent on interviewing and may possibly generate more information about jobs. If a group of employees has similar responsibilities but also unique assignments, the group interviews may be followed by a brief review with those people who have unique assignments. In addition to the detail on jobs that can be obtained through the interview process, another advantage is the opportunity to provide firsthand knowledge about the job analysis to library employees and to answer their questions. In this way, the concern and anxiety related to job analysis can be addressed and minimized.

Job-analysis interviews may be conducted in a variety of ways and the best approach will depend on local needs and conditions. One approach is to have the personnel staff meet with the supervisor and/or incumbent to discuss the job. Or a committee can be established to conduct the interviews and to develop the job information. A committee can be effective in a number of ways, particularly by offering additional assistance to the library personnel office and by playing an important role in public relations for job analysis. Library staff may view committee members as peers and be less defensive in discussing their job duties and requirements. Another useful technique for interviews calls for a public-service employee to conduct job interviews with technical services staff and vice versa—or at least, to have both functional areas represented in each job interview. This technique should assist committee members in maintaining objectivity when conducting job interviews as well as in reducing biases of committee members.

No matter who conducts job-analysis interviews, the success will depend on the training that is provided prior to initiating the process. Interviewers should have good interpersonal and communication skills, they should be trained in how to conduct an interview, and they should have a clear understanding of the purpose and focus of the job interviews. Training for the process of job-analysis interviews should focus on the process and stress the need to be objective. The primary considerations when using the interview technique are to insure that interviewers are well-trained and that there is a definite structure to the interview. A final consideration in planning the interview method for job analysis is to determine how the information obtained in the interview will be recorded. Probably the most effective means is to use a standard set of questions and to record the information received during the interview. A standardized approach will insure that the same basic questions are covered in discussing each job and will provide a structure for the interviewer.

4. JOB OBSERVATION OR AUDIT

Another method for gathering job information is similar to the interview process but requires direct observation of the job activities being performed; this is the job observation or audit. This on-site observation of work being performed is most effective for analyzing positions involving routine and repetitive tasks. It is less effective (if not inappropriate) for jobs that are comprised primarily of tasks involving mental processes and/or entail duties and activities which occur on a cyclical or random basis. For these positions, it is not possible to observe all activities of the job; therefore, complete and accurate job information cannot be obtained. The observation—audit approach can be used to advantage by libraries when an external agent (e.g., consultant, university or state personnel staff) is responsible for collecting job data and the person knows little about library terminology and technology, tools and equipment, or user demands and requirements. An audit in these situations allows the library supervisor an opportunity to "educate" the job analyst and thus to insure a better understanding of library operations and job duties. The job audit can also be used effectively in conjunction with the interview technique in order to obtain a more precise understanding of job activities. In no situation does it seem appropriate to rely solely on a job audit to gather job information since not all aspects of a job are necessarily observable. Therefore, job audits should be supplemented with written documentation and an interview.

5. TASK ANALYSIS

This is another method to gain job information, and it is beginning to gain more use in the library field. The methodology focuses on the specific components or identifiable units of a job rather than the general information on responsibiliites typically provided through job descriptions or questionnaires. A task has been defined in a number of ways but generally is viewed as a discrete unit of work which has a definite beginning and an end. A task may involve decisions, perceptions, and/or physical activity, and be of any degree of complexity. Task analysis allows for each separate component of a job to be described, thus providing the most comprehensive job information.

Two major library studies utilizing task analysis methodology have been conducted: the Illinois Library Task Analysis Project (ILTAP) and the Library Selection Project in California. The study in Illinois, described by Ricking and Booth (1974), was undertaken with the sponsorship of the Illinois Library Association and the American Library Association. It was established to provide a means for determining manpower needs in Illinois libraries, based on an analysis of work being performed. The 18 libraries that participated in the study represented public, school, special, and academic libraries with public libraries representing the largest group in the study.

The California project was conducted by Gerczak (1977) of the Selection Consulting Center, Sacramento, California (a nonprofit governmental research and consulting agency). The project included a consortium of 13 city and county libraries and the California State Library and was established to develop a selection system for library personnel.

In both studies, task lists or inventories were developed to represent all tasks performed by professional and support staff in the libraries. In the Illinois study, over 100 persons were included in the process of identifying tasks and an initial list of 1600 tasks resulted. From this list, subsets of tasks were later identified for three types of libraries: academic, public, and school media libraries. The California project involved 13 professional librarians at four libraries who developed a task-analysis questionnaire which resulted in a listing of tasks under major functional areas. One phase of the California project focused on selection requirements for library positions by defining what is needed to perform tasks identified as critical for an entry-level librarian in terms of knowledge, skills, abilities, personal characteristics, and behaviors. From this effort, 9000 behavior descriptions were recorded with the assistance of the participating librarians. These descriptions were then categorized, according to Gerczak (1977, p. 32) into "meaningful, distinct, and identifiable job content categories (performance dimensions)."

In both studies, the methodology used was influenced by the work of Sidney Fine (1974), who developed a system of task analysis referred to as Functional Job Analysis. This system of job analysis will be reviewed later in this report. Two additional task analysis studies which have been conducted in libraries are significant. Rothenberg *et al.* (1971) describe a study involving 2100 health science libraries in a study designed to analyze manpower utilization in the nation's health science libraries. A job–task index was designed to measure a subject's involvement in 27 library-related tasks and a degree of professionalism was assigned to each job task based on an "assessment of the extent of formalized education needed to perform the specific task." It is important to note that it was found that "educational attainment when taken as the sole independent variable cannot predict job level" (Rothenberg *et al.*, 1971, p. 326).

Another recent study involved analyzing the tasks being performed by public service librarians in a medium-sized academic library. A daily task inventory was obtained from the librarians by having them keep a "minute-by-minute" record of their activities for a normal work week. Ferguson and Taylor assert that

> data obtained from a study similar to the one presented here would allow the library administrator to move duties selectively from one employee to another—from one expensive professional to a less expensive clerical worker—when the changes can prove cost-beneficial. Data such as these will, of course, precipitate and facilitate the type of introspection in which professional librarians should be involved. It is not enough to say a job is

being done. Questions and answers need to be posed about the way an activity is being done and why it is being done (1980, p. 29).

Although this specific study was conducted with a different approach to task analysis than the other studies, it demonstrates the value of obtaining specific and comprehensive information about job duties.

Benedict and Gherman (1980, p. 210) explain the functional job-analysis system developed by Sidney Fine and implemented at the Iowa State University Library as part of a University-wide system.

> At the basis of an integrated personnel system is the task data bank which supplies the informational elements of the other modules of the system. The task bank is made up of a statement for each distinct task which is performed within the library. Instead of having position descriptions made up of unique tasks for each individual or job, the task data bank is an arrangement of tasks of a similar nature in an ascending or descending order of difficulty.

The task descriptions, which are developed by employees and supervisors with assistance from personnel office staff along with supplementary information provided in a job-analysis questionnaire or summary sheet, replace the standard job description while providing far more detail about the activities and requirements of specific tasks and, of course, jobs.

Columbia University Libraries developed a task-analysis approach for analyzing and evaluating 300 support positions. The job data were gathered by having supervisors prepare job descriptions for all support positions with detailed descriptions of each task performed and an indication of the percentage of the time each employee spent on a particular task. These detailed task-based job descriptions were reviewed by incumbents before being referred to the library administrative committee which had been organized to develop a position classification system. The committee sorted the tasks into public and technical services and then into "major tasks" and "minor tasks." Eventually, all tasks were identified and grouped, and an index of tasks was created with a definition for each task. The definitions were cross-indexed with jobs and vice versa. In addition, tasks that had different levels of difficulty were identified and a specific description was written for each level of the task (e.g., bibliographic searching had five levels reflecting the different degrees of complexity of this task).

The University of Connecticut Library used a task-analysis approach to analyze jobs in order to assess staff assignments and to identify jobs which required redesign or reclassification to other job titles or levels. The task information was obtained from each library department or functional unit such as Reference, Circulation, Cataloging, and so forth. The department head identified all major functions in the department and the tasks which supported these functions. Staff then developed task descriptions though few staff had to describe all tasks of their jobs because of the high percentage of shared tasks within a department. This approach offered a number of advantages. It minimized the problem of job information being inflated, which happens too often when staff are asked to describe their own jobs. Secondly, it reduced the time necessary for any one employee to devote to the project since the writing of tasks descriptions was shared. Finally, the approach reduced the anxiety which is often engendered when people feel they must describe and thus defend their jobs. In this task-analysis study, it was recognized that two different types of tasks existed, and different task forms were designed to accommodate the description of routine and nonroutine tasks. Routine tasks were defined as those which would have the same outcome no matter who performed them or when they were performed. The form designed for routine tasks required a step-by-step description of the task. Non-routine tasks were defined as those with a different result on each occurrence because of varying factors or circumstances (e.g., tasks of the reference interview, performance evaluation, book selection). The format of the nonroutine task descriptions was more general with information requested in the following categories: (*a*) purpose of the task; (*b*) description of the criteria or factors which contributed to the outcome of the task; and (*c*) major tools–resources used in completing the task.

In general, the advantages of a task-analysis methodology include:

1. Information on jobs can be broken down into manageable units.
2. Very specific information on jobs at the task level is available.
3. Information on knowledge, skills, abilities as well as tools and resources used in performing each task is available.
4. Data at the task level allows for recognition of the most complex work within a job even when the task may represent only a small percentage of the employee's total time.
5. Job information at the task level is easy to review and manipulate thus allowing for a means to redesign jobs and recognize small changes in jobs. A task approach to job analysis allows for a full analysis of a job without any aspect of the job being overlooked.

The disadvantages of task analysis include the fact that it is likely to be more time-consuming than other approaches to job analysis and that minute analysis of a job may result in losing sight of the value of the coordination of all tasks—the value of the whole. Certainly, the combination of all tasks into a job, and the work environment in which these duties are performed, contribute to the overall complexity of a job and this aspect should not be ignored in a task analysis approach.

To insure a successful use of task analysis, some type of modified position description questionnaire should be considered. The inclusion of such a form can provide the necessary overview of the position with information on supervision received, workload, personal contacts, and so forth. Some means of measuring worker characteristics either at the job or at the task level should also be incorporated into the study. As explained by Benedict and Gherman (1980, p. 211), the functional job-analysis approach requests this information at the task level:

> The third element of the task data sheet is an inventory of skills, knowledge, and abilities which is broken down into two sections: functional and specific. Functional skills, knowledge and abilities include those that are expected of an employee on the first day in the position. They are interpreted as the minimum hiring requirements for the job. Specific skills, knowledge and abilities enable the employee to perform a specific technology or procedure. Generally, they are acquired through on-the-job experience and training.

The choice of methodology to obtain job data is extremely important to the success of the study. Therefore, the limitations and advantages of each method should be examined carefully in relationship to the purpose of the study. Also, since job analysis is a costly process no matter what approach is used, conducting a thorough study is important so that the system will be easy to update and maintain, and a complete reanalysis will not be necessary every few years. There are other considerations when implementing a job-analysis study and these are reviewed briefly.

6. OTHER CONSIDERATIONS IN JOB ANALYSIS

An important aspect of job analysis is the ability to store, retrieve, and update the data as needed. Even when libraries are handling several hundred positions, it is desirable for the information to be organized and stored in such a manner that easy access and updating is feasible. If information is gathered through job descriptions, it is important to decide how it will be coded, indexed, and filed (by job title, functional title, position number, departmental code, major duties, or a combination of these). When a task-analysis approach is used, it is possible to develop a task index with codes to indicate what tasks appear in specific jobs, and also to code individual job descriptions with the task numbers. However, when quantifiable data are obtained, they can easily be stored in a computer file, thus providing easy access to a large volume of job information. According to van Rijn (1979, p. 7), the use of a computer can provide a means for comparing job information and generally allows "the application of a variety of statistical procedures to facilitate the description, analysis and interpretation of the data." For those libraries that have a word-processing system, even the storage of job and task descriptions is possible and simplifies not only retrieval but updating as well.

Once jobs have been analyzed, a determination should be made as to how job information will be reviewed and updated. In most libraries, a review occurs when a supervisor or the incumbent makes a request or the position becomes vacant and is automatically reviewed. Several libraries require that a form be completed when requesting a job review, so that new duties or tasks can be identified. In one library, the "old" job description must be submitted and the specific differences in the previous duties and those now assigned must be identified. Another library asks supervisors to explain the reasons for changes in duties, to identify the position to which the duties formerly belonged, and to identify duties which have been removed from the position under review. These questions not only provide updated information on the job under review but also on other jobs which have been or will be affected by the shift in duties and assignments.

When undertaking a job analysis there may be one or several objectives to the study. Increasingly, organizations are recognizing the value of job analysis in supporting an integrated personnel system which addresses all major personnel functions. Certainly it is desirable, when planning job analysis, to identify in advance whether the results will be adaptable or useful for more than one personnel function.

A primary consideration in implementing a job study is the communication with those who will be involved and/or affected such as managers, supervisors, and job incumbents. An announcement issued from the library director indicating the purpose and scope of the study may be helpful in providing information to staff and letting them know that the project has the full support of the library administrative and managerial team. Specific information on the job analysis should be given to employees including:

1. Objective or purpose of the study: how the data will be used.
2. Responsibility for administering the project: who has responsibility and who will be involved in implementing the project.
3. Time: an estimate of the length of the study and the time required from staff to provide information for the study.
4. Process: what are the steps in the process.
5. Results: what specific results are expected, such as a revised classification system, new job descriptions, a training program, etc. (In particular, if job data are to be used to establish a classification system, staff should be reassured that they will not be downgraded nor suffer any loss of pay if their positions are evaluated at a lower level.)

Effective communication on a subject as sensitive as job analysis often involves a combination of written announcements and staff meetings to inform and to respond to questions and concerns of staff. Job analysis, when implemented, is often perceived as very threatening. Employees are uncertain what effect it will have on their job assignments, salary, and status. Often employees are convinced that their performance is going to be evaluated. Other staff hold the view that no one can understand the process, demands, and complexities of their work. These situations may create resistance and uncooperative attitudes. Therefore, clear communication presented in a supportive context can do a great deal to minimize these reactions and make the process a smooth and efficient one.

In the majority of situations, the job-salary study is handled primarily by staff from the library personnel office or in conjunction with university personnel. The use of staff committees, though, is becoming more prevalent as a means of providing different viewpoints to the process and for establishing greater acceptability among staff by having more than administrative personnel involved. Though the use of consultants for job analysis is less frequent, there are cases in which the university hires a consultant to conduct a study for the library or involving the library staff. The effectiveness of a consultant, or consulting firm, depends in large part on the individual consultants and their knowledge of library activities and requirements. The objections to consultants have centered around their lack of familiarity with library operations, terminology, and job requirements and the elaborate questionnaires used to obtain job information which are confusing to library employees. Advantages that have been identified with using consultants are that the consultant brings the knowledge and expertise of job analysis (and job evaluation) into the library or university and the consultant has the time to conduct a thorough study as well as the necessary objectivity. Quite often a system for job analysis developed by an outside consultant can be most useful when there is nothing already in place and the library or the university must establish a structure for analyzing jobs, a classification, and/or a compensation system. Once a system for gathering job data and analyzing the data has been established, the use of consultants or their precise methodology may be abandoned. When outside consultants are used it is perhaps more important than ever to make sure that library staff are well-informed about the study and that consultants receive orientation to the library before beginning the project.

Indeed, orientation and training for appropriate persons related to job analysis is critical. If university personnel staff or consultants are to conduct the study, the library administration should request the opportunity to provide a presentation to these individuals on the organizational structure of library activities and functions, technology, terminology, work flow, complexities, and the categories of library staff and the nature of their roles in the library. When appropriate, written materials such as an organization chart, descriptions of functions and services, statistics on materials processed and people served, a glossary, and other relevant information should be developed for those outside the library who will be analyzing library jobs. If library staff are to be involved in conducting the job analysis, they should receive training in techniques, methods, and complexitites of job analysis. Most library staff have not had experience in this activity and therefore require preparation. Training might include a reading of selected articles, a review of procedures and approaches used in other organizations, and training—as appropriate—on designing questionnaires, conducting interviews, and organizing and analyzing job data. When possible, experienced personnel from other university departments (e.g., university personnel, business, or psychology department staff) should be asked to talk with library staff responsible for the job analysis to review the major principles and pitfalls and to allow a review of issues and concerns with an expert.

C. Summary

It is clear that there are advantages and disadvantages to any of the job-analysis methodologies. While each approach offers certain advantages, it is clear that in most situations the more detailed and comprehensive the data collection, the more effective the results of the study, including the defense of the results to staff. Job analysis is not a scientific process but one of judgment; therefore, the demands placed upon the methodology is greater.

Among the libraries in this study, there was no clear support for one methodology over another when implementing an initial job analysis. Most of the libraries used a combination of at least two or more methods such as job description and interview, or questionnaire, interview, and observation. Indeed, follow-up interviews and/or on-site observations were used in almost all cases in conjunction with other methods to confirm the written documentation or to acquire a more detailed understanding of performance requirements. Though task analysis was not the most frequent job-analysis method, it clearly is gaining prominence as an important tool, particularly for analysis of support staff positions. Once the initial study is completed, though, almost all libraries rely on a standard job description for updating information on jobs and for reviewing jobs for reclassification.

Job analysis can provide a basic tool for library personnel administrators in responding to a range of complex personnel needs and demands, including long-range planning, recruitment, training and development, and compensation. Job analysis offers a major source of data for interpreting and determining the personnel needs of the organization based on the work which must be accomplished rather than relying on tradition and speculation.

III. JOB EVALUATION

A. The Process of Job Evaluation

Flippo (1966, p. 116) characterized job evaluation as "a systematic and orderly process of determining the worth of a job in relation to other jobs" in the organization. Trieman (1979, p. 1) states that "the term *job evaluation* refers to a formal procedure for hierarchically ordering a set of jobs or positions with respect to their *value* or *worth,* usually for the purpose of setting pay rates. A basic tenet of job evaluation is that it is the job, not the worker, that is evaluated and rated." The evaluation of jobs is probably the most complex and sensitive aspect of personnel administration. Though there exists no scientific system for evaluating job worth, there has been considerable research (Otis and Leukart, 1954; Mecham and McCormick, 1969; Livy, 1975; Fine, 1974; Krzystofiak *et al.,* 1979; Melching and Borcher, 1973; McCormick, 1979; Trieman, 1979) into techniques and methods for establishing a sound analytical approach to this process. The basis for establishing job worth or value in an organization, though, remains one of judgment. After job values have been identified, it is possible to establish a mechanism for evaluating all jobs against the identified values and reducing the subjectivity of the decision making.

A number of concerns relating to job evaluation have been identified; they may be grouped into two categories: factor-related problems and evaluator-related problems.

1. FACTOR–RELATED PROBLEMS

1. The factors to be used in establishing job values should be identified unique to each organization.

Even though job factors (e.g., experience, authority, complexity) tend to be similar among organizations of all types, it would be a mistake for a library to assume that the factors, and the values assigned to the factors, developed in another environment appropriately reflect library jobs and job worth.

2. Factors to be used for job evaluation should be established prior to the job analysis in order to insure an appropriate focus to the data-gathering process.
3. Formal education as a factor in establishing job worth may be artificial in that it adds to the job value but does not necessarily measure

accurately the knowledge required for job performance. Instead, a knowledge factor, which is unrelated to educational degrees, should be considered.
4. The most complex activities of a job should be adequately identified and weighted, since people are hired for their ability to perform the most difficult tasks of a job and should be rewarded on this basis.
5. Dimensions of the work environment such as workload, variety of tasks, pressure and time demands, complexity of tools and resources used, and other similar factors should be considered in weighing the complexity of jobs.
6. Factors related to worker behaviors (e.g., manual dexterity, analytical ability, interpersonal skills) should be identified to ensure that these hidden requirements which contribute to job complexity are recognized.

2. EVALUATOR-RELATED PROBLEMS

1. The identification of factors and the worth of these factors is a judgmental process and therefore special effort must be given to emphasizing objectivity and minimizing personal bias.
2. The results of job evaluation may be skewed if committee members performing the evaluation assume consensus as their primary goal rather than sound and equitable decisions.
3. The evaluation of a job should be separated from an evaluator's opinion of the incumbent and, in particular, evaluators should guard against sex-role stereotyping in determining job worth.

The issue of sex stereotyping and discrimination in job evaluation is coming under particular scrutiny by individual employees, women's groups, unions, and the courts. The EEOC considers sex discrimination and the comparable worth issue to be of major concern and has contracted with the National Academy of Sciences to conduct an evaluation of major job-evaluation systems to determine if sex discrimination is inherent in existing systems. In the preliminary report, the National Academy of Sciences committee reached no definite conclusions, but three major problems were identified (Trieman, 1979, p. 48):

> 1) The relative ranking of jobs tends to be highly dependent upon which factors are used in the evaluation and how heavily each factor is weighed. But the principal procedure for deriving factor weights pegs them to current wage rates and thereby reflects existing sex differences in wage rates. 2) Job evaluation is inherently subjective, making it possible that well-known processes of sex-role stereotyping will be operative in this context as well,

resulting in an under-evaluation of jobs held predominantly by women. 3) Many employers use several job evaluation plans—one for shop jobs, one for office jobs, etc.—a procedure that makes it impossible to compare the worth of jobs in different sectors of a firm.

It is clear that the values that are brought to bear in job evaluation reflect not only the nature and tradition of an organization but also society's values as well particularly in assigning worth to jobs performed primarily by women (e.g., teachers, nurses, librarians). In addition, for those organizations that maintain several classification and compensation systems, difficulties may arise because of the problems of comparing and justifying job worth and pay structure among several employee groups. For instance, universities typically have different classification and pay structures for faculty, professional, clerical, and technical staff. These structures are usually the result of the use of different job factors and job values in evaluating the hierarchical relationship of jobs and in determining compensation. Private companies (as represented in this study) are particularly sensitive to the need to be able to demonstrate the fairness of their compensation system to any government agency that may investigate their practices, and have established, or are moving toward, a single evaluation system for all jobs in the organization.

The need to organize work flow and to assign job responsibilities among library staff has always been a concern of library administrators and staff, particularly in identifying duties appropriate to professional and nonprofessional staff (California Library Association, 1932; American Library Association, 1948; Asheim, 1968; American Library Association, 1970; Ricking and Booth, 1974). The requirement for a systematic means for determining which tasks belong in which job category and level has increased over the past 20 years as libraries have grown in size, scope and complexity. As library organizations have changed, external pressures also have developed which have affected personnel administration directly and indirectly, such as federal and state legislation, unionization, and an increase in participatory management. With these changes has come a corresponding shift away from authoritarian management models. Increasingly, more defensible and objective methods for administrative actions are required, and thus job evaluation becomes an increasingly important activity in libraries.

B. Job Evaluation Methodology

This section discusses the four standard job evaluation methods, which fall into two general categories: nonquantitative and quantitative. The nonquantitative method, which includes the systems of ranking and classification, is the simpler of the two approaches since it involves the comparison of whole jobs rather than specific factors within each job. The quantitative systems utilize a more detailed approach in which specific job factors are identified and then measured by assigning points or other values to arrive at the worth of the job. The two quantitative systems are the point system and the factor-comparison system.

1. RANKING SYSTEM

This system involves the establishment of a hierarchy of jobs based on the worth of the jobs within the organization but without a specific definition of "worth." The system typically involves a comparison of all jobs based on data contained in job descriptions. The process requires that two jobs be compared and a decision made as to which is at a higher level, then another job compared to both of these jobs, and so on. The ranking system can be implemented with a minimum of time and cost if job descriptions already exist in the organization, but it suffers from a number of disadvantages. Flippo (1966, p. 283) says that "its greatest virtue, simplicity, is also a disadvantage, in that measurement is somewhat crude. It is hard to measure whole jobs. In addition, there is no predetermined scale of values, or yardstick, for the judges to use. Each judge has his own set of criteria, and it is difficult to explain the results to a job incumbent."

This system, the simplest of job evaluation methods, works effectively only when a very limited number of jobs is involved since it becomes impractical, if not impossible, to make distinctions if many jobs must be ranked. In the words of Canelas (1977, p. 6):

> it is difficult to utilize this method in large organizations. The larger and more geographically dispersed the library becomes, the more difficult it is to find individuals in the library who know all or many of the jobs well. Another problem is that rankers sometimes tend to think that they do know all of the jobs well and rank almost by title without bothering to consider all of the facts listed in each of the position descriptions. . . . Another problem is that the jobs can presumably be ranked by only one factor, since it's not possible to rank all jobs in a library from highest to lowest if many factors must be taken into consideration. . . . And the single factor chosen—either consciously or unconsciously— was administrative responsibility.

In the National Academy of Science report, Trieman (1979, p. 2) states that "the basic feature of ranking systems is that they involve a comparison of whole jobs with respect to a (usually amorphous) criterion of 'worth'. Ranking methods are not held in high repute in the job evaluation literature."

2. CLASSIFICATION SYSTEM

This approach to evaluating jobs utilizes already-existing job classes or grades which carry specific requirements and descriptions for each level. These descriptions are referred to as "generic" descriptions and are intended to be general enough to cover a range of specific jobs. In this system, jobs are evaluated as whole units by comparing them with the existing classification descriptions, but without considering specific job factors separately. Flippo (1966, p. 285) considers job classification to be an improvement over ranking in that a "predetermined scale of values is provided." Trieman (1979, p. 2) describes the classification methodology critically as an "idealized hierarchical structure" into which each job is fit.

Canelas (1977, p. 2) suggests that "this system can provide a good deal of flexibility because as positions change, or new changes emerge, they may be placed at the appropriate point in the classification structure." Again, in the classification approach, specific factors about a job may be overlooked or given insignificant or inappropriate consideration. As Trieman (1979, p. 2) points out, "jobs with discrepant levels on two or more criteria (e.g., jobs involving very high educational qualifications but not exercising any supervisory responsibility) may not fit into the scheme very well and hence require arbitrary judgments for assignment." A classification system does operate on the "best fit" concept.

There is no doubt, therefore, that a classification system—particularly a large, diverse system such as in a university—is subject to a high margin of error in evaluating jobs which, though similar, may also be very dissimilar in many regards. This will be discussed further in Section D.

3. FACTOR COMPARISON SYSTEM

A factor comparison system is a refined ranking method that relies on two major components: the selection of job factors and the identification of benchmark jobs. Trieman (1979, p. 3) states that

> ...basically, factor comparison systems work as follows: A set of factors on which the evaluation will be based is chosen (these are ordinarily known as "compensable factors"). It is considered desirable to keep the number of factors small—four to seven has been cited as an acceptable range. . . . Second, a set of "benchmark" jobs is chosen; these are jobs about which consensus is presumed to exist regarding relative worth and the relative importance of the various factors determining worth.

The benchmark jobs are compared based on the specific factors and ranked, and then subsequent jobs are compared against these jobs in relation to each factor. Flippo (1966, p. 293) states that "factor comparison thus incorporates a job-to-job type of rating. It is a refinement of simple ranking in that comparisons are accomplished *job to job, by factors* rather than as whole jobs."

Canelas (1977, p. 7) sees a distinct advantage for libraries in using this methdology because once developed the "position classification system is tailor made for the library that develops it; there are excellent instructions available for implementing the system, and it's not difficult to train employees to use the method." Trieman (1979, p. 3), on the other hand, concludes that "factor comparison systems are not widely used. . . . There is considerable consensus in the job evaluation literature that these methods are both cumbersome to execute and highly subjective in their application; moreover, they tend to be unpopular with employees since they are difficult to understand." This conflicts, though, with a previous survey (Miner, 1976) of 158 organizations (manufacturing, nonmanufacturing, and public institutions such as hospitals, education, and government) which found factor comparison used in one-third of the organizations. In addition, the Federal government system (Foss, 1977) for evaluating jobs is based on a factor-comparison methodology governed by standards issued by the United States Civil Service Commission. And a number of libraries have used factor-comparison methodology, which will be discussed in Section D, successfully.

An advantage of the factor-comparison methodology is the specificity resulting from a comparison of specific job factors rather than jobs as a whole, and the flexibility of the system which can respond to changes that occur within the organization and jobs. A disadvantage relates to identifying the benchmark positions and the possibility of relying on traditional views of jobs and their worth. For instance, if a benchmark position has been over- or underrated, the rating of all positions compared to this one will be skewed. Therefore, benchmark jobs should be reviewed thoroughly in order to insure that they are fairly evaluated.

4. POINT SYSTEM

The point-evaluation system is based on identifying specific compensable factors to each of which a weight is assigned. This system, according to Flippo (1966, p. 286), "involves a more detailed, quantitative and analytical approach to the measurement of job worth" since not only are job factors identified but their relative worth is established. As with the factor-comparison system, the identification of job factors and the number to be used should be determined by each organization so that the factors reflect the conditions and values of the particular organization.

After job factors have been selected, a scale of values is constructed in order to measure each factor. It is necessary, first, to establish the total number of points, and then to determine the percentage of points to be allocated to each of the factors. Henderson (1976c, p. 32) has described this process of establishing weights, or values, for the job factors:

> In light of the organization objectives, some factors are obviously more important than others. To account for this difference, it is necessary to weight each factor in terms of its importance to organizational goals and objectives. This weighting or comparison process must be as exact as possible (recognizing that judgments are subjective even when made by experts). To date, the most exact method developed has been that of assigning points to each factor—that is, . . . factors of unequal importance are assigned a different number of points to reflect the relative value of each.

Once the total points have been defined for a given factor, then degrees for that factor can be established with the points distributed along a continuum (factor for decision making would consist of 4 or 5 degrees or levels of freedom and complexity and the points would be distributed among these levels). As each job is evaluated in relation to the point factor system, a total numerical value is arrived at for the job.

As with other job evaluation systems, there are advantages and disadvantages with the point system. Canelas (1977, p. 7) states that

> ...among the advantages are the stability of the scales once developed. Although jobs may change, the scales generally do not unless the library changes its mission. In addition, the scales increase in precision with use. The system is easy to explain to staff who generally accept the values inherent in the scales and staff acceptance is therefore high.

On the other hand, Canelas indicates that the disadvantages include the fact that a "point system is difficult to develop. It is difficult to define the factors and each of their degrees precisely in a way that carries the same meaning for each of the raters. It is also difficult to weight each of the factors in accordance with their importance." Trieman (1979, p. 3) sees a disadvantage in that "the range of possible points is constant across all jobs, which makes a system easier to administer but may introduce excessive rigidity," while acknowledging that "because of the relative simplicity of the procedure, this is the most widely used type of evaluation in the United States."

C. Job Factors

It is apparent from a review of job-evaluation systems that the identification of job factors is a major component of at least two of these systems:

factor-comparison and point systems. Job factors can be described in three major categories, according to Henderson (1976c, p. 28):

> The first category, universal factors, contains descriptions applicable to elements or parts of each job in practically any organization. . . . Because of the broad nature of these universal factors, each is further defined through a second category, or series of subfactors. These subfactors permit the development of profile statements that more precisely define the work elements or specific attributes of a particular job. The breaking down of subfactors into degrees forms the third category. It permits the reflection or measurement of the degree to which each subfactor is important in particular jobs.

Clearly, job factors must be well defined and they must be thoroughly understood in order to avoid duplication and overlap in measuring certain job dimensions, and to prevent oversight of important job elements. Ricking and Booth (1974, p. 102) indicate that criteria such as the following should be used in identifying job factors:

1. The factor should measure significant and distinct characteristics of work.
2. It is applicable to all positions but in varying degrees.
3. It is ratable in terms of recognizable and definable differences in level.
4. It will have minimal overlap with other job factors.

Consistency of language and definition of terms in job evaluation is extremely important. A controlled language reduces semantic problems by having all terms well defined so that it is clear what is being measured and reduces the potential for overlap or duplication in measurement. Functional job analysis is a process which addresses this problem by establishing a conceptual framework for analyzing jobs and providing well-defined terms.

Roter (1973, p. 1033) describes functional job analysis as a scheme which is based

> on the premise that tasks require a worker to utilize cognitive, interpersonal and physical resources in varying degrees. *Cognitive* resources are directed at data, or information, ideas, facts, statistics. *Interpersonal* resources are directed at people, or clients, co workers, customers. *Physical* resources are directed at things, or machines, equipment. . . . Within each of these broad categories, moreover, are various levels of complexity against which tasks may be evaluated. These levels are regularly defined in a hierarchy. . . .

For each of these three major areas with their specific definitions, specific job factors can be established.

Hay Associates, a major consulting firm that has developed a job-evaluation system, has organized job factors in a somewhat different manner by identifying what they consider to be three basic elements or dimensions for any job: know-how, problem-solving, and accountability. Each of these major factors has subfactors against which jobs are evaluated. According to Miner (1976, p. 27), know-how is the sum total of every kind of skill, however acquired, needed for acceptable job performance; problem-solving measures the intensity of the mental process—thinking required by the job for analyzing, evaluating, meeting, reasoning, arriving at and making conclusions; accountability measures the answerability for action and for the consequences of action.

Whatever approach is used to identify, categorize, and define job factors, the important point is that a scheme for establishing and defining factors should be established so that the specific needs and values of the organization are supported, and so that a high degree of specificity exists in factor definition. Even when job factors are well defined, problems may still exist in using the factors. Trieman (1979, p. 32) states that "although in principle a very large set of compensable factors could be developed, in practice most job evaluation systems use more or less the same set of factors. In part, this is due to . . . the propensity for designers of a job evaluation system to copy factors from previously developed plans with only minor modification." Thus, libraries may find that they are accepting factors from another organization's job-evaluation system which is inadequate to measure library jobs, particularly professional positions. The weight assigned to job factors is also a major concern in resolving the question of sex discrimination inherent in job-evaluation systems. For instance, Trieman (1979, p. 33) states that if

> the benchmark jobs used to establish the factor weights are largely men's jobs those factors that mainly differentiate *among women's jobs* will be relegated to minor importance. The result could easily be that women's jobs are concentrated in the bottom of the job worth hierarchy while men's jobs are spread throughout the hierarchy, purely as an artifact of the way the factor weights are determined . . . the way that factor levels are assigned in practice can radically alter the source.

From this brief review of job factors and factor weights, it is clear that considerable attention should be given to the identification of the factors and the determination of their worth and value to the organization. In particular, attention should be given to identifying potential sex stereotyping when determining factors and establishing factor weights. Otherwise, the results of the job evaluation might not be qualitatively any better than one conducted with a ranking or classification methodology.

D. Job Evaluation in Libraries

It is possible to draw conclusions about job-evaluation methodologies and approaches found in libraries through the literature and the research conducted by this author.[2] It is clear that libraries have been and are continuing to devote considerable time and attention to job evaluation and the development of equitable systems for establishing compensation systems. It is equally clear that a struggle continues to find an equitable means not only for determining salary but also for defining a system for job evaluation that is not too cumbersome or complex to administer. The resources that academic libraries—and the universities within which they reside—have available for developing job-evaluation systems are certainly more limited than those in private industry; thus, job-evaluation projects appear too often to be patched together by adapting other organization's systems and/or by using staff on a part-time basis to implement a very complex project. The length of time that it takes to implement and complete a job evaluation study in a library will vary with the size of the organization. One to two years is an average time to complete a study, with additional time taken to resolve grievances that are generated as a result.

In analyzing the job evaluation activities in academic libraries, there are clear indications of what is most prevalent and the changes that are occurring in job evaluation.

The ranking system as a job-evaluation method is not one that is favored in libraries, presumably because academic libraries of any size are unable to use the rather simplistic approach. With the issue of equitable compensation and comparability in salary structures, it is unlikely that libraries will look to the ranking methodology in the future.

On the other hand, the classification system for job evaluation appears to be a heavily used system among libraries with staff size ranging from 40 to 300. In those libraries in which a classification system is used, there is almost always a different system for support staff and professionals, and frequently the support staff are included in the university classification system, whereas librarian positions have a separate system or are included in the university administrative or faculty system. As mentioned, problems with a classification system—particularly when it is large—can be numerous and may have a negative affect on maintaining a fair compensation system. Norman D. Willis and Associates have conducted studies of two major state civil service classification systems (1974, 1976, 1980). The study this firm conducted for the state of Connecticut (1980, p. 2) sought to determine whether "inequities exist within the State's classification system, and to recommend appropriate action." In studying the civil service classification

[2]Data collected in the CLR-sponsored research on job evaluation systems are sensitive information. The anonymity of the libraries will be maintained in order to provide as much information about specific job evaluation systems without compromising a library that participated in this study.

system, which incorporates 2700 classifications for more than 44,600 state employees, the firm (1980, p. 5) first identified a benchmark sampling of 160 classifications in order to provide a "sound representation within each of the major job families and a relatively equal mix among those classifications traditionally occupied predominantly by either male or female employees. Classifications were considered to be predominantly male or female if they are currently populated by 70% or more of either sex." The job evaluation included 125 jobs from the representative classifications and four principal factors were used to evaluate the jobs: knowledge and skills, mental demands, accountability, and working conditions. The basis of this job evaluation pilot study was a point system developed by the firm. One of the conclusions of the study was that as a result of either classification specifications which are too broad or incorrect placement of positions within classifications, the classification system has generated a significant level of internal salary inequity which was particularly reflected in the differences between pay levels for male and female jobs. "Jobs staffed predominantly by men tend to be paid more at comparable levels of evaluated worth than jobs staffed predominantly by women. Jobs staffed by a mix of men and women (less than 70% of either sex) tend to have lower salaries than male dominated jobs and higher than female dominated jobs" (Norman D. Willis, 1980, p. 34).

A study of the civil service classification system of the State of Washington found similar results with regard to salary inequitites because of the classification system (Norman D. Willis, 1974, 1976). From these two major studies, it is clear than when a classification system is used for evaluating a large number of positions (and highly diverse positions), the margin for error increases substantially. Since classification systems are standard in libraries (either developed internally by the library staff or imposed by the institution), it indicates that further analysis should be made of the effectiveness of this system. Even though the classification systems reviewed by Willis and Associates were very large, involving thousands of positions, there is no understanding to date that the problems they identified occur only in such massive classification systems. Whether classification systems provide a sound job evaluation methodology and a basis for equitable compensation should continue to be reviewed.

Several libraries that use a classification system to evaluate jobs did not use this approach in the initial evaluation of jobs and in the establishment of a classification and compensation structure. Instead, either a point or factor–comparison method was used in implementing a job-evaluation project; only after this was completed and a system working was the classification methodology used for evaluating new jobs or jobs submitted for upgrading.

The factor–comparison system is one which is being used increasingly in academic libraries, particularly for professional positions. The literature provides information on several libraries which have used factor comparison methods to evaluate jobs at the professional level (Wilkinson et al., 1975; Position Classification at Michigan, 1979; Duda, 1980).

The University of Western Ontario (Wilkinson, et al., 1975, p. 354) system consisted of two factors: "general factors," which characterize all professional positions, and "ranking factors," which are characterized by the degree to which they are found at the different levels. General factors included the following: (*a*) academic qualifications; (*b*) judgment, which "involves the application of expertise to the reasoned and defensible analysis of alternatives in order to determine a preferable course of action"; (*c*) client relationships—embodying interpersonal change and enrichment; and (*d*) voluntary involvement in professional activities. Wilkinson et al. (1975, p. 354) note that it is the joint presence of these two factors—that distinguishes professional from support positions, since the general factors "are not viable instruments for ranking positions because they are not themselves capable of being conceived of on a consistent growth continuum."

The following factors were identified at Ontario as those that contribute to the position rank: (*a*) degree of expertise required to exercise assigned responsibility and accountability; (*b*) independence and freedom of action; (*c*) level of formal external contact which position requires to be effective; (*d*) planning and development; and (*e*) supervision. Consultants analyzed the job data by using a "grid profile" sheet composed of the four general and the five ranking factors. From the development of the factors on a continuum, general statements were then developed for a classification system with six levels. This classification system was built, and operates, on a factor-comparison methodology.

The University of Michigan Library has developed its present system over a period of more than 10 years. In 1966, the Library was using a point system for evaluating professional positions (Tompkins, 1966). The current method has dropped the point system and instead relies on a factor-comparison approach (Position Classification at Michigan, 1979). Two major factors have been established: scope of assignment and level of responsibility. Each is measured on a number of dimensions or subfactors at three levels of difficulty. Benchmark positions exist, and it is against these positions—using the factors—that professional positions are evaluated. An evaluation worksheet is used by the evaluators, and as a position is evaluated for each factor, the evaluator indicates the degree of difficulty by noting an *A*, *C,* or *E*. Degrees *B* and *D* are not described but may be used by a rater when a position falls between two categories on a factor or compares with one degree of difficulty in one respect and with another degree in another. The degrees of difficulty are described, and these descriptions together with the benchmark positions provide the guidelines within which the evaluators grade the professional positions. An appointed committee of library professionals acts as evaluators in this system. They maintain a "decision book" for later reference and review. Members of the Committee (Position Classification at Michigan, 1979, p. 210) feel that the factor-comparison system "has provided a document sufficiently flexible to provide for . . . expected changes for some time in the future."

Columbia has also developed a position classification system for professional positions which coexists with a system of ranks that is based on individual professional competency and achievements. The Columbia system consists of five position categories with specific factors established as the basis for evaluating and placing positions in the classification. According to Duda (1980, p. 301), the various factors that were identified "indicated an ascending level of responsibility governed by the extent of administrative duties and/or policy-making responsibilities." This system was used to evaluate 135 professional positions.

Other academic libraries, as identified by this author, are using the factor-comparison system though support and professional positions are not included in the same system. A private company that uses the factor-comparison methodology includes all of its 8000 jobs, 10% of which represent benchmark positions. Job data are gathered through the use of a job description and a job-evaluation questionnaire in which specific information is sought regarding the four compensable factors: autonomy and authority, impact, complexity, and operating climate. Supervisors who provide the information are given guidelines that include definition of terms and an explanation of each factor and its dimensions. On the basis of data obtained from the supervisor, a compensation analyst compares the job under review with two other jobs: a benchmark position within the department or division, and a benchmark position outside of the department or division. There are usually a total of four comparisons for every job evaluated. A system of plus (+) and minus (−) symbols is used to indicate the relationship on each factor between the position under review and the benchmark positions. The plus and minus symbols are tallied to provide a final indication of the level of the position and the resulting compensation.

Two important aspects of a factor-comparison system are the information relating to the benchmark positions and the documentation that is developed on job-evaluation decisions. In a number of organizations, benchmark positions are not identified to staff to avoid job descriptions being written to match a benchmark position. More importantly, benchmark positions must be reevaluated on a regular basis to note changes in these positions since they have an impact on the evaluation of all other positions. In factor comparison, documentation is essential to review the basis for a decision in the event of a grievance; also, as a means for reviewing previous thinking and rationale. Libraries that use the factor-comparison system indicate that it provides specificity for evaluating jobs but avoids the possible rigidity of a point system. It is also felt that the factor-comparison system can respond to changes that occur within the organization and specific jobs. A possible disadvantage may be an overreliance on conditions that already exist in the library and an acceptance of the traditional view of job hierarchy.

The point system for evaluating jobs is one that appears to be increasing in use within libraries, particularly for support positions which are evaluated as part of a university-directed evaluation project; only one library identified by the author has developed its own internal point system for support positions.

The library developed a point system with the job data focused at the task level. Based on the detailed task information available, all tasks were first ranked into a hierarchy of complexity and then grouped into six classification levels which were developed as part of the study. A range of numerical values was established for each grade level of the classification system, and the total score or points for a job was determined on a task-by-task basis by multiplying the grade level of the task times the percentage of time spent on the task. A hypothetical situation would be as follows:

Task #10 at grade level 3 is performed by an employee 10%. It would be calculated as:

$$3 \text{ (grade level)} \times 10 \text{ (\%)} = 30 \text{ (score)}$$

The aggregate of task scores for each job provided the total points for the job which then indicated the classification level for the position.

The management committee of the library which designed the system anticipated difficulties in evaluating jobs which contained tasks at multiple levels. Therefore, evaluation principles were developed to provide additional credit or points for certain work requirements and situations to maintain a fair evaluation and, thus, a fair compensation system. The type of situations which were given additional consideration in the evaluation process included: (*a*) the highest-ranking task within a job should be rewarded, since the incumbent is required to have job competencies to perform this task even if for a small percentage of time; (*b*) if 50% of the tasks in a job are at a higher level, then the position is classed at the higher level; and (*c*) additional credit is given for positions in a unit which are physically remote from a supervisor, thus requiring more independent and responsible actions on the part of the incumbent. The specific way in which additional credit was provided for these work situations is confidential; the important point is that the job-evaluation principles were established to recognize the complexity of the total job requirements and the work environment. This job-evaluation system establishes a process for identifying and evaluating at the lowest common denominator—tasks—while at the same time giving careful consideration to the whole job and the environment in which it is performed.

Another important study was conducted on a statewide basis involving the analysis of all library-support positions in state-supported academic libraries. The purpose was to create a more equitable pay relationship between positions in the various libraries and to provide greater consistency in applying classification levels. The Oliver factor ranking system used by the federal government and a number of other state and city governments was adapted for this project. The approach is based on job evaluation by a committee of specialists in the field in which the positions are being evaluated, in this case, libraries. The committee was composed of both librarians and library assistants representing the academic libraries included in the project. The committee defined the factors to be used in evaluating the library-assistant positions and the points and levels associated with each of the factors. A lengthy and detailed job-evaluation questionnaire was developed to obtain job and task information.

The process for evaluating the jobs included the following steps:

1. Each committee member, or rater, individually evaluated each job against the factor guide and assigned points.
2. Each evaluator's rating was listed on a board, and the group discussed the differences among their ratings in order to achieve consensus on each job.
3. Jobs were placed on a grid and benchmark jobs were then identified for each level.
4. Classification specifications were written for each level using these key jobs.

When the position-classification system is complete, it will be related to the state pay plan to establish salary grades. The advantages of this system are that it provides a specific number of factors to be evaluated with specific points assigned to the factor levels. In addition, each job is evaluated on the basis of task-level information as well as additional information about the job such as equipment used, impact of work on departmental unit, instructions and guidelines received, and work relationships. Also the fact that the library assistants are represented on this committee may provide a balance of opinion and perspective to the work of the committee; in such a situation, the committee members should guard against the librarians carrying greater influence on decisions simply because they are librarians.

The disadvantages to the system appear to be that information on the organizational structure and work environment within which the jobs are performed is not considered. Therefore, the size or complexity of a library is not a consideration even though these dimensions do affect individual job complexity and difficulty. In addition, there appears to be no way to give additional credit or points to certain work situations such as the absence of a supervisor which again affects the responsibilities and complexity of an incumbent's job.

In addition to academic libraries, the author visited two private companies that use a point system for evaluating jobs. One company uses the Hay system—which has been in place since the 1950s—and employs more than 10,000 people. The Hay factors have been adapted to the organization and a detailed chart provides the points which have been assigned to the levels of each factor. In this company, there is a 16-level scheme into which all positions of the organization must fit, based on evaluation against the Hay factors. The director of compensation feels that the levels are insufficient and may force too many diverse jobs into a limited range of job levels. The nationwide evaluation of jobs in this company occurs at three distinct levels, with committees reviewing the position at each level. Job data are acquired through a detailed job description–questionnaire submitted by the supervisor. A standing committee at the local "plant" evaluates the job, and then sends a recommendation along to a divisional committee, which repeats the process, taking into account positions in other departments. Finally, the position is reviewed by a committee at the corporate level against the Hay factors in relationship to positions throughout the corporation, and a final decision is reached.

The second private company is implementing a new system to replace a current evaluation system which consists of a point system for nonexecutive and a position comparison and market-survey system for executives. The new system, when completed, will include all 8000 positions in the organization. The system being used is particularly interesting as it is a new development in job evaluation and one not yet heavily utilized or tested. It is the Position Analysis Questionnaire (PAQ) developed by McCormick, Jeannert and Mecham (McCormick, 1974; McCormick *et al.*, 1969). The PAQ is a structured job-analysis questionnaire that can be used for analyzing and evaluating many different types and levels of jobs because it is focused on worker-oriented factors and not specific job duties. Using the PAQ approach allows for statistically derived job-dimension scores to be obtained, thus making it possible to relate positions or jobs to each other on the basis of the job-dimension scores. Jeannert (1980, p. 32) has stated that the

> ...PAQ procedure is also known as the job component method of job evaluation. The structured job analysis questionnaire is made up of 194 items, most of which reflect directly, or at least suggest, the basic human behaviors associated with work. Since the PAQ focuses on job *behaviors,* as opposed to specific tasks or functions, it can be applied to any type of job without regard to level . . . or technological characteristics. . . . the PAQ items are organized to provide a logical framework in which the job analysis can proceed.

The 194-item questionnaire is divided into six major divisions: (*a*) information input (Where and how does the worker get the information that is used in performing the job?); (*b*) mental processes (What reasoning, decision making, planning, and information-processing activities are involved in performing the job?); (*c*) work output (What physical activities does the worker perform and what tools or devices are used?); (*d*) relationships with other persons (What relationships with other people are required in performing the job); (*e*) job context (In what physical and social context is the work performed?); and (*f*) other job characteristics (What activities, conditions, or characteristics other than those described are relevant to the job?).

Through research using the PAQ system, 45 job factors have been identified that fall into these major divisions plus an additional one referred to as "overall dimensions" which includes such items as nontypical work schedules; public or customer-related contacts; working in an unpleasant, hazardous, or demanding environment. According to Jeannert (1980, p. 35), "once a job has been analyzed by means of the PAQ, computerized scoring is available to reduce the 1945 item response to these forty-five job dimension scores to form a job profile. These job dimension scores can be combined statistically to derive a job evaluation score using PAQ points." The points for the evaluation system (and therefore the value given to the factors) are determined by the firm which produces the PAQ, not the organization using the PAQ evaluation system. The questionnaire is standardized and does not alter for each organization. The company implementing the PAQ system (at considerable cost) sees the following advantages:

1. They will establish one system as the basis for evaluating all positions in the company and thus justify the compensation plan.
2. It is desirable to have an evaluation system which is behavioral-based as opposed to specific task- or job-duties based.
3. This will provide a system that addresses not only compensation but also selection, training, and performance evaluation which is the basis for merit awards.
4. The points assigned to the dimensions within the PAQ as well as the scoring and ranking of jobs is performed by the consulting firm through the use of computer programs already established.

Therefore, company personnel feels that this approach for establishing job worth is more objective and not susceptible to company politics and bias and therefore more defensible to government agencies as well as their own employees.

In the National Academy of Science analysis of job-evaluation methodologies, Trieman (1979, p. 26) indicated that the results of independent studies using the PAQ approach indicate a strong correlation between the outcomes of the other evaluation systems and the PAQ. While the designers of the PAQ see this as confirmation that PAQ is an accurate tool, Treiman states that such results "lend substantial credibility to the choice of factors in conventional job evaluation approaches."

The strength of the PAQ approach is considered by Jeannert (1980, p. 41) to be the ability to "translate job analysis data directly to job evaluation information across a wide spectrum of jobs without the need for committees or other procedures susceptible to bias." The PAQ system is expensive, since the implementation as well as maintenance of the system relies on PAQ Services, Inc. for instructional materials, the questionnaire, and the cost of computer time and programs needed for analysis of the data. There are no data available on how costs of implementing the PAQ system compares with other major systems such as that of the Hay system.

A drawback to this system may be the fact that the questionnaire—and thus the factors for evaluating jobs—does not vary and is assumed to contain all the critical factors for all jobs in all types of organizations and work environments. In addition, the value scale of factors has been developed by PAQ Services, Inc., and reflects the values and opinions of the members of the PAQ and not the values of the organization whose positions are being evaluated. This could be particularly problematic for a service organization such as a library if job worth—and factor weights—are more attuned to the business sector. If indeed the results of the PAQ system are almost identical to results of other evaluation systems, then the necessity for such an expensive system should be questioned. Even though the actual evaluation is done by the consulting firm, the implementation of the PAQ system rests with the organization; staff must be available to provide orientation and instruction to staff in completing the form, to enter the data, and generally to oversee the entire system. Another consideration relates to the procedure to be used in moving from a market-survey system for setting salaries to one totally based on the PAQ analysis. This could result in large adjustments in salaries for groups of jobs, particularly those held by women where a market-survey basis for setting salaries has held certain jobs at lower pay rates (e.g., clerical and secretarial jobs). A major disadvantage of the PAQ system, though, is the inability to check the accuracy of employees' responses to the PAQ questionnaire. There is no mechanism for checking whether an employee has exaggerated an answer (and thus inflated the job score) except by comparison against the established job hierarchy. Since the purpose of a job analysis and evaluation system is to establish positions in proper hierarchy or relationship to other positions, it defeats the purpose if the only validity check of job information is to compare results against situations and assumptions that already prevail. The use of the PAQ system and the development of other job-evaluation tools will continue to be of primary interest to personnel administrators as demands grow for more accountability in how compensation for jobs is determined.

Generally, the point-factor system in job evaluation has definite advantages, particularly when a classification or compensation system is to be established where none has existed previously. For libraries, as service organizations, the real concern has to be whether the factors and points assigned to the factors truly reflect the values held by the library. This is particularly important when an external agent is responsible for implementing a job-evaluation system. Even though a point system, like any other system, is based on judgment, it does minimize the personal opinion of individual evaluators as to what is of value to the organization by having well-defined factors and weights as the basis of decision making. In the business of comparing "apples and oranges," the more precise the definitions, the more likely that fairness will result and acceptance on the part of staff will be greater.

E. Summary

Evaluating the worth of jobs is the most complex of personnel activities and one that is fraught with potential problems, including damage to staff morale and possible legal action. As yet, no one evaluation system has been identified as the best for all situations and all types of organizations, although it is clear that the more simplistic and nonquantifiable systems (ranking and classification) are more likely to produce problems than the quantifiable systems (factor comparison and point). It is obvious also that the process of job analysis is crucial to the success of job evaluation; if the job analysis data are poor, then inadequate information will be used for the decision making process in establishing job worth. Therefore, job analysis and job evaluation must be seen as a complete process.

IV. CONCLUSIONS

Problems facing academic library administrators and staff in the foreseeable future are going to be many and diverse, and will require skillful and thoughtful planning to maintain and sustain the vitality, if not survival, of the library's role in the academic community.

As budget constraints become a way of life, increasing pressure will be felt on already strained personnel resources. Library administrators will have to maintain a delicate balance in articulating the critical nature of their needs for additional resources. They will have to point out how library services are suffering without creating an impression among members of the academic community that services have deteriorated to such a level as to be negligible. Concurrently, library administrators have to be responsive to new and changing needs of academic library users, but not at the expense of library staff. It will be necessary for administrators to recognize when staff have been pushed or pulled too far or spread too thin and to limit or reduce services even in the face of criticism and attack from library users. Though planning will not eliminate all problems of the future or assure smooth sailing in academic libraries, it is more likely to minimize confusion and division between the library administrators and its staff and between the library staff and the academic community.

In writing about library financial management during periods of budget constraints, Prentice (1978, p. 1) states that

> ...limitations on funds force library planners to set priorities. All desirable services cannot be provided and some must be sacrificed. How can library planners utilize existing resources so that maximum benefit can be realized from each dollar? What are the library's objectives and have they changed during the past two decades? Will funding limitations change those objectives? How can the library manager go about planning for services in a constricted-budget environment? What methodologies for planning and what types of information are necessary for making the best possible choices?

These, of course, are the questions raised as a result of budget situations, but there are many other pressures on library personnel in a field and a society which is changing at an ever-accelerating pace. These pressures include the integration of new technology into libraries, unionization, pay equity and comparability issues, the issue of educational degrees as exclusionary requirements for library positions, and the increasing demand for greater job and career satisfaction and opportunity. Library planners will be faced with many questions relating to these issues. With new technology will the same number of staff still be needed and what types of skills and abilities will be necessary? Will there be a need for fewer librarians over the next decade and if so, what positions are likely to be affected? To what extent will transfer of staff—with necessary retraining—be required? What are potential impacts on staff due to changes in job content—attitude and morale problems as well as matters of compensation? How will unionization and other legal issues relating to personnel affect library staff in matters such as job assignments and qualifications, professional responsibility, and compensation? To what extent should administrators consider the numerous applicants with doctoral degrees as qualified subject specialists and reference librarians? How will increasing expectations for greater growth and development be met by libraries faced with few, if any, resources for training and development, and limited opportunities for job advancement?

The questions are many and serious. It is clear that none of them can be answered without careful thought and consideration, and none should be considered in isolation. In order to meet the numerous situations in a positive manner, planning becomes essential to the library organization. Flippo (1966, p. 33) has stated that

> though planning is somewhat nebulous in nature it nevertheless is essential for success. It has numerous values, among them the seemingly contradictory advantage of making planning possible. If there is little advance planning, the management task becomes one of "fire fighting," that is, continually handling many small and large emergencies as they occur. This method makes for a highly interesting work day, but it is extremely demanding, physically and emotionally. Integrated and purposeful actions for the organization is lacking.

Library administrators must identify planning strategies appropriate to their organization and establish criteria for evaluating programs and activities. They should determine what information is basic to the planning function and the mechanisms to be used to establish a continuous planning process. Clearly, personnel planning should be integrated into overall organizational planning, since for the former to be effective it will require more than simply an analysis of numbers of staff and turnover rates. Indeed, it is imperative to review the use of personnel in relationship to library programs and activities and goals and objectives as well as within the context of projected budget support and the changing needs of library users. Resistance to planning should be corrected and in its place an enthusiasm and commitment to directing actively the course of the library should be encouraged. Library administrators should find ways to recognize and reward planning efforts rather than crisis management and fire fighting. Planning cannot wait until all the answers are known or all the information is at hand. Planning today does not have to limit flexibility tomorrow. Indeed, planning should be a dynamic process, continually taking into account new facts, figures, and contingencies.

Job analysis and evaluation are tools for library administrators to use in the ongoing planning process. Job analysis provides the essential data for recruitment, training and development, and compensation as well as long-range planning. The data generated through job analysis provide the foundation upon which decisions can be based for the allocation of personnel resources. Job evaluation is the activity most directly related to the issue of compensation, and during the coming years there will be greater pressure on all organizations to clarify, refine, revise, and justify the methods by which they establish the value—and thus the compensation—for jobs within the organization. Because of the newly evolving legal issue of pay comparability, which focuses on female-identified jobs and professions, libraries will be very much in the forefront of this particular battle. Because of this, library administrators may be challenged on their internal decisions regarding salaries (as it relates to salaries awarded men and women not just by position) while at the same time they may be expected to direct the battle on comparability in their own institutions to see much-needed improvements in compensation for library staff.

While a number of library administrators have already made a commitment to planning as part of the organization's program, there is still much to be done to integrate a planning component into the administrative program of academic libraries. As Flippo (1966, p. 45) has pointed out

...values to be derived from planning are the achievement of integrated and goal-directed action, a reduction in the number and seriousness of emergencies, the use of more efficient methods, the facilitation of authority delegation, and the development of standards necessary for accurate control. The planning process is essentially the scientific process of orderly thinking.

REFERENCES

American Library Association, Board of Personnel Administration (1948). "Descriptive List of Professional and Non-Professional Duties in Libraries." American Library Association, Chicago.

American Library Association (1970). "Library Education and Personnel Utilization: A Statement of Policy Adopted by the Council of the ALA, June 30, 1970." American Library Association, Chicago.

Asheim, L. E. (1968). Education and manpower in librarianship. *ALA Bulletin* 63, 1096–118.

Benedict, F. C., and Gherman, P. M. (1980). Implementing an integrated personnel system. *Journal of Academic Librarianship* 6, 210–214.

Breiting, A.; Dorey, M., and Sockbeson, D. (1976). Staff development in college and university libraries. *Special Libraries* 67 (July), 305–310.

Bryant, D. R., Maggard, M. J., and Taylor, R. P. (1973). Manpower planning models and techniques: A descriptive survey. *Business Horizons* 16 (April), 69–78.

Burack, E. H., and Gutteridge, T. G. (1978). Institutional manpower planning: Rhetoric versus reality. *California Management Review* 20 (spring), 13–22.

California Library Association (1932). Professional versus non-professional positions in libraries. *In* "Handbook and Proceedings of the Annual Meeting 1932" pp. 57–62.

Canelas, D. B. (1977) "Position Classification in Libraries and an Introduction to the Library Education and Personnel Utilization Policy." Paper presented at the American Library

Association, Office of Library Personnel Resources/Library Education Division Preconference on Effective Personnel Utilization: LEPU Guidelines and Principles, Detroit, Michigan, 16 June 1977.
Chapman, E. A., St. Pierre, P. L., and Lubans, J. (1970). "Library Systems Analysis Guidelines." Wiley-Interscience, New York.
Clark, P. M. (1973). "Personnel for Research Libraries; Qualifications, Responsibilities and Use, Final Report." ERIC 072 836.
Conroy, B. (1978). "Library Staff Development and Continuing Education: Principles and Practices." Libraries Unlimited, Littleton, Colorado.
Cottom, K. (1980). Minimum qualifications and the law: The issue ticks away for librarians. *American Libraries* 11 (May), 280–281.
Crowe, W. J., Jr. (1977). "A Select Bibliography of Materials Relating to Position Classification in Libraries." Paper prepared for the American Library Association, Office of Library Personnel Resources/Library Education Division Preconference on Effective Personnel Utilization: LEPU Guidelines and Principles, Detroit, Michigan, 16 June 1977.
Dowell, D. R. (1980). Minimum qualifications for librarians: Papers from a symposium. *North Carolina Libraries* 38, (spring), 7–29.
Duda, F. (1980). Columbia's two-track system. *College and Research Libraries* 41 (July), 295–304.
Ferguson, A. W., and Taylor, J. R. (1980). What *are* you doing? An analysis of public services librarians at a medium-sized research library. *Journal of Academic Librarianship* 6 (March), 24–29.
Fine, S. (1974). Functional job analysis: An approach to a technology for manpower planning. *Personnel Journal* 53 (November), 813–818.
Fine, S., and Wiley, W. W. (1971). "An Introduction to Functional Job Analysis: A Scaling of Selected Tasks from the Social Welfare Field." W. E. Upjohn Institute for Employment Research, Kalamazoo, Michigan.
Flippo, E. B. (1966). "Principles of Personnel Management." 2d edition. McGraw-Hill Book Co., New York.
Foss, P. (1977). "General Principles of Position Classification." Paper presented at the American Library Association, Office of Library Personnel Resources/Library Education Division Preconference on Effective Personnel Utilization: LEPU Guidelines and Principles, Detroit, Michigan, 16 June 1977.
Gerczak, A. (1977). "Library Selection Project: Job Analysis Report, Phase I." Selection Consulting Center, Sacramento, California.
Gerczak, A. (1978). "Phase II: Selection Systems Design for Entry-Level Professional Librarians." Selection Consulting Center, Sacramento, California.
Henderson, R. I. (1975a). Job descriptions—critical documents, versatile tools, part 1: Structure and uses. *Supervisory Management* 21 (November), 3–10.
Henderson, R. I. (1975b). Job descriptions—critical documents, versatile tools, part 2: Planning for job analysis. *Supervisory Management* 21 (December), 15–25.
Henderson, R. I. (1976a). Job descriptions—critical documents, versatile tools, part 3: Conducting a job analysis. *Supervisory Management* 21 (January), 26–34.
Henderson, R. I. (1976b). Job descriptions—critical documents, versatile tools, part 4: Getting it on paper. *Supervisory Management* 21 (February), 12–21.
Henderson, R. I. (1976c). Job descriptions—critical documents, versatile tools, part 5: Compensable factors. *Supervisory Management* 21 (March), 27–34.
Jeannert, P. R. (1980). Equitable job evaluation and classification with the position analysis questionnaire. *Compensation Review* 12, 32–41.

Krzystofiak, F., Newman, J. M., and Anderson, G. (1979). A quantified approach to measurement of job content: Procedures and payoffs. *Personnel Psychology* 32, 341–357.

Lee, R. and Lee, C. S. (1971). Personnel planning for a library manpower system. *Library Trends* 20 (July), 19–38.

Livy, B. (1975). "Job Evaluation: A Critical Review." John Wiley, New York.

McCormick, E. J. (1974). "The Application of Structured Job Analysis Information Based on the Position Analysis Questionnaire (PAQ)." Department of Psychological Science, Occupational Research Center, Purdue University, West Lafayette, Indiana.

McCormick, E. J. (1979). "Job Analysis: Methods and Applications." AMACOM, American Management Association, New York.

McCormick, E. J., Mecham, R. C., and Jeannert, P. R. (1969). "Position Analysis Questionnaire." Department of Psychological Science, Occupational Research Center, Purdue University, West Lafayette, Indiana.

Martell, C. R., and Dougherty, R. M. (1978). The role of continuing education and training in human resources development: An administrator's viewpoint. *Journal of Academic Librarianship* 4, (July), 151–155.

Mecham, R. C., and McCormick, E. J. (1969). "The Use in Job Evaluation of Job Elements and Job Dimensions Based on the Position Analysis Questionnaire." Department of Psychological Science, Occupational Research Center, Purdue University, West Lafayette, Indiana.

Melching, W. H., and Borcher, S. D. (1973). "Procedures for Constructing and Using Task Inventories." Research and Development Series 91. Center for Vocational and Technical Education, Columbus, Ohio.

Miner, M. G. (1976). "Job Evaluation Policies and Procedures, PDF Survey No. 113." The Bureau of National Affairs, Inc., Washington, D.C.

Mitchell, B. J. (1973). In-house training of supervisory library assistants in a large academic library. *College and Research Libraries* 34 (March), 144–49.

Norman D. Willis and Associates (1974). "State of Washington Comparable Worth Study." Norman D. Willis & Associates, Seattle, Washington.

Norman D. Willis and Associates (1976). "State of Washington Comparable Worth Study." Norman D. Willis & Associates, Seattle, Washington.

Norman D. Willis and Associates (1980). "Objective Job Evaluation Pilot Study, State of Connecticut." Norman D. Willis & Associates, Seattle, Washington.

Norton, E. H. (1980). EEOC in the 1980's: Taking stock and moving ahead. *Equal Opportunity Forum* 7 (February), 7.

Otis, J. L., and Leukart, R. H. (1954). "Job Evaluation: A Basis for Sound Wage Administration." 2d ed. Prentice-Hall, Englewood Cliffs, New Jersey.

Position classification at Michigan: Another look (1979). *College and Research Libraries* 40 (May), 205–213.

Prentice, A. E. (1978). "Strategies for Survival: Library Financial Management Today." R. R. Bowker Company, Xerox Publishing Division, New York.

Ricking, M., and Booth, R. E. (1974). "Personnel Utilization in Libraries: A Systems Approach." American Library Association, Chicago.

Roter, B. (1973). An integrated framework for personnel utilization and management. *Personnel Journal* 52 (December), 1031–1039.

Rothenberg, L. B., Lucianovic, J., Dronick, D., and Rees, A. M. (1971). A job-task index for evaluating professional utilization in libraries. *Library Quarterly* 41 (October), 320–328.

Schofield, J. L. (1975). Job evaluation, job analysis, job satisfaction and resistance to change. *Library Association Record* 77 (October), 241–243.

Sergean, R. (1977). "Librarianship and Information Work: Job Characteristics and Staffing Needs." Research and Development Reports. The British Library, London.

Sergean, R., and McKay, J. R. (1974). The description and classification of jobs in librarianship and information work. *Library Association Record* 76, (June), 112–115.

Sheldon, B. E., ed. (1973). "Planning and Evaluating Library Training Programs: A Guide for Library Leaders, Staffs and Advisory Groups." The Leadership Training Institute, School of Library Science, Florida State University, Tallahassee, Florida.

Snyder, C. A., and Saunders, N. P. (1978). Continuing education and staff development: Needs assessment, comprehensive program planning and evaluation. *Journal of Academic Librarianship* 4 (July), 144–150.

Sparks, C. P. (1980). "Job Analysis under the Uniform Guidelines Procedures, Standards, Requirements, and Restraints." Paper presented at the Third Annual Conference on EEO Compliance and Human Resource Utilization, University of Chicago, 19 May 1980.

Stone, E. W. (1969). "Factors Related to Professional Development of Librarians." Scarecrow Press, Metuchen, New Jersey.

Taylor, L. R., and Colbert, G. A. (1978). Empirically derived job families as a foundation for the study of validity generalization. *Personnel Psychology* 31, 341–354.

Tompkins, M. M. (1966). Classification evaluation of professional librarian positions in the University of Michigan library. *College and Research Libraries* 27 (May), 175–84.

Trieman, D. J. (1979). "Job Evaluation: An Analytic Review, Interim Report to the Equal Employment Opportunity Commission." National Academy of Science, Washington, D.C.

U.S. Civil Service Commission (1965). Basic training course in position classification: The classification process. Personnel Methods Series 11 (part 2). Government Printing Office, Washington, D.C.

U.S. Department of Labor (1972). "Handbook for Analyzing Jobs." Manpower Administration, U.S. Government Printing Office, Washington, D.C.

U.S. Equal Employment Opportunity Commission, U.S. Civil Service Commission, U.S. Department of Justice and U.S. Department of Labor (1978). Uniform guidelines on employee selection procedures *Federal Register* 43 (166), 38290–38315.

van Rijn, P. (1979). "Job Analyses for Selection: An Overview." Professional Series 79–2. Personnel Research and Development Center, Office of Personnel Management, Washington, D.C.

Walker, J. W. (1968). Trends in manpower management research. *Business Horizons* 11 (August), 36–46.

Wilkinson, J., Plate, K., and Lee, R. (1975). A matrix approach to position classification. *College and Research Libraries* 36 (September), 351–363.

Zweizig, D. L. (1979). Organizational assessment of staff development needs: A model and a case study. *In* "The Evaluation of Continuing Education for Professionals A System View" (P. LeBreton, ed.), pp. 180–196. The University of Washington, Seattle, Washington.

The Role of Information in Governmental Planning

COLLEEN L. COGHLAN*

Minnesota Department of Energy, Planning, and Development

I.	Introduction	99
II.	Governmental Deliberative Activities	100
	A. Deliberative Activities in General	101
	B. Executive Agency Deliberations	105
III.	Health Planning and Resources Development (Public Law 96–79)	106
	A. Authority and Charge	107
	B. Process	110
	C. The Plan	118
IV.	Deliberated Government Documents: A Bibliographic Chain	119
	A. The Documents	119
	B. Bibliographic Chain of Documents	120
V.	Conclusion	125
	References	125

I. INTRODUCTION

This article is concerned with the use and production of information in governmental planning, an activity usually labeled explicitly in law and which, typically, includes deliberations. Deliberation has been defined as

*Present address: Metropolitan State University, St. Paul, Minnesota 55101.

"formal discussion and debate of all sides of an issue"[1] and as a process during which "the reasons for and against a choice of acts are examined and weighed."[2] In the governmental setting, these deliberations include the structured or formal consideration of a problem and possible solutions, and they are important because of their frequency, their wide-ranging effect, and the number of records which they produce. For instance, in 1977, there were 875 Federal advisory committees with 17,400 individual members.[3] State committees add to the numbers, and document production and dispersion loom large even if only one document were produced for each committee member. The explicit labeling of an activity as "planning" is important because it implies a certain framework of assumptions, expectations, and activities. Planning, for instance, is usually understood to include anticipating and preparing for the future. As such, it is a neutral word and a useful concept. "Governmental planning" may not be as neutral because governmental activity of any kind is rarely neutral, and the term "planning" may or may not be in favor at any given time. But the idea of anticipating the future remains useful, even necessary, and precedes virtually every decision. This anticipation of the future may be called "policy analysis," "policy research," or "study." Whatever the activities connected with the government's deliberations about the impact of its actions are called, the activities will continue; they will draw from existing information and produce new information.

II. GOVERNMENTAL DELIBERATIVE ACTIVITIES

The process of deliberation is a procedure for considering information which addresses a problem and leads to one or more possible solutions. Havelock (1971, pp. 1–10) calls this a "knowledge transfer process" which is "best understood as an interaction or linkage between a potential 'user' and a potential 'resource,'" and is able to be analyzed by the formula: *who* says *what* to *whom* by *what channel* to *what effect* for *what purpose*." Placing this knowledge transfer process within the context of the larger topic, knowledge dissemination and utilization, he then proposes an institutional framework for viewing diffusion and utilization macrosystems (see Figure

---

[1] *The American Heritage Dictionary of the English Language*. Boston: American Heritage Publishing Company and Houghton Mifflin Company, 1973, p. 349.

[2] *Black's Law Dictionary*. revised 4th edition. St. Paul, MN: West Publishing Company, 1968, p. 514.

[3] United States Congress. Senate. Committee on Governmental Affairs, *Federal Advisory Committees: Index*, Washington, D.C.: U.S. Government Printing Office, 1978.

1). The framework includes the university (academic departments and professional schools), the scientific community, the service professions, product organizations, service organizations, the consumer, the media and the government, with the latter "hovering over this complex conglomerate of institutional forms . . . attempting, at least, to serve and represent the consumer through influencing the other systems in various ways, 'coordinating' their efforts so that together they will all function as a system to benefit the consumer." (Havelock, 1971, p. 3–7)

Within this large governmental knowledge-transfer activity are the many smaller knowledge-transfer activities in the three branches of government. These latter activities include, among other types of knowledge transfer, the deliberations with which this paper is concerned.

A. Deliberative Activities in General

Although the deliberations of the several branches of government differ greatly in purpose and authority, they are similar in that they all use information, and these information-related activities share certain important characteristics. In each of these activities, participants consider information and produce documents following a prescribed process. The participants consist of deliberators, staff people, and interested parties—some of whom also testify. The deliberators are usually carefully chosen, sometimes elected, and often form a council, committee, task force, jury, or other voting body. The information usually comes from many sources, is of many types, and probably reflects several different points of view, especially if the range of acceptable sources is broad. The number of documents varies with the flexibility and longevity of the process. They are of two kinds: supporting documents—reports, testimony, and statistical analyses—and deliberated documents—a final report or a public law and its earlier versions. This distinction between supporting documents and deliberated documents reflects the authority of the deliberators to change the context of the documents. Supporting documents may or may not be used in later, deliberated documents, but they contain technical information produced by non-deliberators and they stand as presented. Deliberated documents contain analyses and recommendations which have been examined, weighed, and modified by the deliberators. Finally, the process is usually described somewhere—in a law, in a formal statement of activity purpose, and authority, or in the minutes of the first meeting—and it has at least two parts: action and timing. An action is an activity which the participants are authorized to perform. These actions affect the outcome being sought and vary considerably in importance and finality. For instance, being able or being required to vote is more important than being able to comment on a point. Timing

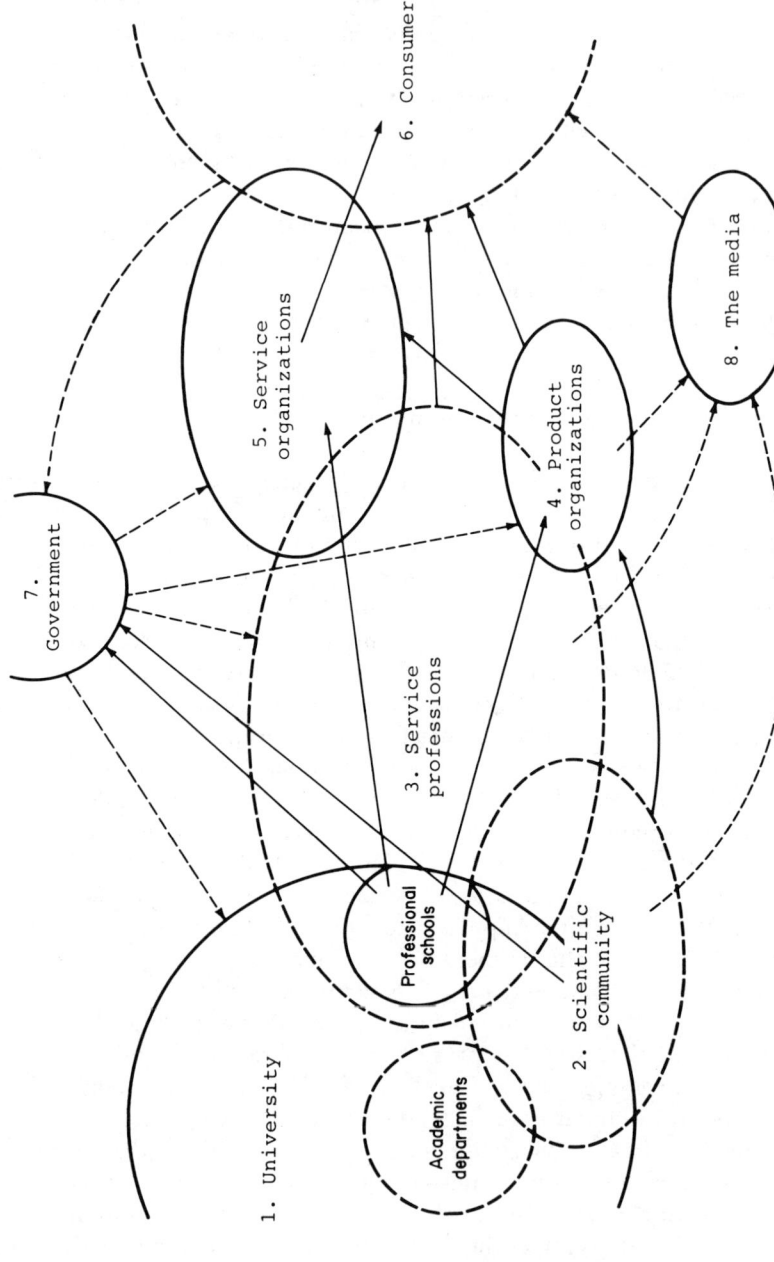

Fig. 1. An institutional framework for viewing diffusion and utilization macrosystems. Source: Havelock, R. G. (1971). "Planning for Innovation." © Center for Research on Utilization of Scientific Knowledge, University of Michigan.

relates not only to the sequence of events but the spacing as well and may be the critical factor in the strategy of interested parties. The events may be labeled differently but they probably assume a sequence based on a problem-solving model like that of Jung and Lippitt (1966):

1. Identification of a concern
2. Diagnosis of the situation
3. Formulating action alternatives
4. Feasibility testing of selected alternatives
5. Adoption and diffusion of good alternatives

A later modification of this model, presented by Lippitt (1971) (Fig. 2) as the "research utilization problem-solving model", suggests that the process, which consists of five steps:

1. Identification of a concern
2. Diagnosis of the situation
3. Formulating action alternatives
4. Feasibility testing of selected alternatives, including training and evaluation
5. Adoption and diffusion of good alternatives

may draw on external knowledge in the form of (1) theory (2) research findings (3) innovations (4) methodology or (5) human resources, or on internal knowledge in the form of (1) priority of needs, objectives (2) diagnostic data (3) manpower resources (4) existing innovations or (5) evaluation of change process and progress. Paraphrasing Havelock, (1971) process reduces to: Who does what to the information when?

Governmental deliberations differ in the several branches but are all pervasive: A judge or jury considers evidence before acting; Congress holds hearings on pending matters; executive agency officials convene task forces to advise them. Of these several types, deliberations within executive agencies[4] may be the most frequent, the least acknowledged, and the most

---

[4]There is no single definition of the term agency. Any given definition usually relates to specific legislation. Generally, executive agency means any executive branch department, independent commission, board, bureau, office or other establishment of the Federal Government, including independent regulatory commissions and boards. . . . Federal agency is a broader term, encompassing executive agencies and establishments in the judicial and legislative branches (except the Senate, the House of Representatives, and activities under the direction of the Architect of the Capitol) (*A Glossary of Terms Used in the Federal Budget Process, and Related Accounting, Economic, and Tax Terms*. 3d Ed. Washington, D.C.: U.S. General Accounting Office, March 1981, p. 32.)

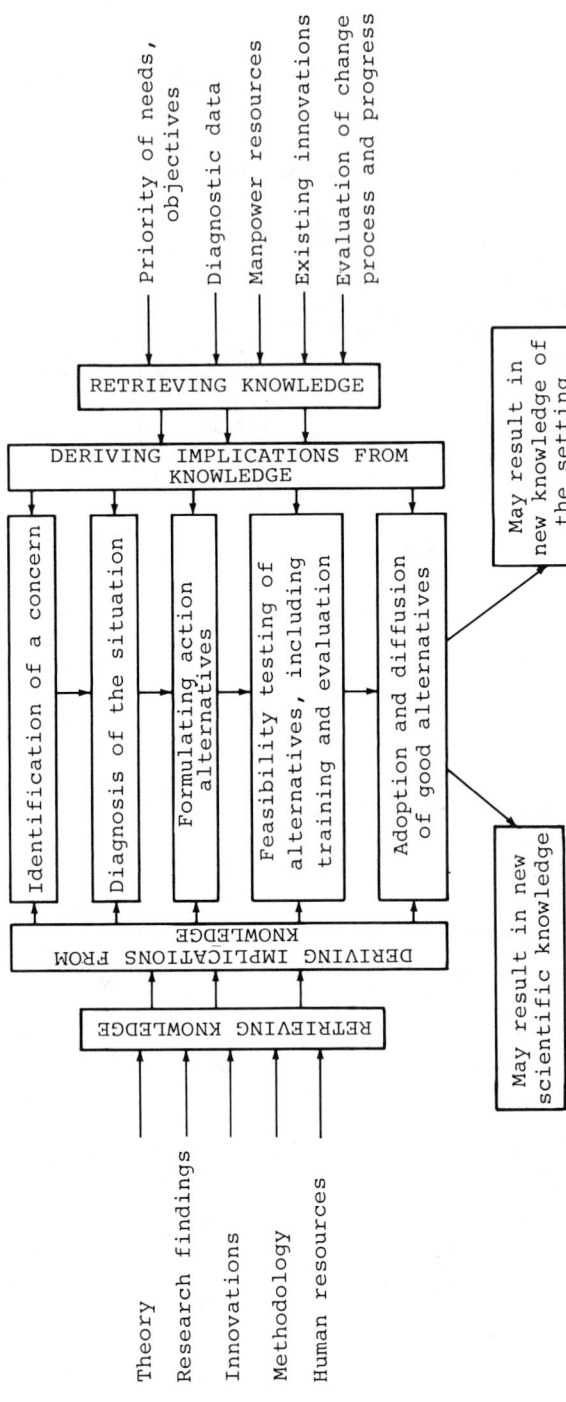

Fig. 2. Research utilization problem-solving model. Source: Lippitt, R. (1971). Research utilization problem-solving model. *In* Havelock, R. G. (1971). "Planning for Innovation." © Center for Research on Utilization of Scientific Knowledge, University of Michigan.

The Role of Information in Governmental Planning 105

amenable to change, and, therefore, most important for citizens to consider. The deliberations analyzed within this paper are those undertaken by persons who are not—for the most part—government employees to help governmental employees make decisions. The emphasis is on the documents which are produced as a result of these deliberations.

B. Executive Agency Deliberations

The executive branch has the fewest routine procedures for its deliberative activities, and the established procedures are likely to vary among the executive agencies. As a result, procedures for introducing information (sources, timing) may require definition of "rules" by the participants or they may be prescribed in more or less detail in a law. If rules must be established, they typically describe both the process and the resulting documents. Although there is variation in the consequent deliberations, there is also pattern. Types of resulting documents form one such pattern; but even with this possible predictability, no organized bibliographic reference to these documents exists. Zwirn (1980a, 1980b) addresses Congressional deliberations in terms of this combination of process and resulting document production, but explicit and constant Congressional rules for procedures make this task less onerous than a comparable analysis of executive agency deliberations. However, Levy (1979) and Ikem (1981) provide a good starting point with a description of the activities and documentation of several deliberative bodies in the United Nations. However, neither relates the practices of these groups to any other groups or to any broader concepts.

The deliberative process always assumes that an authority for the process exists. The authority is the legal foundation upon which the choice of the deliberators and the nature of their deliberations are based. In the executive agency deliberations, it may be a statute[5], a rule, a regulation, or an execu-

---

[5]The authority to convene a group of deliberators may be explicit in substantive or basic law, explicit and also funded in authorizing legislation, or carried out as part of a program of work for which Congress has appropriated funds. "*SUBSTANTIVE LAW:* Statutory public law other than appropriation law; sometimes referred to as basic law. Substantive law usually authorizes, in broad general terms, the executive branch to carry out a program of work. Annual determination as to the amount of the work to be done is usually thereafter embodied in appropriation law. . . ." "*AUTHORIZING LEGISLATION:* Substantive legislation enacted by Congress that sets up or continues the legal operation of a Federal program or agency either indefinitely or for a specific period of time or sanctions a particular type of obligation or expenditure within a program. Authorizing legislation is normally a prerequisite for appropriations. It may place a limit on the amount of budget authority to be included in appropriation acts or it may authorize the appropriation of "such sums as may be necessary." . . . "*APPRO-

tive order. It may be general or specific, explicit or implicit, one time or continuing, but it must exist if credibility is to be maintained and court action by dissatisfied affected persons is to be avoided. The process itself begins with a charge. A charge is an assigned task, a statement of what a group is to do. It includes (*a*) the problem which prompted the activity; (*b*) the actions of the deliberating group (review, comment, develop, advise); and (*c*) the outcome sought (plan, agency policy, report). In terms of Lippitt's model (see Figure 2), the charge is the identification of a concern. Given the authority to convene the group and the charge for the group to consider, the deliberative process begins. As noted earlier, the process has three parts—participants, information, and documents—linked by action and timing. The final outcome sought is the policy or plan, a statement (*a*) which is accepted by the governmental agency; (*b*) with which the agency agrees; and (*c*) on which it will base future actions.

Governmental policy and planning deliberations are frequent and have great impact on the citizenry. As shown above, every deliberation is a process which uses information and creates documents. Because of the possible variation among these processes, an understanding of a particular deliberative process must be based on an analysis of the specific authority which established it.

III. HEALTH PLANNING AND RESOURCES DEVELOPMENT (PUBLIC LAW 96–79)

The current health planning law is Public Law 96–79, titled the Health Planning and Resources Development Act and codified as Titles XV and XVI of the Public Health Service Act as amended by the Health Planning and Resources Development Amendments of 1979.

The health planning law specifies in great detail the participants, the timing of participation, the kinds of information to be used (and produced, if necessary), and the kinds of documents to be developed. The detail of the law doubtless derives from the importance of the subject. It is concerned with (*a*) three major participants: the sellers or providers of, the buyers or

---

PRIATION ACT: A statue, under the jurisdiction of the House and Senate Committees in Appropriations, that generally provides authorization for Federal agencies to incur obligations and to make payment out of the treasury for specified purposes. . . ." This is one form of "spending legislation." (*A Glossary of Terms Used in the Federal Budget Process, and Related Accounting, Economic, and Tax Terms.* 3d Ed. Washington, D.C.: U.S. General Accounting Office, March 1981, p. 32.)

consumers of, and the payers for health care; (*b*) their respective goals of quality of care, access to services, and cost of services; and (*c*) the relationship among the participants.

A. Authority and Charge

The law authorizes, indeed requires, that the Secretary of the Department of Health and Human Services (hereafter referred to as "the Secretary") "issue guidelines concerning national health planning policy" (Section 1501 [a]) which guidelines shall include "(1) standards respecting the appropriate supply, distribution, and organization of health resources . . . [and] (2) national health planning goals developed after consideration of the [established] priorities . . . which goals to the maximum extent practicable shall be expressed in quantitative terms" (Section 1501 [b]). This is the general authority and charge. The rest of this long law (91 pages by one printing) lays out a complex process for accomplishing this charge.

The major activity in this process is the development of regional and state plans. To create these plans, the law establishes and charges (1) deliberating bodies at the regional, state, and national level, two of which figure more prominently in the development of the plans than the other, and (2) three discrete entities which, together with some of the other participants, form an extensive structure for the collection, analysis, and use of data in these plan production activities.

1. DELIBERATIVE BODIES

The regional health-systems agency (hereafter referred to as "regional agency"), and specifically its *governing body,* is responsible for the health planning activities in the regional health-service area. This is a designated area which typically has a population of at least 500,000, a geographic and economic sensitivity, and coordination with other regional boundaries established for other health-related activities (Section 1511 [a]). There is at least one regional agency within each state; some states have more; and some regional agencies cross state boundaries. The regional governing body is responsible for the internal affairs of the regional agency and for the establishment of the regional plan and related reports. Specific responsibilities include:

1. assembling and analyzing data,
2. establishing and at least triennially, reviewing and amending a regional plan,

3. establishing, annually reviewing, and amending an annual implementation plan (Section 1513(b)(1–3)),
4. establishing procedures for and reviewing grant and contract proposals and performance,
5. scheduling at least six well-publicized public meetings a year, including one in each calendar quarter, and
6. preparing an annual report (including the regional plan) and making available certain records and data of the agency (Section 1512(b)(3)(B)).

The authority of the governing body for administration of the agency's activities is clear, and many of its responsibilities are related to producing documents and making information available in other ways.

The activities at the state level are administered by the State Health Planning and Development Agency (hereafter referred to as the state agency) which is advised by the Statewide Health Coordinating Council (hereafter referred to as "Statewide Council"), established under Section 1524(a) to advise the state agency). It is an advisory rather than a governing body. As the law invests both the state agency and the Statewide Council with large parts in the development of the state health plan, this relative degree of authority is of some importance. The Governor's approval or disapproval of the state health plan draws them together.

The Statewide Council is responsible for:

1. establishing a uniform format for regional plans,
2. reviewing and coordinating at least triennially the regional plans,
3. reviewing at least annually the annual implementation plan and the budget of each regional agency in the state and reporting results to the Secretary,
4. preparing, reviewing at least triennially, and revising as necessary a state health plan, and
5. advising the State Agency generally on the performance of its functions.

The major functions of the state agency include the following:

1. "conduct the health planning activities of the State and implement those parts of the State health plan . . . and the [regional] plans . . . which relate to the government of the State,"
2. "determine the statewide health needs,"
3. "prepare, review at least triennially, and revise as necessary a preliminary State health plan which shall be made up of [the regional plans],"

4. revise regional plans as necessary "to achieve their appropriate coordination or to deal more effectively with statewide health needs,"
5. submit the preliminary state health plan to the Statewide Council for approval or disapproval and for use in developing the state health plan, and
6. "assist the Statewide Council . . . generally" (Section 1523(a)(1–3)).

The state agency establishes statewide health needs and develops the preliminary state health plan which must address them. The Statewide Council must consider this preliminary state health plan as it develops and approves the state health plan. The governor then must approve the plan before it becomes the official state health plan. He can disapprove the submitted plan only if it does not effectively meet the statewide health needs. So the state agency and the Statewide Council together develop a state health plan likely to be approved by the governor. The governor is the ultimate state authority. The National Council on Health Planning and Development advises, consults with, and makes recommendations to the Secretary (Section 1503(a)), and as such, has little involvement in and virtually no authority related to the development of plans.

2. DATA AGENCIES

The regional and state plans which are to be developed by these deliberative bodies are to be based on an effective use of pertinent data and analyses, and, to the extent practicable, are to have goals expressed quantitatively. For these information-related activities to occur with some uniformity among all of the regional and state health-plan developers, the law requires that one of the regional staff members have expertise in the gathering and analysis of data (Section 1512(b)(2)(A)(ii)), and that the Secretary provide technical assistance to the regional health-systems agencies and to the state agencies by establishing (1) centers for health planning to provide "such technical and consulting assistance as regional health systems agencies and State agencies may from time to time require, conducting research, studies and analyses of health planning and resources development, and developing health planning approaches, methodologies, policies, and standards. . . ." (Section 1534(a)), and (2) "a national health planning information center to support the health planning and resources development programs . . . ; to provide access to current information in health planning and resources development; and to provide information for use in the analysis of issues and problems related to health planning and resources development" (Section 1533(c)).

The information-related structures established in this law assume and draw upon the existing resources of the Federal government. "The [regional] agency shall to the maximum extent practicable use existing data (including data developed under Federal health programs) and coordinate its activities with the cooperative system" (Section 1513(b)(1)). The "cooperative system" is the Cooperative Health Statistics System, a program of the National Center for Health Statistics in which personnel of the Center coordinate the activities of the states as they collect seven classes of data, including health facilities, health manpower, and vital (birth and death) records. Coordination with the cooperative system is also included as part of the state agency's activities regarding the collection, retrieval, analyses, reporting, and publication of statistical and other information related to health and health care (Section 1522(b)(7)(A)).

The importance of the cooperative system and its parent body, the National Center for Health Statistics, is apparent from this explicit mention in the law and from the titles of serial publications produced by the Center and distributed to health planners: *Vital and Health Statistics Series, Vital Statistics of the United States, Monthly Vital Statistics Report, Advance Data,* and *Statistical Notes for Health Planners.* But other than advocating coordination, the law establishes no legal or budgetary ties between health planning and the National Center for Health Statistics; therefore, it is not discussed further.

B. Process

As noted earlier, the process involves participants using information in prescribed ways to produce plans.

1. PARTICIPANTS

Participants in the process include the members of the three types of deliberative groups already mentioned and several other specified groups. In the following list, any composition required by the law is detailed.

a. Deliberative Groups. Deliberative groups include:

1. the National Council on Health Planning and Development, with 20 members, including government employees, providers of health care, representatives of urban and rural medically underserved populations, and persons who "are exceptionally well qualified to be on the Council" (Section 1503(b)(1)),
2. the regional agency governing body, with an unspecified number of

persons (usually from 10 to 30), a majority of whom are consumers of health care and who broadly represent the sociodemographic characteristics of the area. This majority also includes major purchasers of health care such as labor organizations and business corporations. The rest of the members are residents of the area and providers of health care. The law describes each of these groups in considerable detail (Section 1512(b)(3)(C)),
3. the Statewide Council, which has complex requirements. It must have at least 16 representatives from the regional agencies; a majority of this number must be consumers of health care; and consumers must constitute at least 60% of the whole Council. The governor may appoint such persons (including state officials, public elected officials, and other representatives of governmental authorities within the state) to serve on the Statewide Council as he deems appropriate; however, a majority of the persons appointed by the governor must be consumers of health care who are not also providers of health care. At least one-half of the providers of health care who are members of the Council must be direct providers of health care. Consumer members must include individuals who represent rural and urban medically underserved populations if such populations exist in the state (Section 1524(b)(1)).

b. Nondeliberative Groups. Nondeliberative groups include:

1. regional agency staff, who must have expertise in administration, gathering and analysis of data, health planning, development and use of health and mental health resources, financial and economic analysis, prevention of disease and other public health matters (Section 1512(b)(2)(A))
2. state agency staff, including a professional staff for planning and a professional staff for development (Section 1522(b)(4)(A))
3. the state health authority and state mental health authority (Section 1523(a)(2))
4. a task force of regional and state persons knowledgeable about mental health services including services for alcohol and drug abuse (Section 1513(b)(2)(F)) and Section 1524(c)(2)(D))
5. interested persons including area residents (Section 1513(b)(2))
6. technical assistance personnel to assist agency staff members (Sections 1533 and 1534)
7. the Governor
8. the Secretary of the Department of Health and Human Services who issues the regulations and who holds most of the authority in the law.

With the fixed requirements for the deliberative groups and the explicit mention of the additional groups, most of the components in Havelock's macrosystem are represented in the health planning law. One of Havelock's components not explicitly mentioned is the University, but the technical assistance established in the law and available to the staff suggests that the research activities of this component probably are noted, and the professional school activities are covered by the service professions. The broad representation, especially of consumer groups, does suggest that the government, in the form of the health planning law, is diffusing and utilizing information well, at least in Havelock's terms.

2. INFORMATION

With regard to information, the second component of the process, the health-planning law emphasizes data collection. National, state, and regional health-planning agencies are authorized to collect data for several purposes, some of which are related to health plans.

At the national level, the Secretary is authorized to collect data to determine whether the national guidelines are being met by the goals and implementation activities of regional and state health plans, and to "prescribe the manner in which such data shall be assembled and reported, and the definitions which shall be used" (Section 1501(e)(1)). If the Secretary requires data to determine whether the national guidelines are being met, the regional agency must assemble and report them. It must also

> assemble and analyze data concerning: (A) the status . . . of the health of the residents of the health service area, (B) the status of the health care delivery system in the area and the use of that system by the residents of the area, (C) the effect the area's health care delivery system has on the health of the residents of the area, (D) the number, type, and location of the area's health resources, including health services, manpower, and facilities, (E) the patterns of utilization of the area's health resources, and (F) the environmental and occupational exposure factors affecting immediate and long-term health conditions.

The use of the word *assemble* instead of *collect* is consistent with the law's caution: "the agency shall to the maximum extent practicable use existing data including data developed under Federal health programs" (Section 1513(b)(1)). In addition to these mandated functions, the regional agency also must collect—and may use in its plan—information on the rates charged for each of the 25 most frequently used hospital services in the state, including the average semiprivate and private room rates (Section 1513(h)(1)).

The state agency is basically a coordinator rather than a collector of data. It coordinates its activities with those of the cooperative data-gathering system discussed and "with any entity of the State which reviews the rates or budgets of health care facilities in the State" (Section 1522(b)(7)(A-B)). Moreover, the state agency must prepare an inventory of health-care facilities located in the state, and if the pertinent data are not already collected, the inference is that the state agency should do so.

Following these data-collection activities—the first of the information requirements in the law—come the data-use activities. Three devices are used to assure consistency among all the regional and state health planners as they use the data to develop their plans. The first device is establishment of uniform formats for plans (Section 1524(c)(1)) and uniform systems for calculating several costs, rates, and services. These latter uniform systems include: (*a*) calculating cost of operation and volume of services provided by health-services institutions and rates to be charged to health insurers and other payers; (*b*) a classification system for health-services institutions; and (*c*) a uniform system for reporting by the health-services institutions (Section 1533(d)(1–5)).

The second device is the setting of minimum data requirements for determining the health status of the residents of a health-service area and the determinants of such status; determining the status of the health resources and services of a health-service area; and describing the use of health resources and services within a health-service area (Section 1533(b)(1)). The third device is the establishment of centers for technical assistance (Section 1533(c), 1534).

This technical assistance is of three kinds: "(1) assistance in developing health plans and approaches to planning various types of health services, (2) technical materials, including methodologies, policies, and standards appropriate for use in health planning, and (2) other technical assistance as may be necessary in order that such agencies may properly perform their functions" (Section 1533(a)). Once these data have been collected, they become part of an agency's records, subject to the federal Freedom of Information Act, State Official Records Acts, and certain provisions of the Health Planning and Resources Development Act. Both the regional agency and the state agency must make records and data of the agency (with specified exceptions relating to personnel) available upon request (Section 1512(b)(3)(B), and 1522(b)(6)(C)).

Other than testimony, which cannot be predicted, the only additional planning information is in the records of the public meetings that the deliberators and agencies are required to hold. The number, content, and format of these records are difficult to predict, but their availability is probably required under a state's official records act or the federal Freedom of Information Act. Recognizing the enormity of establishing an organizational structure *and* an information system at the same time, the Health Planning and Resources Development Act also established the previously noted national health-planning information center to help move all of this information among the producers and users created by the law.

3. DOCUMENTS

The documents are the third part of the process. The Health Planning and Resources Development Act also includes authority for several review processes—each of which is likely to produce documents—but this discussion is limited to the documents which come from the planning process.

The National Guidelines for Health Planning, issued and revised in regulation form by the Secretary after review by all the deliberating groups, agency staffs, and other interested parties includes standards and goals which must be addressed in every regional and state plan. These guidelines tie together the contents of separate plans and are the framework for evaluating the health-care delivery systems. The guidelines are reviewed annually by the Secretary and, if a change is warranted, the deliberative process used is that included in the process to make Federal regulations generally, with one addition: the Secretary asks the National Council on Health Planning and Development, the Statewide Councils, the state agencies, the regional agencies, the associations, and the specialty societies representing medical and other health-care providers for early comments and recommendations. The documents which emerge from the guidelines activity after this early comment are published in the *Federal Register* in accordance with Federal requirements. The data that the Secretary may require the regional and state agencies to assemble and report—in a prescribed manner and with prescribed definitions—are used to determine whether the goals established in these guidelines are being met, but no explicit information requirements exist for first establishing the guidelines.

The Regional Plan, issued by the regional agency governing body after deliberation, addresses national priorities, state needs, and the standards and goals of the national guidelines as adapted to regional concerns. The law describes this regional plan and the participants' actions in some detail.

> The regional agency is directed to consider the national guidelines, the priorities, and the data developed as regional requirements and to use the uniform format in establishing and reviewing at least triennially a Regional Plan which shall be a detailed statement of goals (A) describing a healthful environment (primarily with regard to health care equipment and to health services provided by health care institutions, health care facilities and other providers of health care and to other health resources) and health systems in the area which, when developed, will assure that quality health systems in the area which, when developed, will assure that quality health services will be available and accessible in a manner which assures continuity of care, at reasonable cost, for all residents of the area; (B) which are responsive

The Role of Information in Governmental Planning 115

to the unique needs and resources of the area; (C) which take into account the national guidelines for health planning policy and services; (D) which are responsive to statewide health needs; (E) which describe the institutional health services needed to provide for the well-being of persons receiving care within the health service area, including, at a minimum, acute inpatient, . . . rehabilitation, and long-term care services; and (F) which describe other health services needed to provide for the well-being of persons receiving care within the health service area, including, at a minimum, prevention, ambulatory and home health services, treatment for alcohol and drug abuse,

and mental health services. The regional plan shall describe "the number and type of resources," required to meet its goals and "shall state the extent to which existing health care facilities are in need of modernization, conversions to other uses, or closure and the extent to which new health care facilities need to be constructed or acquired" (Section 1513(b)(2)). The regional agency establishes a plan with goals which "take into account" the national guidelines, which "are responsive" to statewide health needs, and to the unique needs and resources of the area "in accordance with" a uniform format. The attempt simultaneously to require consistency and but allow flexibility is apparent in these actions.

Table 1 includes the data and analysis activities which are required first in the regional plans and then in the state plan, which is basically a composite of these regional perspectives. This stage in the development of the plan suggests that the first three steps of Lippitt's problem-solving model (see Figure 2) have been addressed: a concern has been identified (the charge in the law), a situation diagnosed (data gathered and analyzed), and the action alternatives have been formulated. Lippitt's fourth step—feasibility testing of selected alternatives—may be seen in the next stage: deliberations by the regional governing body.

The process of developing the regional plan probably includes a greater number of deliberations, but the law (Section 1513(b)(2)(F) and Section 1512(b)(3)(B)(v)) requires only those noted in Table 2. This same process is required for the *Annual Implementation Plan,* which describes objectives and provides for improving the health of residents in accordance with the special needs of an area. A public notice of activities and call for public comment are required but not an official response. The regional deliberating body holds its hearing and establishes its plan which is reviewed by the Statewide Council before forwarding to the Secretary. The composition of these bodies is so broad that almost any type of constituent would have a voting representative, but this or any other type of exchange is not explicitly required in the law. At the state level, the Statewide Council is directed to "prepare, review at least triennially, and revise as necessary a *State Plan* which shall be made up of" the regional plans, revised if necessary "to achieve their appropriate coordination or to deal more effectively with

TABLE 1
Developing the State Health Plan: An Analysis Based on P.L. 96-79 and Lippitt's Model. Part 1: Predeliberative Activities

Identification of a concern	Diagnosis of the situation			Formulating action alternatives [goals]
	Analysis			
	Data	Processes	Considerations	
Health status of residents →	Set minimum data requirement			To provide health systems
Status and residents' use of health care delivery system →	Set minimum data required, e.g.,			To Provide a Healthful Environment
	number, type and location of health services, manpower, facilities;	Planning methodologies	National guidelines National priorities Statewide health needs	From health care institutions which offer at least acute inpatient services, rehabilitation services, and long term care services
	patterns of resource use;	"Uniform formats"		
	numbers of patient days, patient admissions, outpatient visits, beds operated by an institution	"Uniform systems" for calculations and reporting by institution	Area's unique needs and resources Policies Standards Regional plans incorporated into state plan	From health care facilities, other health care providers, and other health resources which offer other health services, e.g., prevention, ambulatory and home health, alcohol and drug abuse treatment, mental health services
	Costs, volume, and rates of services from each cost center			

TABLE 2
Developing the State Health Plan: An Analysis Based on P.L. 96–79 and Lippitt's Model. Part 2: Deliberative Activities

Participants	Feasibility testing of selected alternatives																	Adoption and diffusion of good alternatives		
	Regional plan											State plan									Final		
	Proposed (Public hearing)					Final					Preliminary				Proposed (Public hearing)							
	Propose	Publish notice	Submit views	Conduct	Revise	Establish	Issue	Review and report	Require revision	Revise	Prepare	Review	Receive	Consider	Prepare	Publish notice	Submit views	Conduct	Recommend	Approve–disapprove	Publish	Revise
Regional governing body	x	x		x	x	x	x															
Statewide council					x	x	x			x												
State agency								x	x		x	x	x	x	x	x		x	x		x	x
Governor																				x		
Communications media (including two newspapers)		x																				
Interested persons (including area residents)			x														x					
State mental health authority																			x			
State health authority																			x			

statewide health needs as determined by the State Agency." The state plan takes account of national priorities and guidelines and state needs, considers the preliminary state plan developed by the state agency, is concerned with the same subjects, and is subject to the same general procedures in its preparation as the regional plan. After deliberation and approval by the Statewide Council, the state plan is sent to the governor for final approval (Section 1524(c)(2)).

The procedures involved in preparing the state plan are quite complicated because of the number of participants and documents. The information-related tasks required by law for the state plan are primarily coordinative. In addition to the uniform format and probable data and statistical foundation similarities, a major incorporation of the regional plans occurs as the preliminary state plan is developed and then reviewed and modified during deliberations. The law does not address similar functions of coordination and review of state plans for a plan at the national level except to require that the Secretary review regional and state plans when conducting his annual review of the national guidelines (Section 1501(d)). Both the regional and state deliberating bodies are charged with issuing, making readily available, or publishing the established plans, but the number, location, and cost of copies is not specified in any way. One possible agency for dissemination is the National Health Planning Information Center which (with a subcontract to National Technical Information Service) collects, organizes, indexes, abstracts, and distributes on demand these documents.

C. The Plan

The outcome of this intensive deliberation is the state plan and supporting regional plans. These negotiated statements include national standards and priorities, state needs, regional adaptations (as necessary) of goals based on data and analyses, and recommended actions to reach the goals. A plan, then, considers the current state of things (data and analysis), projects the ideal or at least a better state of things (standards and priorities), and presents recommendations for achieving that better state (goals and recommended actions). This latter "implementation strategy" is one way of differentiating a plan from a policy and in the case of the Health Planning and Resources Development Act (Public Law 96–79) is a powerful differentiator because the law includes authorities beyond the establishment of the plan. The law also authorizes the regional agencies to issue grants for projects to help meet the goals (Section 1513(c)) and requires the regional agencies, state agency, or Statewide Council to apply the standards in the plan to the several reviews also authorized in the law (Section 1513(e-g),

1523(a)(4–6), 1524(c)(6)). These additional authorities have provoked comments that the law is more a regulatory than planning law. At this point, in terms of Lippitt's problem-solving model, the feasibility of the alternative goals has been tested (by deliberation) and the good alternatives have been adopted and diffused.

IV. DELIBERATED GOVERNMENT DOCUMENTS: A BIBLIOGRAPHIC CHAIN

Governmental decisions are not isolated events. They are always preceded by a law which provides authority, and they are usually preceded by deliberations which provide credibility, some adaptability, and ultimately more "popular authority." These deliberations, following the legislative deliberations which established the law, constitute a second, more specific, look at what needs to be done and a series of activities which begins with a charge and ends with a policy or plan at least accepted and at most approved and used by the agency official issuing the charge. Although the procedures vary, certain steps almost always occur and typically are marked by the appearance of a document—an evolutionary document, if you will—based on a preceding document and probably leading to yet another version. This evolution seems to have certain predictable elements in it.

A. The Documents

The documents are of five types: background paper, draft, preliminary statement, proposed document, and approved (or final) document. A *background paper* is usually prepared by staff members or experts under contract. It presents information and typically does not present a point of view. It may be an excellent summation of extensive data about the topic of the charge.

A *draft* is an untried or undeliberated statement, usually presented in the manner and form of the final document. It is based on the charge and on the background papers and typically includes options for action, but it does not indicate which option is preferred. It is developed by staff and used by the deliberators to refine the information presented and the method of presentation. In Lippitt's terms, the emphases in the draft are on the identification of the concern and the diagnosis of the situation. The action alternatives are formulated but not tested.

A *preliminary statement* is a deliberated draft which includes multiple options for actions. The format is that established in the drafts. It bears the

Table 3
Deliberated Documents: Type and Contents

Types of documents	Contents of documents			
	Analysis		Recommendations	
	Undeliberated	Deliberated	Undeliberated	Deliberated
Background papers	X	—	—	—
Draft	X	—	X	—
Preliminary statement	—	X	X	—
Proposed document	—	X	—	X
Approved document	—	X	—	X

deliberators' names and thus represents their ideas rather than those of a staff person; however, it has probably been written by a staff person and is generally distributed more widely for comments. The narrative portions are in virtually final form; comments about the several options will be the major subject of deliberation. These deliberations which hone and weigh the options are a preliminary form of feasibility testing.

The *proposed document* is the same as the preliminary statement except that favored options have been designated. It is acceptable to deliberators as it stands. Public comment will be the only reason to change either the analyses or recommended actions. This public comment is an advanced form of feasibility testing.

The *approved document* is the final version, approved by the deliberators, and ready to be forwarded to the agency official(s) in charge of the relevant activity.

Once the background papers have been developed and incorporated into the first draft, the evolving documents used in the deliberative process will have two major parts: (*a*) the analysis, which establishes and explores various dimensions of the problem; and (*b*) the recommendations, which propose, then explore, several solutions. Typically one, but sometimes both of the parts will be the major subject of the deliberation. The analysis is usually deliberated and approved before the recommendations are considered by the group. Table 3 summarizes these points.

B. Bibliographic Chain of Documents

The concept of a chain of linked documents representing a process during which an idea is modified is certainly not a new one. Scientific information has long been viewed in this way, and research to document the validity of the view has been going on for at least the last 20 years (Garvey and Griffith, 1979; De Solla Price, 1965). In fact, a "community" or "network" of scientists or an "invisible college" is defined in part by the activities of its members related to their production of documents. After a closer look at the scientific bibliographic chain, a governmental bibliographic chain will be proposed.

1. SCIENTIFIC INFORMATION

Scientific information becomes public knowledge, argues Ziman (1968), when it has been evaluated sufficiently by those able to judge it. This "evaluation" is more frequently called "peer review," and it occurs several different times as an idea is explored, then explained in different parts of the scientific literature. Journal articles and, later, books are the two major publishing forms used by scientists, but proposals (for funding) and preprints (of conference papers) are two other forms which are reviewed before they are accepted either for funding or for delivery at a conference. The journal article may be "reevaluated" and included in its entirety in a collection of readings or in the form of a reference in an annual review or a state-of-the-art essay. The expanded presentation characteristic of a book may become part of the "body of knowledge" included in an encyclopedia or other general reference work.

Doyle and Grimes (1972) present a hypothetical model of this evolutionary process by which ideas are developed, recorded, sorted, and sometimes admitted into a collective "Body of Knowledge" (see Fig. 3). Each step of the process is distinguished by production of a document or "package," in other words, a "link" in the bibliographic chain. The initial idea is developed into human resources and institutional resources in Phase I, into work-in-progress, unpublished studies, periodicals, reports and monographs, annual reviews and state-of-the-art reports, and books and encyclopedic summaries in Phase II, and into indexing and abstracting services, annual reviews and state-of-the-art reports and bibliographic reviews in Phase III, before being admitted into the "body of knowledge". The process includes the development of (*a*) primary documents in which the original author refines or expands the original idea; (*b*) secondary documents which list, index, abstract, or otherwise describe but do not evaluate the original idea; and (*c*) tertiary documents which evaluate and sometimes include part or all of the original idea.

Garvey and Griffith (1979) present an empirically developed model of the dissemination process from the time of initiation of work to integration

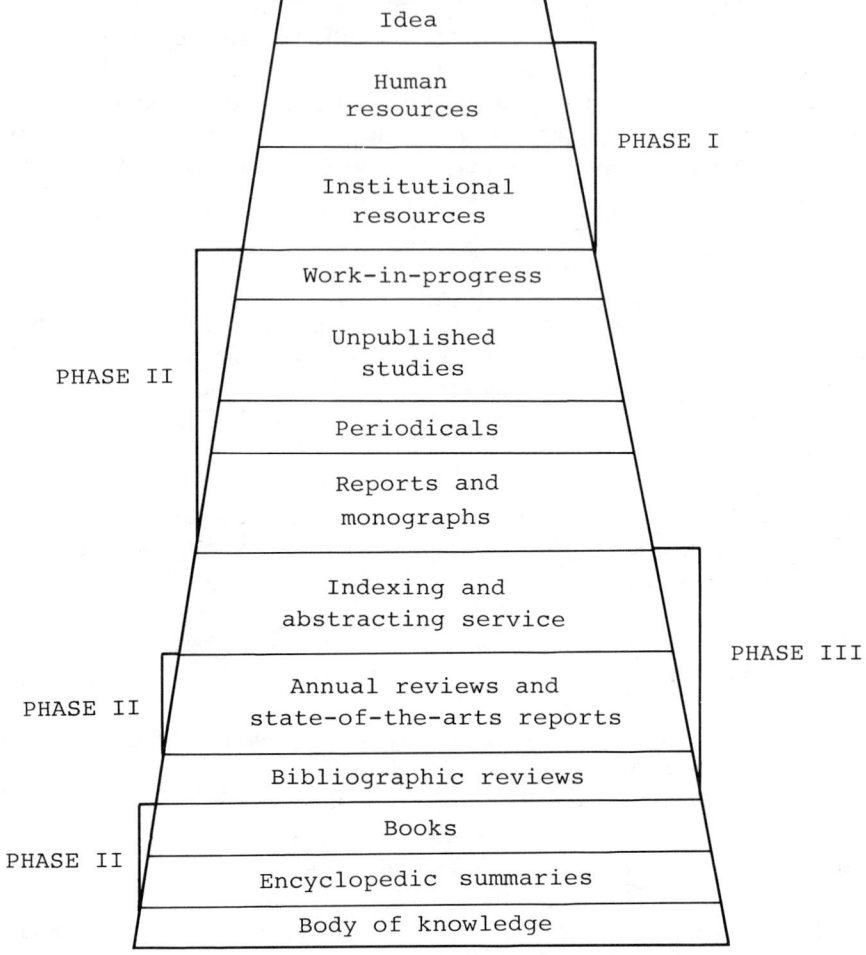

Fig. 3. A bibliographic chain. Reprinted by permission of the American Library Association from The progression of educational information, by James Doyle and George H. Grimes, *in* "Bibliographic Control of Nonprint Media," ed. by Pearce S. Grove and Evelyn G. Clement, p. 44. Copyright © 1972 by the American Library Association.

into the fund of scientific knowledge (Figure 4). The model, based on the process in psychology, posits the following stages:

1. The initiation of work, resulting in reports of preliminary findings
2. The completion of work, resulting in reports to a variety of audiences, including local societies and national conventions, with publication in conference proceedings and, later, an abstract journal

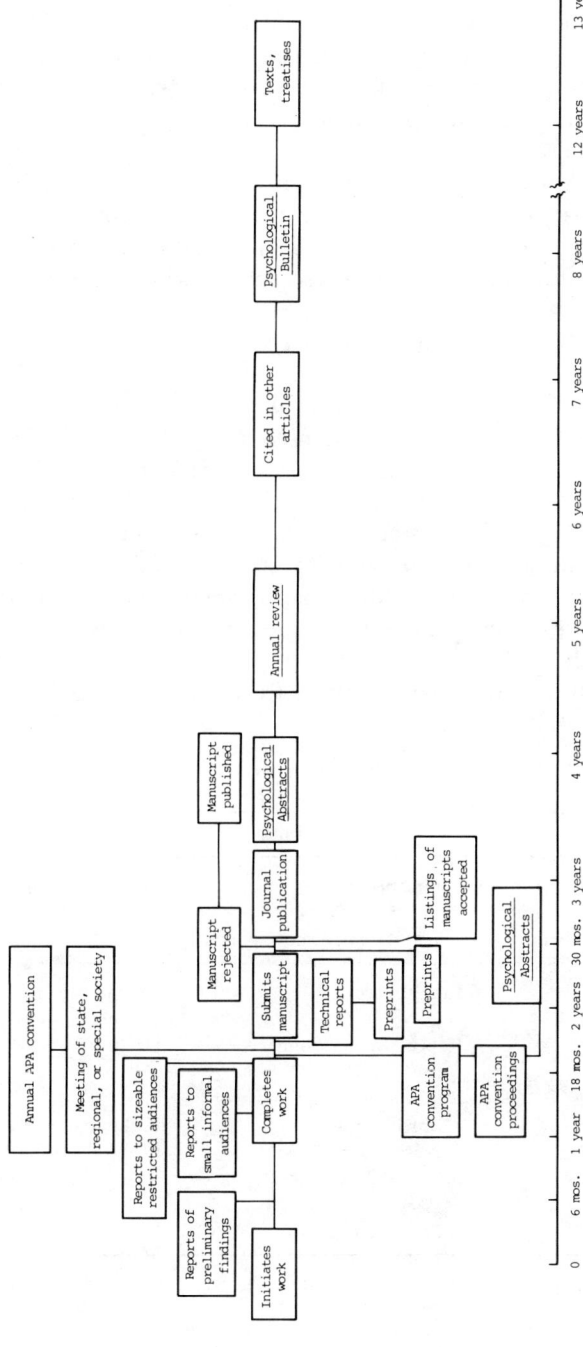

Fig. 4. The dissemination process in psychology. Source: Garvey, W. D. and Griffith, B. C. (1979). Communication and Information Processing within Scientific Disciplines. *In* "Communication: The Essence of Science" (W. D. Garvey). Pergamon Press, Elmsford, New York.

3. Dissemination of findings as a technical report
4. Submission of manuscript for journal publication, with subsequent notice in an abstract journal, an annual review, citation in other articles, and eventual incorporation in texts and treatises. Both models assume several reviews of the documents. Both models assume that within the reviewed statements is an evolving idea. Both models assume a broader audience with each reviewed document. Both models assign particular significance to the journal article as the transition from the informal to the formal communication process.

2. GOVERNMENT INFORMATION

Government information becomes public policy after a charge has been deliberated sufficiently by those appointed and those concerned. Like the models of the scientific communication structure just noted, the sequence of documents produced from these governmental deliberations assumes several reviews, an evolving statement of analysis and recommendations, and a broader audience with each review. Like the published journal article, the plan finally approved by the higher authority has more credibility in the larger communities of government and specialized publics. Based on these similarities, Table 4 lists the products in the bibliographic chain of governmental deliberations which parallel those from the two models of the scien-

TABLE 4
Comparison of Documents Produced in Scientific Communication and in Governmental Deliberations

Scientific communication		Governmental Deliberations
From Doyle and Grimes	From Garvey and Griffith	
Idea*	Initiates work*	Charge plus background papers
Work in progress	Reports of preliminary findings	Draft
Unpublished studies	Reports of completed work:	
	Small group	Preliminary statement
	National meeting	Proposed document
	Submitted manuscript	Approved document (forwarded to authority)
Journal article	Journal article	Policy–plan

*If formal proposal exists, it may be considered the first document in the scientific communication chain.

tific information chain. Although a finally approved plan may be comparable to a journal article in terms of prior review, it is not at all comparable to the continuing evolution and review which both models of scientific communication illustrate. There is simply no device to secure a continuing review and broadening audience for the plan.

V. CONCLUSION

This article has attempted to rationalize and thus make predictable the process(es) by which executive agency deliberations occur. A problem-solving model (Jung and Lippitt, 1966; Havelock, 1971) of knowledge transfer has been used to analyze the deliberative process established in the National Health Planning and Resources Development Act and Amendments (Public Law 96–79) and to identify a sequence of documents. These documents have been described in terms of their information requirements, the persons who are concerned with them, and their evolving content. Finally, they have been compared to the products or documents described in two models of the scientific communication process (Garvey and Griffith, 1979; Doyle and Grimes, 1972). The deliberative documents share with the products of the scientific communication process the requirement of multiple review and the possibility of a variety of product forms, but there are profound differences between them in post-approval–post-publication evaluation and accessibility. There is no single system for bibliographic control of the deliberative documents, resulting in a variety of degrees of control based on varying mandates in a variety of laws, a subject which it has not been possible to consider here.

REFERENCES

De Solla Price, D. J. (1965). Networks of scientific papers. *Science* 149, 510–515.
Doyle, J., and Grimes, G. H. (1972). The progression of educational information. *In* Bibliographic Control of Nonprint Media" (P. S. Grove and E. G. Clement, eds.), pp. 44–47. American Library Association, Chicago.
Garvey, W. D., and Griffith, B. C. (1979). Communication and information processing within scientific disciplines: Empirical findings for psychology. *In* "Communication: The Essence of Science" (W. D. Garvey, ed.), pp. 127–147. Pergamon Press, New York.
Havelock, R. G. (1971). "Planning for Innovation." Center for Research on Utilization of Scientific Knowledge, University of Michigan, Ann Arbor, Michigan.

Ikem, J. E. (1981). Documentation of UN and OAU. *International Library Review* 13, 287–300.
Jung, C., and Lippitt, R. (1966). The study of change as a concept—in research utilization. *Theory into Practice* 5, 25–29.
Levy, E. (1979). Documentation of subsidiary bodies of the economic and social council. *Government Publications Review* 6, 135–137.
Lippitt, R. (1971). Research Utilization Problem-Solving Model. In *Planning for Innovation* (R. G. Havelock), pp. 10–63. Center for Research on Utilization of Scientific Knowledge, University of Michigan, Ann Arbor, Michigan.
Ziman, J. (1968). "Public Knowledge." Cambridge University Press, New York.
Zwirn, J. (1980a). Congressional bills. *Government Publications Review* 7A, 17–25.
Zwirn, J. (1980b). Congressional committee reports. *Government Publications Review* 7A, 319–327.

The Journal Literature of Librarianship

RICHARD D. JOHNSON

*State University of New York
College at Oneonta*

I.	Introduction	127
II.	The Journals	128
	A. The Number of Journals	128
	B. Guides to the Journals	129
	C. Varieties of Journals	130
	D. Summary	131
III.	Subjects and Methodologies	132
IV.	Authorship	134
V.	Critical Reception of the Literature	138
VI.	Editor and Author	140
	A. Review of Manuscripts	141
	B. Time Lags in Publishing	142
	C. Copyright	143
VII.	Interest of the Profession in Writing	143
VIII.	Book Reviewing	145
IX.	Indexing and Abstracting Services	146
X.	Conclusion	147
	References	148

I. INTRODUCTION

The journals of librarianship are the principal means for prompt communication of professional information. Librarians use a variety of informal channels as well, such as meetings and personal communications, and these methods can be more current and meaningful because of the personal relationships involved. Still, the journal remains one medium available to all members of the profession. Except for the cost of subscription, which remains the principal barrier to the full sharing of such literature, journals play a major role in the improvement of libraries and in the professional development of librarians.

The purpose of this review is to examine the journal literature of the profession. Emphasis will be placed on journals serving librarians although there will be some necessary discussion of related journals in information science. Emphasis will be placed on experiences in the United States during the post-World-War-II years. Comments offered on the journal literature often are applied to monograph literature as well. Thus, any discussion of journals in librarianship will have some application to other forms of publication in the profession.

II. THE JOURNALS

A. The Number of Journals

Although the literature of librarianship, both books and journals, may seem quite small when compared to the range and number of publications developed for other professions and disciplines, there has been a steady increase in the number of journals, newsletters, and other serial publications available to librarians. This very growth has proved a continuing concern to critics of the literature.

In his paper for a conference on the bibliographic control of library literature, Little (1968, pp. 3–6) demonstrates the dramatic growth in the number of library periodicals. Working solely with extant publications, he identifies 17 journals at the turn of the century. Of these, seven were published in the United States and four in Great Britain. By 1946, this total had grown to 169 titles, 115 in English and 54 in foreign languages. During the post-World-War-II years, 306 titles were added between 1947 and 1966. Little, in 1968, was able to point out that 63.75% of all journals in existence then began publication since World War II.

As a response to this tremendous growth, Little notes that 14 of the 18 indexing and abstracting services covering this field have been established since 1950. Little confines himself to library periodicals of substance, omitting various newsletters or publications of library staff associations, and his final total for relevant periodicals totals 480, 266 in English and 214 in foreign languages.

The twentieth edition of *Ulrich's International Periodicals Directory* (1981) employs a broader definition in its listing of periodicals under the heading, "Library and Information Services." This section lists a total of approximately 950 titles, including a variety of newsletters in addition to journals of substance.

Tegler (1979, p. 16) reports differing estimates on the number of journals in the field, with counts ranging from 520 to 1000.

B. Guides to the Journals

Other guides to the journal literature of librarianship have proved more selective. Katz and Richards in the third edition of their *Magazines for Libraries* (1978) provide a section listing 126 titles of journals in librarianship, with brief evaluative annotations for each. (A separate section gives a listing of library newsletters and bulletins.)

Even more selective is Lee's "Library Periodicals in Review" (1979), a section in one issue of *Serials Review,* which provides brief reviews (by individual reviewers) for 30 principal journals.

Hernon *et al., Library and Library-Related Publications: A Directory of Publishing Opportunities in Journals, Serials, and Annuals* (1973) presents a comprehensive, detailed listing of 160 library and library-related journals. As the title indicates, this guide is meant to serve potential authors.

A similar function is filled by the new publication by Stevens and Stevens, *Author's Guide to Journals in Library and Information Science* (1982). This volume gives information on the publication policies and procedures followed by each of the journals included and, accordingly, now substantially replaces the earler publication by Hernon *et al.*

Taylor (1978) in his listing of subjects of interest to library periodicals also provides data on 102 journals, including general information on manuscript submission.

Besides the descriptive and directory information available through these various guides, several recent historical accounts have related journals to the larger subject of library literature. The centennial of the American Library Association in 1976 provided the occasion for three accounts: Danton (1976) gives an historical account of the library press, including both monographs and journals; Kaser (1976) presents an overview of publications related to academic librarianship, including its journals; and Edgar (1978) assesses library periodicals over the century.

More recently, Bobinski (1979) served as the editor for two issues of *Drexel Library Quarterly,* devoted to "The Literature of Librarianship and Information Science." In these issues, Shields (1979) surveys national and state periodicals, calling upon his own experiences as a former editor of *American Libraries* and of the *Ohio Library Association Bulletin.* Melin (1979), herself an editor of two journals, reviews the more specialized journals by type of library, type of activity, special interest, and research. Tegler (1979) reviews the indexing and abstracting services for the field.

C. Varieties of Journals

An examination of such guides, bibliographies, and historical and descriptive accounts reveals the great variety of journals serving librarianship. Not only do the periodicals give a general coverage for all kinds of libraries, as in *Library Journal,* but they can focus on one kind of library, such as in *College & Research Libraries* or in *Public Libraries*. They can cover specialties within the profession, as in *The Serials Librarian* or *Library Resources & Technical Services,* or serve the reference librarian, as with *RQ.* Some journals, like *Library Trends* and *Drexel Library Quarterly,* devote each issue to articles related to a single topic. Two journals, *Library Quarterly* and *Library Research,* openly profess a dedication to serious controlled inquiry, while other periodicals, such as *Wilson Library Bulletin,* may report on news of the profession. Others, for example, *American Libraries,* also report news of the professional association for which they serve as an official organ. Many journals also serve an alerting function to the literature of the profession by including book reviews or listings of new publications.

Publishers for these journals also show variety. Commercial publishers, such as the R. R. Bowker Company, H. W. Wilson Company, Pergamon Press, Haworth Press, John Wiley, Ablex, and Pierian Press publish journals for the field.

Library schools and their parent universities, such as the University of Chicago, University of Illinois, and Drexel University, also issue journals. A trade association, the Library Binding Institute, publishes a general journal, *Library Scene,* which also features items of interest to its membership.

Government agencies as well as individual libraries publish an assortment of newsletters and journals reporting on their activities and their resources.

Professional associations have made a major contribution by their publishing activities with a variety of newsletters and periodicals. A perquisite of membership, the association publication, be it newsletter or journal, sometimes is the individual's principal link to the organization—and often serves as the motive for the person's continuing membership. The American Library Association has developed a major group of newsletters and journals for most of its divisions. These periodicals have been one force in giving a separate identity to the individual units.

D. Summary

Viewing the journals of librarianship as a group, one can venture numerous generalizations about them. Compared to many other fields, these journals have a very limited circulation. Only two, *Library Journal* and *American Libraries,* have a circulation in excess of 30,000, and there are few periodicals with a circulation higher than 10,000.

Many journals receive some form of subsidy to support their publication. Those serving as an organ for an association may receive a subvention from the association; often, the association will set aside a portion of a member's dues for the journal or newsletter. A publication issued from a college or university may receive support in terms of office space, clerical staff, and released time for a faculty member to serve as editor. Except for a few journals, there is no full-time paid editorial staff, and any honorarium received by the editor or authors does not compensate for the amount of time and effort given to the publication. Thus, the journals rest on the unpaid contributions from a number of members of the profession. Rewards received are primarily non-monetary—a sense of personal accomplishment, heightened respect from one's peers, evidence of achievement to assist in one's personal advancement.

Except for several newsletters and some of the more popular journals and association organs, the periodicals are generally issued on a quarterly basis. But even with that infrequency of issue, publication schedules are sometimes ignored. For a number of journals, the date on the issue cover bears little relationship to the actual date of publication. When one studies time lags in the role of a journal in reviewing books or the time lag for an indexing or abstracting service to list the journal's contents, one must take into account, not the date on the issue, but the date the publisher mails the journal or when the subscriber receives it.

Because of the great importance of volunteer contributions in library publications, there is considerable turnover among editorial staffs. Some associations place a limit on the length of term for their unpaid journal editors. In this way more members can have opportunities to participate in professional activities, but such limitations may have adverse effects in terms of irregular and interrupted publication patterns and in uneven quality in the journal.

There is no control of the publication of new journals in librarianship.

The law of the marketplace holds, and new journals appear with no coordination or relationship to existing journals. Witness the 15 journals in librarianship recently published or announced by Haworth Press. As shown in this article, critics of the journals have noted this proliferation as one major concern.

III. SUBJECTS AND METHODOLOGIES

Some periodicals in librarianship inform readers of the "tools of the trade." Such reviewing media include *Booklist* and *Choice*, the sections with reviews in *Library Journal* or the reviews of reference works in *RQ, Wilson Library Bulletin*, or semiannually in *College & Research Libraries*.

Other periodicals are primarily newsletters that alert readers to developments in a given field. For example, *Advanced Technology Libraries*, published by Knowledge Industry Publications, reports on computer applications in libraries; the *Washington Newsletter*, issued by the Washington Office of the American Library Association, informs readers of proposed legislation or federal regulations affecting libraries. Other journals may emphasize articles, generally prepared by outside contributors, with information of some professional interest to other librarians. Some periodicals include an assortment of pieces—articles, news items, and reviews.

Principal interest has focused on the journal articles themselves—their quality, patterns of authorship, and editorial review procedures. However, there has been little controlled investigation to date on the subjects covered in journal articles or the methodologies employed.

Beals (1942) prepared the classic statement for librarianship on the kinds of literature published. Presenting a paper on the "Implications of Communications Research for the Public Library" at the 1941 Institute of the University of Chicago's Graduate Library School, he described the three principal types of library publications concerning the social value of public libraries. These types are relevant as well to other fields of librarianship. In Beals' words, "they are glad tidings, testimony, and research."

"Glad tidings" are of two kinds: the first, "speculative essays of what might, could, would, or should be true" of librarianship, and the second, announcements of something "about to be done or very recently undertaken" (p. 165). Beals comments that a large proportion of library literature consists of glad tidings. Although he admits that such writings may "usefully extend the librarian's powers of imagination and invention in the search for perfection in an imperfect world" (p. 165), still, in his view, they present no valid evidence.

"Testimony" includes "retrospective accounts of something done, or benefits conferred" (p. 166). Beals notes that, when written, such testimony is often phrased in the first person plural, as a writer describes what a group has done. The proof offered for testimony is experience, which Beals cautions can serve as "the sole source of error as well as of truth." Thus, he warns that "all testimony based on undifferentiated experience needs careful scrutiny" (p. 166).

"Research" represents Beals' third classification. He warns that research is not restricted to statistical studies but includes "any study in which a problem is defined and analyzed into its constituent parts, in which valid data are collected and related to relevant factors, in which hypotheses are formed and, through testing, rejected, amended, or proved" (p. 167).

Although Beals limited his glad tidings classification to those writings that are "anticipatory and optimistic," a related classification not noted by Beals may be described as "bad tidings" or warnings of unwished-for happenings if a prescribed course is not followed.

Writing for another profession, Stamatakos (1979) supplies a classification for published literature similar to Beals. Again there are three groupings—expository, descriptive, and empirical. In the expository paper, the writer takes a position on a subject, presenting tidings, whether good or bad, based on research and review. The descriptive paper is akin to Beals' "testimony," and the empirical paper is based on formal research, "abstracted dissertations and other kinds of data-based papers" (p. 7).

In his historical review of the literature of academic librarianship, Kaser (1976 p. 125) presents still another classification—one linked to changes over time as a profession grows and develops. He identifies five stages: first, simple descriptions of conditions or operations in a single institution; second, trial generalizations based on experiences in several institutions; third, testing these trial generalizations through a survey of other libraries. All these steps have so far been descriptive in character. But, in a fourth stage, "prescriptive statements can for the first time with some authority be made." Finally, through later writings, the prescriptions are refined, consensus secured, and standards for the profession achieved.

Although he does not list formally the individual subjects covered in the literature, Kaser (1976) acknowledges that his major impression is "that there is little that is ever truly new in the field." Such subjects as "cooperation, status, evaluation, concern for service, and virtually all other motivating issues have been around for a long time" (p. 125).

In an attempt to discover changes in library research methodologies over time, Kim and Kim (1979) compare 432 articles published in *College & Research Libraries* from 1957 to 1966 with 402 articles published in the decade 1967–1976. They demonstrate a major increase in studies employing quantitative methods such as counting, numerical, or other statistical procedures, with descriptive research—notably survey research—being the most heavily used. Frequency distributions and percentages are the basic methods employed, with only a few articles using more sophisticated forms of analysis.

A novel approach to determining the subject coverage of library journals may be seen in the work of Taylor (1978). Editors of 102 journals were given a checklist of 143 subjects and asked to indicate those on which they would welcome articles. The nine most popular subjects—checked by more than 41 editors—included automation of library processes, censorship, education for librarianship, audio-visual materials and services, computers and computer applications, copyright and authorship, continuing education, networks of libraries, and acquisitions. The resulting document provides a shopping list for a prospective author. In addition to the listing of subjects by "popularity," there is a list showing which journals are interested in each. A separate list by journal titles indicates the subjects each desires as well as additional data about that periodical's requirements for manuscript submission.

Even with such beginnings as given in these accounts, major work remains to be undertaken in librarianship on the subjects selected for treatment in the professional literature as well as the methodologies employed.

IV. AUTHORSHIP

Although we have as yet no detailed studies on the subjects included in the literature, several scholars have studied patterns of authorship in the profession. The studies generally do not distinguish between book and journal article authorship; hence, one must assume the results presented from such inquiries can be generalized for all kinds of publications.

In his two studies, Bloomfield (1966, 1979) identifies a positive relationship between advanced academic degrees and amount of publishing. Selecting various groups of librarians—those with a doctorate in librarianship, those with a doctorate in another subject, those who had written a master's thesis in librarianship, library school faculty, authors in librarianship selected at random, and librarians selected at random from the *American Library Directory*—he demonstrates that those librarians with doctorates, whether in librarianship or in another subject, are the most prolific authors as represented by citations in *Library Literature*. In his second study (1979), he indicates that, from a random sample of librarians chosen from the

American Library Directory, 38% had written at least one piece subsequently indexed in *Library Literature.*

Bloomfield was pleased with this last finding because it indicates to him that more librarians write for publication than had previously been thought. The *American Library Directory,* however, is a directory of libraries, not of librarians, and the librarians listed in it generally hold a major role in the administrative hierarchy of a given library. Thus, any sample of librarians selected from it will be prejudiced in favor of the principal staff in a library.

One novel feature in Bloomfield's research (1979) is his willingness to name names. The result is two lists showing the 10 most prolific authors holding library science doctorates and the eight most prolific authors with nonlibrary science doctoral degrees. Comparing his second study to his first (1966), he notes the appearance of the same names on each list and concludes that "it might be said that those with talent for writing continue their writing at a more or less uniform rate" (1979, p. 28). Concluding his own historical review of the literature, Kaser (1976) felt obliged to comment "that a very small segment of the profession at any given moment is the fountainhead of a very large share of the writing in the field" (p. 125).

Concentration of authorship among a small group of writers has been demonstrated also in other fields. Statistical formulations to describe this concentration are based on the 1926 paper of Alfred J. Lotka on authorship in chemistry and physics and have been subsequently named Lotka's law. Lotka proposed an inverse-square law, which may be summarized in that "for every 100 authors contributing, one article each, there would be 25 others contributing two articles each ($100/2^2 = 25$), about 11 contributing 3 articles each ($100/3^2 = 11.1$), about six contributing 4 articles each ($100/4^2 = 6.25$), and so on" (Subramanyam, 1981, p. 168).

Potter (1981) provides a summary and critique of other demonstrations attempting to apply Lotka's law to different disciplines. He notes several studies conducted in librarianship and information science: Voos (1974) on information science, Schorr (1974) on library science, and Schorr (1975) on map librarianship. Subramanyam (1981), undertaking another study on concentration of authorship in librarianship and the application of Lotka's law, attempts to correct some of the errors ascribed to Schorr (1974). Schorr has based his study on authorship in two journals only (*Library Quarterly* and *College & Research Libraries*) and proposed an inverse-quadruple power law. Subramanyam, using the index, *Library Literature,* as his source for authorship, came up with an inverse-cube law. Comparing his findings with those of Lotka, he notes "that the proportion of authors contributing only one paper is about 81 percent of the total number of authors. This figure was about 60 percent in Lotka's study of the literature of chemistry and physics" (p. 170).

Watson (1977) employs a different approach to her study of publication activity. Limiting herself to librarians in 10 large United States university libraries, she secured publication lists for each library and biographical data on the librarians. Like Bloomfield, she identifies a positive relationship between advanced degrees and publishing. She has also found that library administrators, branch and department heads, and subject and technical specialists in these libraries (the positions most likely to be listed in the *American Library Directory*) produce the majority of contributions—out of proportion to their numbers. Whereas this group in Watson's sample represents only about 50% of the library population, they are responsible for approximately 85% of the publications. The other 50%, the group Watson identifies as "supervised librarians with no subject specialty," is responsible for the remaining 15%.

Watson questions the administrators' greater productivity and suggests two alternative answers: First, it is possible that these more productive administrators "have gained their positions of responsibility because they are more competent and more motivated than other professionals." Or, second, their high productivity may be "due, in part, to the autonomy such librarians have traditionally enjoyed in university libraries. Since they can control their work schedules, they can allot time to research that librarians in large departments and under direct supervision cannot" (p. 383).

Bloomfield (1979) restricts his inquiry into publishing activity to items listed in *Library Literature* (basically professional literature). Watson (1977), looking at all publishing activity, found 69% of publishing in periodicals—with 39% in library periodicals and 30% in subject journals. If Bloomfield had looked at nonlibrary publishing activity as well, his findings on librarian productivity certainly would have been higher.

In their consideration of academic library research as reported in articles in *College & Research Libraries* from 1957 to 1976, Kim and Kim (1979) also consider authorship. Comparing authors of articles in the first decade, 1957–1966, with those in the second decade, 1967–1976, they report that in the former, library administrators—directors, assistant directors, and supervisors of major library services—dominate the issues, having written 65.7% of the articles. In the latter, they note increasing numbers of contributions from "rank and file librarians—defined as librarians, bibliographers, supervisors of reference, cataloging, and acquisition divisions" (p. 380). This group prepared 46.6% of the articles as compared with 47.2% by the administrators.

One cannot directly compare these findings to those of Watson because of the differing methodology and definitions. Because of their smaller number, administrators continue as the more productive authors.

Olsgaard and Olsgaard (1980) use still another approach in their investigation of authorship. In their study of the characteristics of authors represented over a 10-year period in five major journals (*College & Research Libraries, Library Journal, Library Quarterly, Library Trends,* and *RQ*), they determined that men are represented as authors out of proportion to their number in the population of librarians in the United States. Although men constitute 16% of the librarian work force, they represent 69.5% of the authors in *College & Research Libraries,* 62.5% for *Library Journal,* 78.8% for *Library Quarterly,* 67.3% for *Library Trends,* and 58.7% for *RQ*.

As to occupations represented, library school faculty members publish more in these journals than their size in the population would suggest, and nonlibrarians publishing in these journals range from 16.6% in *College & Research Libraries* to 28.9% in *Library Journal.* Among practicing librarians, academic librarians are represented more times in the five journals than either public or other librarians.

Olsgaard and Olsgaard (1980) introduce one element not present in other studies of authorship: geographic distribution. From their study, they show that the Northeast and Midwest regions are represented "with a positive ratio of contributors in relation to their national norm" (p. 52). The West matches the national norm, and the Southeast and Southwest show a negative ratio.

Like Watson, Burlingame and Repp (1981) consider solely academic librarians in their study of publishing. Based on a mail survey of two groups of academic librarians—the first an "author group" (those who had published at least one article in a recognized professional journal during the 1970s) and the second a "nonauthor group" (selected from the 1979 *ALA Membership Directory*), their findings confirm several conclusions from the earlier studies. Those individuals with doctorates publish more than those without, and men publish more than women. Authors are more likely than nonauthors to be actively involved in professional activities such as attendance at national meetings and holding office in national associations. They do not, however, address the relationship of authorship to administrative position in a library.

These several studies of authorship, despite their differing methodologies, suggest some of the characteristics of librarians as writers. One may apply these characteristics to the journal literature of the field: librarians with a doctorate are more likely to be published; men are more represented than women as authors; academic librarians tend to publish more than other librarians; library school faculty are more heavily represented as authors than their numbers in the work force would indicate; and library administrators are more likely to publish than nonadministrators.

V. CRITICAL RECEPTION OF THE LITERATURE

Wilson (1953) reviewed library literature in an overall sense for the 30-year period, 1923–1953, with particular reference to education for librarianship. He concludes that the professional literature of 1953 has been "lengthened and enriched to a degree undreamed of" three decades earlier (p. 140). He notes particularly the impact on the literature of librarianship of publications in other fields, principally education and the social sciences. With such influences, research articles appearing in professional journals have had a healthful influence on librarianship—familiarizing librarians with research methods, stimulating investigation by other librarians, convincing scholars in other fields of the importance of graduate study in librarianship, and filling the profession's need to reshape and revitalize its theories and practices. Similarly, he notes the healthful influence of long critical essays and carefully considered book reviews on the literature of librarianship.

In the following decade, Bundy (1961) surveyed a sample of public library administrators on their views and use of the professional periodicals. She concludes that the journals are an important source of information guiding administrators in day-to-day library operations and can serve as a catalyst to bring about change. She cautions, however, that the journals seem to make a lesser contribution in goal setting and major policymaking.

Such favorable comments on the improvements in, and usefulness of, library literature represent a minority opinion when one samples other considerations of the literature.

Thompson (1961) entitles his remarks "The Sad State of Library Literature" and offers as his principal recommendation the elimination or combination of existing journals. Blake (1961) uses these words and phrases to describe library literature: "as arid as it is voluminous"; "pompous utterances, petty subject matter, the incomprehensible style"; "prissiness"; "timidity"; and "atrocious style." Becker (1957) employs satire as he offers advice on "How to Write Effectively for a Library Periodical."

Katz's report (1967) on a survey of a group of library school faculty, librarians, and library school students begins with this capsule criticism: "Library literature is timid, rotten, unimaginative, vague, repulsive and debased" (p. 176). He employs this survey as a basis to warn library schools not to begin any publishing program.

In the following year, Little (1968) summarized criticism of library literature up to that date under six major points: poor literary style and execution, superfluity and repetition, belaboring of the obvious, paucity of significantly new ideas, absence of a scholarly approach, and lack of evidence of research.

Although Moon (1969) would have agreed with each of these criticisms, he points out that "the deadliest disease afflicting the library press is proliferation" (p. 4104). He recommends that at least one in three periodicals cease publication. He points out these evils associated with the overabundance of journals: spreading too thin the limited amount of good materials, spreading too thin the advertising support, diverting into an obscure publication an article that merits a larger audience, and making it possible for almost any piece of writing, no matter how bad, to be published.

Realizing that his recommendations to reduce the number of journals would not be accepted, Moon next advises journals not to be afraid to publish thinner issues and to be tougher in acceptance decisions. He also counsels journals to emphasize "useful hard news and current information" (p. 4106). With his experience still fresh from his own recent editorship of *Library Journal,* Moon describes his successes with that journal, principally related to a lively, individual, opinionated, passionate treatment of the current issues in the profession.

Moon describes the array of manuscripts submitted to a library periodical editor as "this incredible stream of garbage," and Jones (1976) used that image as the title for his own critique of British library journals.

Although Shores does not specifically cite Moon's recommendation to cut the number of library periodicals, he argues (1972) in favor of the proliferation of library periodicals. He justifies them as "insurance for intellectual freedom." He holds that a new and subtler form of censorship threatens the periodicals, because of the development of two establishments—one for the *status quo,* one for activist protest—and asserts that outlets for other viewpoints are on the decline.

McGrath (1972) employs another means that might be called upon to justify more journals. After checking three sources of unpublished research materials, he offers the cautious conclusion "that there is enough material in the American library research environment to fill another journal—perhaps a quarterly—or to fill an equivalent number of pages in an existing journal" (p. 25).

In her description of library periodicals, Collier (1974a) emphasizes the practical and functional nature of the literature. Thus in looking at academic librarians' quest for parity with formal teaching faculty, she concludes that the professional literature indicates that the concerns of the librarian do not correspond to those of the teacher. Her article has occasioned letters by Eshelman and Hamlin (1974), plus a reply by Collier (1974b).

The late Leon Carnovsky, for many years editor of *Library Quarterly,* presented in several articles a more balanced view on the quality of library periodicals (1955, 1956, 1964). Writing more than a decade before Moon, he notes the growth in the number of professional periodicals. But he does not see this increase as necessarily an evil. The new journals will "stimulate more writing, and much of it is good" (1955, p. 265). He admits that no library periodical is all good or all bad and believes that "our exasperation with the dull and unreadable articles makes a deeper impress than does our satisfaction with the good one" (1956, p. 69).

Danton (1976) also discusses journal quality and proliferation in his historical review. By and large, he agrees, the negative comments exceed the positive. But he concludes that "the accusations of dullness and unoriginality no longer quite hold water." He cites as examples of excellence *American Libraries, Library Journal,* and *Wilson Library Bulletin* and notes that "much of the material in *College & Research Libraries* (CRL) and LQ [*Library Quarterly*] is not dull except to those to whom all scholarship is dull" (p. 157).

Although Richardson (1977) does not address quality specifically, he considers the readability of library periodicals by appling the test for readability of Flesch to 15 journals, using samples of articles from an issue of each periodical for 1974. His findings indicate that *School Library Journal* is the easiest to read, followed by *American Libraries.* At the other end of the scale, *Library Trends* proves the most difficult to read, with *School Media Quarterly, Journal of the American Society for Information Science, Journal of Education for Librarianship,* and *College & Research Libraries* grouped with the more difficult journals. It is also shown that *Library Quarterly* is only slightly more difficult to read than *Library Journal.* It must be remembered that these findings are based on a single sample.

VI. EDITOR AND AUTHOR

Carnovsky (1956) commented on the important role of editors of library periodicals. "They can do much to encourage and stimulate the creation of significant and informative writing" (p. 72).

Except for Moon's broad overview of what he accomplished at *Library Journal* (1969), detailed published accounts on editorial procedures at the various library periodicals are lacking. Rayward (1980), for one, however, provides a valuable summary of the editing and publishing of *Library Quarterly.* Otherwise, the basic information on editorial procedures is included in the journal's instructions to prospective authors or summarized in such guides as Hernon, *et al.* (1973) or in Stevens and Stevens (1982).

A. Review of Manuscripts

Concerned about the quality of library literature, O'Connor and Van Orden (1978) have undertaken their own survey of publishing to determine what chance an author has to publish an unsolicited manuscript in one of the nation's principal library periodicals. They limit their sample to 33 English language journals published in the United States and Canada that accept unsolicited contributions. Several major journals, such as *Library Trends* and *Drexel Library Quarterly,* which include commissioned articles only, are thus eliminated. The researchers then (in the fall of 1976) sent questionnaires to the journals, requesting information on the number of unsolicited manuscripts received each year, the number accepted, and the procedures followed in reviewing a manuscript for possible publication.

Editors reported a broad range of unsolicited manuscripts received annually, ranging from 650 for *Library Journal,* 300 for *School Library Journal,* and 250 for *Audiovisual Instruction,* down to 10 each received by the *Bulletin of the American Society for Information Science, Information Reports/Bibliography,* and *Microform Review.* (One journal, *Argus,* reports receiving three unsolicited manuscripts and accepted all for publication.)

Acceptance rates by the journals ranged from 95% at *Journal of Micrographics* (15 manuscripts received), 80% at *Microform Review* (10 manuscripts received), 60% at *Information Processing and Management* (70 manuscripts received), down to 5% at *American Libraries* (200 manuscripts received), 5% at *Wilson Library Bulletin* (250 manuscripts received), and 3% at *School Library Journal* (300 manuscripts received). *Library Journal* reported accepting 10% of the 650 manuscripts submitted. The overall acceptance rate for the 33 journals was 22.7%

O'Connor and Van Orden are concerned that 77.3% of all unsolicited manuscripts are rejected. Citing Meadows (1974, p. 38) they note that in the pure sciences the rejection rate is only 25%, whereas library manuscripts seem more like those in the humanities and arts where rejection rates may exceed 75%.

The basic source for these comparative figures is Zuckerman and Merton (1971). They report in detail on the referee system and the rate of rejection in journal publishing. They present a table showing rejection rates for 16 different disciplines, ranging from a 90% rejection rate in history, 86% in language and literature, 85% in philosophy, 84% in political science, and 78% in sociology to lows of 29% in the biological sciences, 24% in physics, 22% in geology, and 20% in linguistics. Zuckerman and Merton offer this conclusion:

> The pattern of differences between fields and within fields can be described in the same rule of thumb: the more humanistically oriented the journal, the higher the rate of rejecting

manuscripts for publication; the more experimentally and observationally oriented, with an emphasis on rigour of observation and analysis, the lower the rate of rejection (1978, p. 77).

In a second part of their inquiry on library journals, O'Connor and Van Orden queried editors on their reviewing procedures and then grouped the journals in six categories: for 10 journals, the editor solely makes the decision to accept or reject a manuscript; for another 10 journals, the editor makes the decision with the aid of an editorial staff; for five journals, the editor has an advisory staff; for two journals, it is stated that an editorial board makes the decision; the six remaining journals employ a refereeing process: three with referees knowing the author's identity and three with the referees not knowing who the author is—the double-blind refereeing process.

O'Connor and Van Orden (1978) recognize that refereeing offers no immediate panacea for the production of quality articles. A longer time is required for editorial review, and the various referees may use differing standards. In the double-blind process, there is the problem of adequately masking the author's identity, and it has been known, at times, for referees to steal ideas from the papers they judge. Even so, the two researchers believe the advantages are greater because decisons on publication will be more objective.

Still, there are differing standards among referees. Here, O'Connor and Van Orden see a need for each journal to prepare and publish a detailed statement of purpose and criteria used to judge manuscripts. Only in this way will potential authors know what to expect from a given journal, and—as O'Connor and Van Orden believe—the quality of manuscripts submitted will improve.

O'Connor and Van Orden have made a major contribution to librarianship with this initial study on journal review procedures. There is, however, some lack of clarity in their original questionnaire as well as in the answers from some journals. One may question how detailed and accurate are the records which any given journal maintains on manuscript submissions.

Increasingly, as in all human relationships, the relationship of author and editor in library periodicals is becoming more formalized. The various reviewing and refereeing devices the journals now use are bringing objectivity to the relationship. It is incumbent upon the editor to retain a human dimension and warmth in working with authors.

B. Time Lags in Publishing

Once an editor does accept a manuscript, there is a further delay before actual publication, delay that depends on the number of other accepted manuscripts awaiting publication. The journals responding to O'Connor and Van Orden (1978) reported an average length of five months between acceptance and publication. Given the additional time required for the initial review, an average of two months, this can mean that an author beginning the composition of a reasonably short manuscript may not see it published until one year later. This time can be lengthened if the manuscript is rejected by one journal and submitted to another for a second review or if the journal experiences any publication delays.

C. Copyright

Authors of articles in library periodicals receive little if any financial remuneration for their writing. The Copyright Revision Act of 1976 (Title 17 U.S. Code) does, however, make a major change in copyright for journal articles. Section 201(c), "Contributions to Collective Works," vests copyright initially in the author of the article. The journal itself has only the privilege of distributing the article in the journal, "any revision of that collective work, and any later collective work in the same series."

In order that publishers may retain some control over material in their journals, such as the right to microfilm for preservation purposes, many now request that authors assign copyright to the publisher, either on submission of the manuscript or upon acceptance for publication. In return, the publisher agrees to protect the rights and interests of the author.

VII. INTEREST OF THE PROFESSION IN WRITING

Particularly among academic librarians, publication is looked upon as one means to obtain advancement or security of employment. A list of publications can prove a valuable addition to a librarian's resume when seeking a new position. Some librarians have questioned whether the ability to achieve publication has any relevance to job performance. Campbell (1977), for example, reports his rejection by a university library for a position because of the "demand for substantial activity in the areas of research and publication." He held, however, that the position he applied for, as head of an undergraduate library, should require a commitment of service to students and not "doing research and getting it published."

Two recent surveys of academic library practices do not indicate any widespread requirement for writing and publishing. Although Byerly

(1980) points out that half of the Ohio academic library directors responding to him report at least one member on their staffs published in the previous two years, there was no stated requirement in any library for publication. In their survey of 96 university libraries (members of the Association of Research Libraries (ARL)), Rayman and Goudy (1980) report that only 15% of the institutions expected their librarians to publish.

Watson (1977) questions how academic librarians with full work schedules can allocate time for research and writing. She suggests the possibility of naming research as an assigned responsibility for staff members. Such a procedure has been followed in the Ohio State University Libraries with each staff member's job including a regular 20% time allotment for research and professional development (Miller *et al.,* 1976).

Two surveys from the 1960s give some data on encouragement by college and university libraries for writing and publishing. Jesse and Mitchell (1968) found that less than one-half of the university libraries surveyed and only one college library give release time to staff members for independent research projects, with the remaining libraries giving more qualified answers to this question. More than half of the university libraries give help in the form of free photocopying or clerical assistance. Kellam and Barker (1968) report from their survey of ARL and other university libraries overall encouragement for writing. Three-quarters of the libraries permit staff free time to prepare articles, and the most common recognition given is to take publications into account when considering promotions, salary increases, or tenure decisions.

With increasing interest and encouragement and at times a requirement to publish, the profession has responded in several helpful ways. National and regional groups sponsor programs and workshops on writing. For example, the New England Chapter of the Association of College and Research Libraries (ACRL) held a 1975 conference on writing and publishing, featuring editors of several national journals and library school faculty (Harreld, 1975). At this conference Stueart (1976) pointed out that librarian writers are missing some potential markets. They are too inward-looking and write only for each other. Librarians could have a much greater impact with their writing were they to write for nonlibrary periodicals as well.

The Librarians Association of the University of North Carolina at Chapel Hill sponsored a 1979 conference on research, featuring papers on methodology (Magrill, 1980), funding (Gwynn, 1980), and writing (Rayward, 1980). At the 1980 ALA conference, three divisions—the Association for Library Service to Children, Young Adult Services Division, and the Public Library Association—sponsored a preconference on research with papers on methods (Carter, 1981), costing (Lynch, 1981), and reporting results (Rayward, 1981). The subsequent publication of papers from these meetings in professional journals provides a wider dissemination for the guidelines, instructions, and ideas offered.

At its 1981 national conference in Minneapolis, ACRL introduced as part of its continuing education program a one-day workshop on "Writing the Journal Article and Getting It Published."

Stevens has been particularly active in encouraging and assisting librarians to write for publication. Through journal articles (Stevens, 1979) and his guide to journals (Stevens and Stevens, 1982, pp. 11–26), he provides useful aids and hints to potential authors. More important, he led the New England Academic Librarians' Writing Seminar (Stevens, 1980), which provided an opportunity for a group of librarians to meet together over a period of several years to learn from one another and to improve their writing skills.

For other fields, Andrews (1980) gives advice to special librarians on ways in which to get published, and Rayward (1981) focuses his comments primarily to librarians working with children and young adults. In their recent manual on research in librarianship, Busha and Harter (1980, pp. 371–391) provide a useful chapter on how to write and then publish the results of one's research.

A Library Periodicals Round Table was active in the American Library Association during the 1950s and issued a newsletter from 1954 to 1958. The Public Relations Section of the then Library Administration Division subsequently took over the interests of the round table, and attention subsided. In 1980, ALA authorized a temporary Membership Initiative Group on Library and Information Literature (LIL'MIG); this group continues some of the interests of the earlier round table (LIL'MIG, 1981).

VIII. BOOK REVIEWING

Some library periodicals concentrate on general book reviews (*Booklist* and *Choice*); others have major sections devoted to them (*Library Journal*). Periodicals such as these can serve as basic selection tools for a library.

Other journals have sections devoted to reviews, announcements, and listings of new professional works. Reviewing of books in librarianship has presented another opportunity for librarians to write and to publish.

Chen and Galvin (1975) have presented the major summary on the current state of book reviewing in librarianship. Selecting 222 English language monographs in library and information science published in 1971, they searched for reviews of these titles in 22 library periodicals for the years 1971, 1972, and the first 6 months of 1973. They were able to locate reviews for 164 of these titles (74%) in at least one of the journals. The periodical with the greatest number of reviews was *Library Journal* with 87. There was considerable duplication for individual titles, with 99 reviewed in more than one journal.

An average of 8.46 months occurred between publication of the work and appearance of a review. The time lag varied for the journals, ranging from 5.4 months for *Wilson Library Bulletin* and 5.8 months for *Booklist* to 10.8 months for *Library Quarterly* and 12.1 months for *College & Research Libraries*.

As was demonstrated in earlier studies of general book reviewing, most reviews are favorable, and reviews in library periodicals are no exception, with 70.9% favorable. When one adds to this total the reviews offering no evaluation at all, a total of 81% were either favorable or presented no evaluation.

Chen and Galvin present three basic functions for professional book reviewing: alerting, selection, and peer appraisal. They conclude that reviews of library literature make a major contribution in the alerting function but are of limited value as selection tools or in peer appraisal.

IX. INDEXING AND ABSTRACTING SERVICES

Accessibility of the journal literature of librarianship depends on its bibliographic control through a series of secondary services that list and describe it. Current and comprehensive coverage of the literature is desired. In librarianship and related information science, individuals, associations, and publishers have provided a variety of indexes and abstracting services. Although they duplicate one another in their coverage of some journals, they still have not given the comprehensive coverage or the currency needed.

Tegler (1979) has provided an excellent and current summary of the state of indexing and abstracting services. She describes the seven principal services currently available—all but two are English language publications.

Library Literature, indexing some 200 different journals, is the standard American guide to the literature. *Library and Information Science Abstracts* is its English counterpart, even though there are substantial differences. *Information Science Abstracts* and *Computer and Control Abstracts* represent related interests. *CALL: Current Awareness Library Literature* reproduces title pages of journals and contains editorial comments by its editor–publisher Samuel Goldstein. Unfortunately, its publication pattern has proved erratic.

The French *Bulletin Signaletique, Part 101: Sciences de l'Information, Docu-

mentation and the Russian *Referativnyi Zhurnal, Section 59*, complete Tegler's basic list.

She also notes several supporting services of value to the literature of librarianship: *Science Citation Index, Social Sciences Citation Index,* and *Current Index to Journals in Education (CIJE)*.

Tegler calls attention to several studies of overlap in journal coverage by the secondary services, and all studies reach the same conclusion: "One must use several services in order to gain satisfactory access to the literature" (p. 7).

Tegler concludes her survey of the services by recalling the 1968 Conference on the Bibliographic Control of Library Science Literature held at the State University of New York at Albany (1968, 1970). Despite the numerous recommendations offered there for the improvement and coordination of existing publications, for new publications, and for an international study group, she records that "no significant change ever took place . . . within three to four months of the conference, the recommendations were all but forgotten" (p. 19).

X. CONCLUSION

A summary view of the journal literature of librarianship shows a group of 500–1000 periodicals, newsletters, and other kinds of journals serving a broad array of interests and issued by a great variety of publishers. There is no coordination or control of their issuance, and the number of journals continues to grow.

They are primarily amateur and volunteer endeavors—editors also filling full-time library positions and authors writing manuscripts in their spare time. Hence, patterns in publication are erratic.

The profession has yet to study the subjects covered and methodologies employed in the articles, but studies of authorship demonstrate that those librarians with advanced degrees or in major administrative positions are more likely to write and to be published.

The journal literature has received an unfavorable press, but even so the seminal study of manuscript reviewing demonstrates a rejection rate of 77.2% If one dislikes the material that has been published, one can only question what the unpublished manuscripts look like.

The profession is most supportive of its members' writing and publishing, and the meetings and conferences held as well as articles and publications on writing indicate that encouragement.

Book reviewing in the journals covers the relevant literature only in part, and the various indexing and abstracting services give but partial control to the literature of librarianship.

Although there are promises that the electronic journal can replace the periodical in conventional print form (Singleton, 1981), experiments to date (Senders, 1981) have not been particularly successful. The print journal, even with all of its problems, remains a reliable, portable, easily available, and inexpensive medium for professional communication.

REFERENCES

Andrews, T. (1980). The special librarian as author. *In* "Special Librarianship: A New Reader" (E. B. Jackson, ed.), pp. 477–489. Scarecrow Press, Metuchen, New Jersey.

Beals, R. A. (1942). Implications of communications research for the public library. *In* "Print, Radio, and Film in a Democracy: Ten Papers on the Administration of Mass Communications in the Public Interest" (D. Waples, ed.), pp. 159–181. University of Chicago Press, Chicago.

Becker, P. G. (1957). How to write effectively for a library periodical. *Wilson Library Bulletin* 31, 539, 559.

Blake, F. M. (1961). A look at library literature. *Wilson Library Bulletin* 35, 715, 720.

Bloomfield, M. (1966). The writing habits of librarians. *College & Research Libraries* 27, 109–119.

Bloomfield, M. (1979). A quantitative study of the publishing characteristics of librarians. *Drexel Library Quarterly* 15 (July), 24–49.

Bobinski, G. S., ed (1979). The literature of librarianship and information science. *Drexel Library Quarterly* 15 (January), 1–100; (July), 1–119.

Bundy, M. L. (1961). Public library administrators view their professional periodicals. *Illinois Libraries* 43, 397–420.

Burlingame, D. F., and Repp, J. (1981). Factors Associated with Academic Librarians' Publishing in the '70's: Prologue for the '80's. In "Options for the 80s." Second National ACRL Conference. Minneapolis.

Busha, C. H., and Harter, S. P. (1980). "Research Methods in Librarianship: Techniques and Interpretation." Academic Press, New York.

Byerly, G. (1980). The faculty status of academic librarians in Ohio. *College & Research Libraries* 41, 422–429.

Campbell, J. (1977). Publish or perish, library-style. *Wilson Library Bulletin* 52, 250.

Carnovsky, L. (1955). Standards for library periodicals. *Library Journal* 80, 264–268.

Carnovsky, L. (1956). Library periodicals: Objectives—theory and practice. *I.L.A. Record* 9, 69–72.

Carnovsky, L. (1964). Publishing the results of research in librarianship. *Library Trends* 13, 126–140.

Carter, J. R. (1981). Practical research for practicing librarians. *Top of the News* 37, 128–137.

Chen, C. C., and Galvin, T. J. (1975). Reviewing the literature of librarianship: A state of the art report. *In* "American Reference Books Annual" 6, pp. xxxi–xlv. Libraries Unlimited, Littleton, Colorado.

Collier, B. (1974a). The library journals: Putting things in order. *Change* 6 (May), 59–61.

Collier, B. (1974b). Bonnie Collier replies. *Change* 6 (September), 61.

Conference on the Bibliographic Control of Library Science Literature (1968). "Part 1: Short Summary of Papers and Proceedings; Part 2: Summary of Recommendations." State University of New York at Albany, Albany, New York. ERIC ED 050 737.

Conference on the Bibliographic Control of Library Science Literature (1970). "Proceedings, Edited, from Stenotype and Audiotape Recordings, by David Mitchell and Beverly Choate." State University of New York at Albany, Albany, New York. ERIC ED 050 738.

Danton, J. P. (1976). The library press. *Library Trends* **25**, 153–176.

Edgar, N. L. (1978). Library periodical literature: A centennial assessment. *The Serials Librarian* **2**, 341–350.

Eshelman, W. R., and Hamlin, A. T. (1974). Library journals. *Change* **6** (September), 60–61.

Gwynn, N. E. (1980). Funding library research. *College & Research Libraries* **41**, 207–209.

Harreld, J. M. (1975). Report on the conference on writing and publishing for librarians. *College & Research Libraries News* **36**, 177–179.

Hernon, P., Pastine, M., and Williams, S. L. (1973). "Library and Library-Related Publications: A Directory of Publishing Opportunities in Journals, Serials, and Annuals." Libraries Unlimited, Littleton, Colorado.

Jesse, W. H., and Mitchell, A. E. (1968). Professional staff opportunities for study and research. *College & Research Libraries* **29**, 87–100.

Jones, G. (1976). 'This incredible stream of garbage': The library journals, 1876–1975. *The Indexer* **10**, 9–14.

Kaser, D. (1976). A century of academic librarianship as reflected in its literature. *College & Research Libraries* **37**, 110–127. (Reprinted in "Libraries for Teaching, Libraries for Research: Essays for a Century," [R. D. Johnson, ed.), pp. 219–236. American Library Association, Chicago, 1977.)

Katz, B., and Richards, B. C. (1978). "Magazines for Libraries." 3d ed. Bowker, New York.

Katz, W. (1967). Publications. *Drexel Library Quarterly* **3**, 176–184.

Kellam, W. P., and Barker, D. L. (1968). Activities and opportunities of university librarians for full participation in the educational enterprise. *College & Research Libraries* **29**, 195–199.

Kim, S. D., and Kim, M. T. (1979). Academic library research: A twenty year perspective. *In* "New Horizons for Academic Libraries" (R. D. Stueart and R. D. Johnson, eds.), pp. 375–383. K. G. Saur, New York.

Lee, J. M., ed. (1979). Library periodicals in review. *Serials Review* **5**, 7–39.

LIL'MIG (1981). *Library Journal* **106**, 616.

Little, T. M. (1968). "Use and users of library literature." Paper prepared for the Conference on the Bibliographic Control of Library Science Literature, State University of New York at Albany, 19–20 April 1968. State University of New York at Albany, Albany, New York. ERIC ED 050 745.

Lynch, M. J. (1981). Costing small-scale research. *Top of the News* **37**, 138–144.

McGrath, W. E. (1972). "An Estimate of the Amount of Research Required to Fill a New Journal of Library Science and Three Estimates of the Amount of Research Available." Library Research Round Table, American Library Association, Chicago. ERIC ED 081 453.

Magrill, R. M. (1980). Conducting library research. *College & Research Libraries* **41**, 200–206.

Meadows, A. J. (1974). "Communication in Science." Butterworths, London.

Melin, N. J. (1979). The specialization of library periodical literature: Its development and status. *Drexel Library Quarterly* **15** (January), 25–51.

Miller, S. L., Gapen, K., Hoadley, I. B., and Poli, R. (1976). To be or not to be: An academic library research committee. *The Journal of Academic Librarianship* **2** (March), 20–24.

Moon, E. (1969). The library press. *Library Journal* **94**, 4104–4109.
O'Connor, D., and Van Orden, P. (1978). Getting into print. *College & Research Libraries* **39**, 389–396.
Olsgaard, J. N., and Olsgaard, J. K. (1980). Authorship in five library periodicals. *College & Research Libraries* **41**, 49–53.
Potter, W. G. (1981). Lotka's law revisited. *Library Trends* **30**, 21–39.
Rayman, R., and Goudy, F. W. (1980). Research and publication requirements in university libraries. *College & Research Libraries* **41**, 43–48.
Rayward, W. B. (1980). Publishing library research. *College & Research Libraries* **41**, 210–219.
Rayward, W. B. (1981). Reporting the results of research: To inform others, to improve practice, and to add to knowledge in the field. *Top of the News* **37**, 145–156.
Richardson, J. V., Jr. (1977). Readability and readership of journals in library science. *The Journal of Academic Librarianship* **3**, 20–22.
Schorr, A. E. (1974). Lotka's law and library science. *RQ* **14**, 32–33.
Schorr, A. E. (1975). Lotka's law and map librarianship. *Journal of the American Society for Information Science* **26**, 189–190.
Senders, J. W. (1981). I have seen the future, and it doesn't work: The electronic journal experiment. *In* "Scholarly Publishing in an Era of Change: Proceedings of the Second Annual Meeting, Society for Scholarly Publishing, Minneapolis, Minnesota, June 2–4, 1980" (E. G. Langlois, ed.), pp. 8–9. Society for Scholarly Publishing, Washington, D.C.
Shields, G. R. (1979). The library press: National and state magazines. *Drexel Library Quarterly* **15** (January), 3–24.
Shores, L. (1972). Press proliferation: A word for more. *RQ* **11**, 297–299.
Singleton, A. (1981). The electronic journal and its relatives. *Scholarly Publishing* **13**, 3–18.
Stamatakos, L. C. (1979). Seven critical steps in writing for publication. *Southern College Personnel Association Journal* **2** (Winter), 7–13.
Stevens, N. D. (1979). Writing for publication. *Collection Management* **3**, 21–29.
Stevens, N. D., ed. (1980). "Essays from the New England Academic Librarians' Writing Seminar." Scarecrow Press, Metuchen, New Jersey.
Stevens, N. D., and Stevens, N. B. (1982). "Author's Guide to Journals in Library and Information Science." Haworth Press, New York.
Stueart, R. D. (1976). Writing the journal article. *College & Research Libraries* **37**, 153–157.
Subramanyam, K. (1981). Lotka's law and library literature. *Library Research* **3**, 167–170.
Taylor, K. I. (1978). "Subjects of Articles Sought by Editors of Library and Information Science Periodicals: A Survey of 102 State, Regional, National and International Professional Publications." Graduate Department of Library Science, Villanova University, Villanova, Pennsylvania.
Tegler, P. (1979). The indexes and abstracts of library and information science. *Drexel Library Quarterly* **15** (July), 2 23.
Thompson, D. E. (1961). The sad state of library literature. *ALA Bulletin* **55**, 642–644.
Ulrich's International Periodicals Directory" (1981). 20th ed. Bowker, New York.
Voos, H. (1974). Lotka and information science. *Journal of the American Society for Information Science* **25**, 270–272.
Watson, P. De S. (1977). Publication activity among academic librarians. *College & Research Libraries* **38**, 375–384.
Wilson, L. R. (1953). The challenge of library literature to education for librarianship, 1923–1953. *In* "Challenges to Librarianship" (L. Shores, ed.), pp. 125–140. Wm. C. Brown Co., Dubuque, Iowa.
Zuckerman, H., and Merton, R. K. (1971). Patterns of evaluation in science: Institutionalization, structure and functions of the referee system. *Minerva* **9**, 66–100.

A Guide for Searching in Anglo-American Main-Entry Catalogs

ELIZABETH L. TATE

Rockville, Maryland

I.	Catalogs and Catalog Codes	151
II.	Bibliographic Citations	152
III.	Changing Main Entry Patterns	153
	A. Choice of Entry for Monographs	153
	B. Form of Entry	162
	C. Serials	168
	D. Conference Publications	169
IV.	Conclusion	171
	References	172

I. CATALOGS AND CATALOG CODES

The completion of the monumental *National Union Catalog: Pre-1956 Imprints* in January 1981 marked the end of an era in this country—the era of the single-entry catalog. The availability of the REMARC Database in October 1980 heralded a new era, the era of the on-line catalog with multiple access points for retrospective as well as current records. However, the extra access points provided by machine-readable tapes or by indexes printed from tapes may not be available to all who wish to consult the hundreds of volumes of the national union author catalogs. This guide has been prepared to assist in searching these and other catalogs that offer only a main-entry approach.

Five catalog codes have governed the construction of the entries that appear in many catalogs in this country. The five tomes that sit upon catalogers' reference shelves give the appearance of discrete entities. In reality, catalog codes—or, rather, cataloging rules—are a continuum. As catalogers encounter publications that do not fit, or do not seem to fit, the generalized instructions of the codes, additions and modifications to the rules are issued. These changes are crystallized from time to time into a new edition for convenience. Of particular interest to the searcher consulting the single-entry catalog are the changes that have affected the choice and/or form of the main entry (i.e., the complete catalog record of an item under the heading designated by a catalog code as the principal entry, usually the name of a person or a corporate body).

The sources for the changes outlined in this guide are the five codes and the three publications for announcing changes between editions. The brief references by which each has been cited in the text can be interpreted by means of the "Key to Principal Sources" at the end of the article. Specific rule numbers have been given only for exact quotations or for cases in which the indexes to the codes do not easily locate the relevant rules.

II. BIBLIOGRAPHIC CITATIONS

This guide has been designed to assist the person approaching a main-entry catalog with a bibliographic citation. The efficiency with which a searcher can translate a citation into the corresponding main entry depends not only on the catalog rules that have determined the heading but on the characteristics of the citation as well. Three characteristics of citations affect their findability: (1) accuracy, (2) completeness, and (3) purpose. Of these, accuracy is not of concern here. The second characteristic, completeness, does affect the ease with which the best access point can be selected. Citations vary in completeness from cryptic legal references like "Earp's Appeal, 28 Pa St. 368" to detailed models like this one from the *MLA Handbook* (Gibaldi and Achtert, 1980, pp. 108–109):

> Coulson, Jessie, trans. *Crime and Punishment.*
> By Feodor Dostoevsky. Ed. George Gibian.
> New York: Norton, 1964.

However, even though the bibliographic data in a citation may be plentiful, it can still fail to provide the information necessary to identify responsibility for the intellectual content of the work, which is the cataloger's primary concern in choosing a main entry. The second example illustrates the third characteristic that accounts for differences between catalog main entries and citation entry elements. Citations customarily describe only the item consulted; few citations relate that item to other versions of the work. A catalog main entry, on the other hand, is designed to collocate entries for all versions of a work in a collection.

The rules in the codes are many, but the number of cases covered by some of them are few. The selection of the ones mentioned here has been based on an examination of two random samples of citations (Tate, 1963, 1981). The kinds of citations in the samples suggest that the searcher most frequently needs information about the changing main-entry patterns for three types of works: (1) works of personal authorship, which predominate, (2) works involving corporate responsibility, which are the most troublesome even though they constitute a small proportion (about 20% in each sample), and (3) conference publications and other serials, citations to which appear to be increasing. Only the changes between 1908 and 1980 that significantly affect the findability of main entries have been described. The guide has been organized in terms of the kinds of data in citations.

III. CHANGING MAIN-ENTRY PATTERNS

A. Choice of Entry for Monographs

1. ONE AUTHOR

Many citations, fortunately, are references to works of simple personal authorship. For works of single personal authorship, the author has always been preferred as main entry, so the choice of access point will present the searcher no problem if the person named in the citation is in fact the author and not an editor or compiler. Until recently, the same could have been said of the single corporate author, but with the 1978 code, corporate main entry has been restricted on the basis of document content. Thus for the work cited below, which does not concern the administrative affairs of the association, main entry will be title instead of corporate body.

CHARTING THE AMERICAN LUMBER INDUSTRY, National Lumber Manufacturers' Association, Washington D.C.

2. TWO OR THREE AUTHORS

The rules for works of joint authorship in the 1908 code categorically required entry under the author named first on the title page, followed by the name of the second author or "and others." The concept of principal responsibility was introduced in the 1941 code for works in which the contribution of each author constitutes a distinct part (Rule 3a). It results occasionally in entry under an author other than the first named. Even though principal responsibility has now become the basic criterion for choosing a main entry, the author named first in the citation is a reasonable starting point.

3. MORE THAN THREE AUTHORS

When authorship is shared by more than three, main entry may be under the first named author or it may be under title. While the 1908 code makes no differentiation on the basis of number, the 1941 code specifies title main entry for certain composite works with more than three authors (Rule 3b). In the 1967 code, title is to be the main entry for works with more than three but with no principal author and no editor. In a citation, the name of an author followed by "and others" should suggest the possibility of a title main entry, especially for recent imprints.

4. COMPILERS

A recent change in the rules for edited compilations or collections necessitates a change in searching strategy. The 1908 code recommended entry under the name of the compiler or editor unless that person's contribution was slight and the name did not appear prominently in the publication. Though the rules were stated in different terms, this provision was continued until 1975, when title main entry became mandatory for all edited compilations with a collective title (CS No. 112, p. 5). The publication date in the citation, therefore, should determine whether the first search is title or compiler.

However, before that decision is faced, the searcher must recognize the work cited as a compilation. The role of the compiler is not always spelled out as these citations illustrate.

Nichol Smith's *Eighteenth Century Essays,* p. 270
Chansons du quinzième siècle, G. Paris, p. 29.
Joh. Müller, Quellenschriften und Geschichte des deutsch-sprachlichen Unterrichtes bis zur Mitte des 16. Jahrhunderts. Gotha. 1882.

Words in the title suggesting contents that include discrete, individually authored items such as *Essays, Chansons,* or *Quellenschriften* can alert the searcher to the possibility of title main entry, especially for recent publications. The bibliography is another type of compilation that may appear in the catalog under either the name of the compiler, personal or corporate, or the title.

The searcher needs to be wary of a pitfall in looking for one specific type of edited compilation published prior to 1967. If the citation indicates that the work is a festschrift and that it has been "published by a society or an institution in honor of a person or to celebrate an anniversary," the search should begin with the heading for the corporate body (1908, rule 126 [2]). For example, the citation that reads

Kaminka, Armand
    Festschrift Armand Kaminka zum 70. Geb.–Wien:
Verl. d. Wiener Maimonides-Inst. 1937. XV, 148;
58; bibliogr.

has been cataloged according to this rule under the heading: "Vienna. Maimonides Institut."

Even though this rule for festschriften, fortunately, disappeared from the 1967 code, main entry under corporate heading remained a possibility under that code for compilations prepared and edited by a corporate body.

5. EDITORS

Many citations identify an editor. The editor's responsibility for the intellectual content of the work is not identical in each case; however, the cataloger's choice of main entry is determined by the level of responsibility. Some named as editors fill the role of compiler as this citation illustrates.

> Luther Gulick and Lyndall Urwick (eds.) Papers on the Science of Administration (New York: Institute of Public Administration, Columbia University, 1937), p. 33.

The searching strategies for collections are applicable to this category. Three citations illustrate a second type of edited work.

> Cepari, V.: *Life of St. Aloysius,* edited by Fr. Schroeder, S.J., and in English by Fr. F. Goldie, S.J., 1891.
> J. C. Beaglehole, ed., *The Journals of Captain James Cook* and *The Endeavour Journal of Joseph Banks, 1768–1771*
> Murphy G.: Income tax, sur-tax, profits tax, 4th ed. London 1948.

In each case, the editor has contributed to a pre-existing work. The 1908 code succinctly states the principle of entry found in all the codes: "Enter a revision under the name of the original author unless it has become substantially a new work" (Rule 19). The third example illustrates the difficulties of defining "substantially a new work," for it is a work by William Roger Carter, the fourth edition of which was prepared by G. W. Murphy. More objective criteria for recognizing a substantially new work have been introduced into the 1978 code. The edition statement can alert the searcher to the need for more information when search under the citation entry element has failed.

The preexisting work to which an editor contributes is not necessarily a work of personal authorship. "Birch, *Charters of Lincoln,* viii" cites a work of corporate authorship, the city of Lincoln, England, while the anonymous *Acta Sanctorum* has been referenced in this citation.

See H. Delehaye, *Synaxarium Ecclesiae Constantinopolitanae, Acta Sanctorum, Prophylaeum Novembris,* Brussels, 1902, pp. 571–4.

With neither main entry under a personal name, the searcher is obliged to derive the heading by analyzing the title.

6. TRANSLATORS

Carefully prepared citations mention the translator, especially if his or her name has appeared on the title page. Main entry under the heading appropriate to the original work has consistently been prescribed by the codes with only two exceptions. A collection of translations from various authors by a single translator is treated as a collection and is subject to the variations outlined in Section III,A,4. The 1967 and 1978 codes exempt "free translations" from the basic rule, preferring entry under translator instead. Here again, searching problems can originate in the failure of some citations to identify the translator's role, e.g.:

The Yoga-Sutra of Patanjali . . . . M. J. Dvidedi.
One Hundred Poems of Kabir: Rabindranath Tagore.

A title that mentions a classic or an anonymous epic or includes the name of an ancient or medieval writer should alert the searcher to the possibility of main entry under the heading appropriate for the original work. Some citations to these types of works give an editor or translator as the entry element; others cite the work under the title, e.g., "Iliade, XIV, 278–279." or as in this reference to a medieval mystery play:

Das Adamsspiel, Anglonormannisches Mysterium des XII. Jahrh.,
herausgegeben von Dr. Karl Grass, Oberlehrer am Realgymnasium

zu Düren (Rheinland). Zweite verbesserte Auflage (*Romanische Bibliothek,* vi), Halle a. S., 1907.

7. OTHER CONTRIBUTORS TO PREEXISTING WORKS

a. Commentators. Citations to commentaries offer the searcher the option of search under the heading for the original or under the heading for a subsequent contributor:

Peake's Commentary on the Bible. Gen ed. and New Testament ed., Matthew Black. Old Testament ed., H. H. Rowley. London, N.Y., Nelson, 1962. 1126 p. maps.

The 1908 code provided unequivocal guidance: "When the text of a work is given with a commentary, the work is to be cataloged under the name of the author of the text" (Rule 13). The 1941 code introduced the option of entry under the commentator if the text is subordinate, while the 1967 code made the decision dependent on the presentation of the work on the title page (see also CS No. 111, pp. 2–3).

b. Authors of Related Works. Recent changes in the rules for related works will modify the searcher's approach to main entries for continuations, supplements, indexes, etc. An index, according to the 1908 code, should be recorded on the same entry as the work indexed, a practice continued until 1976. A supplement issued with its own title was to be entered under the name of its own author. The 1941 code extended the use of the "dash entry" to supplements not independent of the original work. Thus the work cited as "Addenda ad Eckhelli, Vindob. 1826, p. 7" is covered by the entry for Joseph Eckhel's *Doctrina Numorum Veterum,* whereas the book cited as "The useful plants of West tropical Afrika Dalziel, 1937. Londres." is cataloged under Dalziel, even though it is an appendix to the *Flora of West Tropical Africa,* by J. Hutchinson and J. M. Dalziel. Problems in programming for "dash entries" in machine-readable records prompted the Library of Congress to abandon that practice in 1975 (CS No. 114, pp. 4–5; No. 118, pp. 7–8; No. 119, pp. 15–18) and independent entry is prescribed by the 1978 code for all related works.

One type of related work, the libretto, has posed puzzling questions about authorship responsibility. The 1908 code regarded the librettist as the author, while the 1941 code prescribed entry under composer to assemble the musical unit in the catalog (App. VIII, Rule 21). Entry under composer will be continued by the Library of Congress under the alternative rule provided by the 1978 code (CSB No. 2, p. 25).

The composer served as main entry under the 1908 code for the thematic index. a practice revised in the 1941 code by a directive to enter thematic catalogs under compiler, or under publisher if no compiler is named (App. VIII, Rule 31). With no special rules in the 1967 and 1978 codes, the searching strategies for compilations become applicable.

c. Other Secondary Contributors. Two citations suggest kinds of authorship responsibility different from those already discussed. The first reads

> The letters of Samuel Clemens to his wife, reproduced here, are from *My Father, Mark Twain,* by Clara Clemens. Copyright by Harper & Brothers, publishers.

The second reads

> THE BALTIC REPUBLICS
> Published by the National Council of
> American–Soviet Friendship 44 pages.
> Based on "The Baltic Ridle" [sic] by
> Gregory Meiksins.—10c.

Each was possible only because of the previous work of another author, yet each is more than just an edition or translation of that work. The principle underlying the many rules in the five codes is to select as main entry the heading appropriate to the pre-existing work unless the later work has modified the original so significantly that a substantially new work has been created. A change from one literary form to another is regarded as a substantial change, as are parodies and imitations. But abridgments, outlines, and other condensations are entered under the author of the original. Adaptations and paraphrases also were entered under the original author under the 1941 rules, but are regarded as substantially new works by the 1967 code. For biographies that incorporate primary source material, the selection of the main entry was based primarily on the content of the work in the 1941 code. The 1967 rule gives more weight to the title page presentation of the work and should bring greater correspondence between main entry and citation-entry element. Modifications of music and art works follow the principle mentioned above with one exception. Engravings that reproduce the work of another artist have been entered under the original artist until the 1967 code (Rule 261B) specified the subsequent artist.

8. OTHER AUTHORSHIP ROLES

Numerous rules in the five codes under a variety of captions provide for collaborative works, the contributions to which differ in kind. Either the author named first on the title page or the principal contributor is the main entry prescribed by most of these rules. The concept of "principal contributor" in the 1978 code encompasses the spirits whose observations are reported in mediumistic writings, a category not even mentioned in the 1908 code—a matter of little importance because of the small number of spirit communications. Of greater importance to the searcher is the fact that the cataloger's identification of principal contributor may very well differ from that of the person preparing the citation

> Houdon, Jean-Antoine. *Statue of Voltaire.* Comédie Française, Paris. Illus. 51 in *Literature through Art: A New Approach to French Literature.* By Helmut A. Hatzfeld. New York: Oxford Univ. Press, 1952.

The fragment of a work relating to the subject under discussion is of paramount importance to the citer, whereas the entry prepared by the cataloger must represent the work as a whole.

9. CORPORATE AUTHORS

a. Personal versus Corporate Responsibility. When a corporate body shares the responsibility for the creation of a work, a different choice confronts the searcher. The searcher is obliged by citations like the following to select either a personal name or a corporate body for the first search.

> Lord, N.W., Experimental work conducted in the chemical laboratory of the United States Geological Survey fuel-testing plant at St. Louis, Mo., Jan. 1, 1905, to July 31, 1906: U.S. Geol. Survey Bull. 323, 49 pp., 1907.
> K. T. Compton and F. L. Mohler, *Critical Potentials.* (1924.) (Bulletin of Nat. Research Council; Washington.)

When the citer makes the choice, a personal name is likely to be the entry element. Catalogers' choices have been guided by a series of rules that attacked the problem piecemeal until Lubetzky saw the crux of the question. The 1908 code specified personal author entry for "reports made to a department by a person who is not an official" (Rule 60) and for reports from exploring expeditions that were clearly works of single or shared personal authorship (Rule 111). The 1941 code added to the list "scientific papers, addresses, and other publications, not administrative or routine in character" but it also required corporate entry for "reports which are prepared by an official as a part of his routine duty" (Rule 75). Unfortunately, the two are not mutually exclusive and, in practice, catalogers at that time tended to favor corporate entry. Thus, the first work cited, according to this rule, would appear under the name of the agency, while the second is entered under "National Research Council. *Committee on Ionization Potentials and Related Subjects,*" of which the two personal authors were official members (for further discussion of parent body or subordinate unit as the heading, see p. 162). With the reorientation of the 1967 code, the work of consultants and single reports "that embody the results of scholarly investigation or scientific research" were exempted from corporate authorship and the corporate heading was not to be preferred for borderline cases (Rule 17). Corporate main entry has been even further restricted by the 1978 code. Once again, the imprint date becomes an important clue to search strategy.

Citations to some legal materials necessitate a choice between a personal name and a corporate heading. Prior to the 1978 code, a citation like "The Catherine of Dover, 2. Hag. Ad. 145" could be found only after translation into the heading "Gt. Brit. *High Court of Admiralty.*" If the work were to be cataloged today, the main entry would be under the name of the court reporter, John Haggard. Only the legal specialist can easily translate such brief data into searchable headings without the kind of assistance offered by the *Manual of Legal Citations* (University of London, Institute of Advanced Legal Studies), *Effective Legal Research* (Price and Bitner) or other guides described in Marion's "Sources for Determining Citation Practice for Court Reports throughout the World."

The possibility of a corporate main entry must be divined from some citations

Banks and Banking. By J. J. Maclaren, Toronto. 1908.

Much of the content of this work is suggested by the subtitle: "The Bank Act, Canada, and Amending Acts, with Notes, Authorities and Decisions, and the Law Relating to Warehouse Receipts, Bills of Lading, etc. Also the Savings Bank Act, the Act Incorporating the Canadian Bankers' Association, the By-laws of the Association, and the Winding Up Act." Under all the codes, the relative proportions of legal source material and commentary determine the choice of main entry, although here again catalogers tended to prefer corporate headings under the 1949 code. It is well to remember that an unsuccessful search under the personal name in the citation might profitably be followed by search under the appropriate heading for the legal content, e.g.,

Canada. *Laws, statutes, etc.*

Personal author main entry has consistently been preferred for one other category of legal material, namely, documents relating to trials involving individuals. The few rules scattered through the 1908 code were supplemented in 1909 and 1910 by rules on cards for "Briefs," "Contested Elections," "Impeachment Trials" and "Courts-Martial and Courts of Inquiry" and incorporated into the 1941 code with one minor change. Main entry headings for civil actions, which had included the names of both parties (Brooks, William, *vs.* Byam, Ezekiel) were reduced to the name of the party to the suit given first on the title page. Though the criterion for choice of main entry for civil suits was significantly changed in the 1967 code, the results are often the same. Quite different headings, however, result from the 1967 rule for pleas and briefs which requires entry under the name of the party to the case instead of the attorney.

b. Form Subheadings versus Uniform Titles. The 1978 code brought a major change for catalogers that will probably be of little benefit to searchers. In lieu of the form subheadings "Charter", "Constitution", "Laws, statutes, etc.", "Ordinances, etc.", "Treaties, etc.", following names of jurisdictions, and "Liturgy and ritual" following the denominational names of churches, the entry will consist of two parts: the name of the jurisdiction or church as entry, followed by a uniform title based on the individual work being cataloged. However, the second element of the main entry is of little concern to the searcher until the first element has been unearthed—no easy task as is shown by these three citations, quoted in their entirety:

R. decreto 24 febbraio 1924, n. 225 (Punto franco di Fiume)
Verordnung vom 24. Juni 1916, RGB1. Nr. 195, über die
    Generalvormundschaft.
Dingley Act (Act of July 24, 1897, par. 415).

Once the searcher has ferreted out of these cryptic references the most likely jurisdiction, he or she is on the road to success and need only remember that after 1981 form subheadings will no longer be used and uniform titles will serve to organize the files.

When searching treaties one should not forget that under the 1941 and 1949 codes, multilateral treaties or conventions signed at international conferences were entered under the name of the conference. Otherwise, the search might very well begin with the home country, if it is a signatory. However, the preference accorded the home country for the entry of bilateral and trilateral treaties in the 1967 code has been discontinued in the 1978 code, making it necessary to search under the first country named in the citation or under the one whose catalog entry is first in English alphabetical order. The rules for treaties in the five codes are too detailed and complex to be summarized briefly and should be consulted by the searcher.

c. *Parent Body versus Subordinate Unit.* The citation below illustrates a third problem in devising a searching strategy for works of corporate authorship.

Vide Relatórios do Banco de Portugal.

Even though a citation may name a corporate body, it will not necessarily mention the subordinate unit that issued the work, in this case the bank's Conselho de Administração. The criterion for including this type of subordinate unit in the main entry heading has evolved in a direction that should simplify searching. The first effort to cope with the problem recommends the inclusion of the subordinate unit unless "the extent or anticipated extent of the material under the heading does not warrant subdivision. In particular, if the functions of the subordinate unit are concerned with the administration of the agency of which it forms a part . . . the subheading is generally omitted" (CS No. 33, pp. 4–5). This 1954 rule revision governed practice until the 1967 code, which emphasized subordinate units by making only one exception to the inclusion of the subordinate unit, namely, the kind that "simply acts as the information or publication agent for the parent body" (Rule 18A). The 1978 code bases the decision on the attribution of authorship in the chief source of information (Rule 21.1B4). The Library of Congress is not recataloging entries originally made under the parent body when the appropriate subdivision is now established (CSB No. 3, pp. 8–9). These variations in practice make it necessary to continue a search through the subordinate units of a corporate body for a citation not found under the parent body.

The changing patterns in the main entries prescribed by five codes have been summarized to aid in selecting the citation data with which to begin the search for works of personal or corporate authorship. Having decided on the most probable main entry, the searcher must next head for the right letter of the alphabet in the catalog. In some cases, changes in the catalog rules will determine the direction to take.

B. Form of Entry

Devising a heading for the name selected as main entry is a two-pronged problem for the cataloger who must decide which variant is to be used and which part of that variant is to be the entry element. The searcher, on the other hand, has only the variant in the citation with which to work and must approach the catalog by way of some arrangement of those data. Cross references, obligatory under all the codes, facilitate the searching. For these reasons, changes in the rules for choice of variant will not be discussed.

Publication date has been designated as a reliable clue to the choice of main entry. Because of the Library of Congress policy of superimposition it is a considerably less reliable clue to the form of entry to be anticipated under the 1967 code.[1] Though dates are still a factor, it is the age of the author that is most likely to indicate whether the entry will accord with the earlier rules or with the 1967 code. For corporate authors in particular, many previously established headings were continued after the appearance of AACR1.

1. PERSONAL NAMES

The random samples on which this guide is based indicate that most of the personal names encountered in citations in a general library in the United States are modern Occidental names, consisting of a surname and one or more forenames. Under all codes, the surname is the entry element; rules for surnames composed of more than one word have in general produced consistent results even though they may be worded differently. One exception relates to the names of married Portuguese women. The first statement of the rule in the 1941 code recommended entry under the first part of the compound surname as a general practice, e.g., Michaëlis de Vasconcellos, Carolina (Rule 59f2); by 1949 it was clear that Portuguese usage, though inconsistent, favored entry under the last part of the name (Rule 46F2); the change then made was continued thereafter (1967, Rule 46B3b; 1978, Rule 22.5C5). Since all of the rules for compound surnames and for surnames with a prefix permit a heading contrary to the rules if it accords with the owner's preference, search under an element other than the customary one may sometimes be necessary.

The 1967 and 1978 codes accept as an integral part of the surname a place name regularly used with a hyphen after the surname. The searcher on the trail of earlier entries will need to remember that some seemingly compound surnames, like Müller-Breslau, are in fact single surnames.

The placement of a patronymic in a heading can affect searching strategy. Exceptions to the usual pattern are found in a rule for Romanian names in the 1967 code (Rule 48) and in the earlier LC practice of entering Icelandic names under patronymic, later discontinued, as announced in the summer

---

[1]The Library of Congress in January 1967 announced its adoption of a policy called "superimposition." Under this policy, the rules in the 1967 code for choice of entry were applied only to works new to the Library of Congress, while the rules for form of entry were applied only to headings being established for the first time (CS No. 79, p. 1). As a consequence, headings, especially headings for corporate bodies, formulated under earlier codes, have persisted in the catalogs in spite of changes in the rules.

of 1974 (CS No. 110, pp. 2–3) Since few Icelandic names include a surname, entries will be found under the personal name: Snæbjorn Jónsson.

Unused forenames have been banned by all of the codes, though they may sometimes be found in headings. Until recently, a first forename represented by an initial has been completed whenever possible; before the 1967 code, other initials also were completed. To reflect the author's preference, a change in the 1978 code introduces a style of entry that gives initials in lieu of forenames (Rule 22.3A). On Library of Congress cards, however, under the provisions of Rule 22.16A, the full forenames will follow the initials whenever the information is readily available (CSB No. 8, p. 13). Accordingly, the heading "Priestley, John Boynton, 1894– " has been revised to read "Priestley, J. B. (John Boynton), 1894– " (CSB No. 11, p. 76). Headings under the 1978 code will reflect predominant usage even to the extent of omitting forenames entirely as is illustrated by the revised heading "Molière, 1622–1673" (CSB No. 7, p. 6; see also CSB No. 11, p. 26).

Unfortunately, the new headings will not necessarily correspond to the cited form. Some present-day publishers instruct authors to reduce all forenames to initials in references. And even when full documentation is encouraged, few writers care about the preferences of a prolific author and most are content to accept the name as given on the item cited. Two citations to the same author from two different sources can serve as an illustration. One gave the name as "Gregory, T. E. G.," while the other read "T. E. Gregory." The predominant identification in the author's publications leads to the heading "Gregory, T. E. (Theodore Emanuel)" under present rules. Since Gregory used two spellings of his first forename and was knighted in 1942, the heading produced by the 1949 code is "Gregory, *Sir* Theodor Emanuel Gugenheim, 1890– ." Comparing these citations and headings suggests that a search should not be abandoned until all possible permutations and combinations of forenames and initials have been explored.

2. CORPORATE BODIES

a. Entry under Place. A major change in the 1967 code gives better correspondence between citation data and catalog entry. By eliminating the distinction between "societies" and "institutions", the two latest codes eliminate the need to search nongovernmental corporate headings under a place name. It should be noted, however, that corporate headings established prior to 1967 were continued without revision until the adoption of the 1978 code. It is difficult to generalize the earlier rules that required entry under place but perhaps these tips may assist the searcher in analyzing the citation.

Earlier entries are likely to be under place if the name of the corporate body is generic and if, at the same time, it suggests substantial physical facilities with a specific location (e.g., "Universidad," "Bibliothèque," "Art Museum," "Aéroport," "Ursuline Convent," "Zoologischer Garten," "First National Bank," "Public School 48"). Entry under location is a possibility also if the corporate body has a strong place association, even though the physical facilities are not extensive. Examples specifically enumerated by the 1949 code include boards of trade, exhibitions, radio stations, university and union league clubs, volunteer fire companies, mercantile library associations, guilds, and cemeteries. The place name that constitutes the entry element mirrors the primary geographical or jurisdictional association. Most of the categories listed above were entered under the name of a city or town. But if the organization is oriented toward a political jurisdiction rather than a geographic location, the entry element may be the name of a state, county, province, etc. In particular, a corporate body in the United States or Canada, receiving tax support below the national level, may very well be entered under the name of the jurisdiction. Those likely to appear in citations include government supported institutions of higher learning, hospitals, libraries, and agricultural experiment stations, with all Canadian stations entered under Canada, however (1949, Rule 106B). Many state historical and agricultural societies also will be found under the name of the state.

Lubetzky wrote that a "closer examination of the rules for entry of societies and institutions will reveal a diversity of method which defies any reasonable explanation" (p. 24) and no further reminder of the rules and the exceptions will be attempted here except to note that a searcher in pursuit of the heading for a Carnegie or Passmore–Edwards public library should look under place, even though the corporate name begins with a proper noun (1908, Rule 99).

b. Initials, Initialisms and Abbreviations in Corporate Names. For many corporate bodies in the private sector, the heading will appear directly under the name. Some of these names begin with a personal name. The 1908 code (Rule 83) and the 1978 code (Rule 24.1) enter this type of name as it appears. The 1908 code does make an exception of the private school known only by the proprietor's name and of business firms. The 1967 code begins the heading with the surname and inverts the other names only if the corporate name begins with an initial or abbreviation (Rule 67A). The 1941 and 1949 codes invert all forename elements for business firms and corporations. Institutions appear under a full forename, but a forename element consisting of initials only is omitted entirely; the same treatment was extended to foundations, endowments, and funds by the 1949 code. Thus the searcher may have to look, for example, under

> A. K. Smiley Public Library, *Redlands, Cal.*
> Smiley Public Library, *Redlands, Calif.*
> Smiley (A. K.) Public Library

If the treatment of initials has perplexed catalogers, the question of initialisms has been even more of a conundrum. Since a rule first appeared in the 1941 code, the heading for a society could consist of an initialism or acronym if that was the form the society customarily used. Few societies during the first half of this century consistently identified their publications by means of an initialism or acronym only, and the preference for entry under corporate (i.e., official) name is seen in most headings until recently. The 1978 code permits the use of a brief form, including an initialism or acronym, if no other form of name is predominant (Rule 24.2d) with the result that headings like "AWS Committee on Definitions and Symbols" will replace the more complete versions like "American Welding Society. Committee on Definitions and Symbols" (CSB No. 8; p. 15). Other clues in the citation, such as the publisher's name or a series title, can help the searcher expand an initialism into the complete name that functions as entry element in many headings.

The names of some prestigious corporate bodies begin with an adjective or its abbreviation denoting royal privilege. Prior to the 1978 code words like "Real" or "König." were omitted from headings, or ignored in filing (1908, Rule 78) except in English names or in names such as "Koninklijke Bibliotheek" that would be reduced to a common word or phrase without it. Here publication date can guide the person searching a citation like this one:

> *Studia Palæographica. A contribution to the history of early Latin minuscule and to the dating of Visigothic mss.,* dans *Sitzungsberichte der König. Bayer. Akademie der Wissenschaften,* 1910, 12. Abhandl., p. 31.

c. *Hierarchy.* Sometimes a citation will present the name of a corporate body as it appears on the publication, giving the searcher more than enough information about its organizational relationships and hierarchical structure. With a citation that reads "U.S. Dept. of Health, Education, and Welfare, National Institute of Education, Educational Resources Information Center," the searcher is obliged to decide whether to start with *U, D, N,* or *E.* The possibility of direct entry is much greater with the two latest codes, not only for government agencies but for other types of corporate body as well. A distinctive name that includes no terms implying subordination is a strong clue that should prompt the searcher to anticipate direct entry. For example, the heading that once appeared in the catalog as "Great Britain. National Coal Board. Mining Research Establishment" has now been revised to read "Mining Research Establishment (Great Britain)" (CSB No. 8, p. 18). One constant worth remembering is the fact that all of the codes have required entry under jurisdiction for agencies that fulfill the legislative, executive, and judicial functions of government.

With a corporate name like those just mentioned, the searcher has another problem. How much of the hierarchy will need to be taken into account in the effort to reach the desired heading? The 1908 code disposed of the problem with two instructions: "Enter government bureaus or offices subordinate to a department directly under the country, not as subheadings under the department. . . . Minor divisions and offices are usually to be subordinated to the bureaus or departments of which they form a part" (Rule 59). Other than to omit the concept of "minor," no change was made until 1954 when a rule revision permitted direct entry of a subordinate unit under the name of the jurisdiction unless the name was too nondescript to identify the unit (CS No. 33, p. 4–5). Here again, the searching strategy will depend on the probable date the heading was established, with those for organizations existing before 1954 likely to contain more levels of hierarchy.

Indeed, the imprint date is likely to be one of very few clues the citation offers the searcher. A wealth of information about a corporate body is a rarity in a citation. A publication that proved to be a Senate document prepared by the Federal Trade Commission was cited as

> Sixty-seventh Congress, 2nd Session, Prices of Tobacco Products, 1922.

It would appear under the heading for the Commission according to all the codes except the 1978 code, which produces a title main entry. Information has been grudgingly given in this citation also:

> From the *Report of the Consultative Committee on Secondary Education* 1938. (Given with the permission of the Controller of H. M. Stationery Office.)

Without that parenthetical statement it might never have been found under "Gt. Brit. *Board of Education. Consultative Committee.*"

For both personal and corporate authors, another obstacle to successful searching may be met in citations to nonroman alphabet names, especially those that originate in foreign publications. The headings in catalog entries have been romanized by Library of Congress tables, whereas a different table may have been used for the name in the citation, giving for some names differing beginning letters. The spelling of a personal or corporate name, similarly, can be changed through successive translations and romanizations. The romanization of a citation to a Ukrainian edition of Wilhelm Wundt's *Einführung in die Psychologie,* for example, produces the spelling "Vundt" for the author's surname.

C. Serials

Since a serial differs from a monograph in publishing pattern and not in conditions of authorship, the distinction between serials and monographs has been dropped in the rules for entry in the 1978 code. The distinction remains, however, in bibliographic citations. For that reason, a few words about serials are appropriate, even though many of the searching strategies noted are applicable.

The principle of separate entries for successive serial titles, initiated in the 1967 code and continued in the 1978 code, is a major change that benefits both cataloger and searcher. It does not affect searching strategy, however, since the variant in the citation has to be the starting point.

Searching for serials issued by corporate bodies does require a strategy that should vary with the probable date of cataloging. This citation provides an excellent example.

Ann. Mo. Bot. Gard. 15: 169–240. 1928.

The entry for this journal under the three earliest codes is "St. Louis. Missouri Botanical Garden." Had it been cataloged after Rule 98 in AACR1 was revised in May 1974, the entry would have been "Missouri Botanical Garden" (CS No. 109, pp. 3–5) And the rule for corporate entry in the 1978 code will give "Annals of the Missouri Botanical Garden." Here is a second example, also abbreviated—as are so many journal citations.

Wash. Agr. Exp. Sta. Bul. 243. 1930.

The imprint date recommends a first search under "Washington (State) Agricultural Experiment Station, *Pullman.*" For an entry cataloged after 1967, the searcher would need to go to the other end of the alphabet and look for "Agricultural Experiment Station, Pullman, Wash." And after 1981, the goal should be "Bulletin / State College of Washington, Agricultural Experiment Station." Since application of the rule for corporate main entry in the 1978 code may result in more title main entries for serials, the searcher will need to remember that the arrangement of the chief source of information in the first issue will determine the presentation of data in the catalog entry. Since the citation will not necessarily conform, it will be a good idea, especially with nondistinctive titles, to search the title with and without grammatical connectives, like "of," "of the" or "from."

The entire citation to the agricultural experiment station bulletin read:

> Holtz, H. F. Effect of calcium and phosphorous content of various soil series of western Washington upon the calcium and phosphorous composition of oats, red clover, and white clover. Wash. Agr. Exp. Sta. Bull. 243. 1930.

The fact that the only LC entry for this pamphlet is a collective entry for the series can be a reminder to the searcher to analyze citations of this type not only as monographs but also as serials. Agricultural experiment station bulletins, in particular, since 1909, have been given collective entries only (Cds, "Agricultural Experiment Station Bulletins (State)").

Another bit of incidental intelligence about serials may occasionally prove useful to the searcher. Before the 1967 code appeared, a collection of extracts by various authors from a single serial was entered under the name of the serial, as was a separately cataloged special number of a periodical. Thus, *The Vogue Book of Menus and Recipes for Entertaining at Home,* by Jessica Daves, "with Tatiana McKenna and the editors of Vogue" will be found under the heading "Vogue."

D. Conference Publications

Conference proceedings are a particularly difficult type of publication to catalog and to search. Finding the entries is a matter of knowing not only the rule changes but also the actual practices in applying the rules. Today's catalogers know that a conference publication may be a monograph or a serial. It may or may not have named contributors. There may be one or more named editors or none at all. The conference that issues the publication may meet regularly or only once. It may have one, several, or no sponsors. All or some of the sponsors may change with every meeting or they may remain the same. The conference may have no name at all, or a name that is identical with that of the sponsor, or a general name along with a specific name that varies from meeting to meeting. For example, too many cooks are readily apparent at the International Conference on Energy Storage, Compression, and Switching, held at Asti–Torino, Italy, in 1974 and sponsored by the Instituto Elettrotecnico Nazionale Galileo Ferraris, the

Stevens Institute of Technology and the Consiglio Nazionale delle Ricerche, the proceedings of which, published with the title *Energy Storage, Compression, and Switching,* were edited by W. H. Bostick, V. Nardi, and O. S. F. Zucker.

The authors of the 1908 code cannot have dreamed of all these possibilities when they disposed of the problems of conferences with three directives.

> Enter conventions, conferences, and assemblies of societies, political parties, religious denominations, etc. under the names of these bodies. . . . Enter conventions and conferences of bodies which have no existence beyond the convention under the name of the convention. If no name can be found, enter under the place of meeting and supply a name descriptive of the character of the convention (Rule 105).

The first two outline a basic searching strategy that is still workable. Look under the name of the conference, omitting initial words such as "biennial" that indicate the frequency of the meetings. But if the name of the conference consists of the name of an organization with the addition of a word or phrase denoting the meeting in general terms, look under the heading for the organization with the meeting name as a subheading. An example from the 1908 code reads "International co-operative alliance. *2d congress, Paris, 1896*" (Rule 105). Here is one that appears in the 1978 code: "International Labour Organisation. *European Regional Conference (2nd : 1968 : Geneva)* (Rule 24.13).

The third directive tackles one of the most harassing problems of cataloging conferences, "What is a name?" The searcher will find several different answers in the entries added to the catalog between 1908 and 1962. One answer is that of the 1908 code, which produced headings like "Boston. Woman's rights meeting, 1859" (Rule 105). The idea of supplying a name led to a second answer, the conference name constructed out of the title. Thus, the title page that read "Pediatrics and the emotional needs of the child, as discussed by pediatricians and psychiatrists at Hershey, Pa., March 6–8, 1947" inspired the heading "Conference on Pediatrics and the Emotional Needs of the Child, Hershey, Pa., 1947." A third answer was to enter the conference publication under the first-named sponsor.

In May 1962, the Library of Congress adopted some better solutions that can be translated into a searching strategy. If the name in the citation is nebulous, consider the conference unnamed. Nebulous names are characterized by the indefinite article, the use of lower case instead of capital letters in the name, and names that are general descriptions (CS No. 57; p.5) For publications of an unnamed conference cataloged between 1962 and 1975, search under editor; for those without an editor and for all cataloged after 1975, prefer title. For example, title serves as main entry for this work: "Wage determination: papers presented at an international conference, Paris, 3rd–6th July 1973."

A solution to another of these problems was adopted in October 1964. If a conference has both a specific name and a more general name associating it with a series of meetings, the specific name will be selected for the main-entry heading (CS No. 66, p. 4) so that the main entry for the proceedings of Symposium A–10, XII Pacific Science Congress, appears under the heading "Symposium on Nature Conservation in the Pacific, Canberra, Australia, 1971" and not under "Pacific Science Congress, 12th, Canberra, Australia, 1971."

The last tip for searching conference publications is based on knowledge of an LC cataloging policy of many years ago. The crisis in cataloging prompted LC, like many other libraries, to adopt shortcuts. One shortcut practiced for a brief period at the Library was that of serial entry for conference proceedings and papers, with a cataloger's note to bring out the fact that some of the volumes had individual titles. For this reason, it is worthwhile to look for a serial entry with a general title, like "Proceedings," if the individual title given in the citation is not found under the conference heading.

IV. CONCLUSION

By the end of this decade, computer terminals will undoubtedly offer library patrons throughout the country multiple access points to our major national bibliography. Meanwhile, in numerous libraries, the efficient use of single-entry catalogs will still require a knowledge of the changes that have occurred in the structure of main entries over the years.

Synthesizing rules from five catalog codes into a brief guide inevitably means many oversimplifications and omissions. Indeed, no effort has been made to include the rules the cataloger needs to handle the difficult but unusual cases. Nor has any effort been made to note all the exceptions to the principal rules, because the two samples on which the paper is based clearly indicate that few bibliographic citations contain the information with which to judge the applicability of those exceptions. But this guide will have served its purpose if it helps the searcher translate the information provided by citations into searching strategies that will take account of the changing theories of main entry developed over the years in an attempt to cope with the problems of bibliographic control.

REFERENCES

Key to Principal Sources

1908 code = "Catalog Rules: Author and Title Entries." American ed. American Library Association Publishing Board, Boston.
1941 code = "A.L.A. Catalog Rules: Author and Title Entries." prelim. American 2d ed. Catalog Code Revision Committee, American Library Association, Chicago.
1949 code = "A.L.A. Cataloging Rules for Author and Title Entries." 2d ed. Division of Cataloging and Classification, American Library Association, Chicago.
1967 code = "Anglo-American Cataloging Rules." North American text. American Library Association, Chicago.
1978 code = "Anglo-American Cataloguing Rules." 2d ed. American Library Association, Chicago.
Cds = "L. of C. Cat. rules (suppl.)" Issued occasionally on 3" × 5" cards. Library of Congress, 1904?–1933?
CS = "Cataloging Service." Library of Congress, Washington, D.C. No. 33 (September 1954); No. 57 (June 1962); No. 66 (October 1964); No. 79 (January 1967); No. 109 (May 1974); No. 110 (summer 1974); No. 111 (fall 1974); No. 112 (winter 1975); No. 114 (summer 1975); No. 118 (summer 1976); No. 119 (fall 1976).
CSB = Cataloging Service Bulletin. Processing Services, Library of Congress, Washington, D.C. No. 2 (fall 1978); No. 3 (winter 1979); No. 7 (winter 1980); No. 8 (spring 1980); No. 11 (winter 1981).

Other References

Gibaldi, J. and Achtert, W. S. (1980). "MLA Handbook for Writers of Research Papers, Theses, and Dissertations." student ed. Modern Language Association, New York.
Lubetzky, S. (1953). "Cataloging Rules and Principles." Processing Dept., Library of Congress, Washington, D.C.
Marion, P. C. (1981). Sources for determining citation practice for court reports throughout the world. *Library Resources & Technical Services* 25, 139–148.
Price, M. O., and Bitner, H. (1969). "Effective Legal Research." 3d ed. Little, Boston.
Tate, E. (1963). Main entries and citations. *Library Quarterly* 33, 172–191.
Tate, E. (1981). "A Cataloger's View of the Puzzle." Paper presented at the RASD Catalog Use Committee program "Citation to Catalog: Piecing Together the Bibliographic Puzzle," American Library Assn. Annual Conference, San Francisco, June 29.
University of London, Institute of Advanced Legal Studies (1959). "Manual of Legal Citations."

The Colonial Legacy in West African Libraries: A Comparative Analysis

MARY N. MAACK*
University of Minnesota

I.	Methodology and Background................................	174
	A. Comparative Analysis......................................	174
	B. Geographical and Cultural Setting........................	176
	C. Pre-Colonial Era	180
II.	The Colonial Era: 1890–1945................................	183
	A. From Exploration to Administration	183
	B. Research Needs and Library Development	185
	C. European Education and General Libraries in Africa	190
	D. Libraries and Librarianship in the Colonial Context	197
III.	Decolonization: 1945–1960..................................	199
	A. Africa in the Postwar Period.............................	199
	B. Higher Education and Academic Libraries	201
	C. Research Needs and Library Development	207
	D. Popular Education and Public Libraries.....................	211
	E. The Library Profession...................................	219
	F. European Library Traditions in Africa......................	226
IV.	The Colonial Legacy: A Comparative Analysis....................	231
	A. Administrative Organization	231
	B. Social Agencies	233
	C. Economic Infrastructure.................................	234
	D. The Cultural Legacy	236
	E. Adaptation and Innovation	238
	References...	240

*Present address: Ecole Nationale Supérieure des Bibliothèques, Villeurbanne, France.

I. METHODOLOGY AND BACKGROUND

Books, serials, and written documents have become significant instruments in the rapid transformation of Africa. Within a single generation, the largely preliterate societies of the colonial era gave way to new states in which status, wealth, and power were no longer ascribed by caste or lineage. Instead, leadership and social mobility are now achieved through Westernized education that enables individuals to function in an environment dominated by bureaucracy, commerce, and modern technology. As the African elite moves from a minimal use of written communication to heavy dependance on print media, libraries are beginning to be viewed as tools in national development.

A. Comparative Analysis

The literature of librarianship in Africa has increased significantly within the last decade and now includes a number of dissertations and other research reports as well as directories, surveys, and descriptive articles. The present study is the first attempt to use the techniques of comparative librarianship to analyze the overall pattern of library service that has emerged in the new states of West Africa. Four countries have been chosen for study: two former French territories, the Ivory Coast and Senegal, and two member states of the British Commonwealth, Ghana and Nigeria (Fig. 1). Because these new states continue to maintain close ties with the former colonial powers, library development since independence has been greatly influenced by French and British practices introduced during the formative period from 1945 to 1960. The four countries selected for study represent the two countries from each linguistic group with the greatest library development.

The purpose of this study is to investigate the historical evolution of libraries within each country; to establish similarities and differences among the four countries; and to offer a simultaneous comparison, focusing on the causal factors that have led to markedly different approaches to national library planning. Since the earliest libraries containing printed materials were established under European rule, they were shaped by a complex interplay of internal forces related to the sociocultural conditions in the colony and external forces deriving from the attitudes, policies, and economic involvement of the metropolitan power. The first part of the study describes the growth of libraries in the context of varying social determinants that have shaped the history of the four countries prior to indepen-

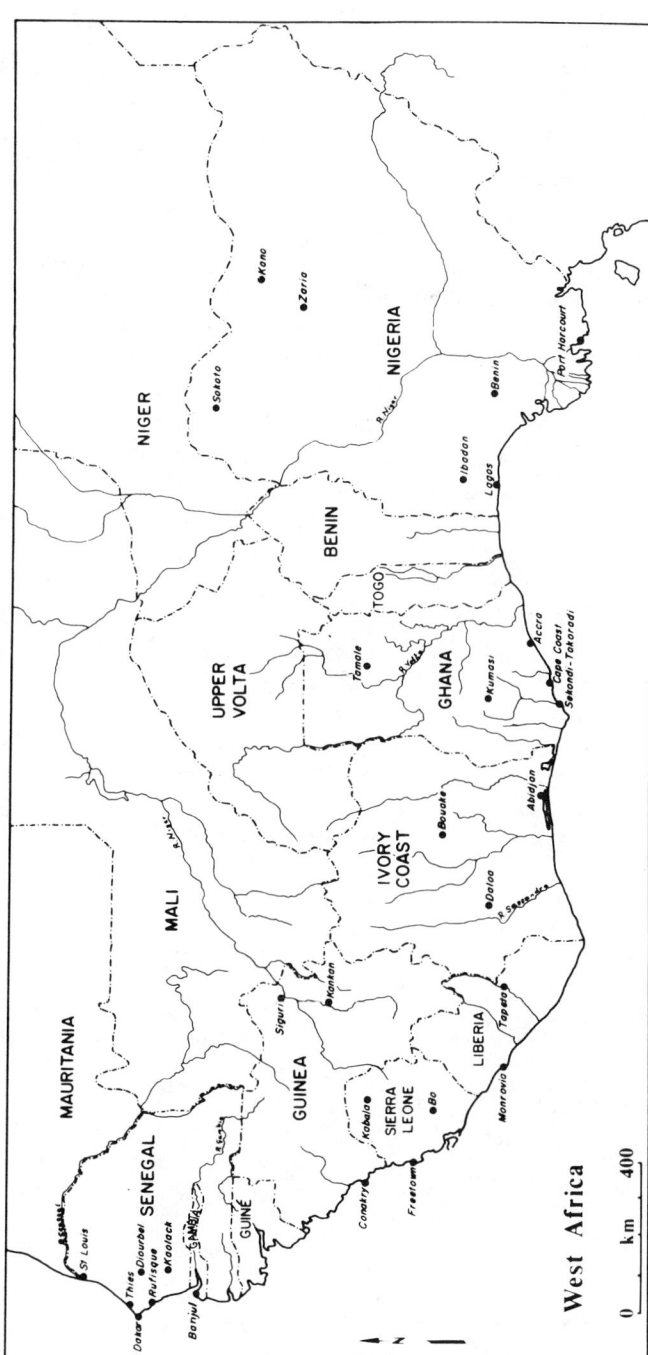

Fig. 1. Other cities mentioned in the text are Legon, a suburb of Accra, Ghana; Kaduna, located in north central Nigeria, 130 miles southwest of Kano; Yaba, 2.5 miles northwest of Lagos, Nigeria. Source: John Dunn (ed.), *West African States: Failure and Promise*. Cambridge: Cambridge University Press, 1978.

dence. For each country, consideration is given to its (a) economic and social evolution; (b) political institutions and ideologies; and (c) educational progress—including schooling at all levels from literacy training to postgraduate research. Two additional factors of direct importance to library development are also considered: the role of librarians and library promoters and the influence of international exchange and foreign aid.

Comparative analysis of these four countries reveals that each has selected somewhat different priorities and has established a legislative and social framework for library development that departs from that of the former mother country. Quantitative analysis of two African library directories compiled under UNESCO auspices in 1963 (Tables 1 and 2) and 1975 provides one means of evaluating the growth of different types of libraries since independence. However, statistics of this nature must be seen as indicative of the rate of library growth, not as an accurate representation of total library resources. It is only through an intensive review of primary and secondary literature from the region that library needs can be identified and the effectiveness of library service can be assessed.

B. Geographical and Cultural Setting

As indicated in Table 3, Ghana, Nigeria, the Ivory Coast, and Senegal differ considerably in size, population, ethnic diversity, economic development, and educational attainment. However, comparison of library systems within these countries reveals many similarities that have resulted from the

TABLE 1
Total Library Resources, 1963[a]

Country/population	Libraries	Staff Professional	Nonprofessional	Book stock (volumes)	Ratio of book stock in libraries to population
Ghana 6,726,815	29	37	179	717,000	1:11
Ivory Coast 3,340,000	20	2	13	33,200	1:98
Nigeria 55,510,054	35	64	295	588,200	1:105
Senegal 3,100,000	39	25	38	279,300	1:90
	123	128	525	1,617,700	

[a]Source: Dadzie, E. W. and Strickland, J. T. (1965) *Directory of Archives, Libraries and Schools of Librarianship.*

TABLE 2
Library Resources, 1963, by Type of Library[a]

Country	Academic & research libraries			Special libraries			Public libraries		
	Number	Volumes	Staff	Number	Volumes	Staff	Number	Volumes	Staff
Ghana	5	210,134	15/53	7	24,600	8/15	17	483,400	14/111
Ivory Coast	7	18,000	1/N.A.	9	5,200[b]	0/3	4	10,000	1/10
Nigeria	6	279,300	32/133	18	48,700	8/39	11	260,200	24/123
Senegal	9	203,200	18/32	20	24,200	3/2	10	51,900	4/4
Total	27	710,634	66/218	55			42		

[a]Source: Dadzie, E. W. and Strickland, J. T. (1965) *Directory of Archives, Libraries and Schools of Librarianship.*
[b]Figures not available for four libraries.

TABLE 3
Selected Characteristics of the Four Countries, 1980[a]

Country	Size (mi²)	Population	Primary school en-rollment (%)	Linguistic groups Est. total	Linguistic groups Major	Religion (%)		Urbanization (%) major cities		Principal commodities
Ghana	95,100	11,000,000	—	75	4	Traditional Islamic Christian None	38 13 42 7	Accra Kumasai Tamale	30 636,000 260,000 83,000	Cocoa Coconuts
Ivory Coast	124,000	7,613,000	50	65	5	Traditional Islamic Christian	65 23 12	Abidjan Bouaké Daloa	over 33 1,389,000 808,000 369,000	Coffee Cocoa
Nigeria	356,669	72,217,000	34	250	10	Traditional Islamic Christian	18 47 35	Lagos Ibadon Ogbomosho	23 1,060,000 847,000 432,000	Groundnuts Cocoa Crude petroleum
Senegal	75,955	5,381,000	40	N.A.	5	Traditional Islamic Christian	5 90 5	Dakar Thiès Kaolack	25 800,000 117,000 106,000	Groundnuts

[a]Source: *Africa South of the Sahara, 1980–81* (10th ed.). London: Europa Publications, 1980.

fact that certain social and economic conditions are common to the region. First, all four countries emerged from colonial rule with few nationals trained for political leadership, or for scientific, technical, or professional positions. Thus higher education, secondary education, and technical–vocational training became an immediate prerequisite to national development. At the same time, all four governments have made intensive efforts to increase primary school enrollment, and all have conducted literacy campaigns—but with limited success.

This emphasis on education is closely related to new economic priorities, such as the development of light industry, especially food processing and goods for local consumption. However, like most of tropical Africa, these countries are still closely tied to the colonial economic system which fostered the export of primary resources such as cocoa, coffee, palm oil, ground nuts, forest products, and minerals. Except for Nigeria—now the world's eighth largest producer of crude oil—West Africa's economy is predominantly agricultural. Both Senegal and Ghana suffer from their dependence on a monocrop export commodity. Although there is greater diversity of crops and forest products in Nigeria and the Ivory Coast, the projected 1990 per capita income for both countries is under $1000 (Zartman 1979, pp. 76–77).

Economic development in West Africa is circumscribed by climate and geography. There are two major climatic zones in the 900-mile expanse from the northern border of Senegal and Mauretania to the southeastern coast of Nigeria. Stretching from Senegal and Mali through the northern reaches of Ghana and Nigeria is the Sudanese zone—a flat, grassy, savannah land of sufficient rainfall, punctuated by intermittent clumps of baobab trees. Within West Africa, there is immense variation in rainfall, ranging from 10 inches annually in northern Senegal to 150 inches on the Ghanaian coast. In the southern portion of Nigeria, the Ivory Coast, and Ghana, tropical forests are dense, sunless, and humid, with few scattered villages in clearings.

Cultural diversity within this region is even more striking than the variation in climate. Among nearly 400 different linguistic groups (Table 3), there is an astounding variety of religious beliefs, customs, and social organization. In Ghana, the Ga peoples have remained fragmented in small townships with no chief office and no formal political hierarchy; the Ewe had chiefdoms but have not developed large-scale political units; the Akan peoples have maintained a complex hierarchical political structure with powerful royal lineages and an indigenous bureaucracy (Foster, 1965, pp. 27–29). Kingdoms were also common in the Senegambian region where each Wolof state had a strong paramount chief and a hierarchial social structure consisting of nobles, free peasants, castes of artisans, and slaves.

By 1350, the Wolof had united into a loose federation known as the Djolof Empire. Sudanese peoples also created stable, extensive states; the province of Bornu in northern Nigeria was ruled by one dynasty for over 1000 years. Other Islamic peoples like the Hausa were not united until the *jihads* (Holy wars) of the nineteenth century. However, the anthropologist George Murdock comments that the Hausa peoples "as a result of long experience in the trans-Saharan trade, have achieved a cultural unity comparable to that of the great nations of Europe in modern times. . . ." (1959, p. 137).

C. Pre-Colonial Era

West African peoples, from those living in the "stateless societies" of Ghana to the subjects of the vast Sudanese empires all placed great importance on oral traditions, "those testimonies of the past deliberately transmitted from mouth to mouth" (Vansina, 1960, p. 46).

A body of written literature, made up largely of religious commentaries and devotional poetry, was produced by Hausa and Fulani authors, but none of these Islamic societies developed beyond the protoliterate stage where writing was confined to a narrow elite. The restricted access to written works and the total absence of printing also inhibited the growth and dissemination of objective knowledge. The Ghanaian scholar S. I. Kotei comments that "the inability to communicate language in writing profoundly affects the technology of the intellect of a people" (1972, p. 2). Western society's ability to transmit ideas with speed and precision also encouraged an appreciation for exact sequences and measurement. This in turn accelerated the progress of the technology that gave European powers a great advantage in the conquest of Africa. By the turn of the century, French and British troops had contained—or subdued—most military resistance to colonial rule in West Africa. Resistance to the "moral conquest"[1] represented by Western education (with its print-oriented culture) was to persist well into the twentieth century.

1. PRELITERATE SOCIETY

Kotei notes that "there was a reluctance, characteristic of all preliterate societies, to accept a mode of communication which posed a threat to the accustomed habits of life and thought in the community" (1975, p. 176).

A strong preference for oral communication persists even in the urban

---

[1] *Une conquête morale* is the title of Georges Hardy's influential book on French education in Africa. The term was frequently used by French writers after its publication in 1920.

setting because of the value African peoples have placed on oral traditions in transmitting to the next generation their material culture, their customs and standards for social behavior, and their intellectual heritage or *Weltanschauung* (Goody and Watt, 1968, p. 28). Oral traditions thus provide the cohesive force which bind the people to one another and to their common past.

A few Europeans began to appreciate the diversity of oral traditions during the colonial period, and in 1933 the French administrator Henry Labouret published a typology of literary traditions, dividing them into four broad classes: myths, legends, epics, and stories (quoted in Cornevin, 1976, p. 92). Much later, Jan Vansina, the Belgian ethnohistorian, created a broader typology that consisted of (a) formulae (titles, slogans, didactic formulae, etc.); (b) poetry (historical, panegyric, religious, personal); (c) lists (place names, personal names—genealogies, king lists); (d) tales (general and local history, myths, stories and personal recollections); and (e) commentaries (legal, auxiliary, sporadic) [1965, p. 144].

Memorization of these different kinds of traditions was institutionalized, and certain individuals were rigorously trained and held responsible for the accurate recitation of specific genealogies, commentaries, or historical narratives. Thus, the organization of information among preliterate peoples corresponded to their social organization; while many proverbs, maxims, and stories were known to everyone, knowledge of other more complex or politically significant traditions was assigned to individuals by virtue of their rank or caste. Although such an arrangement allowed effective access to specific kinds of information, it had the disadvantage of being intellectually labor-intensive, leaving little opportunity for the development of abstract logic such as that involved in mathematics or philosophy.

Oral traditions may be subject to certain kinds of distortions, but their longevity is attested by the fact that many *griots* (a caste of praise singers) in the Senegambia region can recite genealogies that go back over 20 generations. However, once the chain of transmission is broken, it can never be repaired. There is more truth than poetry in the frequently quoted statement by Malian author Amadou Hampeté Ba: "Un vieillard qui meurt est une bibliothèque qui brûle." (An old man who dies is a library that burns.) (quoted in Cornevin 1976, p. 95). In recent times, the permanent loss of traditional wisdom and culture has been greatest among those groups where members of the younger generation migrated to the city and lost interest in conserving their ancestral heritage.

Indigenous alphabets were developed by three West African peoples—Vai, Nsibidi, and Bamoun—but their use was so limited and transient that "their study belongs strictly to palaeography" (Kotei, 1975, p. 175). Although there is no evidence of writing systems among other non-Islamic peoples, most Africans actually lived on the "margins of literacy" in societies that had an awareness of writing but in most cases included only a few literate individuals or groups (Goody, 1968a, pp. 4–5). By the late nineteenth century, most West Africans either had some contact with Europeans on the coast or with the Islamic theocracies to the northwest. Yet even prolonged association with literate societies did not stimulate the adoption of writing. Based on his anthropological field work in northern Ghana, Goody concluded that the Lo Dagaa "saw in the Muslims capacity to write a more effective means of supernatural communication" (Goody, 1968b, p. 201). Despite the magical powers attributed to written talismans, these people made no attempt to learn Arabic or to use Arabic characters to write their own language.

Kotei suggests that in West Africa, Islamic books were "regarded as the esoteric possession of a class which should be feared rather than emulated" (1975, p. 176). This attitude of distrust was later extended to books imported by Europeans. Thus, the use of alphabetic writing systems (Arabic or Roman) was initially perceived as an alien, impersonal mode of communication, not as a force for intellectual progress.

2. CONDITIONAL OR RESTRICTED LITERACY

Publishing in West Africa began with the advent of Islam in the eleventh century, and by the seventeenth century both foreign and locally produced manuscripts were available in centers of the trans-Saharan trade (Wilks, 1968, p. 170). There are early references to the existence of splendid private libraries in major seats of learning like Timbuktu (in modern Mali) and Sankore (in northern Nigeria). Learning also flourished in the Sudanese empire of Songhay during the sixteenth century, and one writer commented: "Amongst the possessions of the rich, good libraries and good horses would seem . . . to have been most valued" (Shaw, 1905, p. 207). A small class of literate Muslims continued to exist in the western Sudan, and certain Fulani religious leaders, like Uthman Dan Fodio (d. 1817), authored numerous works.

Since the early years of the twentieth century, Koranic schools and *medersas* (Muslim institutions for advanced study) have been frequently described by colonial administrators, anthropologists, and other Africanists. On the basis of field work among the Dyula of the western Sudan, Wilks concluded that a minority of those pupils who attended Koranic schools acquired a good command of Arabic, progressing to "the study of grammar, syntax and reading basic works; . . . many [others] . . . leave school able to read and write Arabic even if imperfectly" (1968, p. 166). At about the same time, based on research in Gonja towns in northern Ghana, Goody observed that the elementary class at Koranic schools in this area "was not taught to *read* but to recite simply using the letters as mnemonics for what was to come next." (1968b, p. 222). This kind of rote learning, sometimes involving the recitation of Arabic phrases not understood by the pupils, was observed by Paul Marty, a Colonial administrator who conducted numerous studies on Islam in French West Africa. (Marty, 1914, p. 51–58). While some Muslim people like the Fulani developed elites of highly literate theologians and scholars, certain sects such as the Mourides in eastern Senegal actually discouraged reading among their followers.

Although the degree to which literacy was diffused among the population varied greatly across western Sudan, scholars agree that few of these Islamic states had progressed beyond a protoliterate stage in which reading was purposely restricted to a selected elite. Goody further remarked a tendency to secrecy "that even gathers round the Qur'ān itself, increasing its magical efficacity as well as the power of its custodians" (1968a, p. 11). In Africa, as in medieval Europe, learning was linked with religion and magic; most writing was done in a foreign language, and literacy was confined to an oligarchy of nobles and clerics.

II. THE COLONIAL ERA: 1890–1945

A. From Exploration to Administration

The Portugese first explored the western coast of Africa in the fifteenth century, but nearly 400 years elapsed before European power in the region began to rival that of Islamic rulers. During the first half of the nineteenth century, the strength of Islam in the Sudan increased as Muslim reformers lead a series of Holy Wars (*jihads*) against "pagan" and nominally Islamic states. In 1857 when the French forces of General Louis Faideherb met the troops of the Muslim reformer, Al Haji Umar, the clash began between the two opposing imperialisms—African–Muslim and European–Christian.

Prior to the 1850s, European control seldom extended beyond a few coastal enclaves where merchants traded cloth and other manufactured products for ivory, palm oil, gold, and slaves. After the slave trade was legally abolished by Britain (1807) and France (1818), there was some attempt to promote tropical agriculture in the Senegal River valley. Since 1779, the French government had administered the island city of Saint Louis, along with a few other posts and factories, but before Faideherb's appointment, little attempt was made to extend French control to the interior.

The British government had even less involvement in Africa than France, and chartered companies were given a free hand in establishing relationships with local rulers. However, the chartered company's intervention in local politics culminated in 1861 when Britain finally decided to annex Lagos as its first Crown Colony in West Africa. Government involvement in the region continued, and in 1874, the southern provinces of the Gold Coast were incorporated as a colony. Although European military expansion had increased during the third quarter of the nineteenth century, by 1879, more than 90% of the continent was still ruled by Africans (Oliver and Atmore, 1967, p. 103). It was during the 1880s and 1890s that this situation was completely reversed and most of Africa came under European control.

The belated but rapid conquest of the continent was largely the result of new political rivalries in Europe. Both Belgium and Germany, which had entered the African arena as latecomers, insisted that new rules supercede the informal "spheres of influence" that other powers had maintained since the Napoleonic wars. At the Conference of Berlin in 1884, it was agreed that claims to the African coastline must be backed by "the establishment of an effective degree of authority" over the adjacent region (Oliver and Atmore, 1967, p. 111). The Berlin Conference thus marked the advent of a "scramble for Africa" by European powers who reshaped the political and economic boundaries of the continent.

The French government, which had been a reluctant participant in Faideherb's forays, soon became involved, from 1888 to 1893, in the conquest of western Sudan. At the same time, France sent forces to subdue resistance in the southern forest region, and by 1889, the Ivory Coast was declared a French protectorate. The British also consolidated their position in West Africa, and after the military occupation of the Ashanti Kingdom in 1896, all of the Gold Coast came under British "protection." Meanwhile, the government ended the charter of the Royal Niger Company and sent military expeditions into northern Nigeria. Local resistance continued for some time, but by 1902 the British were masters of the northern Hausa peoples as well as the Yoruba to the west of the Niger delta and the Ibo in the southeast. However, it was not until 1914 that the North and South were almalgamated to form a single colony known as Nigeria.

Between 1900 and World War I, the colonial boundaries of most modern African states were set, and the administrative machinery of European rule began to function. The highly centralized system of government that the French had created in Senegal was gradually extended to other territories brought under French control. In 1895, all of France's West African possessions were joined in a federation known as Afrique Occidentale Française (AOF). The small port city of Dakar on the Senegalese coast became the federal capital in 1902. During the rest of the colonial period, Senegal remained the most favored of the French colonies—both because of its longer association with France and because of the benefits brought by the presence of the capital. Administratively, however, Senegal was equal to the other members of the federation. These colonies were divided into a number of administrative *cercles,* each headed by a *commandant* who answered to a lieutenant governor, who in turn reported to the governor general in Dakar. The latter alone had the right to approve all major policy decisions.

In contrast to the French pattern of direct administration, the British established a system of government known as "indirect rule." This meant that the governance of their Colonies was "shared between the . . . Government . . . and the Emirate or tribe or other native group forming a Native Administration" with its own police, courts, and treasury (Crocker, 1936, p. 12). While the situation in the Gold Coast was described as "a mixture of direct and indirect rule with a steady bias towards the latter" (Hailey, 1938, p. 465), the colony emerged with a fairly strong central government. Nigeria, on the other hand, had a relatively weak federal government in Lagos that did not foster much interaction between the southern and the northern provinces. In both Nigeria and the Gold Coast, the practice of governing through traditional African leaders encouraged the maintenance of strong ethnic ties and stimulated regional rivalries.

While the political structure of the British and French colonies differed greatly, the economic policies of the two powers were much the same. In both Paris and London, the main concern was that the colonies should pay for themselves; thus, most public funds invested in African development came from loans raised by the respective colonial governments. The largest share of these monies went to railway and port construction, followed by road building, water, electricity supplies, and sanitation systems. Last came social services—such as health clinics, schools, and, in a few instances, libraries.

B. Research Needs and Library Development

In summarizing early West African library development, Kotei remarked that "at no time before the War did the Government take any important action in library establishment that was not initiated by . . . benevolent institutions . . . except for those [special libraries] that were instrumental in promoting the Colonial System" (Kotei, 1972, pp. 162–163). Although special and research libraries received some government funding, their limited and sporadic development reflected the low priority given to scientific inquiry by colonial policymakers.

1. BASIC AND APPLIED RESEARCH IN FRANCOPHONE AFRICA

The need for scientific books and periodicals was recognized quite early by French colonists. Although no specific requests for books date back to Michel Adanson's botanical research in Senegal (1745–1753), the fact that the young botanist was forced to devise his own classification system provides an early illustration of the problem of carrying out research in isolation from other scientists (Lacroix, 1938). Although there was an attempt to acquire scientific books for the Colonial library in Saint Louis during the 1820s, this collection suffered neglect after agricultural experimentation was phased out in 1829. By the late nineteenth century, a few scientific publications were being regularly received in the colony. Thus, Adanson's practice of collecting data that would later be reexamined and published in France remained the dominant pattern of scientific research in Senegal until the turn of the century.

After the creation of the AOF, researchers and technicians were brought to Africa to staff agencies for sanitation, agriculture, forestry, geology, and public health. By 1907, a number of these scientists joined with administrators and local doctors to form the Société de Géographie of the AOF. This society dissolved after two years, but the idea of a learned society that could serve as a coordinating agency for research remained alive. In 1915 Governor General François Clozel, a noted scholar and book lover, founded the Comité d'Etudes Historique et Scientifique (CEHS) of the AOF. This group was charged with coordinating government-sponsored research in the AOF, encouraging individual research, publishing scholarly papers, and issuing an annotated bibliography. Under Clozel's presidency, the executive committee of CEHS began to function as a library committee.

The CEHS library (originally the library of the Governor General) was then administered by the AOF archivist, Claude Faure. Faure had been appointed in 1913, at the initiative of Governor General Ponty, who wished to see local historical documents properly cared for. Because Faure was the only staff member with library training,[2] he was put in charge of the library as well as the archives. Faure also served as secretary of CEHS and worked with the executive committee in developing a scientific collection.

Until CEHS disbanded in 1937, its officers recommended new books and periodicals for purchase and authorized exchanges with other learned societies in France and its colonies. However, the library grew slowly, reflecting the amateur, part-time nature of CEHS, whose members often relied on

[2] Faure was a graduate of the École des Chartes, the prestigious French archival training school. There was no other formal library training available in France at this time and many of the most prominent French librarians were *chartistes*.

the small specialized collections in their offices or pursued part of their research during home leave in France. Thus, after 20 years under the committee's direction, the library of the Government General contained just over 3000 books and was lacking many relevant monographs.

Meanwhile, CEHS made two attempts to inventory the small special libraries in the various agencies of the government general. Only a few inventories were received by the committee in 1923, but the idea of creating a union list was revived by CEHS secretary Albert Charton in 1932. At that time, 10 library inventories were compiled. Together, all 10 collections totaled no more than 3,000 books, and there was very little duplication between them ("Catalogues," 1932). Many of these special libraries continued to exist, but a survey conducted two decades later showed that none contained over 3000 volumes (Répertoire, 1954).

The turning point for library development in the AOF came with the foundation of the Institut Français d'Afrique Noire (IFAN)—the first multidisciplinary research institute in tropical Africa. Governor General Brévié, founder of IFAN, saw the institute as continuing the coordinating function of CEHS while developing its own research program to be carried out by a full-time staff of scientists and research assistants. Brévié, who drafted IFAN's statutes, also made sure the institute was explicitly charged with setting up museums, archives, libraries, and scientific collections that would supply "la documentation nécessaire à l'étude . . . des questions intéressant l'Afrique Occidentale Française (Arrêté, 1936).

Theodore Monod, an energetic and versatile young scholar, was named director of IFAN in 1938. When he arrived in Dakar, Monod made the establishment of a good collection of scientific publications one of his first priorities. He soon convinced Governor General de Coppet greatly to increase funding for the library. Thus, the book budget that had been only 10,000 francs in the early 1930s was raised to 194,000 francs in 1938 to allow for binding and for the purchase of out-of-print works as well as new acquisitions. From 1939 through the war years, the annual allocation was set at 100,000 francs. Although Monod complained from time to time that he lacked enough funds to buy all the works needed for the institute, this was nonetheless a substantial enough sum to allow the IFAN library to triple the size of its collection in one decade, from 7,000 volumes in 1939 to 21,000 in 1949 (Institut Français d'Afrique Noire, 1949).

Although Monod supplied direction and continuity to the library, the archivist of the governor general was given the responsibility for the library's technical services and administration. The first archivist to serve as IFAN librarian was André Villard, who, like Faure, had studied at the Ecole des Chartes in Paris. It was under Villard's direction that the IFAN library became a bona fide research collection, organized and maintained according to contemporary French library practices. The provision for an adequate annual budget, the continuous and systematic acquisition of scientific works, the effective cataloging of books, and the indexing of periodicals—all were characteristics of a library capable of meeting the research needs at the new institute.

2. SCIENCE AND RESEARCH LIBRARIES IN GHANA AND NIGERIA

There was no equivalent to IFAN in British West Africa, but in many other ways, the development of libraries for scientific research followed a similar pattern. As in the AOF, special libraries were set up in government agencies around the turn of the century. One of the earliest government libraries in Nigeria was a law library established in Lagos in 1900 (Aguolu, 1977b, p. 138). There were also small legal collections in the Gold Coast, and in the 1930s a research library containing works on customary law and English common law was established at the Supreme Court. This collection was maintained by a judicial secretary.

In addition to these collections, which grew out of an administrative need for legal documents, there were special libraries that reflected the colonial government's interest in applied research in fields like tropical medicine. However, the development of such collections often lagged behind research needs. The director of the newly established Medical Research Institute at Yaba (near Lagos) commented in 1910: "In the West African Colonies there is as yet no collection of scientific books or journals available for consultation on any subject. An adequate library is, therefore, an absolute necessity here" (quoted by Aguolu, 1977b, p. 139). The Gold Coast fared somewhat better, and in 1908 the *Annual Report* of the Accra Laboratory stated that there were "good books which can be consulted" (Tettey, 1960, p. 245). However, it was not until 1914 that a pathologist in charge of this laboratory began to organize the library and systematically build up its collection. By World War I, a second Nigerian medical library was established at the Medical Headquarters in Lagos. Some progress occurred in the 1920s, and there was a continuing effort to build good journal collections in Accra and Yaba. The latter library also benefited from American aid from 1929 to 1933 when the Yellow Fever Commission of the International Health Division of the Rockefeller Foundation contributed a considerable number of valuable reports, pamphlets, and offprints (Cannon, 1954, p. 184–185).

Most of the other early libraries in the Gold Coast and Nigeria were created in response to research interest in minerals or tropical agriculture. One of the first was the library of the British Cotton Growers Association

Research Station established in 1905. Between the two wars, other special libraries were set up in agencies such as the Nigerian Geological Survey at Kaduna (1919); the National Department of Veterinary Research at Vom, Nigeria (1924); the Samaru Research Station in northern Nigeria (1925); the Gold Coast Agriculture Department (1926); and the Gold Coast Geological Department (1925) (Aguolu, 1977a; Kotei, 1972). On the eve of the World War II, two important regional institutes were also created. The first of these was the Cocoa Research Institute set up in 1938 to study methods of improving production and combating swollen shoot disease. Its library soon became the best specialized library in the Gold Coast and one of the best collections on cocoa in the world (Kotei, 1972, p. 172). Meanwhile, in Nigeria the West African Institute for Oil–Palm Research was set up at Benin in 1939. It too acquired a highly specialized library collection.

The belated establishment of such research institutes and the limited development of special libraries was a result of the fact that the European powers "devoted a minimal amount to research into and improvement of the agriculture of West Africa, even though this was the basis of these economies" (Crowder, 1968, p. 275). Furthermore, research that was done often had limited application because results were not disseminated beyond the colony. In a lengthy report, in 1938, E. B. Worthington sharply criticized the "waste of research," observing that the data gathered by scientists were often published in annual departmental reports, bulletins, pamphlets, and occasional papers—publications not specifically designed to give information to other researchers and frequently not available to the scientific community.

Worthington also was concerned about the inaccessibility of unpublished data gathered by medical, agricultural, and administrative officers. He remarked: "Some officers have collected notes of great scientific value about the people, their customs, food, diseases, etc. The bulk of these notes are kept in the files of district offices where they are not easily unearthed and may never be remembered [when needed] at a later date" (1938, p. 22). This situation obtained in British colonies, which had no archival program until after World War II. However, in the Gold Coast, J. T. Furley (Secretary of State for Native Affairs from 1917 to 1923) began to build a collection of documents in his office. This was not a central depository, as in Dakar, but Furley put a great deal of energy into the project and acquired photostats of certain materials from European archives at his own expense (Kotei, 1972, p. 176). Furley also built up a small book collection, but neither the Gold Coast or Nigeria had an Africanist collection that could rival the IFAN library in Dakar.

Meanwhile, those researchers who wished to place their work in a broader context were forced to consult European libraries during home leave.

Worthington noted that the Royal Botanical Gardens at Kew served as headquarters for Empire botanical investigations, the Imperial Forestry Institute at Oxford had a staff of experts on African forests, and research in tropical medicine was carried out by the London School of Hygiene and Tropical Medicine and the Liverpool School of Tropical Medicine (1938, pp. 145, 179, 467–68). Libraries in these institutions contained more materials relevant to African research than any collection in Nigeria or the Gold Coast. The pattern of turning to European establishments for research training and documentation persisted in the postwar period, leading Kotei to comment (1972) "The cumulative effect of these practices has been that today there are richer collections of both published and unpublished studies [relating to Africa] in British, American and European libraries than in Ghana—except for cocoa" (p. 173).

The practice of gathering raw data from Africa but refining and publishing it elsewhere was a part of process some African scholars have termed "academic colonialism" (Bengolea and Akiwowo, 1974). This pattern of scientific research retarded library development, and the lack of local library resources, in turn, inhibited the progress researchers could make while resident in Africa. France made some attempt to break this cycle with the establishment of CEHS in 1915, and later, with the creation of IFAN, which became involved with effective library development and scholarly publishing. However, before World War II, France had a smaller scientific staff in the AOF than Britain had in her West African Colonies (Worthington, 1938). Thus, scientists from both countries would have agreed with Worthington's assessment that "a development based on a real understanding of Africa's potentialities has hardly yet began, and will be impossible until the necessity of scientific research is recognized" (1938, p. 24).

C. European Education and General Libraries in Africa

Like research, most educational efforts supported by the colonial governments had a highly pragmatic orientation. Almost no public funding was available for the education of Africans until the turn of the century when both the British and French found themselves in possession of vast West African territories deemed unsuitable for large-scale European settlement. This situation forced both countries to confront the problem of preparing Africans to serve as interpreters, teachers, and clerks. While the educational policy of the two European powers was aimed at producing such "African auxiliaries," their approach differed in both philosophy and practice. In the AOF a highly centralized school system—patterned after that in France—

was established; the majority of schools was directly supported by the state, and all instruction was given in French. British educational policy in Africa likewise reflected the evolution of schools in Great Britain, where both religious movements and self-education were important. Remi Clignet further comments that British educational institutions had gradually come "under the loose control of local government rather than under the strict tutelage of central authority; this model was exported to Africa, [where] the spread of education was for a long time exclusively dependent upon private initiative" (Clignet, 1970, p. 430).

Because of this laissez-faire attitude, educational initiative in British Africa came mainly from missionaries, who in turn had an impact on library development in the region. The French, on the other hand, discouraged missionary efforts in the AOF (where Muslims dominated the population); thus, those "public libraries" that developed in French West Africa were supported either by the government or by private clubs.

1. THE CRUSADE FOR POPULAR LIBRARIES IN THE AOF

The first *bibliothèque publique* in Saint Louis antedated the first French school by more than a decade. An 1803 inventory of the library kept in the courthouse of Saint Louis revealed a collection of 1351 volumes, including works on science, philosophy, religion, and literature, as well as reference books and multivolume collections of authors such as Molière, Racine, Montaigne, Diderot, and Voltaire. A small municipal library continued to exist in Saint Louis during most of the nineteenth century; there is no evidence that its use was restricted to Europeans (Maack, 1981b, pp. 12–16). However, very few Africans had any access to Western education at this time, even though the first French school had been set up in Senegal in 1816.

Significant expansion of schooling came in 1903 when an Inspectorate of Education was set up in the AOF. The new federal school system consisted of four levels: a primary level—as broadly available as possible—but limited to training in the French language, hygiene, and vocational skills; a second level for lower government employees and clerks; a third level for higher-status assistants; and finally, the equivalent of metropolitan education for a selected elite. This system reflected France's new educational policy, expressed in the phrase "instruire les masses et dégager l'élite," i.e. "instruct the masses and disengage the elite" (by assimilating them into French culture). Because the West African empire had expanded to include peoples from hundreds of different ethnic groups, the republican ideal of assimilating all French subjects was replaced with a more pragmatic alternative—the selective assimilation of a narrow elite.

Due to the meager financing for education, this elite developed slowly. Thus, surveys of "public" libraries done in 1919 and 1928 revealed that colonial administrators were most concerned with the reading needs of Europeans. They therefore regarded the meager municipal collections and club libraries as sufficient and offered no suggestions for their improvement.

Small libraries also existed in the *cercles,* and in 1931 Governor General Jules Brévié issued a circular encouraging the lieutenant governors of each colony to foster the development of such collections (Brévié, 1931, p. 454–455). Brévié, a career officer, was quite familiar with life in distant French outposts where such tiny libraries provided the only link with the intellectual life of Europe. Most of Brévié's remarks centered on the reading needs of French personnel, but he did comment that the library should be open to all residents of the *cercle* and should even include children's books. Despite Brévié's intention that African reading needs be considered, the lieutenant governors of Senegal and the Ivory Coast both attributed the absence of libraries in certain *cercles* to the small number of Europeans resident there (Maack, 1981a, p. 214). It was not until the late 1930s that the educational service in the Ivory Coast and Senegal first attempted to set up circulating libraries for African readers. At the same time, there were also a few experiments with library service by mail, in which books were sent free of charge to European and African instructors or administrators working in isolated posts. Some of these circulating libraries were quite successful, and by 1939 the inspector of education for the AOF proposed the development of a popular lending library in each higher primary school (Maack, 1981b, p. 47).

The strongest champion of public library development at this time was André Villard. Shortly after his appointment as AOF archivist in 1937, Villard toured the municipal library in Saint Louis. By the late 1930s, Saint Louis contained a few African families who had been literate in French for several generations, in addition to a Westernized *metisse* community (of mixed African and European descent) and a population of over 1000 Europeans. Saint Louisiens—who had also enjoyed some access to a municipal or colonial library since the nineteenth century—were more oriented toward reading than other residents of French African cities. However, on his first visit to the library, Villard found its quarters in disrepair and its budget inadequate to meet the needs of the community (Villard, 1937b). He reported this to the Governor of Senegal, who agreed to increase the library budget dramatically in 1938. Villard then arranged for the Senegalese librarian, Fara Cissé, to come to Dakar for rudimentary library training. Throughout his tenure as archivist, Villard visited the library in Saint Louis regularly and offered Cissé advice for its improvement. During the late

1930s and early 1940s, Cissé reported on the growing popularity of this library, which served 30–50 readers per day and circulated an average of 10,000 books annually (Cissé, 1941).

Villard soon became convinced that cities other than Saint Louis could benefit from library service, and in 1937 he began a campaign to establish popular libraries for young African wage earners living in other parts of the AOF. The extraordinary success of a Dakar bookstore "selling cheap editions of the best and the worst books" seemed ample proof of an avid desire to read among these Westernized Africans (Villard, 1937a). However, Villard feared that for many of the literate clerks and errand boys, the French primary school had provided a superficial and sometimes distorted understanding of Western culture. Therefore, he strongly advocated that popular libraries provide good literature that would shape the taste of these readers, rather than cater to their whims. While his concept of the library was certainly paternalistic, it was also rooted in the belief that the library should be a continuation of the school.

Although Villard foresaw numerous problems, he proceeded to draw up a detailed program for the establishment of popular libraries throughout the AOF (Villard, 1937a). Villard's proposal was ambitious and modest at the same time. It was modest in that he recommended setting up such libraries at a minimal cost by employing local teachers as "librarians", by using already-existing buildings, and by offering convenient but limited hours. However, the proposal was quite ambitious in the sense that it advocated the establishment of libraries throughout French West Africa at a time when very little money was allotted for cultural or educational insitutions in a region in which less than 5% of the total population was literate in French.

Despite the cost involved, Villard's plan and his innovative ideas about the cultural role of popular libraries were well received by the officials in the AOF, where a new vision of a Franco-African culture had recently emerged. One of the chief proponents of this new doctrine was Brévié who wrote in 1935, "however pressing may be the need for economic change . . . our [first] mission in Africa is to bring about a cultural renaissance, a piece of creative work in human material, an association of two races" (quoted in Mumford and Orde-Brown, 1937, p. 96). A generation of administrators imbued with such ideals was not insensitive to the role of books in extending French culture; thus, Villard's appeal that good popular libraries might "prepare for the future by shaping the conscience of an entire country" did not fall on deaf ears. The intellectual and social climate was favorable for his proposed undertaking, but the timing could not have been worse. In 1939, when Villard's library campaign seemed on the verge of success, France entered World War II and cultural programs in the colonies were abruptly tabled.

2. PUBLIC LIBRARY INITIATIVES IN THE GOLD COAST AND NIGERIA

When the war broke out, neither the British nor the French colonies in West Africa had any public library service aside from what was provided by a few municipal, school, or club libraries. Library development in the Gold Coast prior to 1946 was almost entirely due to private initiative. Missionary education had had a significant impact on the coastal regions by the mid-nineteenth century, and a small group of wealthy Christian Africans was able to study in England. Described as "black Victorians," this select group adopted Western dress and culture and joined the literary society set up by Father J. P. Brown in 1859 (Kotei, 1972, p. 184). Brown also established the Cape Coast Book Club and soon similar societies were founded in other towns, notably Accra, Sekondi, and Elmina. Kotei comments that "the clubs introduced to the Gold Coast the concept of the modern public library, but their stocks did not form the nucleus of our public library system because the cultural distance between their founders and the rest of the population was too large" (1972, p. 105). Indeed, contemporary critics of these clubs attributed their failure to their leaders' "supercilious attitudes, frivolity [and] ostentatious behavior". As these early book clubs faltered and disappeared, members of the elite continued to build libraries which they sometimes opened to friends.

By the 1870s, more book clubs sprang up, but these were less exclusive. One, the Accra Young Men's Free and Mutual Improvement Society, was sponsored by the Methodist mission. While the membership in such groups was transitory, the involvement of the missions was not, since book clubs were a logical byproduct of mission schools and mission publishing programs.

Protestant missions were established in the Gold Coast in the 1820s, and by the 1840s all the major English denominations were represented. Four of these groups later set up presses (the Scottish Press, the English Church Mission Press, the Methodist Book Depot, and the Catholic Mission Press) that produced catechisms, evangelical works, and a number of books in local vernaculars (Brown, 1975, pp. 114–115). Of even greater significance was the growth of mission schools. By 1881, there were 137 schools in the Gold Coast run by missions, but only two schools that were run by the government (Evans, 1956, p. 9). The first Director of Education for the colony was appointed in 1890, and after 1900 the government began to open schools in areas unreached by the missions. Government expenditure on education increased during the interwar years, but most of these funds went to subsidize mission schools that met official inspection standards.

Although the missions had limited resources, they showed a continuing interest in promoting books and libraries. One of the more successful efforts was the foundation of the West African Literature Society by the Gold Coast Methodist Mission. This society issued locally published works that focused on regional topics and were written by West Africans. Some of the missions also had circulating libraries, and in 1929 such collections were able to receive donations of books from the International Council for Christian Literature for Africa (ICCLA). The Council was also instrumental in persuading the Carnegie Corporation of New York to aid West African Libraries. ICCLA secretary Margaret Wrong compiled a list of basic books for African mission libraries and later was requested to prepare a survey of libraries in British West Africa for the Carnegie Corporation in 1939.

Meanwhile, a local philanthropist, Rev. John Aglionby, Lord Bishop of Accra, turned his attention to public libraries. Aglionby was a dynamic churchman who was responsible for the creation of over 300 African churches and numerous village schools in the Gold Coast. His concern for libraries stemmed from motives of "altruism and enlightened religious interest overlaid with strong educational purpose" (Kotei, 1972, p. 147). In 1928, Aglionby announced his intention to start a lending library in Accra and requested donations of suitable books on religion, history, travel, and literature as well as biographies, boys' books, and good fiction. Aglionby received eight crates of books and set up a library of 6000 volumes open to anyone (Evans, 1964, p. 7). The collection was originally housed at the Bishop's Boys' School, but in 1933 Aglionby addressed the government with a request that a library building be provided by the colony.

As the discussions of a building dragged on, Aglionby opened a small lending library in his home, where he offered parishioners free access to his own books (Evans, 1956, p. 10). This experience further convinced him that the growing demand for books could be met only by the establishment of a genuine public library with government support. Therefore, in 1935 he wrote to the Governor General, offering £1000 toward the creation of a public library and suggesting that other donations be solicited. After some discussion, the government accepted Aglionby's offer and agreed that a library wing be added to the King George V Memorial Hall which was then under construction. Shortly after the building was completed, a severe earthquake struck Accra, badly damaging the colonial secretariat. The library wing of the new building was then taken over by the government offices, and no further attempt was made to create a public library until the end of World War II. In commenting on this impasse, Evans remarked that the catastrophe may have been "fortunate . . . as there was no trained librarian, and to attempt to organize a library service without trained personnel would have been a big mistake" (Evans, 1956, p. 10).

Nigeria, likewise, had no trained librarian prior to World War II, and the limited library development that occurred there was also due to philanthropy and the efforts of the missions. Because Nigeria's economy was less developed than that of the Gold Coast, private initiative in education assumed even greater importance. Until 1898, all education in Nigeria was under the direct control of missionaries, and as late as 1942, 97% of all students were enrolled in mission schools (Coleman, 1958, p. 113). The Nigerian government did inspect and subsidize qualified mission schools; however, at no time prior to World War II did the colony allot more than 4.3% of its total budget to education. This policy created a great disparity between the Southern Province where mission activity was vigorous and the Muslim North where Christian missionaries were almost totally excluded. Thus in 1937 there were over 220,000 pupils in Southern primary and secondary schools but only 20,000 enrolled in the populous Northern Provinces (Coleman, 1958, p. 134). It is little wonder that Margaret Wrong recommended separate library policies for North and South Nigeria in her 1939 report to the Carnegie Corporation (Wrong, 1939).

At the time of Wrong's survey, Nigeria was the only West African colony to have received Carnegie funds. The first grant of $6000 "for library development" was given in 1932 after the Carnegie Corporation had been approached by Sir Allan Burns, then Deputy Chief Secretary to the Nigerian Government. Prior to this, Burns had "tried in vain to persuade the governor that government funds could well be spent on a public library for Lagos" (quoted in Aguolu, 1977a, p. 478). Once the Carnegie grant was received, Burns and an ad hoc library committee decided to set up a subscription library in Lagos. This library had little impact on the literate African community because of high subscription fees; in 1939 its membership listed 145 Europeans and 11 Africans (Wrong, 1939, p. 1). Although the use of the grant for this kind of library had probably not been anticipated by the Carnegie Corporation, it nonetheless remained on the library scene in Nigeria "assisting with surveys, subsidizing projects [and] financing investigations" (Harris, 1970, p. 30). However, the real impact of Carnegie assistance did not come until after World War II.

Meanwhile, a few wealthy Nigerians began to build book collections which they opened to friends. One of these individuals, Tom Jones, collected numerous books and government documents that he presented to the government to be used as a reference library. Some time between 1910 and 1920, this collection was turned into an unsuccessful subscription library tucked away in a dilapidated building (Aguolu, 1977a, p. 141). The most remarkable Nigerian book collector was Henry Carr who became the first African Commissioner of Lagos Colony in 1920. When he died in 1945, he left behind "a collection of 18,000 containing practically all standard works in the humanities and arts" (Flood, 1951, p. 31). Described as the largest personal library ever assembled by a West African, this library was opened to Carr's friends during his lifetime.

In addition to private and subscription libraries, there were small "libraries" in Nigerian mission stations and schools. However, such collections sometimes consisted of no more than a copy of the Holy Bible, five pamphlets entitled *The Adventures of Tarzan,* and a popular novel called *The Sorrows of Satan* (Omolewa, 1974, p. 30). A few libraries also were sponsored by the Department of Education. However, an examination of the records of such libraries in Lagos, Kaduna, and Enugu revealed that Europeans formed the majority of the readership (Omolewa, 1974, p. 33).

D. Libraries and Librarianship in the Colonial Context

During the first 50 years of colonial rule in West Africa, the framework was established for the subsequent economic, social, and political evolution of the region. In French West Africa, a highly centralized form of administration carried over to education, research, and library development. Early efforts were made to coordinate research, to prepare union lists of special libraries, and to plan a system of popular libraries for the entire federation. In addition, the AOF archivist—as the only trained professional working in the region—was expected to tour member colonies to give advice on library and archival matters.

Because the archivist could seldom visit the archives in each capital, little progress was made if the lieutenant governors did not employ competent, full-time personnel. André Villard felt that the situation in these territorial archives could not be stabilized unless a group of young African archivists were trained in Dakar and sent to each colony. With the enthusiastic support of Governor General de Coppet, Villard set up a training program for secondary school graduates in 1937. This program was carefully tailored to the needs of the African colonies where the archivist would also be in charge of the administrative library and, perhaps, would be responsible for organizing a local public library as well. Since there were few specialists to care for ethnographic objects, Villard added a session on museology to his training program. In addition to attending lectures, students did practice work in classification, inventory, and book acquisition. The first four trainees served in Dakar from November 1937 to November 1938 during a period when the AOF archives were being reorganized in their new quarters. These clerk–archivists were then assigned to posts in Guinea, the Ivory Coast, Niger, and Togo.

Villard was not able to continue the training program during the war, but he established a precedent that was followed by each of his successors. As a result of Villard's work, archival management and library administration in the modern sense were established in French West Africa, but only in the federal archives, the IFAN library, and a few smaller collections administered by African librarian–archivists trained in Dakar. It was not until the postwar years that other collections in the region began to be systematically organized and developed.

The first full-time professional librarian was appointed in the Gold Coast in 1945 and in Nigeria in 1948. Prior to this time, a British librarian, Ethel Fegan, was commissioned by the Carnegie Corporation to report on library needs in British West Africa. She arrived at the Gold Coast in 1942 where her duties included visiting colleges and other educational institutions and providing introductory training for African library assistants. She also reorganized the Achimota College Library which had a number of general readers as well as students and teachers.

After a year in West Africa, Fegan presented a report to the Carnegie Corporation and the Colonial Office, emphasizing the need for trained librarians and recommending that a temporary training school be set up (Evans, 1964, p. 136). The Colonial Office approved the recommendation for a library school and in 1944 Fegan and Kate Ferguson arrived in Achimota to organize a 9-month course for librarians from the British West African Colonies (Sierre Leone, Nigeria, and the Gold Coast). The program was financed jointly by the three colonial governments, the Carnegie Corporation, and the British Council.[3] Twelve students—six from the Gold Coast, four from Nigeria and two from Sierre Leone—attended lectures on librarianship, audited general lectures in the college, and did practical work in the Achimota School Library (Pitcher, 1970, p. 15). At the end of the course in June 1945, the students sat for the entrance examination of the British Library Association.

Fegan had originally recommended that library training be given for 3 years, but the Gold Coast Library Advisory Committee decided to terminate the school after a single session. The committee justified the decision on the basis that "the prospect of the establishment of further libraries in which librarians may be employed are at the present time, remote" (quoted in Obi, 1974, p. 409). A decade and a half passed before a permanent library school was set up in Ibadan, Nigeria; in the interim, the remaining Carnegie funds were used to send a few West Africans to England for library training.

In library education, as in general education and public library develop-

---

[3]The British Council founded in 1934, is a chartered voluntary organization that receives grants-in-aid from the Foreign Office.

ment, the British colonial governments did not take action until there was some initiative by missions or private philanthropy. Libraries in Nigeria and the Gold Coast had benefited only modestly from philanthropy by the end of World War II. When the Anglo-American philanthropic tradition was introduced in British West Africa, there was no comparable tradition in the AOF where the stimulus for the creation or improvement of libraries was usually chaneled through the government. This practice followed the pattern of library development in France, where the central government played an important role, while private donations were described as "sporadic and generally modest" (Comte, 1977, p. 87).

By 1945, the limited philanthropy received by the Gold Coast and Nigeria had not resulted in much better public library service than that available in French West Africa. In fact, it may be argued that the best public library in the region was the collection Villard had reorganized in Saint Louis, Senegal. At the same time, Senegal, which was the site of IFAN and a number of specialized research agencies including IFAN, also had more scholarly books than the other colonies. The Gold Coast, with several important special libraries and a collection of over 11,000 volumes at Achimota College, would have ranked well ahead of Nigeria or the Ivory Coast in library service.

III. DECOLONIZATION: 1945–1960

A. Africa in the Postwar Period

The slow, halting pace of change in West Africa gained sudden and irreversible momentum after World War II, causing the decade and a half before independence to be "by far the most active period in the history of colonial rule" (Oliver and Atmore, 1967, p. 213). These years were equally marked by a strong undercurrent of nationalism and decolonization, which resulted in new attitudes, policies, and economic priorities.

The most visible and dramatic change came in the economic sphere. First, the postwar boom in raw material prices helped to create a surplus in government funds that enabled colonial authorities to embark on ambitious development schemes. Secondly, both Britain and France abandoned the idea that the colonies could experience vigorous development without metropolitan aid. The 1945 Colonial Development and Welfare Act enabled the British government to spend on colonial projects sums that were astronomical by prewar standards. For example, this act provided 23 million of the 55 million allotted for Nigeria's first 10-year development plan

(1946–1955) (Crowder, 1968, p. 503). Meanwhile, French West Africa benefited from a similar fund known by its acronym "FIDES." Through this program, France provided official aid on a scale much larger than Britain; for the period from 1946 to 1955, over £277 million in FIDES funds went to subsidize the development plans of the AOF territories (Oliver and Atmore, 1967, p. 215).

The new economic policies of the colonial powers were in part due to the fact that these governments maintained their wartime levels of taxation and thus had vastly increased revenues to invest on social benefits at home and abroad. Development plans in both Britain and France placed great emphasis on education, professional training, and research. This meant that the colonies were soon able to draw technical assistance from a larger pool of highly trained European personnel; thus, the European population in West Africa (working in both the public and private sector) grew significantly after the war.

Increased European aid and technical assistance was also a response to criticism of colonial exploitation and international pressure for self-government. In signing the Atlantic Charter in 1941, Britain had officially recognized "the right of all people to choose the form of government under which they live." This commitment, along with promises made by Britain when recruiting Africans to the war effort, made it imperative that the British prepare the way for African independence.

Although there was virtually no fighting in West Africa, the AOF Colonies also contributed significantly to the Allied effort after breaking away from the Vichy regime in 1942. Two years later, DeGaulle himself declared that it was in the colonies that Free France had "found her refuge and the starting point for her liberation. . . ." As a result, he felt there would be "henceforth a permanent bond between the Mother Country and the empire" (quoted in Crowder, 1968, p. 499). The Gaullist emphasis on the interdependence of France and her overseas territories clearly emerged at the conference of colonial governors held in Brazzaville in 1944. The participants in this conference strongly disapproved of independence but they advocated French aid for social and economic development, adopted the long-range goal of universal primary education, and established guidelines for greater self-government within the French empire.

As both Britain and France offered more political opportunities to Africans, a new group of nationalist leaders came to power. These men included Nnamdi Azikiwe of Nigeria, Kwame Nkrumah of the Gold Coast, Léopold Senghor of Senegal and Félix Houphouët-Boigny of the Ivory Coast. Although all four men proved very successful in reaching the newly enfranchized, largely illiterate masses, their rise to power was also based on their education and their ability to meet Colonial officials as equals. Both

Nkrumah and Azikiwe had studied in British and American universities, while Senghor was the first African to have received an *aggrégation*[4] in France. Houphouët-Boigny, who was educated in Africa, had served in the French assembly before becoming president of the Ivory Coast. All four leaders were convinced of the value of education, and advocated the expansion of schooling at all levels, including the creation of African universities.

B. Higher Education and Academic Libraries

1. BRITISH WEST AFRICA

At the end of World War II, 259 West Africans were enrolled in British universities and there were no degree-granting institutions in either Nigeria or the Gold Coast (Kotei, 1972, p. 392). In 1924, a postsecondary program had been set up at Achimota College, in the Gold Coast, "with the goal of preparing the way for higher education" (Ashby, 1966, p. 188), but a report on the status of the Achimota program in 1938 concluded that there were too few qualified recruits from the secondary schools and too few suitable posts for graduates to justify upgrading the school to university status (Ashby, 1966, p. 202). A similar situation existed in Nigeria where Yaba Medical School (founded in 1930) and later Yaba Higher College (founded in 1934) existed without degree programs. Courses in agriculture, medicine, surveying, veterinary science, education, and forestry were offered at Yaba, but students received certificates or diplomas that had no recognition outside Nigeria.

Because of dissatisfaction with these programs, which were generally considered to be second-rate, most Nigerian and Ghanaian leaders welcomed the 1945 report of the Asquith Commission on Higher Education in the Colonies that recommended the creation of university colleges in the colonies. These colleges were to be administered by the University of London, which was to devise their curricula and award London degrees to their students. The Asquith Commission also emphasized the university's research mission and "the paramount importance of building up a university library [in the colonies] to rank with university libraries elsewhere" (quoted in Ekpe, 1979, p. 12). As a result of the priority given to libraries, the Inter-University Council, created by the Asquith Commission, included a library advisor (funded by the Carnegie Corporation) whose role was to aid with all aspects of library planning and collection development.

---

[4]A competitive state examination in France, taken after the completion of the second university degree.

Only a few African educators objected to the Asquith principle of creating colleges tied to British standards (with emphasis on liberal arts and research), but the report of the Elliot Commission on Higher Education in West Africa proved more controversial. In 1946, the Labor Government chose to ignore the Commission's majority report calling for the creation of three university colleges to be located in the Gold Coast, Nigeria, and Sierra Leone. However, the government's intention to set up only one college in Ibadan, Nigeria, met with strong nationalistic objections in the Gold Coast. Finally, Britain conceded and established a second university college in Legon. Thus, in 1948, both Nigerians and Ghanaians received their first opportunity to earn university degrees without going abroad.

As Ashby commented later, "the African wanted a replica of the British university at its best; the expatriate staff had no other model to offer" (1964, p. 234). However, the principle of transplanting the British system to a totally different sociocultural climate remained open to criticism. F. C. Epke, a Nigerian librarian, faults British educators for their failure to respond to local needs. He observes that at the University College in Ibadan:

> Applied research into health, agriculture, industry and cultures of the country received little or no attention. It took the university eight years after its foundation to establish a department of education, ten years to offer courses in economics, geology, anthropology, sociology, Islamic/Arabic studies. . . . Whereas many courses of local relevance were not offered, the Colonial Office made money available . . . to mount colonial research projects in British universities. The result is a far greater output of publications and accumulation of library materials in British Universities than in colonial universities (1979, p. 13).

While a number of British libraries undoubtedly had richer collections of Africana than were available in Ibadan at independence, the university college library did begin to acquire materials on African subjects prior to their introduction into the curriculum.

Some important publications on West Africa were acquired with the purchase of the 18,000 volume collection belonging to Henry Carr and the private library of nationalist leader Herbert Macaulay, which brought the university college a good collection of government publications relating to West Africa. A collection donated by the family of a former British governor supplied the library with works on Nigerian linguistics and culture, and the 15,000 volumes given by Frederick Dyke formed the nucleus of the library's scientific collection on tropical agriculture and related topics.

In 1948, when John Harris, the first librarian, arrived he found 30,000 volumes from various donations and private collections in addition to 10,000 volumes from Yaba Higher College. These books "lay unsorted in varying stages of decay, crowded into wooden buildings, unprotected from . . . insects, moulds, virus diseases, alterations of dry and damp, and the all pervading laterite dust" (Harris, 1965, p. 253). An experienced academic librarian from New Zealand, Harris immediately began to bring order to what he later described as "a scene of book chaos." By December 1949 Harris and his small staff had catalogued, classified, and shelved 10,000 volumes. This was the first of many remarkable accomplishments for Harris, who was described by one Nigerian colleague as "the father of Nigerian librarianship" (Aguolu, 1978, p. 251), and by another as a man of immense energy "who bestrode the entire Nigerian library scene like a colossus" (Aboyade, 1973, p. 131).

Harris also had the foresight to develop systematically the collection of Africana that he correctly saw as "*the* research centre of the library" (Harris, 1965, p. 258). Therefore, his acquisition policy was to "(1) comprehend *everything Nigerian;* (2) include *everything significant* relating to West Africa as a whole; (3) include as much other Africana as possible" (Harris, 1965, p. 258). In order to facilitate the acquisition of Nigerian books, Harris persuaded the government to pass a Publications Ordinance in 1950 that made the Ibadan library the legal depository collection. Harris also supervised the publication of the Nigerian national bibliography until 1968, solicited donations, compiled lists of desiderata, and recruited an Arabist who was able to acquire 250 indigenous Arabic manuscripts from individuals in Northern Nigeria (see Kensdale, 1955).

In addition to an outstanding collection on Africa, the Ibadan library included "the most comprehensive [collection of bibliographies] in West Africa" and was "a well rounded general library representing the most significant world literature [and] the basic literature and standard textbooks required for teaching purposes"; in 1957 its holdings totalled approximately 100,000 volumes (Lancour, 1958, p. 8). By this time the library was housed in a new building, and Harris was assisted by a staff of nearly 50, including six professionals.

In his effort to transform the Ibadan collection into the first-ranking library of West Africa, Harris was aided by Kenneth Mellanby, the first Principal of the University College (1947–1953), who asserted that "a proper library is an essential part of a university in any country, but in West Africa it is even more important" (quoted by Aguolu, 1977b, p. 191). Prior to Harris' appointment, Mellanby began to order books for the library and purchased the first Microcards used in the British Commonwealth. Once Harris arrived, Mellanby gave him a free hand to develop the library to meet the future research needs of the university.

David Balme, the first principal of the university college in the Gold Coast, was much less open to the development of a collection of Africana than Mellanby. A classicist by training, Balme stated in his inaugural address: "there is only one modern civilization. It happens to have started in

Greece . . . and it spread first through Europe. I don't think we need weep when national cultures go. . . . It is only a matter of pride in superficial things" (quoted in Ashby, 1966, p. 241). Under Balme's direction, a very traditional humanities curriculum was implemented at the university college, and the library, named in Balme's honor, was built to meet the needs of such a program.

The creation of an academic library was begun in 1948 by Ethel Fegan, who transferred 3,000 volumes from Achimota College to form the nucleus of the new collection. Fegan, then in her seventies, served for a few months before the arrival of Elise Walker, a trained librarian with experience at the British Ministry of Town and Country Planning (Armstrong, 1971, p. 299). During her first 5 years, Walker acquired 55,000 books and subscribed to 1900 serials (Dean, 1967, p. 80). In 1959 when the library moved from its temporary quarters in Achimota to its new building in Legon, its collection contained approximately 115,000 volumes.

Although British funding for the Balme library collection was much greater than for Ibadan, the Ghanaian library received less important gifts (Ekpe, 1979, p. 12). The Atoms for Peace Collection donated by the United States did not relate to research or curriculum needs at the school. Other gifts from British colleges were small, and there were no major donations of Africana from individuals. As a result, there were complaints in the early 1960s that the book stock was obsolete, and "reflected the European academic bias of the administration" (Kotei, 1972, p. 411).

Following the British model, science and technology were not taught at the university college, but were relegated to a separate institution—the Kumasi College of Technology, founded in 1952. In the same year, the Nigerian College of Arts, Science and Technology was created with separate branches in Zaria, Enugu, and Ibadan. Nigeria and the Gold Coast each received a $10,000 grant from the Carnegie Corporation to set up appropriate libraries in the two technical colleges (Lancour, 1958, p. 9–10). These libraries collected course-related publications on pharmacology, engineering, architecture, commerce, agriculture, and education. Research was not emphasized at the technical colleges, and their collections grew much more slowly than those of the university colleges in Ibadan and Legon.

When independence was achieved by Ghana in 1957 and by Nigeria in 1960, both countries had university colleges with academic libraries created along British lines. However, the American presence was also felt, through the activities of the Carnegie Corporation, and through the influence of a number of nationalist leaders who had studied in the United States. In identifying the three factors that were decisive in the development of higher education and libraries in West Africa, John Dean ranks the impetus of nationalist leaders first, followed by support from the British government, with the impact of external agencies in third place (Dean, 1970, pp. 115–117). These three forces combined to create a library structure in Anglophone Africa that was shaped by British precedents but was at the same time influenced by both internal and external forces.

2. FRENCH WEST AFRICA

There are many parallels in the development of the University of Dakar and the universities in Ibadan and Legon. However, outside aid and influence was minimal in Francophone Africa, and the aspirations of nationalist leaders in all cases were based on their educational experience in France or in the AOF.

The Ecole William Ponty, located near Dakar, offered postsecondary training to teachers, administrators, and medical assistants. Although it did not award French academic degrees, it was less criticized than Yaba or Achimota, partly because fewer Africans had the opportunity to compare its program with higher education abroad. This situation changed in 1945 when France set up a scholarship program that enabled hundreds of African students to enroll in French universities. However, another 5 years passed before France decided to create a center for higher education in the AOF. Known as l'Institut des Hautes Etudes (IHE), this school was both a response to the immediate educational needs of the region and a first step toward the creation of a full-scale university in Dakar. Despite the long-range goal for extending the university institute, its early years were difficult. Before 1957, there was no central campus or library, few adequate laboratories, and virtually no research support.

From 1953 to 1957, African students strenuously protested the loose standards for faculty recruitment and the difficulty of attracting and keeping well-qualified professors in Dakar. They insisted that without qualified instructors, it was more difficult for them to pass the examinations set by the universities of Bordeaux and Paris and therefore to be graded on the same standards as those in France. Senghor and other African leaders backed the students' demand that a future university in Dakar adhere in every way to the standards set in metropolitan universities. In the end, French authorities bent to this pressure, and in February of 1957 a decree was issued establishing the University of Dakar as the first full-fledged French university overseas.

Many social and cultural problems were to follow as a consequence of creating a French university in Africa, but the administrative situation demanded an immediate response. By the time the decree establishing the university took effect, the 1956 *Loi–Cadre,* which gave the individual French–African territories authority over education, was already in force.

At this point, it was decided that higher education would remain under the authority of the AOF. Even when the federation was dissolved in 1958, colonial administrators and African leaders agreed that the new university should retain its inter-African role and its close ties with the French Ministry of National Education.

In 1960, after the independence of Senegal, the university became a public institution of the new state. However, at this time, Senegalese authorities requested that the University of Dakar continue to be administered "as the eighteenth university of France" (Ashby, 1964, p. 49). Thus, the university continued to be financed by the French, Dakar faculty retained their status within the French corps of university professors, and admissions regulations, examinations, degrees, and curriculum remained the same as those in France.

As the Institut des Hautes Etudes in Dakar was being transformed into a bona fide French university, library resources were being acquired to support the changing needs of the academic community. At the time of its creation, IHE inherited a collection of 2000–3000 titles from the Ecole Africaine de Médecine. Since most of these works were on medicine or tropical diseases, it soon became apparent that a general library would have to be set up to serve the other three schools. In 1950, an instructor was charged with creating the nucleus of a collection for law, letters, and science. Finally, in 1952, a trained French librarian, Suzanne Séguin, was brought to Dakar ("Bibliotheque," 1974, p. 4).

One of Séguin's first tasks was to catalog the growing collection by French cataloging rules. Séguin also formulated a more systematic collection development policy. In addition to purchasing works related to the curriculum, she began to build up a basic collection of reference books and bibliographies. A variety of other materials was ordered, with first priority given to works on French West and French Equatorial Africa and second priority to Anglophone West Africa. Out-of-print materials on the exploration and colonization of Africa were also acquired. Altogether, acquisitions averaged about 10,000 volumes per year in the mid-1950s.

During her first two years, Séguin was aided by a French instructor, a French typist, and two Africans who had only primary school certificates. In addition to lacking sufficient support staff, Séguin was confronted with the challenge of laying the groundwork for a new academic library with few professional colleagues in the region. Four years after her arrival in Dakar, a visiting library expert from Paris paid special tribute to Séguin's pioneering work, "accomplished alone, and under difficult conditions" (Hahn, 1956, p. 508). In 1954, two more French librarians were recruited for positions in the law library and the medical library in Dakar.

When IHE was preparing for university status in 1956, the Direction des

Bibliothèques in Paris sent André Hahn to Dakar to plan the scope and structure of a proposed "federal university library," to serve the AOF capital as well as the academic community. After assessing the situation in Dakar, Hahn strongly urged the creation of a central university library as opposed to housing the separate collections in each *faculté,* as was often the case in France. Hahn's recommendation was approved and the cornerstone of the new library was laid on December 10, 1959. This ceremony was described later by the library's first *conservateur en chef,* Jean Rousset de Pina, as "a purely symbolic gesture, but also an act of faith" (1966, p. 294). Because of the uncertainties surrounding the university's future role at the time of independence, funds for further construction were withheld until 1961. Meanwhile, normal funding continued for materials and operating expenses. From 1957 to 1960, 41,000 volumes were added, giving the library collection over 80,000 volumes of books and journals at the time of independence.

Although the University of Dakar continued to recruit students from other Francophone states, the growing sense of nationalism in these countries led to demands for separate higher education facilities. The Ivorian leader, Houphouët–Boigny, was an ardent nationalist; under his leadership the Ivory Coast was one of the first states to press for independence. In 1959, after the dissolution of the AOF, the Centre d'Enseignement Supérieur was set up in the Ivorian capital of Abidjan. Like the IHE in Dakar, this school trained students who sat for examinations administered by the Université de Paris. The Ivorian school did not achieve university status until 1964, and its library facilities were minimal, with under 7000 books at the time of independence.

C. Research Needs and Library Development

1. FRANCOPHONE AFRICA

At the time of independence, the Ivory Coast lacked an infrastructure of government agencies or institutes to carry out applied research. A 1953 directory of special libraries in tropical Africa lists two independent research institutes in the colony: the Centre de Récherches Agronomiques in Bingerville and the Institut d'Enseignement et Recherches Tropicales near Abidjan. In addition, there was also a CENTRIFAN in Abidjan, founded during the war as a territorial branch of the IFAN headquarters in Dakar. Its program developed slowly, and by 1953, it reported a library collection of under 2000 volumes (Répertoire, 1954). This was, at the time, the largest library in the country.

Although the 1950s did not bring great improvement to the Ivorian library situation during this decade, several other institutes for applied research were set up as branches of French institutes for the study of tropical agriculture and forest products. By the time of independence, the Ivory Coast had centers for the study of tropical forests, veterinary medicine and livestock breeding, cotton and exotic textiles, oil-bearing plants, rubber, cocoa, and coffee. All these institutes were supported by the French government and reflected the dramatic growth in the budget of France's central research agency, the Centre National de la Récherche Scientifique (CNRS).

Senegal also benefited from the growth of French research. A few specialized institutes were set up in the 1950s; in some instances, existing research centers were taken over by newly created French agencies such as the Institut de Récherches Agronomiques Tropicales. However, the presence of several AOF agencies (such as the Direction Fédérale des Mines et de la Géologie) ensured better provision of research facilities and special libraries in Senegal than in most west African colonies, as indicated in the 1953 directory which revealed that Senegal alone had 13 scientific libraries, while the other seven AOF territories had 13 such collections between them.

Most of the special collections in Senegal were inadequate, with 30–50 periodical titles and less than 1000 books. However, researchers working in agencies near Dakar had the advantage of drawing on the IFAN library which contained 29,000 volumes of books and 2087 serials in 1953.

The 1950s were a period of continuing growth for the institute's research program and for its library. At the time of IFAN's fifteenth anniversary, Monod was able to write that scientific research in the AOF had at last come to be regarded as "une activité légitime, normale et nécessaire" (Institut Français d'Afrique Noire, 1953). From 1945 to 1960, more support was given to applied research by the French government and the Government General of the AOF, but none of the French or federal agencies in the AOF could compare with IFAN in terms of staff, laboratory facilities, or library resources. IFAN cooperated with other scientific agencies in Africa and produced some statistical data needed for planning, but Monod insisted that the scope of IFAN's work should not be limited to short-term utilitarian projects. Although official support was gradually beginning to shift from basic research to applied research in the 1950s, Monod's prominence enabled him to maintain IFAN's position at the pinnacle of the AOF scientific establishment ("Historique," 1961).

The postwar decade was not without problems, but most of the IFAN reports from these years acknowledged generous financial support from the Government General of the AOF. This enabled the institute to build up impressive museum collections on ethnography, African art, and natural history. A special film production unit was also set up, but the photography collection (established in the 1930s) remained a part of the library. Each year, over 2000 negatives were contributed to this collection and, by 1959, IFAN's *photothèque* contained 40,000 negatives. To keep up with the flood of printed and pictorial material, the library staff was increased in size; in 1948, Renée Laurens, a trained librarian from the French "corps de bibliothécaires," was appointed to the IFAN post. Under her direction, indexing of Africanist periodicals was undertaken and special bibliographies were compiled and published.

The IFAN library also took on the additional responsibility of being a legal depository collection for materials published in the AOF. When the legal deposit decree was passed in 1946, periodical publishing had already begun to flourish in Dakar and other urban centers where journalism was stimulated by African political activities. In the 1950s, the IFAN library annually processed 4000–5000 individual issues of local serials as well as a few booklets and pamphlets. Since commercial book publishing was practically nonexistent in the AOF at this time, IFAN still received few books directly through legal deposit. However, copies of depository items were sent to the Bibliothèque Nationale in France which, in exchange, sent IFAN copies of French monographs dealing with Africa from its national depository collection. Through this combination of purchase, exchange, and legal deposit, the IFAN library nearly doubled its holdings within the decade; by 1959, it contained more than 40,000 books and pamphlets and over 2500 serial titles.

Saint Louis also had an IFAN branch that concentrated on research concerning Senegal and Mauretania. This CENTRIFAN began to function in 1947 when a program of research in ethnography, sociology, and geography was initiated by its first director. As the research program of the center expanded during the early 1950s, its library acquired from 500 to 700 new books and 118 current periodicals each year. In addition to recent scientific works, the library also contained official publications, colonial journals, and a few scholarly works dating back to the sixteenth century. These older materials were acquired in 1949 when the municipal library of Saint Louis was transferred to IFAN (Maack, 1981b, p. 62–63). Thus in 1954, when the library was moved to the new CENTRIFAN building, it contained over 6000 scientific books.

2. THE GOLD COAST AND NIGERIA

The British, like the French, greatly increased their support for both fundamental and applied research after World War II. During the 1930s, much of the important scientific and ethnographic work in British colonies had been financed by the Rockefeller Foundation, either directly, through fellowships, or indirectly through the International African Institute in London. The first encyclopedic survey of the region, prepared by Lord Hailey in 1938, was largely funded by the Carnegie Corporation. Hailey urged that a government research fund be established and in 1940 the need for this was recognized in the first Colonial Development and Welfare Act: "Many colonies can not finance out of their own resources the research and survey work . . . and the expansion of administrative and technical staffs which are necessary for their full and vigorous development" (Oliver and Atmore, 1967, p. 215). At Hailey's insistance, £1 million per year was designated for African research after 1945 (Mair, 1965, p. 16).

The Colonial Research Committee (CRC), headed by Lord Hailey, allotted some of these funds to individuals (through Colonial Research Fellowships) and to organizations in the United Kingdom such as the International African Institute. CRC also developed a policy that research in Africa should be organized on a regional rather than a national basis. A coordinating body, the West African Council, was set up in 1945 with its secretariat in Accra. The two regional centers—organized during the war for the study of cocoa and for research on oil palm—came under the council. Other regional institutes later set up in Nigeria included a center for trypanosomiasis research, an institute for meteorological research, and the West African Institute for Social and Economic Research. The latter center, founded in 1951, was the only British institute for social research in the region. (Hailey, 1957, p. 1608) However, its function as a West African body was short-lived. In 1956, its staff and facilities were divided between the Economic Research unit attached to the University College in the Gold Coast and the Nigerian Institute of Social and Economic Research affiliated with the University College at Ibadan.

After the independence of Ghana in 1957, the regional role of the institutes for applied research gradually ended. The library resources of these research centers were not divided, but became integrated into the local university library, or were inherited by a successor agency—such as the Cocoa Research Institute, which was later administered by the Ghana Academy of Science. By the early 1960s, the institute library, with 3500 volumes, was one of the largest of the agricultural research collections in West Africa.

Despite the fact that Accra had been the site of the research council, Ghana reported fewer special library resources than Nigeria in 1962–1963. Because of its greater size and diversity, Nigeria had more centers for agricultural research and training. Its largest special collection, however, was the 12,000-volume library at the Federal Laboratory Service at Yaba.

This collection was cataloged and reorganized in 1947 by Hilda Clark, who was sent on a three month mission from Britain by the Medical Research Council (Cannon, 1954, p. 185). The collection at Yaba was subsequently combined with the Federal Medical Library in nearby Lagos and a Nigerian librarian was put in charge of the collection.

The employment of trained librarians in special libraries dates from the 1950s, and by 1963, Ghana and Nigeria each reported eight professionals working in such collections. However, a report of 1963 indicates that special libraries were "still at an early stage of development . . . one can not speak of library service except in few cases" (University and special libraries, 1963, p. 215).

D. Popular Education and Public Libraries

1. THE GOLD COAST LIBRARY BOARD

In just five years after independence, Ghanaian public libraries reported holdings 20 times as large as special libraries and over twice as large as academic libraries (Dadzie and Strickland, 1965). The high priority given to public libraries in the Gold Coast was due largely to the combined effort and enthusiasm of the library pioneer Bishop Aglionby, British Council librarian Evelyn Evans, and Prime Minister Kwame Nkrumah.

The first step toward nationwide public library service came in 1945 when Evelyn J. Evans took charge of the British Council library and reading room in Accra. Before coming to Africa, Evans had nearly a decade and a half of professional experience, including four years as Deputy City Librarian at York ("Profile," 1963). Eager to see library service extended beyond Accra, Evans soon began to tour the country with a mobile library; by 1946, she had distributed 55 book boxes to community centers, schools, clubs, social centers, and mines.

The success of these efforts was noted by the Governor-General; at his invitation, the British Council's representatives became part of the Gold Coast Library Advisory Committee. In this capacity, the British Council also became involved with the Aglionby Library which was opened under Evans's direction in 1946. Because Bishop Aglionby wished this library to become a central library for the Gold Coast, Evans continued her work by extending service to other towns and rural areas (Evans, 1964, p. 31). By 1949, the original collection of 5000 volumes had grown to 28,000 volumes, the first children's service had been established, and there were 158 book boxes in circulation. These assets became the property of the newly constituted Gold Coast Library Board in January 1950.

The Library Board Ordinance which created the new public library system received unanimous approval by the Legislative Council of the colony in April 1949 and was immediately accepted by the Colonial Secretary who thought that the extension of libraries "would afford the people of the Gold Coast a valuable cultural asset" (Kotei, 1972, p. 378). While the public library tradition exemplified in the ordinance was clearly British, the Library Board was unique in that it had national powers and was not specifically confined to public library development. The explicit function of the board was "to establish, equip, manage and maintain libraries in the Gold Coast and to take all steps as may be necessary to carry out such duty"; a decade and a half later, Evans commented that the ordinance's simplicity had "proven its worth" (Evans, 1964, pp. 38, 42).

The Library Board was established at the beginning of the Gold Coast's first five-year development plan, and library provision became an accepted part of the country's educational program. In this, the board also benefited from the personal support of Nkrumah as well as the interest of members of his cabinet. In the words of Nkrumah:

> When my colleagues and I took office in 1951 . . . we decided . . . to plan a system of education that would be in keeping with the requirements of the economic, social and cultural upliftment of the country. . . . The provision of library facilities for everybody throughout the length and breadth of the country was recognized as an essential element in this national scheme of educational advancement (Evans, 1964, p. xiii).

The commitment of Nkrumah and his government is eloquently shown in the funding given the Library Board. For its first year (1950–1951), the Board had £15,750 in government support; library funding was progressively increased to £103,310 in 1955–1956; and to £169,350 in 1960–1961 (Evans, 1964, pp. 58–59). This level of support enabled the board to increase its stock and to build a large central library in Accra, two regional libraries, and several branches.

Between 1951 and 1960 when the estimated rate of literacy rose from 7.5% to nearly 20% (Dowuona–Hammond, 1963, p. 203), library registration increased tenfold, from 3,200 to 32,000; at the same time, circulation increased even more dramatically—from 40,000 to 691,000 books ("Ghana Library Board's Report," 1961, p. 755). Over half of the registered borrowers were children, and among the adults were many people attending courses or preparing for external degrees. Kotei points out that all studies of reading patterns in the Gold Coast from the 1940s to 1970s, without exception, confirmed that "all categories of library users read primarily and predominantly for utilitarian purposes . . . to pass examinations . . . improve their social and educational mobility . . . and assist in the economic development of the nation" (1972, p. 279). The lack of sufficient published African literature, the difficulties in reading in a foreign language, and the African orientation toward oral expression and communal activity have all been acknowledged as major obstacles to leisure reading. However, the steady growth in book circulation in Ghana provided an indication that these obstacles are not insurmountable. Nkrumah's emphasis on "the desirability of developing in [Ghana] the power of intelligent reading" also played a part in the remarkable growth of his country's library service (Evans, 1964, p. 134).

In commenting on the Library Board's funding, Evans stressed that "complete internal self-help and interest is probably one of the reasons that has made the whole project a success. As a desire and need of the people of Ghana, the growth [came] from within the country itself" (Evans, 1964, p. 56). Outside help was supplemental and included a Carnegie grant for staff training and some funding from the Commonwealth Education and Welfare Trust to expand children's facilities and build a regional library in Kumasi. However, while philanthropy played a minor role in the continuity and growth of Ghanaian public library service, its impact prior to the Board's establishment can not be ignored. The gift of Aglionby and the contribution of the British Council had a catalytic effect on the Colonial government, and helped to place library service on an official basis at the time the Nkrumah government was launching its accelerated education program.

2. NIGERIAN PUBLIC LIBRARIES

Public library development in Nigeria lagged far behind that in the Gold Coast because of less effective philanthropy, less local pressure for librarians, and general apathy on the part of Colonial authorities. The British government had first attempted to supply reading matter to West Africans through the efforts of the Public Relations Department, which established reading rooms in many towns during the war. This was part of a British propaganda campaign that "courted [Africans] assiduously through radio, pamphlets, [and] films" (Crowder, 1968, p. 483). Once the war ended, there were attempts in Nigeria to transform these reading rooms into public libraries. Carnegie funding was used to supply books to certain reading rooms in the north, but in 1957, the region's Chief Inspector of Education described these "libraries" as "a dismal shadow of what they should be" (quoted in Omolewa, 1974, p. 32). With limited hours, unlighted facilities, and inappropriate staff, the reading rooms could not develop into a network of small public libraries.

Meanwhile, a Standing Committee to Advise the Government on the Provision of Libraries was set up in 1940 after the Nigerian government had reluctantly agreed to accept a Carnegie grant for libraries. This Standing Committee reconvened in 1945 and recommended a three-point program that entailed the establishment of local libraries by local authorities, the creation of regional central libraries, and the organization of a national central library. Three years later, this proposal was approved by the Secretary to the Government in Lagos but was never implemented. By 1950, no federal revenues had been made available for public library service; instead, one Colonial official commented that the government continued to rely on "cheap grants from the Carnegie Corporation, the British Council or anyone else" (quoted by White, 1964, p. 2). As a result of this practice, there was no attempt to include libraries in the national planning process.

Following Colonial precedents, the first representative government—the Nigerian Council of Ministers—decided in 1952 that "it must be regional, local and private organizations, which increase library facilities throughout the territory" (White, 1964, p. 3). The three regional governments created in 1951 (north, east, and west) were therefore free to adopt whatever provisions they saw fit. In 1955, Harris, commented: "Of the three regions, the North has an established library service but no legislation, the East has legislation but no service. While the West has neither" (quoted by Nwoye, 1977, p. 12).

At the urging of Harris, a working party was set up to seek the passage of library legislation for the western region and a site was approved for a regional library. Unfortunately, no real progress occurred and library development in this region was "unplanned, uncoordinated and unbalanced. Each town, city or locality did what it could . . . [afford] without reference to or co-operation with neighboring libraries" [Adegoke, 1973, p. 418]. In 1956, Nigerian library leader S. B. Aje noted that the public library in the regional capital, Ibadan, failed to meet the needs of the public "because of inaccessibility, inefficient service machinery and inadequate collections" (Aje, 1956, p. 79). The Ministry of Education was responsible for this collection which contained 23,000 volumes by 1959 (Okorie, 1959, p. 163).

It was also the Education Department that provided for library service in the Northern Region. This service was launched in 1952 by an energetic British librarian, Joan Allen (Gunton, 1961, p. 150). With a staff of three, Allen set up a regional library at Kaduna and organized a book-box service that served over a 150 agencies including schools, native administration centers, trade centers, and cultural associations. In 1957–1958, the regional library in Kaduna, with a book stock of 45,000 volumes, recorded a circulation of 75,323 (Okorie, 1959, p. 151). While this was much below the facilities and circulation for the Ghana Library Board, it represented the best service then available in Nigeria.

In May 1958, the first regional bookmobile service began in eastern Nigeria. This project had been in the planning stage since 1955 when the Eastern Region passed a library board law patterned after the library legislation in the Gold Coast. The first step in assessing the region's library needs was taken in March 1956. At that time, Kalu Okorie, the first Nigerian to attain the fellowship of the British Library Association, was commissioned to conduct a library survey. After touring the region he recommended a four-part program:

(1) that regional library headquarters be established in Enugu
(2) that five divisional libraries with mobile service be set up
(3) that bookmobiles designed for the tropics be acquired; and
(4) that a postal book service be provided for isolated areas (Okorie, 1960, p. 4101).

This project was approved by the library board which immediately sought assistance from UNESCO for the establishment of a pilot library at Enugu. UNESCO supplied the services of a library expert, Stanley Horrocks, Borough Librarian of Reading, England. Other UNESCO support included the purchase of the first bookmobile, additional financial aid, and the provision of fellowships for Nigerian staff to train overseas. In return, the regional government agreed to allocate a minimum sum of $175,000 over the five-year period from 1957 through 1961. At the time, this commitment represented, by far, the largest sum in public funds ever allotted for library development in Nigeria.

The library board's effort to obtain an adequate level of funding was facilitated by the Premier of the Eastern Region, Nnamadi Azikiwe. Well known as a journalist and nationalist leader, Azikiwe was largely responsible for establishing intensive educational program in the Eastern Region. Azikiwe, who had studied in the United States at Lincoln University and the University of Pennsylvania, was also an ardent advocate of the public library, which he referred to as the "University of the people" (quoted in Adegoke, 1973, p. 414). Azikiwe played a key role in the passage of the region's 1955 public library law and he later presided over the opening of the new £50,000 central library in Enugu in March 1959. At that time, Azikiwe stated "I feel the public library . . . is almost as much a requirement for any community of people as the food they eat" (quoted in Horrocks, 1962, p. 81). Horrocks himself felt that this nationalistic enthusiasm for libraries was shared by much of the community. He noted during his tours that the construction of library facilities "was taken for granted both in Afikop and in all the other places we visited. . . . This undoubted enthusiasm for a library . . . came direct from the people" (Horrocks, 1962a, p. 82).

Although just 13% of the literate population of Enugu registered at the central library, nearly 175,000 volumes were circulated during its first two years of operation. A survey of library use in 1961 revealed that Nigerians were "active not avid borrowers," that they often used the reading room without checking out books, and that they read books "more as tools of study than as an important leisure time activity" (Horrocks, 1962b, pp. 245–246). Nearly 46,000 books were available from the Enugu Regional Central Library by the time of independence, and each reader was allowed to borrow two books at a time.

As a result of UNESCO aid and government support, Enugu with a population of 80,000, was better served than Lagos, the federal capital, with 276,000 people. The Lagos Library, set up with Carnegie funding in 1932, continued to exist as a subscription library with limited membership and no professional staff. Meanwhile, in 1946 the British Council and the Lagos Town Council jointly sponsored another collection known as the Lagos Public Library. This library was completely taken over by the Town Council in 1950 when the British Council began to divest itself of public library activities in the Colonies. However, the remarkable transformation of the British Council Library in Accra was in no way duplicated in the Nigerian capital. By 1959, the Lagos Municipal Library and its branch in Yaba had a collection of only 11,000 volumes and served about 1500 readers annually (Okorie, 1959, p. 164).

3. FRANCOPHONE AFRICA

Like Lagos, Dakar (with over 230,000 inhabitants in 1955) did not have library service befitting a federal capital with a large number of literate government employees, teachers, and business leaders. In 1952, the Dakar municipal library was described as "existing in name only" with books that were in such poor condition that they could not be circulated (UNESCO Seminar, 1952). As a result, residents were dependent on libraries set up by private groups. One of the largest collections of this type was sponsored by the Alliance Française. Although the Senegalese section was affiliated with the Alliance Française headquarters in Paris, it received little direct aid from France and was forced to support its activities and its library from fees and donations. The Dakar library was opened in 1946; by 1958, it had 8,000 volumes. Although this was the largest general library available in the city, the high registration fee prohibited most literate Africans from using the collection (Maack, 1978, p. 378).

A small but more accessible library was established in 1951 as an offshoot of the Clairafrique bookstore. This library had low borrowing fees because it was supported partially by the Catholic Centre Culturel Daniel Brottier.

During the period before independence, when there was a great deal of intellectual and political ferment in Senegal, public lectures at the Brottier center drew crowds of up to 500 persons and brought many readers to the Clairafrique library. However, with the establishment of study groups, youth organizations, cultural associations, and unions concerned with the education of workers, a greater demand for books was created than could be met by existing libraries. Amadou Matar M'bow, a professor and political activist, commented that despite the high cost of books, African politicians, intellectuals, and labor leaders collected "small personal libraries whose books passed from hand to hand" (M'bow, 1961).

The growing interest in books among literate Senegalese was also evident in the use of the CENTRIFAN library in Saint Louis. This library contained the city's former municipal collection as well as scientific books acquired for the research institute. In 1954, it was moved to the new CENTRIFAN building where it was given a separate wing. A French librarian noted in 1958 that this attractive library "would excite the envy of many librarians in the Metropole [i.e., France] (Hirsch–Pecault, 1958, p. 76). However, she also remarked that the 14 seats in the reading room were often insufficient to accommodate the library's active clientele. By 1956 there were some 600 registered users drawn mainly from the African and European civil servants employed by the governments of Senegal and Mauretania. In that year, 6350 novels and popular nonfiction works were borrowed, along with 500 scientific works; this averaged over 10 loans per registrant. French best sellers were described as being of little interest to Sengalese readers who preferred works on Islam, modern African literature, nonfiction dealing with Africa, and French classics. (Hirsch–Pecault, 1958, p. 76)

A municipal library was set up in Abidjan in 1952. By the time of independence, this library held less than 5000 volumes, but there were plans to develop a special collection on law and philosophy to serve the needs of postsecondary students living near the library. While a few administrative collections and club libraries existed in other cities in the AOF, these collections were meager and often depended on the interst of a few administrators; once those individuals left, such "libraries" generally fell into disuse.

Outside urban centers, there were still a number of *cercle* libraries. Although these tiny collections were generally set up by and for the local European personnel, Robert Cornevin, a colonial administrator who served in Africa during the 1940s, noted that the "*bibliothèque de cercle* sometimes opened its doors to Westernized Africans who had no other source [for reading material] aside from the school library or the private collection of the teacher" (1976, p. 127). The AOF archivist, Margerite Verdat (who served from 1945 to 1948), encouraged the development of good general collections in each *cercle* by trying to persuade local administrators of the importance of such collections, and by offering bibliographic aid and introductory training to those responsible for the small isolated libraries. When Verdat left IFAN in 1948, attempts to give technical assistance to *cercle* libraries had to be abandoned.

There were no further efforts from Dakar to stimulate or coordinate local development. However, in 1953, just before the UNESCO regional seminar on the development of public libraries in Africa, André Masson, an inspector general from the Direction des Bibliothèques in Paris (and former *conservateur* of libraries and archives in Indochina), undertook a study tour in Africa. Masson was well impressed with the work of the Gold Coast Library Board and that of the *Bibliothèque Centrale* in Morocco, with its branches and bookmobiles. Based on his own observations and on the recommendations of the Ibadan seminar, Masson outlined a plan for public library service in Francophone Africa (Masson, 1954). His tour of Nigeria and the AOF had convinced Masson that small isolated collections, by themselves, were completely ineffectual. Therefore, he advocated the creation of a central public library in Dakar to serve as the headquarters of a system with branches, bookmobiles, and a service of book boxes for rural areas. The central library was to serve Dakar users by providing a large reading room that would allow for open access to a general collection of books. Altogether, Masson suggested a book stock of 36,000 volumes.

Although this recommended collection was roughly half as large as that of the Gold Coast Library Board, it would have represented a large, unprecedented investment on the part of France and the Governor General. The AOF authorities, who were preoccupied with other projects (including the rapid expansion of primary schools), took no action on Masson's proposal, nor did they request UNESCO aid. At the time of the *Loi–Cadre* in 1956, public library development remained at a standstill. Mahtar M'bow, who then served as minister of education for Senegal, attributed the failure to request UNESCO aid for libraries to the attitude of Paris toward the French Union, especially "its policy of not allowing any international organization to become involved in the internal affairs of its overseas territories (M'bow, 1961). While this may well have been a factor, account must be taken also of the negative French attitude toward public libraries—both in terms of government commitment and popular response (Richter, 1977; Barnett, 1973).

By the 1950s, comprehensive library planning and the progressive development of public library systems were new to most Frenchmen, who continued to identify libraries with learned institutes. Given the limited development of free, state-supported libraries in France at this time, it is not surprising that when André Han, a second official from the Direction des Bibliothèques, visited Dakar in 1956, he surmised that one of the major obstacles to the creation of public libraries was the lack of interest on the part of Europeans and of French-educated Africans (Hahn, 1956, p. 513). Hahn had been urged by André Masson to examine the possibility of creating a network of public libraries. However, after observing the situation in Dakar, Hahn concluded that it was best to concentrate on library service aimed at young people and adults with at least four years of secondary school. He suggested that the university library include a department for general literature and reference material that would be open to all readers with enough education to take advantage of such a collection.

Hahn's proposal gained support from Rector Jean Capelle who advocated a federal university library at Dakar with "a stature equal to that of Afrique Occidentale Francaise" (Rousset de Pina, 1966, p. 297). However, when the cornerstone of the new university library was laid three years later, the AOF had ceased to exist, the university budget was cut back, and its central library was reduced to half the size that had been originally planned. Thus, there was no provision made for service to general readers.

Since colonial authorities did not follow through on any of the proposals made by French library experts, Senegal and the Ivory Coast attained independence with no public library infrastructure and no tradition of significant government support for any *bibliothèque publique* that was not attached to a research institute. Lacking a model of effective public library service, the two new governments were reluctant to invest in an institution whose value was unproven.

E. The Library Profession

1. FRANCOPHONE AFRICA

The AOF government's failure to respond to UNESCO's initiatives for public library development did not prevent these new ideas from circulating in the region. The four week UNESCO Seminar held in Ibadan in 1953 was attended by 29 librarians and educators, but only three of these individuals worked in the AOF. Nonetheless, the publication of UNESCO recommendations and recent information on the state of public library development in other countries soon stimulated interest among librarians and educators in Francophone Africa.

One of the strongest proponents of the UNESCO recommendations was E. W. K. Dadzie, a Togolese librarian–archivst who was trained in Dakar by Verdat. After six years as director of the Mauretanian archives in Saint Louis, Senegal, Dadzie became the first French-speaking African to be selected as a UNESCO fellow. This fellowship enabled Dadzie to undertake a nine-month study tour of public libraries, adult education facilities and literacy training programs in France, Scandinavia, and the Gold Coast.

The visit to Scandinavia introduced Dadzie to Anglo–American concepts of librarianship, and on his tour of the Gold Coast, he was deeply impressed by the potential of free public libraries adapted to an African environment. In 1956, Dadzie returned to his post in Saint Louis where he began to discuss the value of public libraries with African friends—educators, civil servants, and a few professionals. These people soon agreed that the time had come to press for public libraries in Francophone Africa. Documents from the 1953 UNESCO conference clearly revealed the disparity between the forward-looking program of the Gold Coast Library Board and the absence of real public library service in the AOF (UNESCO Seminar . . . , 1954). Although they were aware that France might be reluctant to accept UNESCO aid, Dadzie and his associates felt that local advocacy of libraries, combined with some support from the Direction des Bibliothèques in Paris, could stimulate the federal and territorial governments to fund library development.

With this goal in mind, 15 men and women agreed (on September 13, 1957) to serve as the provisional executive board of a new organization known as Association pour le Développement des Bibliothèques Publiques en Afrique (ADBPA).[5] The membership of this board of seven officers and eight technical advisors reflected something of the cosmopolitan atmosphere of Saint Louis, which, as the capital of both Senegal and Mauretania, drew civil servants, professionals, and technicians and educators who had come from different territories within the French Union. Teachers dominated the board, and only three of the 15 members had any library experience or training. The proportion of professional librarians and archivists serving as officers and advisors of ADBPA rose from 20% to 54% during the association's first decade of existence. However, in the beginning, there were so few persons in Africa who had professional training or full-time library positions that it would have been impossible to found a library association that did not include interested persons from a variety of occupations.

While the inclusion of nonlibrarians was a practical necessity, Dadzie also felt that it was good strategy to solicit membership of cultural and political leaders who might influence the government to support the association's goals and whose names would, in any case, lend prestige to the cause. A few highly placed government officials and a handful of Senegalese intellectuals did join ADBPA, but in the early years, teachers and civil servants were more numerous than any other group. The nature of ADBPA's membership meant that the association's primary goal was not to provide a forum

---

[5]Documentation is drawn from the AIDBA archives. For fuller discussion and complete citations, see Maack, 1981b, chapters 5 and 10.

for professional dialogue at the local level, but to bring together all individuals conscious of the potential role of books and libraries in Africa and to coordinate their efforts in promoting public libraries. ADBPA activities, therefore, included publicity aimed both at promoting libraries and encouraging reading—such as public conferences, study circles, films, and theater.

The first ADBPA conference, a six-day institute on libraries in French-speaking Africa, took place in November 1959. As the first meeting to bring together persons concerned with library development in this region, the conference received support from the High Commissioner of the AOF and from Senegalese officials as well as the rector University of Dakar.

The conference program consisted of lectures, public meetings, work sessions, and study tours that were attended by 39 participants from Senegal, France, Togo, Mauretania, Guinea, the French Sudan, and Dahomey. Although persons taking part in the conference were drawn from a variety of occupations (including a housewife, an insurance agent, an economist, and meteorologist), the majority of participants were actively involved with libraries. More than half the participants were African, but since so few had library training, only one Mauretanian and one Togolese gave presentations.

Since its foundation, ADBPA has actively lobbied African governments to pass comprehensive library legislation. Recommendations were addressed to the territorial governments in 1958 and 1959 requesting that each one create an autonomous library directorate attached to the Ministry of Education; that a model public library be established in each capital; and that a 4-year plan for the development of urban and rural library service be established; that each country create a network of libraries consisting of a national library, research libraries, and public libraries; it was further recommended that these libraries be organized according to international standards suggested by UNESCO. A copy of the 1959 resolutions was sent to each head of state along with proposals for comprehensive library legislation and for a 12-year library development plan. However, within a few months all 13 Francophone territories had become autonomous. Although some heads of state (such as Léopold Senghor) favored library development in principle, no attention was given to such considerations at the time of independence.

By June 1960, it was apparent that the structure of the ADBPA needed to be modified to reflect the new political situation in Africa. Originally conceived within the context of the AOF, the association had drawn its officers and membership from several territories and had worked to implement certain policies on the federal level. On the eve of independence, the Senegalese section was temporarily given the authority to act as a "central section" that would encourage the creation of other national sections and coordinate their activities. Meanwhile, Dadzie had already organized a Togolese section during a home leave in 1958. The membership of this section had reached 55 by January 1960, but its ties with the central section were tenuous.

Because the leaders of ADBPA hoped to encourage the formation of other national associations, they amended their original statutes by creating an international executive board of fifteen members. After the Mauretanian section was formed in June 1960, the board drew its officers from three sections, plus a *section d'attente* for members living in countries with no national affiliate. The international bureau, presided over by Amadou Mahtar M'bow, included five Senegalese, four Togolese, four Mauretanians, one Nigerian, and one Frenchman. Since no other national sections were formed under the 1960 statutes, Senegal, Mauretania, and Togo remained the center of AIDBA's efforts.

In addition to providing an international framework for the activities of the association, the 1960 constitution officially extended the organization's concerns to all types of libraries. This actually "legitimized" the direction the association had already begun to take. When the first conference was held in 1959, participants discussed all types of libraries and prepared final resolutions that clearly expressed their view that public library development must be a part of a broader plan including national, academic, and research libraries. To reflect the new structure and extended concerns of the association, its name was changed to the Association Internationale pour le Développement des Bibliothèques en Afrique, with the acronym AIDBA.

AIDBA's international vocation was expressed both in the association's efforts to bring together librarians from various African states and in its attempts to solicit aid for African libraries from abroad. Contacts were sought with UNESCO, with French library authorities, and with librarians in other countries that had advanced library systems. Therefore, in 1961 AIDBA leaders were delighted to have an opportunity to participate in the first Afro–Scandinavian library conference. When planning for this conference began in September 1960, the AIDBA secretariat suggested topics, chose African participants, and made travel arrangements for representatives from 12 countries. Of the 27 African delegates who arrived in Copenhagen on October 2, 1961, two-thirds came from Francophone states. However, since Nigeria, Ghana, Sierre Leone, Kenya, and the Sudan also sent representatives, the conference provided the first opportunity for many African librarians from former French territories to exchange views with colleagues from the British Commonwealth, where public libraries were more developed.

Although all types of libraries were discussed, the major focus of the conference was on public library needs in Africa and on possibilities for cooperation between African states and the Scandinavian countries. At the final meeting, delegates drafted general recommendations for library legislation and planning to be addressed to African governments and recommendations for future Afro–Scandinavian cooperation to be presented by Denmark to the other Scandinavian states.

AIDBA held other inter-African conferences after 1961, but it was only the Senegalese section that proved to be a viable national association. Despite its limited size (it grew from 21 members in 1957 to 74 in 1967) and meager funding, the establishment of AIDBA should be regarded as the first stage in the creation of a small but vocal library profession in Senegal (Maack, 1978, pp. 464, 498).

Originally founded as an organization to promote public libraries rather than a professional association, AIDBA came to see its double mission as improving library service and advancing librarianship. During its brief history, it engaged in many of the activities that librarians in developed countries expect of their professional associations. One major difference, however, was in the area of standards. Creating libraries to meet African needs was a central theme of most AIDBA conferences, but the association's main concern was with the adaptation of standards developed by UNESCO or by library associations from industrialized nations. AIDBA therefore directed its efforts toward convincing African governments to implement UNESCO suggestions for libraries and library planning rather than urging them to create their own standards. Although AIDBA's early lobbying met with little success, this did not discourage Dadzie who felt that patience was prerequisite "in a field which is very important but does not appear so to the government" (quoted in Maack, 1981b, p. 189).

2. THE WEST AFRICAN LIBRARY ASSOCIATION

Like its Francophone counterpart, the West African Library Association (WALA) was created in response to the recommendation of the Ibadan seminar that "librarians working in various regions of Africa should take practical steps to form dynamic professional associations as rapidly as possible" (UNESCO Seminar . . . , 1954, p. E8). The founding committee of WALA actually met during the Ibadan conference, and the formation of the new association was cited by UNESCO as "an immediate outcome of the seminar" (UNESCO Seminar . . . , 1954, p. E9).

The primary objectives of WALA were "to unite all persons in West Africa interested in librarianship and to provide the medium for discussion and exchange of ideas" (Aguolu, 1975, p. 254). The association was open to anyone, but from the beginning, librarians assumed most of the leadership positions. The founding committee of the association consisted of 11 individuals, four of whom were expatriate librarians; three African librarians were also members along with two educators, one administrative officer, and one publisher's representative.

During WALA's eight-year existance, nonlibrarians continued to play a role, and two of these individuals—D. A. Cannon, a physician, and Alhaji Gwandu, a political leader—served as presidents. However, it was the expatriate librarians who most often were elected as officers or councillors; between 1954 and 1962, nearly ⅗ of the 85 council seats were held by expatriates. John Harris, who convened the first meeting of the founding committee, served two terms as president (1954 and 1958), three terms as vice-president, and two additional terms as a councillor. Evelyn Evans served three terms on the council (including one term as president), and another British librarian, Jessie Carnell, from the technical college in Kumasi, held the presidency for two terms.

Africans regularly served on the council, and Kalu Okorie of Nigeria was elected as an officer every year for eight years. However, it was not until 1961 that Okorie became the first African librarian to hold the presidency of WALA (Oderinde, 1970, p. 104). The fact that Africans did not immediately form a majority of WALA leadership was due, in part, to their limited opportunities for advanced training. At the time WALA was founded, the only West Africans holding the Fellowship of the Library Association were Okorie and G. M. Pitcher of Ghana (Nyarko, 1979, p. 2). A grant from the Carnegie Corporation enabled the Gold Coast Library Board to send 17 Ghanaians to England for library education between 1950 and 1961 (Benge, 1967, p. 225). In-service training was also offered by the board in Accra, and by a few other libraries or library systems, such as the University College Library in Ibadan. In addition, WALA persuaded the federal and regional governments of Nigeria to award some fellowships for library education abroad. Even though relatively few Africans had access to library training prior to 1960, the personal membership in WALA rose from 107 in 1954 to 159 in 1956 and 226 in 1961.

A few individuals from Sierre Leone and Gambia joined WALA, but the great majority of members were from the Gold Coast or Nigeria. There fore, the annual association meetings alternated between Lagos, Accra, Ibadan, and Kumasi. Twenty-seven Nigerians and seven Ghanaians participated in the inaugural conference held in Lagos in 1954. Because distances between the member countries were great, future conferences also drew heavy participation from the host country, but attracted relatively few librarians from the other parts of West Africa.

The need to maintain contact among members who could not meet together regularly led John Harris to launch *West African Libraries* in March 1954. This publication continued to appear at irregular intervals from 1955 to 1962 (later as *WALA News*) published by Ibadan University Press. During this period, it was the only library journal published in tropical Africa. Altogether 16 issues appeared—approximately two per year. An analysis of the contents of these issues revealed that the majority of articles were papers, reports, and other conference proceedings. However, the Ghanaian library educator, observed: "The standard of articles was generally high, although initially many were largely straightforward accounts of the existing library services. Others were however real contributions to library thought" [Nyarko, 1979, p. 4]. The association published no monographs, in part because of its limited budget.

WALA depended largely on membership dues and received no money from public funds or from outside agencies. However, the association did not hesitate to approach the Carnegie Corporation in 1955 with the request that the corporation "establish four Scholarships a year in the territories of the Gold Coast and Nigeria for training, at a library school in the United Kingdom or the United States, for library assistants who have at least passed one part of the [Library Association] registration examinations" (quoted by Aina, 1979, p. 60).

Rather than acting on this request, the Carnegie Corporation commissioned Harold Lancour, Associate Dean of the Library School at the University of Illinois, to survey libraries in British West Africa and recommend a coherent plan for library education. The president and officers of WALA helped organize Lancour's tour of the region when he arrived in October 1957. Lancour was therefore aware of differences within the council; he also knew that the Ghana division of WALA preferred to see a grant established for scholarships that would allow West Africans to study in England (Lancour, 1958, p. 27). Although he suggested several possible options to the Carnegie Corporation, Lancour strongly recommend the establishment of "a post-graduate West African Institute of Librarianship at University College in Ibadan" (1958, p. 31).

This proposal was favorably received by the Nigerian division of WALA, but it was not palatable to the Ghana Division (nor to the Ghanaian Library Board). As preparations for a library school at Ibadan got underway, the tension between the two divisions grew. In 1959, Harris stated in his presidential address: "I am faced with the unhappy fact that I speak only for Nigeria. The nature of our constitution makes us a divided body, an Association of Divisions. . . . We have not yet learnt to act in a united way as an association (quoted in Oderinde, 1970, p. 68). WALA continued to exist for 3 more years before it split into two separate national associations.

In working to promote library legislation, WALA was also more successful on a divisional level than as an interterritorial association. Nonetheless, at the 1956 conference, it was decided that WALA should present recommendations to the governments of Gambia, Federal Nigeria, Sierre Leone, and Southern Cameroon urging them to adopt legislation patterned on the Gold Coast Library Board Ordinance of 1949. These recommendations were not acted on immediately, but the Nigeria Division was able to achieve some success in other discussions with the federal government. Although the division did not have an official charter, in 1956, it formally protested the adoption of a federal salary scale that did not accord professional status to individuals who had qualified as chartered librarians or as Fellows of the British Library Association. After this situation was rectified, the Nigerian Division continued to maintain close contact with the Federal Minority of Establishments in order "to explore ways of improving the career prospects for librarians" (Oderinde, 1970, p. 86).

The division also approached the regional governments, urging them to pass public library legislation. Its single success was the passage of the Eastern Nigeria Library Board Law in 1955. The other two regions could not be persuaded to adopt similar laws, nor was the federal government ready to pass national legislation. However, in 1958 the Nigerian Division convinced federal authorities to establish a Library Advisory Committee. This committee subsequently played a vital role in the establishment of the National Library.

F. European Library Traditions in Africa

Because WALA and AIDBA were relatively small interterritorial associations, neither was closely patterned after the Library Association (LA) or the Association des Bibliothécaires Français (ABF). Nonetheless, many of the differences between the two African associations grew from roots in their British or French heritage.

The establishment of a register of qualified librarians was not attempted by WALA because of the cost of specialized staff and other expenses involved in creating syllabi and administering examinations (Lancour, 1958, p. 29). Thus WALA, unlike the LA, was a purely voluntary association. It was nonetheless tied to the Library Association because many of its leaders held British credentials and fought to see that these were recognized by colonial authorities in Africa. AIDBA, on the other hand, never considered the question of qualifying examinations. Instead, the Francophone association sought official recognition for the profession by drafting an appropriate civil service scale for librarians and presenting this document to the Senegalese government. (The decree was passed in Senegal in 1969.) This was also the pattern followed by the ABF, which had no power to certify French librarians. However, the ties between ABF and AIDBA were extremely tenuous. Few, if any, Africans joined ABF before independence, and only one French librarian resident in Senegal in 1957 was an ABF member.

During the postwar years, most qualified French librarians passed a state examination after a period of apprenticeship and self-directed study. Outside of the Ecole des Chartes, which still emphasized archives administration and palaeography over library management, and a course on bibliography offered by Louise-Noëlle Malclès at the Sorbonne library, there was no formal training available to prospective French librarians. As a result of this brief exposure to librarianship and the voluntary nature of ABF membership, beginning librarians were not prepared to view library-association activity as an essential element in their professional life. In addition, many of the first French librarians working in the AOF had little previous library experience, and thus had not yet had the opportunity to become involved with library association activity in France. Certain young librarians like Séguin (the first professional to serve at the university libraries in Dakar) willingly participated in AIDBA but did not assume a leadership role. WALA, in contrast, was able to draw on individuals like Harris, who had served as President of the New Zealand Library Association, and Evans, who had been professionally active for many years before coming to Africa. The prestige of these two individuals also contributed to WALA's lobbying efforts since both expatriate librarians had good contacts in government circles.

Like the French association, AIDBA sought to promote national library legislation in Franchphone states; therefore, it seldom dealt directly with lower levels of government nor did it press for the passage of enabling laws. WALA also worked for national legislation in British territories, but its greatest success came with the passage of the regional library law in Eastern Nigeria. AIDBA's failure to persuade Francophone states to adopt a similar statute was attributed by Dadzie to the government's general lack of concern for libraries. Dadzie's perseverence in the face of this continuing apathy may well have grown out of a knowledge that ABF had campaigned for a national library directorate for over 30 years before the Direction des Bibliothèques de France was created in 1945.

AIDBA's inter-African conferences and the papers produced for these meetings were undoubtedly the association's greatest contribution to librarianship in Francophone Africa. Although no journal was published by AIDBA prior to 1960, these mimeographed conference papers were sent on request to librarians unable to attend the meetings. The *WALA News* also served to disseminate the conference proceedings of that association, but other articles appeared from time to time. WALA's more effective publication record was in part due to Harris' abilities and perseverance as an editor. However, the journal's durability was also a result of WALA's larger membership which provided more potential authors and more adequate funding.

Although AIDBA received occasional grants from public funds and small donations from private bodies, its budget depended largely on membership dues. During its first year, the Francophone association had only 21 members, whereas WALA recruited 107 individuals in 1954. By 1961, the Nigeria Division had 145 members and the Ghana Division enrolled 74 individuals, but it was not until 1967 that the Senegalese section of AIDBA could attract a membership of 74. The disparity between the two inter-African associations paralleled the divergence between the LA and the ABF. In 1957, the French association had 589 members while its British counterpart enrolled 4707. Four years later both associations had grown, but ABF had only 767 members in 1961 as compared to 5800 members in the LA (Boissard, 1975, p. 308; Jain, 1971, pp. 16–17).

Even allowing for the difference between the membership in a certifying body and in a purely voluntary association, the disparity between the number of librarians in the two countries remained enormous. It was noted in 1960 that there were 1400 British librarians overseas—mostly in the newer Commonwealth countries (Kotei, 1972, p. 472). Such a contribution in personnel would have been totally impossible for the French, who were struggling to train enough professionals to staff their own rapidly expanding libraries.

The number of trained librarians in France and Britain naturally reflected the number of posts available, and the number of posts in each country in turn reflected the level and nature of library service. In Britain, the Library Association's charter was granted in 1898, at a time of rapid public library development. Thus, one objective in the charter specifically called for the association "to promote the establishment of reference and lending service for use by the public." As public librarians formed "the backbone of the Association," it was this group "who showed the deepest concern to elaborate a coherent body of professional theory" (Cowley, 1933, p. 132; MacKenna, 1964, p. 618). The influence of the public library sector was also seen in the LA syllabi and examination, which tended to stress a strong public service orientation in librarianship. In France, however, the movement for public libraries occurred much later, and library posts were not numerous in academic, municipal, and research libraries, where little service was given to readers.

When the ABF was founded in 1906, French librarianship was just beginning to emerge from an archival tradition, characterized by an emphasis on conservation rather than use, a reluctance to adopt any relative classification system for books, and a general lack of concern for reader service. During the first 30 years of its history, many ABF leaders were graduates of the

Ecole des Chartes, and those librarians in charge of municipal libraries often saw their chief responsibility as the preservation of the city's rare books—not service to general readers. Some *chartistes,* however, were leaders in the movement to transform French municipal libraries into free public libraries. Thus, the two AOF archivists, André Villard and Margerite Verdat, were not outside the French tradition in their efforts to stimulate the creation of popular libraries.

Despite a commitment to public libraries in Africa, the AOF archivists and other French librarians brought an archival orientation to the organization of libraries. As in French research libraries, the IFAN collection was arranged by size, format, and order of acquisition rather than by subject. A similar system was later adopted at the university libraries in Dakar where the collections were divided by *faculté* (law, medicine, science, and liberal arts); books for each *faculté* were then assigned fixed-location numbers (rather than relative classification numbers) and were placed in central stacks closed to readers. Only the reference works located in the reading rooms were arranged by the Universal Decimal Classification. Many academic and research librarians in France and Francophone Africa strongly opposed the idea of open access, partly because they lacked sufficient staff to classify the books and maintain their order on the shelves.

In contrast, the university college libraries in Legon and Ibadan immediately began to assign classification numbers to their collection. The Ghanaian library adopted the Library of Congress Classification, but in Ibadan the Bliss Bibliographic Classification was initially used. Reference service was also introduced in these libraries, which had more clerical staff than the university libraries in Dakar, thus allowing librarians to spend more time in public service.

The 14 librarians assigned to the University of Dakar library in 1962–1963 represented a generous commitment on the part of the Direction des Bibliothèques at a time when there were only 202 university librarians in the entire French corps of librarians. With 20 universities drawing on this limited personnel, even an important library such as that at the University of Lille was forced to manage with 11 professionals (Poindron, 1964, p. 534). At the same time in Britain, the University and Research Section of the Library Association had a membership of 2500 persons. While some of these individuals served in national or special libraries, there were still several hundred chartered librarians employed in the 29 college and university libraries of Britain (MacKenna, 1964, pp. 607, 620). The university libraries in Legon and Ibadan were not as generously staffed as their counterparts in Britain, but they were run by individuals who saw reference service as an important professional duty, along with cataloging and acquisition. Although bibliographic instruction and reader service were not completely lacking in Dakar, the new library building was designed in such a way that there was no central reference desk; furthermore, the offices of the librarians were located in an area that was relatively inaccessible to readers (Maack, 1981b, p. 134). This was a concrete expression of a concept of librarianship in which reader service was not an integral role of the librarian.

While the growth of the university library collections in Legon, Ibadan, and Dakar was quite similar (the first two libraries each reported 160,000 volumes in 1962, the latter 125,000 volumes), public library development was very different in each country. In 1962, an enormous disparity existed in the size and number of public libraries in the Anglophone states, where they received government support, and in the Francophone states, where most libraries for general readers were privately sponsored. However, it must be noted that there was also a marked contrast between the solid progress made in Ghana and the uneven service offered in Nigeria.

By the early 1960s, Ghanian public libraries held close to half a million books to serve a population of 7 million, while Nigeria, with over 55 million people, had public library collections of just over a quarter of a million volumes. Both countries created public libraries that grew out of British traditions, but these bore different fruit in the two former colonies.

The implementation of the Gold Coast Library Board Ordinance occurred just 100 years after the passage of the British Public Libraries Act in 1850. In some ways, the circumstances in the mother country and the colony were similar when their respective library laws were adopted. British library leader Lionel McColvin observed that the passage of the Act of 1850 was

> the personal achievement of well-informed, indomitable enthusiasts. Apart from these there was no *demand* for public libraries. The people did not ask for public libraries. Why *should* they do so?—they had no idea of what a public library could do or mean. . . . In other words here is, definitely, a case when supply created demand, not where demand created supply (1956, p. 23).

In the Gold Coast, the small group of library enthusiasts had seen what public libraries could do in Britain and America, and they succeeded remarkably well in translating this idea to Africa where those without experience abroad knew nothing about public libraries.

Although Anglo-American library philosophy and practice were evident in the Gold Coast, the legislation departed from British and American precedents in that the board was national and had no ties to local governing bodies. In Nigeria, the weakness of the central government and the apathy of colonial authorities made it impossible to pass national public library legislation. The attempt to initiate regional and municipal service met with mixed success. In the Eastern Region where the Library Board had strong political support and UNESCO aid, it was possible to offer a level of service that created an increasing demand for books. Elsewhere, library promoters were unable to obtain sufficient political support or outside funding to foster the growth of a local public library movement.

In Francophone Africa, the small cadre of library enthusiasts were faced with government apathy and the lack of a well-established model of public library service in France. The French municipal library tradition, which featured a popular lending library attached to a scholarly collection, was transferred to Africa, where CENTRIFAN libraries sometimes had a circulating collection of novels and general books. However, aside from the library in Saint Louis, this arrangement was not effective. Meanwhile, in France, the postwar period brought a remarkable extension of modern public library service organized by the Direction des Bibliothèques. Despite the efforts of library officials like Masson to extend this work to Africa, the influence of the directorate did not reach beyond the university library. However, the catalytic role that the Direction des Bibliothèques was filling in France did not go unnoticed by African library promoters; thus, one of AIDBA's continuing goals was to see a similar directorate set up in each Francophone state.

IV. THE COLONIAL LEGACY: A COMPARATIVE ANALYSIS

The marked differences in library philosophy, in technical procedures, and in professional organization that characterized librarianship in Britain and France were transplanted to Africa when the first Western libraries were established. However, the nature of librarianship inherited by the Anglophone and Francophone states must be seen as one element in a broader colonial legacy that shaped the library environment in West Africa. This legacy included the administrative and political structure of each country, the social agencies created before independence, the economic infrastructure, and finally, the cultural priorities transmitted by the governing power.

A. Administrative Organization

The administrative structure of a country is important because it determines the channels of decision making, the roles of different levels of government in library development, and the presence or absence of continuity in policy. In comparing public library history in France, Great Britain, and the United States, Jean Hassenforder concludes that the "one essential condition" is national leadership: "the political and administrative authorities must be won over to the cause of public libraries and must understand the usefulness and need for them. Otherwise the libraries will remain minor institutions doomed to vegetate, for lack of facilities and funds" (1968, p. 19). This statement is perhaps more true in West Africa than in Britain or the United States (where local governments assumed major responsibility for public libraries).

In the Gold Coast, countrywide library service was achieved largely because of support at the highest levels of national leadership where administrative authority was concentrated. Nigeria, on the other hand, had inherited a weak federal government which was unwilling to assume any responsibility for libraries until a relatively weak National Library Act was passed in 1964 (Nwoye, 1977, pp. 6–8). Furthermore, the regional rivalry which grew out of Nigeria's administrative structure stimulated the creation of 12 universities after independence (and hence, spurred academic library development) but it did not foster any competition in the creation of public library systems (Bozimo, 1979).

The British system of indirect rule—involving the use of indigenous political organization—left a legacy of regional tension and instability in Ghana and Nigeria which both experienced political coups, periods of prolonged military rule, and considerable governmental reorganization. This was especially true in Nigeria where the three regions were divided into 12 states in 1967, on the eve of the civil war. Further reorganization occurred at the end of the war in 1970, and six years later, an additional seven states were created, making a total of 19 units of government responsible for library development.

The regionalism which plagued British West Africa was largely absent from the French-speaking states where local political structures had been suppressed or refashioned to fit within the French scheme of administration. Although Francophone leaders like Senghor have shown a strong commitment to preserving African cultural traditions, there has been no attempt to revive precolonial political institutions in Senegal or the Ivory Coast. Instead, the French administrative structure has been preserved virtually intact as noted by Robert Delavignett, a historian and former colonial administrator:

> At the very base of each republic the independence movement maintained the same administrative core that had existed during the colonial epoch. Only the names had changed: the circle was now called the department, and the *commandant de cercle* the prefect. The colonial administrative engine had not been consigned to the scrap-heap; it had merely been painted in African colors (1970, p. 276).

Not only have the Francophone states maintained a continuity in governmental structure, they have also enjoyed great stability in leadership; both Senghor and Houphouët-Boigny have held the presidency of their respective countries for two decades.

Given the political stability and the highly centralized nature of the two Francophone states, it is not surprising that both Senegal and the Ivory Coast adopted national library legislation. In the latter state, the Central Library of the Ivory Coast was created by decree in 1964 and was given the role of building up "a network of secondary libraries called regional libraries based in the main towns" (Library Legislation, 1968, p. 72). Although funding was insufficient to allow the library to fulfill this role, in 1967 another decree was issued creating a Service of Libraries and Publications "to plan and organize the development of [all types of] libraries" (Liguer-Labouet, 1975, p. 160). The following year a national library was founded. Meanwhile, in Senegal the passage of national library legislation did not occur until 1976 when three decrees were issued calling for the creation of a national library system, including all types of libraries, and the establishment of a national library (see Maack, 1981b, pp. 227–228).

Although library promoters in Senegal and the Ivory Coast succeeded in passing relatively comprehensive library legislation, in neither case were they able to persuade the government to provide sufficient financial support to implement the decrees effectively. Thus by the mid-1970s, both Ghana and Nigeria had better library resources than the Francophone states, even though library development in both English-speaking countries had been retarded during periods of political upheaval.

B. Social Agencies

Although the political and administrative legacy was an important determinant of African library development, it was the survival of social agencies created during the colonial period that led to the direct continuity of certain types of library service. These agencies included universities and other institutions of higher education, research centers, and public library systems. In instances where adequate, well-organized libraries already existed, their growth generally proceeded along the same lines. It was easier to maintain the momentum of public library development in a country like Ghana, which had a well-organized national system at independence, than to create such a system in a country like the Ivory Coast, which lacked any mechanism for supplying books to general readers who could not use the municipal library in Abidjan. Thus in 1968 the French librarian Fanny Lalande-Isnard observed that in Africa libraries "developed rapidly in countries where an efficient organization already existed" but often failed to develop where it was necessary for the government to create new structures (1968, p. 243).

It is therefore important to consider the colonial government's failure to create certain types of agencies as part of the legacy inherited by African states. For example, the lack of Africanist research institutes in the British colonies meant that there were no major collections of Africana in the region, aside from the library at the university college in Ibadan. In 1961 an Africana collection was begun at the Balme Library in Legon and the Padmore Research Library on African Affairs was set up in Accra. However, these two Africanist libraries lagged behind the collections at Ibadan and the IFAN library in Dakar.

While the presence or absence of research institutes directly affected only the intellectual elite, the failure to create enough primary schools to enroll all school-age children meant that the West African countries achieved independence at a level of "conditional literacy." Literacy continued to involve reading in a second language throughout Francophone Africa, where instruction in state schools was entirely in French. Vernacular languages were taught at the lower primary level in Ghana and Nigeria, but there was too little material published in these languages to make them important vehicles in national development. By 1980, there was little indication that English and French would soon be replaced as national languages in West Africa. Meanwhile, their continued use is an important factor both in determining the reading needs and preferences of the elite and in acting as an obstacle to the rapid achievement of mass literacy. While colonial education policy in all four countries effectively limited reading to a narrow elite before World War II, the postwar expansion of schools was a first step toward creating societies where literacy was not restricted intentionally for political reasons.

C. Economic Infrastructure

The one economic activity most closely related to education and literacy is the book industry. Greater mission activity in Nigeria and Ghana resulted in more vernacular publishing by the religious presses in those states than in Francophone Africa. However, there was very little commercial publishing before World War II, and no scholarly press existed until Harris created the University of Ibadan Press in 1949. Meanwhile, in the AOF, IFAN began publishing scholarly monographs in 1938; however, the region had little Arabic language publication, even less vernacular publishing, and almost no commercial book production in French.

Since independence, Nigeria has become the largest book producer in the region with some 1000 titles per year during the early 1970s (Tamuno, 1973, p. 9). Meanwhile, a government-sponsored press has been set up in Ghana, and Senegal and the Ivory Coast jointly hold the majority of shares in Nouvelles Editions Africans, a company established in 1972 in conjunction with the French publisher Hachette. Progress has been made by all four countries, but because of the low level of local production, they must continue to import books from Britain and France at a cost that is 40–45% over list price because of transportation costs.

The need to import books and other manufactured products from abroad was one element in the colonial legacy of economic dependency. African colonies were first drawn into the world market as exporters of raw materials for European industry. Prior to 1940, colonial authorities did not encourage the development of local industry nor did they seek to modernize the agricultural sector. After the war, economic progress became the focus of each African government's development plans, but these programs were themselves dependent on foreign investment or aid from abroad.

Such aid has also been crucial in certain areas of library development and the easier access to support from foreign foundations helped to make library progress greater in Nigeria than in Senegal or the Ivory Coast. Nigeria benefited from more Carnegie Corporation support than other West African countries, and it also succeeded in obtaining UNESCO aid to develop school and public libraries. In setting up its national library, Nigeria later received funding from the Ford Foundation. Ghana used Carnegie grants for library-training fellowships and for its technical college library, but the government chose not to seek much outside funding for libraries. Senegal likewise sought little library aid aside from UNESCO support to establish a regional library school in Dakar. Senegal did obtain a few technical assistance personnel from Canada and later received an engineering library (as part of the Ecole Polytechnique financed by Canada), but other direct aid to libraries was minimal. The Ivory Coast also obtained Canadian aid to construct its national library; it was the only Francophone state to receive UNESCO aid for a public library pilot project.

Access to foreign aid combined with internal economic conditions have determined each country's ability to finance libraries. However, in comparing Ghana and the Ivory Coast, it is obvious that economic factors can not account for the disparity in library development in the two countries. By 1975, the Ivory Coast had a slightly higher per capita income than Ghana, was experiencing more rapid economic growth, and had a primary school enrollment of 75% as opposed to 58% in Ghana. Yet the total book stock of Ivory Coast libraries (listed in the 1974–1975 UNESCO directory) was less than 300,000 volumes. At the same time, library collections in Ghana totaled well over a million and a half volumes, and Ghanaian public libraries had 11 times as many books as those in the Ivory Coast.

D. The Cultural Legacy

Unlike economic characteristics, the cultural legacy of colonialism can neither be quantified nor expressed in concrete terms. It remains elusive, intangible, yet pervasive. In one sense, this heritage represents the *Weltanschauung* or world view that each new state espoused as its leaders translated Western thought and values into an African idiom. For example, Senghor's doctrine of *négritude,* expressed as the "revaluation of African culture," was both a reaction to French assimilationist philosophy and an acceptance of the French value system in which one's national heritage was to be preserved and cherished. Pride in French culture was transmitted during the colonial era as part of the *mission civilatrice.* This concept was not an integral part of British colonial thought, and as the Ugandan scholar Ali Mazrui notes, "there is, in fact, far less talk of 'our British heritage' among English-speaking Africans than of 'our French cultural background' among . . . former French subjects" (1978, p. 12).

The colonial cultural legacy, however, includes both philosophy and action. It might therefore be expressed by the term *mentalité* as used by French historians to mean "l'ensemble d'habitudes et d'attitudes"—the totality of attitudes and behavior (Hassenforder, 1967, p. 195). One type of behavior that most clearly expressed the cultural impact of colonialism was creative writing. Mazrui comments (1978):

> The French have a greater preoccupation with expressing themselves through artistic and philosophic media. It is a total national orientation. . . . If then these two colonial powers bequeathed to their possessions abroad the essence of their own ways of life it was not surprising that French-speaking Africans tended, at least for a while, to be more culturally expressive than their English-speaking counterparts. Both groups of Africans might therefore be regarded as reflections of the total cultural orientations of the countries which ruled them (p. 12).

Like literature, libraries are shaped by the value orientation of their coeval culture. The high value placed by the French on their national heritage was conducive to the creation of great national research libraries and archives in France. In Senegal, these values resulted in an emphasis on both African culture and on the Franco-African heritage. This influenced the Senghor government to support the Senegalese and federal archives; to place a national library in the third development plan; and to sponsor the creation of an audiovisual archive for the collection and preservation of tapes, films, slides, and photographs that would document African traditional culture. There was a lack of emphasis on such activities in the English-speaking countries, where archival repositories were not established until the postwar period, where no systematic programs for collecting traditional literature had been implemented, and where Africanist libraries developed much later. Even the creation of a Nigerian national library showed a different orientation, and one publication by the library bore the revealing title: *The National Library of Nigeria: A Tool For Economic Development* (1970).

In the British Commonwealth there was, on the whole, a much more pragmatic attitude toward libraries which were seen as instruments of education and of economic progress, and not primarily as repositories of the national heritage. This is illustrated in the public library philosophy expressed by British library leaders.

L. Stanley Jast, who served as LA president in 1930 wrote: "England and the British Empire and the United States *know* that community libraries, free in every sense but that of support, are essential for the intellectual happiness and welfare of a free people" (quoted in McColvin, 1942, p. 1). This idea was further elaborated by Lionel McColvin in his proposals for postwar reorganization of the public library system: "Failure to provide . . . [public] library service is wasteful to the community and to civilization—wasteful because . . . those who would find in books the means to increased prosperity, satisfaction and happiness are denied this advantage" (1942, p. 1). These same sentiments were echoed by Kwame Nkrumah, who wrote in 1964: "Books must be readily available to satisfy the demands of people, whatever their age or their ability, so that through reading they can derive information, enjoyment, and a broader outlook" (Evans, 1964, pp. xiii–xiv).

The faith in the social utility of libraries in Commonwealth countries led to an investment in public libraries that was much greater than in French-speaking countries. Thus, in 1933, when British public library service was described as "practically coterminus with national boundaries," Gabriel Henriot, former ABF president, remarked that "the question of popular libraries has hardly been submitted to public opinion and public library service exists in France only in an embryonic state" (Cowley, 1933, p. 133; Henriot, 1933, p. 108). About the same time, another ABF president and eminent library promoter, Henri Lemaître, remarked that "the very word library (bibliothèque), because of its scholarly connotation, has become so forbidding to many that another expression was sought. . . . it was thus that the phrase public reading (lecture publique) was created" (quoted in Richter, 1977, p. 2).

Africans studying in France between the two wars found few examples of dynamic public libraries, whereas a number of Nigerians and Ghanaians who studied abroad became strong advocates of the kind of public library service they had seen in action. Nkrumah commented in 1956: "when my studies took me to the United States of America and England, I realized how vital to the student and indeed to every man and woman, was a good library" (Evans, 1964, p. 49). Even though the British were slow to export their public library system to West Africa, the existence of a model for such service was an important element in the cultural legacy of the colonies.

E. Adaptation and Innovation

Two very different library traditions took root in West Africa at the end of the colonial era. At that time, to paraphrase Sir Eric Ashby, African leaders wanted a replica of metropolitan library service at its best; the expatriate librarians had no other model to offer. Yet, it soon became apparent that a model of service that grew out of different social and cultural conditions could not be transplanted without adaptation to local needs.

Many of the first expatriate librarians understood the importance of adapting libraries to the geography and climate as well as the social and intellectual conditions of developing countries. From 1940 to 1960 when the foundations of modern librarianship were laid, Africana collections were built in Dakar and Ibadan, bookmobile service was initiated for the scattered settlements in Eastern Nigeria, and librarians in Ghana attempted to meet readers' demand for nonfiction books. However, during this period of experimentation, the urgency of creating library service allowed little time to reflect on the role of libraries in relationship to African culture and society.

In the two decades since independence, African and expatriate librarians have given much more attention to the impact of books and libraries in Africa. During this period, a number of dissertations have explored the past and present role of oral tradition, visual perception, and literacy in Africa (Aguolu, 1977b; Bozimo, 1979; Kotei, 1972; Maack, 1978; Shodeinde, 1978). Many of these recent studies are based on what Basil Davidson describes as "the belief that the new history of Africa flows out of the old history of Africa, and is otherwise inexplicable. This standpoint sees the 'colonial period' . . . as an interlude of complex and often contradictory consequences, precisely because the new imperialism did not operate within a vacuum but within the packed arena of on-going African society" (1978, p. 18).

Greater appreciation for this continuity has also been shown by expatriate writers. For example, Regine Fontaine from the Bureau du Livre in Paris observes that reading in Africa is a colonial importation alien to African society: "a silent and solitary activity, reading fits poorly into a culture dominated by oral expression and a sense of community. It is considered a culture-object . . . a sum of knowledge which belongs to the master, the professor, and in a general way, to the colonizer" (1974, p. 17).

Somewhat earlier, this same theme was discussed by R. C. Benge, who served as a library educator in Ghana:

> The communal basis for social life . . . is bound to affect not only reading habits, but the creating and appreciation for imaginative literature. The European novel was developed because as a literary form it was dealing with the individual . . . as a person over and above, and often against organized society. . . . I think it is true to say this way of thinking tends to be alien to African social life. . . . The concept of "self" is quite different (1963, p. 211).

While this perceptive analysis offers one explanation for the strong preference for nonfiction among Africans, it does not imply that this is necessarily a static condition. Benge also notes that already there had been a gradual change in reading patterns in Ghana; by 1960, for the first time, fiction represented over 50% of all books circulated by the library board (1963, p. 210). While changing reading patterns and growing circulation figures reflected the rapid evolution of African society, some African librarians were also examining the role of the public library in communities that still include many illiterates. A Nigerian librarian, J. Chidi Anyim, remarks:

> I consider it very wrong to run our public libraries as if our clientele were a reading public. Our culture is essentially oral. In traditional society, the center of activity is the town-square—an arena pulsating with sustained civic and cultural activity drawing its audience from the entire community. Our public libraries must become the equivalent of our village squares if they are to fill their mission in Nigeria (1972, p. 16).

Anyim's view of the public library as a cultural center was also shared by Théodore N'diaye, a Senegalese library educator, who believed that public library services should not be limited to an elite but should reach the masses through use of audiovisual media, which are more closely akin to the oral expression of traditional culture. He wrote:

> In this perspective, the African public library will certainly be a source of information, for self-education, for meeting, a place where every member of the community can find a response to his needs; but the library will also be a center for literacy training, for artistic endeavors and literary exchange, for reading alone or in a group, for listening to music, for exhibits and other cultural events. The African public library . . . it is simply *l'arbre à palabre* [the traditional tree where the village gathers] (1973, p. 4).

N'diaye based these goals for the public library on the principle that "each civilization's structure calls for its own mode of cultural expression." By creating libraries that would also be communal meeting places like the time-honored *arbre à palabre,* N'diaye believed that they could form an integral part of the community life, serving as a source for the conservation and diffusion of African traditions as well as a source for exposure to Western ideas. Thus, he foresaw the library as playing a part in the evolution of a new culture that would be both modern and African.

The striking similarity in the views independently expressed by N'diaye and Anyim may herald a new era of African librarianship that departs from British and French models in an attempt to grapple with problems unique to Africa. The search for new solutions does not necessarily mean abandoning the efforts of library pioneers, but involves a reassessment of library services in light of a better understanding of African needs. As John Harris noted, the first generation of professional librarians in West Africa had to start building not "from scratch . . . [but] miles behind scratch" (1965, p. 253). For the next generation of African librarians, the task would involve innovation but also synthesis, building on earlier foundations a structure that reflects the colonial and pre-colonial heritage of Africa but serves the needs of a rapidly changing society.

REFERENCES

Aboyade, B. O. (1973). The university library and related fields. *In* "The University of Ibadan 1948–1973: A History of the First Twenty-five Years" (J. F. Ade Ajayi and T. N. Tamuno, eds.), pp. 127–150. Ibadan University Press, Ibadan, Nigeria.

Adegoke, A. (1973). The evolution of libraries in Nigeria. *International Library Review* 5, 407–452.

Aguolu, C. C. (1975). Library associations in West Africa and the concept of a profession. *Nigerian Libraries* 11, 253–261. (Reprinted in *International Library Review* 8, 23–31.)

Aguolu, C. C. (1977a). The foundations of modern libraries in Nigeria. *International Library Review* 9, 461–483.

Aguolu, C. C. (1977b). "Libraries of Learning and Research in Nigerian Higher Education: Emergence, Roles and Responsibilities." Unpublished dissertation, University of California, Berkeley.

Aguolu, C. C. (1978). Father of Nigerian librarianship. *New Library World* 79, 251–253.

Aina, L. O. (1979). Factors affecting development of librarianship in Nigeria. *International Library Review* 11, 57–67.

Aje, S. B. (1956). Public libraries in Western Nigeria. *WALA News* 2, 78–84.

Anyim, J. C. (1972). Public libraries as cultural centers. *Nigerian Libraries* 8, 15–19.

Armstrong, C. W. (1971). "The Role of Information Resources in National Development: A Descriptive Study and Analyses of Library Resources in West Africa." Unpublished dissertation, University of Pittsburgh.

Arrêté créant l'Institut Français d'Afrique Noire (1936). *Bulletin du comité d'etudes historiques et scientifiques de l'AOF* **19**, 388.
Ashby, E. (1964). "African Universities and Western Tradition." Harvard University Press, Cambridge, Massachusetts.
Ashby, E. (1966). "Universities: British Indian and African, a Study in the Ecology of Higher Education." Weidenfeld and Nicolson, London.
Barnett, G. K. (1973). "The History of Public Libraries in France from the Revolution to 1939." Unpublished thesis submitted for the Fellowship of the Library Association, London.
Benge, R. C. (1963). Some notes on reading in Ghana. *Library World* **64**, 210–213.
Benge, R. C. (1967). Library education in Ghana 1961–67. *Library Association Record* **69**, 225–229.
Bengolea, R. P., and Akiwowo, A. (1974). Problems in peripheral regions. *International Social Science Journal* **26**, 411–426.
"Bibliotheque universitaire de Dakar" (1974). Grand Imprimerie Africaine, Dakar, Senegal.
Boissard, G. (1975). Do women hold the reins of power in French libraries? *UNESCO Bulletin for Libraries* **29**, 306–314.
Bozimo, D. (1979). "Cooperation among University Libraries in Nigeria – Problems, Perspectives, Prospects: Implications for National Planning." Unpublished dissertation, Columbia University.
Brévié, J. (1931). Circular reprinted in Notes et informations. *Bulletin du comité d'etudes historiques et scientifiques de l'AOF* **14**, 454–455.
Brown, A. R. (1975). State publishing in Ghana: Has it benefitted Ghana? *In* "Publishing in Africa in the Seventies (E. Oluwasanmi, E. McLean and H. Zell, eds.), pp. 113–127. University of Ife Press. Ile-Ife, Nigeria.
Cannon, D. A. (1954). The development of medical library facilities in Nigeria. *Libri* **3**, 184–187.
"Catalogues des bibliothèques" (1932). Dossier 16/0-7 in the Archives d'Afrique Occidentale Française, Dakar, Senegal.
Cissé, F. (1941). "Notes statistiques sur la marche de la bibliothèque de Saint Louis pendant l'année 1940 et les 5 premiers mois de 1941." Dossier 16/0-12 in the Archives d'Afrique Occidentale Française, Dakar, Senegal.
Clignet, R. (1970). Inadequacies of the notion of assimilation in African education. *Journal of Modern African Studies* **8**, 425–444.
Coleman, J. S. (1958). "Nigeria, Background to Nationalism." University of California Press, Berkeley.
Comte, H. (1977). "Les Bibliothèques publiques en France." Press de l'Ecole Nationale Supérieure de Bibliothèques, Lyon, France.
Cornevin, R. (1976). "Literatures d'afrique noire de langue française." Presses Universitaires de France, Paris.
Cowley, J. D. (1933). Great Britain. *In* "Popular Libraries of the World" (A. Bostwick, ed.), pp. 122–134. American Library Association, Chicago.
Crocker, W. R. (1936). "Nigeria, a Critique of British Colonial Administration." Allen and Unwin, London.
Crowder, M. (1968). "West Africa under Colonial Rule." Northwestern University Press, Evanston, Illinois.
Dadzie, E. W., and Strickland, J. T. (1965). "Directory of Archives, Libraries and Schools of Librarianship." UNESCO, Paris.
Davidson, B. (1978). "Let Freedom Come: Africa in Modern History." Little, Brown and Company, Boston.

Dean, J. (1967). The Balme Library, University of Ghana: History, structure, and development, 1948–1965. *Nigerian Libraries* 3, 79–92.
Dean, J. (1970). Organization and services of university libraries in West Africa. *In* "Comparative and International Librarianship: Essays on Themes and Problems (M. Jackson, ed.), pp. 111–118. Greenwood Press, Westport, Conn.
Delavignett, R. (1970). French colonial policy in black Africa. *In* "Colonialism in Africa" (L. H. Gann and P. Duignan, eds.), v. 2, pp. 251–285. Cambridge University Press, Cambridge, Massachusetts.
"Development of Public Libraries in Africa, the Ibadan Seminar" (1954). UNESCO, Paris.
Dowuona-Hammond, A. J. (1963). Foreword (Ghana issue). *Library World* 64, 203–204.
Ekpe, F. C. (1979). The colonial situation and library development in Nigeria. *International Library Review* 11, 5–18.
Evans, E. (1956). "The Development of Public Library Services in the Gold Coast." Library Association, London.
Evans, E. (1961). Library resources in English speaking countries of West Africa. *UNESCO Bulletin for Libraries* 15, 227–31.
Evans. E. (1963a). Ghana and its libraries. *Libri* 12, 364–368.
Evans, E. (1963b). The Ghana Library Board. *Library World* 64, 205–209.
Evans, E. (1964). "A Tropical Library Service." André Deutsch, London.
Flood, R. A. (1951). "Public Libraries in the Colonies." Library Association, London.
Fontaine, R. (1974). Le Problem du livre face au lecteur en Afrique. *Co-opération et développement* 48, 16–23.
Foster, P. (1965). "Education and Social Change in Ghana." University of Chicago Press, Chicago.
Ghana Library Board's Report for 1959–1960 (1961). *Wilson Library Bulletin* 38, 755.
Goody, J. (1968a). Introduction. *In* "Literacy in Traditional Society" (J. Goody, ed.), pp. 1–26. Cambridge University Press, Cambridge, Massachusetts.
Goody, J. (1968b). Restricted literacy in northern Ghana. *In* "Literacy in Traditional Society" (J. Goody, ed.), pp. 198–264. Cambridge University Press, Cambridge, Massachusetts.
Goody, J., and Watt, I. (1968). The consequences of literacy. *In* "Literacy in Traditional Society" (J. Goody, ed.), pp. 27–68. Cambridge University Press, Cambridge, Massachusetts.
Gunton, D. H. (1961). Library in the tropics: A history and blueprint. *Library Association Record* 63, 149–154.
Hahn, A. (1956). L'oeuvre éducative, les bibliothèques et la lecture publique en Afrique Occidentale Française, impressions de mission. *Bulletin des Bibliothèques de France* 1, 499–514.
Hailey, W. M. H. (1938). "An African Survey: A Study of Problems Arising in Africa South of the Sahara." Oxford University Press, London.
Hailey, W. M. H. (1957). "An African Survey: A Study of Problems Arising in Africa South of the Sahara." Revised edition. Oxford University Press, London.
Hardy, G. (1920). *Une Conquête morale: L'Enseignement au Sénégal de 1817 à 1854.* Emile Larose, Paris.
Harris, J. (1965). Ibadan University Library: Some notes on its birth and growth. *Library Association Record* 67, 253–263.
Harris, J. (1970). Libraries and librarianship at mid-century. *Nigerian Libraries* 6, 26–40.
Hassenforder, J. (1967). "Développement comparé des bibliothèques publiques en France, en Grande-Bretagne et aux Etas-Unis dans la seconde moitié de XIXe siécle (1850–1915)." Cercle de la Librairie, Paris.

Hassenforder, J. (1968). Comparative studies and the development of public libraries. *UNESCO Bulletin for Libraries* 22, 13–19.
Henriot, G. (1933). France. *In* "Popular Libraries of the World" (A. Bostwick, ed.), pp. 100–109. American Library Association, Chicago.
Hirsch-Pecault, C. (1958). Une Bibliothèque d'Afrique Noire: Saint-Louis du Sénégal. *Bulletin d'informations de l'Association des Bibliothécaires Français* 26, 75–78.
Historique de l'Institut Français d'Afrique Noire (1961). *Notes africaines* 90, 34–44.
Horrocks, S. (1962a). Enugu journey. *Library World* 64, 81–85.
Horrocks, S. (1962b). Reading for self-improvement in Eastern Nigeria. *UNESCO Bulletin for Libraries* 16, 244–246.
Institut français d'Afrique Noire (1949). "Rapport annuel." Dakar, Senegal.
Institut français d'Afrique Noire (1953). "Rapport annuel." Dakar, Senegal.
Jain, T. C. (1971). "Professional Associations and Development of Librarianship: Case Studies of the Library Association and the American Library Association." Metropolitan Book Company, Delhi, India.
Kensdale, W. E. N. (1955). The Arabic manuscript collection of the library of the University College of Ibadan, Nigeria. *WALA News* 2, 21–25.
Kotei, S. I. A. (1972). "The Social Determinants of Library Development in Ghana". Unpublished thesis, University of London.
Kotei, S. I. A. (1975). Some cultural and social factors of book reading and publishing in Africa. *In* "Publishing in Africa in the Seventies" (E. Oluwasanmi, E. McLean and H. Zell, eds.), pp. 174–208. University of Ife Press, Ile-Ife, Nigeria.
Kotei, S. I. A. (1977). Some variables of comparison between developed and developing library systems. *International Library Review* 9, 249–267.
Lalande-Isnard, F. (1968). The development of libraries in Africa. *UNESCO Bulletin for Libraries* 22, 241–246.
Lancour, H. (1958). Libraries in British West Africa: A report of a survey for the Carnegie corporation of New York. University of Illinois Library School, Urbana *Occasional Papers* 53.
Library legislation in the developing territories of Africa (1968). *Libri* 18, 51–78.
Liguer-Labouet, K. L. (1975). Ivory Coast, Libraries in *In* "Encyclopedia of Library and Information Science" 20, pp. 1–49. Marcel Dekker, New York.
MacKenna, R. O. (1964). Recent developments in university librarianship in Great Britain. *Library Trends* 12, 606–623.
McColvin, L. R. (1942). "The Public Library System of Great Britain: A Report on Its Present Condition with Proposals for Post-War Reorganization." Library Association, London.
McColvin, L. R. (1956). "The Chance to Read: Public Libraries in the World Today." Phoenix House, London.
Maack, M. N. (1978). "A History of Libraries, Archives and Documentation Centers in Senegal from their Colonial Beginnings to 1975." Unpublished dissertation, Columbia University.
Maack, M. N. (1981a). Libraries for the general public in French-speaking Africa: Their cultural role. *Journal of Library History* 16, 210–225.
Maack, M. N. (1981b). "Libraries in Senegal: Continuity and Change in an Emerging Nation." American Library Association, Chicago.
Mair, L. (1965). The social sciences in Africa south of the Sahara: The British contribution. *In* "Africa: Social Problems of Change and Conflict" (P. L. van den Berghe, ed.), pp. 15–35. Chandler Publishing Company, San Francisco.
Marty, P. (1914). La Medersa de Saint-Louis. *Revue du monde musulman* 7, 1–107.

Masson, A. (1954). "Project de lancement de la lecture publiqué en Afrique Occidentale Française avec l'aide du FIDES et de l'UNESCO." Unpublished report in the archives of the Association Internationale pour le Développement des Bibliothèques Africaines, Dakar, Senegal.

Mazrui, A. A. (1978). "Political Values and the Educated Class in Africa." University of California Press, Berkeley.

M'bow, A. M. (1961). "Rapport sur les origines historiques et l'extension du mouvement pour les bibliothèques en Afrique tropicale d'expression française." Paper presented at the First Afro-Scandinavian Conference, Copenhagen, 2–11 October.

Mumford, W. B., and Orde-Brown, G. (1937). "Africans Learn to be French: A Review of Educational Activities in the Seven Federated Colonies of French West Africa." Evans Brothers, London.

Murdock, G. (1959). "Africa, Its Peoples and Their Culture History." McGraw-Hill, New York.

"The National Library of Nigeria: A Tool for Economic Development" (1970). National Library of Nigeria, Lagos, Nigeria.

N'diaye, T. (1973). "Réflexions sur la mission de la bibliothèque publiqué africaine." Ecole des Bibliothecaires, Archivistes et Documentalistes, Dakar, Senegal.

Nwoye, S. C. (1977). Nigeria, libraries in *In* "Encyclopedia of Library and Information Science" 20, pp. 1–49. Marcel Dekker, New York.

Nwoye, S. C. (1979). "Consequences of Extending a Country's Library Legislation to the Inclusion of Academic Libraries, with Special Reference to Nigeria." Paper presented at the 45th Conference of the International Federation of Library Associations and Institutions, Copenhagen, Denmark, 27 August–1 September. ERIC-ED 185994.

Nyarko, K. (1979). "Library Literature in English-Speaking West Africa: Its Achievements, Problems and Prospects." Paper presented at the 45th Conference of the International Federation of Library Associations and Institutions, Copenhagen, 27 August–1 September. ERIC-ED 186006.

Obi, D. (1974). "The Curriculum Needs of the Sub-Saharan African Library School: A Study in Comparative Education for Librarianship". Unpublished dissertation, University of Pittsburgh.

Oderinde, N. O. (1970). Our professional association 1948–1968. *Nigerian Libraries* 6, 65–105.

Okorie, K. (1959). Problems of public library development in Nigeria. *Library World* 68, 161–165.

Okorie, K. (1960). A chance to read in Eastern Nigeria. *Library Journal* 85, 4100–4103.

Oliver, R., and Atmore, A. (1967). "Africa since 1800." Cambridge University Press, Cambridge, Massachusetts.

Omolewa, M. (1974). Adult readers in Nigerian libraries, 1932–1960: A study of library use in colonial Nigeria. *Nigerian Libraries* 10, 29–40.

Pitcher, G. M. (1970). Libraries and librarianship in Ghana, 1944–1969. *Ghana Library Journal* 4, 10–18.

Poindron, P. (1964). French university libraries. *Library Trends* 12, 528–538.

Profile of Evelyn J. A. Evans (1963). *Library World* 64, 224–225.

"Répertoire des bibliothèques scientifiques et techniques en Afrique au sud du Sahara" (1954). CSA publication 10. Conseil Scientifique pour l'Afrique au Sud du Sahara, London.

Richter, N. (1977). Histoire de la lecture publique in France. *Bulletin des bibliothèques de France* 22, 1–24.

Rousset de Pina, J. (1966). La nouvelle bibliothèque centrale de l'Université de Dakar. *Bulletin des bibliothèques de France* **11**, 293–304.

Shaw, F. (1905). "A Tropical Dependency: An Outline of the Ancient History of the Western Sudan with an Account of the Settlement of Northern Nigeria." Nisbet, London.

Shodeinde, A. O. (1978). "Recognition, Interpretation, and Style Preference of Pictures: A Comparison between Nigerian Urban and Nigerian Rural Illiterates." Unpublished dissertation, Southern Illinois University.

Tamuno, O. G. (1973). Printing and publishing in Nigeria: A historical survey. *Nigerian Libraries* **9**, 1–12.

Tettey, C. (1960). Medical library services in English-speaking West Africa. *WALA News* **3**, 245–249.

UNESCO seminar on the development of public libraries in Africa (1952). *UNESCO Bulletin for Libraries* **6**, E135–E138.

UNESCO seminar on the development of public library services in Africa (1954). *UNESCO Bulletin for Libraries* **8**, E8–E10.

University and special libraries in Ghana (1963). *Library World* **64**, 214–217, 226.

Vansina, J. (1960). Recording the oral history of the Bakuma, I: Methods. *Journal of African History* **1**, 46–53.

Vansina, J. (1965). "Oral Tradition: A Study in Historical Methodology." Routledge et Kegan Paul, London.

Villard, A. (1937a). "Rapport à M. le Gouverneur Général de l'AOF." Unpublished report dated 14 June 1937, Dossier 16/0-12 in the Archives d'Afrique Occidentale Française, Dakar, Senegal.

Villard, A. (1937b). "Suite de rapport de juin 1937." Unpublished report dated December 1937, Dossier 16/0-12 in the Archives d'Afrique Occidentale Française, Dakar, Senegal.

White, C. (1964). "The National Library of Nigeria: Growth of the Idea, Problems, Progress." Nigerian Federal Ministry of Information, Lagos.

Wilks, I. (1968). The transmission of Islamic learning in the Western Sudan. *In* "Literacy in Traditional Society" (J. Goody, ed.), pp. 161–197. Cambridge University Press, Cambridge, Massachusetts.

Worthington, E. B. (1938). "Science in Africa, a Review of Scientific Research Relating to Tropical and Southern Africa." Oxford University Press, London.

Wrong, M. (1939). "West Africa: Library Development." The Carnegie Corporation for the Colonial Office, New York.

Zartman, W. I. (1979). Social and political trends in Africa in the 1980s. *In* "Africa in the 1980s, a Continent in Crisis" (C. Legum, ed.), pp. 69–119. McGraw-Hill, New York.

Zidouemba, D. (1977). "Directory of Documentation, Libraries and Archives Services in Africa." UNESCO, Paris.

Information Access By Blind and Physically Handicapped Persons

ALFRED D. HAGLE

Library of Congress
Washington, D.C.

I.	Introduction	248
II.	Frequency of Impairment	248
III.	Resources and Services	250
	A. The National Library Service	250
	B. Braille Production and Tactile Technology	252
	C. Compositor's Tapes	255
	D. Optical Character Recognition	256
	E. Tangible Graphic Displays	256
	F. Direct Access Reading Aids	257
	G. Optacon	259
	H. Braille Computer Terminals	259
	I. Optical Scanners	260
	J. Tone Output Reading Machines	261
	K. Phonograph—Talking Book Machine	263
	L. Cassette Technology	265
	M. Indexing	267
	N. Recorded Encyclopedia	268
	O. Newspapers, Radio Reading	268
	P. Hearing Impairments	269
IV.	Bibliographic Control	271
V.	International Cooperation	272

VI.	Conclusion	273
	References	274

I. INTRODUCTION

Major handicaps are experienced most keenly by those individuals whose impairment restricts their capability for independence in mobility, communication (whether speech, reading, or writing), self-care, self-direction, or work skills. It is the communication skills that constitute the primary focus of this article, although it may be recognized at the outset that the ability to exchange spoken and written messages is perhaps the most important precondition to employment, education, and participation in the cultural and civic affairs of the community. Handicapped persons, especially those who are severely so, have over the last century been the beneficiaries of many efforts to solve their problem of inadequate communication skills. Braille is one such example, and use of sound recordings has been helpful. For one reason or another, other systems of communication failed to gain wide acceptance among those they were intended to help. They were too complex, too difficult to learn, too expensive to produce, and the like, and they disappeared from the scene. Many ideas for new communications systems survive, such as the electronic scanning of printed material and translating it into tactile or audible signals, but application of these ideas to the reading and communication of handicapped persons has had to wait for the development of the necessary technological capability. Recent developments, particularly in computer technology, hold promise that elimination of communication barriers can be achieved, at least to a considerable degree. Some of these developments will be discussed in the pages that follow.

II. FREQUENCY OF IMPAIRMENT

The terms "handicap" and impairment" have no specific medical definition. Legal definition of functional impairment can be found in laws or regulations of various agencies of government which will, assuming that the criteria set forth are met, provide access to needed services or funds. These definitions conform with the particular purposes and functions of specific agencies, which determine the kind and extent of materials, services, funds, or equipment provided for the impaired person's communication needs.

It is this particularity that enables an agency or organization serving handicapped or impaired persons to determine statistically, using survey techniques, the potential number of persons who could possibly benefit from their services. At the same time, this particularity seems to preclude the accumulation of accurate data concerning the overall number of impaired persons whose residual limiting condition from whatever cause—injury, congenital condition, or disease—are unable to take their place in the life and activities of the community.

The most recent statistics on impairment reflect information dating from 1977 (U.S. National Center for Health Statistics, 1981). Except as noted otherwise, the following figures are drawn from the cited report. In 1977, an estimated 11.4 million persons had visual impairments, including about 1.4 million with "severe visual impairment"—defined as an inability to see newsprint with corrective lenses or with no useful vision in one or both eyes. The prevalence rates tended to be highest for persons 65 years of age and over for both severe and less severe visual impairments.

Of the number of visually impaired persons, nearly 500,000 persons, according to a 1978 estimate, are legally blind (National Society for the Prevention of Blindness, 1980). When discussing blindness, it should be remembered that there are two definitions—medical and legal. According to the medical definition, blindness is the "lack or loss of ability to see, lack or perception of visual stimuli due to disorders of the organs of sight or to lesions in certain areas of the brain." (Dorland's, 1974, p. 209) Legal blindness is defined as visual acuity, as determined by competent authority, which measures 20/200 or less in the better eye with correcting lenses, or the widest diameter of the visual field subtends an angular distance no greater than 20 degrees.

The legal definition of blindness represents an economic definition derived from Title X of the Social Security Act. It is based on an arbitrary point below which individuals are presumed to be unable to perform economically.

In 1977, approximately 1.5 million persons suffered from complete or partial paralysis, representing a rate of 7.2 impairments per 1000 persons. Complete or partial paralysis was proportionately most prevalent among persons 65 years of age or over. Complete paralysis of the extremities and trunk accounted for almost one-half of the persons paralyzed. Slightly over one-half of those paralyzed had cerebral palsy or partial paralysis of the extremities of trunk.

It is estimated that there were 16.2 million hearing impairments (including tinnitus), about half of which involved both ears. In general, the rate of hearing impairments was highest for persons 65 years of age and over.

Speech impairments are estimated at about 2 million or a rate of 9.4 per 1,000 persons.

About 358,000 persons had major extremities missing; 1.9 million had minor extremities missing. These figures represent rates per 1000 persons of 1.7 and 8.8, respectively. Rates of missing major extremities rose with age and were relatively higher for males than females. Injury accounted for most of the missing extremities.

Approximately 9 million nonparalytic orthopedic impairments of the back or spine, 7 million of the lower extremity or hip, 2.5 million of the upper extremity of shoulder, and 1 million multiple or other nonparalytic orthopedic impairments of the limbs, back, or trunk are reported.

For the purposes of identifying eligible handicapped persons who are not users of special library services and of assessing the effectiveness of the present Library of Congress program—offered through the National Library Service for the Blind and Physically Handicapped (hereafter, National Library Service)—a national survey was completed for the Library by the American Foundation for the Blind (American Foundation for the Blind, 1980, Vol. 1). According to this survey, an estimated 3 million persons in the United States are eligible for service. Two-thirds of them are blind or visually handicapped, and about half of those persons in extended-care institutions and hospitals are eligible for free reading services; about half of the eligible population is 65 or older.

In addition to this general survey, a survey of about 10,000 users of the National Library Service conducted in September 1979 found that of a total of 4415 respondents, 50% are 65 years or older, 64% have a visual handicap only, and 29% have multiple handicaps (*Market Facts*, 1981).

III. RESOURCES AND SERVICES

A. The National Library Service

The primary source of braille and recorded books and magazines for general reading is the Library of Congress program, funded by Congressional appropriations. These materials, and the equipment with which to use them, are provided on a free loan basis to eligible persons, defined as those who cannot read a page of conventional print, hold a book, or turn a book's pages. As in the case in most programs, eligibility is established by a statement from a certifying authority, a physician, social worker, teacher, or the like. For those who are eligible, the National Library Service provides access to an extensive collection of reading materials and music scores, textbooks, and instructional materials in braille, large print, and on disc and cassette recordings through a cooperating network of 56 regional and 101 subregional libraries where the books are housed, circulated, and supplemented to meet local needs. To assist these agencies in coping with increased storage and distribution problems, four multistate service centers are working with the National Library Service. Each serves approximately 13 contiguous states to store and circulate Library of Congress materials on a contractual basis. The four centers also maintain and circulate collections of infrequently used materials, including back issues of periodicals as well as older braille and recorded book titles. In addition, 16 other agencies assist in initial processing of applications and assignment of specially designed talking book machines which provide blind and physically handicapped readers with a means of reading the books and magazines produced for the program.

During fiscal year 1981—the fiftieth anniversary year of the Library of Congress reading program for blind and physically handicapped individuals—readership rose to more than 800,000 and circulation of braille and recorded books and magazines increased to more than 18 million.

Titles selected are similar to those found in an average public library and the objective is to have a wide variety of subjects and reading levels represented. The high cost of producing braille and recorded titles in sufficient quantity limits selection to those books judged likely to be very popular. When a title is selected for the Library of Congress program, the text is reproduced without any omissions except those required by the format. Information from the book jacket about the author is also included. For periodicals, all editorial text is reproduced; advertisements are omitted to conform with the free mailing privilege regulations. All materials copied are produced under contract according to Library of Congress specifications. A few titles are purchased from sources in the United States and abroad, such as braille books from the Royal National Institute for the Blind in England. The five principal braille presses engaged in producing books and magazines under contract with the federal government are:

1. American Printing House for the Blind (APH), Louisville, Kentucky
2. Clovernook Printing House for the Blind (CPH), Cincinnati, Ohio
3. National Braille Press (NBP), Boston, Massachusetts
4. Triformation (TRI), Stuart, Florida
5. Volunteer Services for the Blind (VSB), Philadelphia, Pennsylvania

In addition, APH and the American Foundation for the Blind (AFB), New York City, New York, handle the complete manufacturing process for books and magazines on discs.

Blind or handicapped readers may find variety in the special format collections, but the number of titles in any subject category is meager compared to the abundance enjoyed by those who can read regular print. The collection of available mass-produced books, that is, books produced in quantity for distribution to all network libraries, now consists of about 5000 individual titles.

Complementing these network services are the transcriptions of educational, vocational, and religious materials provided by nonprofit agencies, community-service organizations, and church publishing houses. Generally, these groups produce single copies of titles at the specific request of blind or physically handicapped students or professionals or for specific purposes. It is through their efforts that handicapped readers have the larger degree of choice and the opportunity to have their specialized information needs met.

Commercial sources offer a wealth of recorded material to complement the free recordings from the Library of Congress network and other agencies. Many of these recordings are packaged in appealing multimedia kits such as discs or cassettes accompanied by books.

Recording for the Blind (RFB), a nonprofit, voluntary organization located in New York City, lends recorded academic texts on cassettes at no cost to eligible readers, serving students at all levels, from elementary to graduate, and professional. The RFB library offers more than 60,000 titles, with new books added at the rate of 5,000 per year. RFB cassettes may be played on both the Library of Congress machine and a cassette player–recorder sold by the American Printing House for the Blind.

B. Braille Production and Tactile Technology

Present research and testing efforts are exploring new ways to produce braille copy to reduce production costs, decrease the time involved in getting a book to a reader, and to reduce the bulkiness[1] of the braille books, thereby saving on storage space requirements and costs.

While it is expensive to produce, braille retains many advantages of print not found in recordings. Braille readers can read more selectively and can

---

[1]Books produced by braille presses are interpointed (both sides of the page). Volunteer-produced books with braille on only one side of the page require twice as many volumes, and thus, twice as much shelf space. Even interpointed braille is bulky. An average press braille book requires three volumes and occupies a space 12 in. high by 12 in. deep by 7.5 in. wide.

engage in search and retrieval that readers of recorded material may find much more difficult. A serious disadvantage of braille is that most blind persons neither read nor transcribe in braille.

In both reading and production of braille, the number of letters contained in a printed text has been substantially reduced through the use of contractions. The present official guide in the United States, *Standard English Braille, American Edition,* uses contradictions to eliminate much of the redundancy by dropping units (letters) not considered significant linguistically. Some words attain a startling brevity, e.g. "tomorrow" is reduced in Grade 2 contracted braille to "tm." The present system contains nearly 200 words or letter combinations. The result is the creation of a complicated code which deters many from engaging in the training necessary to become skilled braille readers.

Before 1960, all production of braille materials in multiple copies used the technology developed in the nineteenth century.[2] Multiple copies were made by embossing pages from iron or zinc plates on modified ink-printer presses, and human operators—stereograph operators who are able to use braille—were required to emboss the plates and operate the presses (Cylke, 1981, p. 63). Labor was a major component in the cost of producing braille materials.

The number of copies of a braille edition is very small in comparison to the production runs of commercial printing presses, and the cost per volume of braille materials is high. Limited demand could never be expected to justify sufficient increases in the number of copies produced to lower unit costs, and producers have sought reduction of costs in more efficient production technology, thereby eliminating much of the expensive labor costs. This development is directly related to greater integration of blind individuals into the general community; as more job opportunities and more vocational choices are open to blind individuals, fewer have chosen to become operators of braille stereograph machines and the shortage of these skilled workers has given impetus to technical advances.

By the 1960s, braille books and other reading materials began to be produced using high-speed embossing machinery and computers for translation of text into braille and storage of the text.

Triformation Systems, a specialty electronic firm in Florida, under contract with the Library of Congress redesigned the braille-page embosser to

---

[2] An exception is the process in use for the last 20 years by which a few copies of a paper master could be made by using a vacuum-forming machine and specially prepared plastic sheets. But some braille readers have complained that the plastic sheets are uncomfortable under the fingers. Attempts to find a substitute have not been successful, but an effort is underway to identify the cause of the discomfort and to seek a better formulation of the plastic.

permit high-speed production of plates. This embosser turns out about 40 master zinc braille plates an hour. Previously, it took one day to produce the same amount of work using a hand-operated stereograph machine. Prototypes developed by Triformation Systems have been incorporated into a new system for computer translation of print to braille at the Clovernook Home and School for the Blind in Cincinnati.

Development of braille-production systems—using computers—has taken several approaches. These systems vary in the degree to which the production process has been automated. All use a record of the text on magnetic tape or other magnetic media for storage, correction of errors, and reproduction of the text. The systems differ, however, in the form of the text used by the computer and the translator and braille-embossing functions.

Usually, an operator types the text on a keyboard terminal attached to the computer. The complete computerized systems include translation into braille from the text in alphanumeric format. When the system does not include translation into braille, the text is recorded using a "Perkins Braille Writer"-like keyboard of six dot keys and a spare key.

Advanced automated technologies take advantage of computerized systems currently used in the publishing industry which include storage of texts on a magnetic medium. Often, this text can be used directly in braille production systems, bypassing the need to rerecord the text. Although some modification of text is unavoidable, this can be automated by using a computer program.

John Berryman (1981), in his excellent article, provides a detailed description of the production process used in computerized braille production. He states that automation of embossing varies in degree and method. Two main categories of embossers have been developed: those that emboss paper and those that emboss metallic plates. Most computerized braille-production systems have at least one paper embosser, which can be used for proofreading or for low-volume production. Most emboss on only one side of the paper, but some can emboss on both sides by interpointing.

Metallic plate-embossing terminals are used for high-volume production runs. In braille publishing, high volume is 50–100 copies for books and 500–2000 copies for periodicals. The embossed plates are transferred to modified printing presses for press braille production. Some systems use braille-line images on magnetic cassettes (or punch cards), which are the used used to drive modified stereotyping machines to produce embossed plates.

Computer technique is used to produce several braille newspapers and magazines in the United States, Germany, and other countries. Probably, it is most highly automated in the production of bank statements. The banks provide their research unit with magnetic tapes on which the details to be embossed are stored, and a completely automated system reads data from the tapes, translates it, and embosses the bank statements (Berryman, 1981, p. 261). Many of these installations are multipurpose—braille production is only one of the computer's functions.

C. Compositor's Tapes

Braille is produced from machine-readable tapes, the storage medium used to drive the phototypesetting equipment for print books, in some advanced systems.

The magazine *National Geographic* has been produced by the Library of Congress, using compositor's tapes. Success with this effort led to production of the book *Helen and Teacher,* by Joseph Lash in 1980. *Helen and Teacher* in braille was ready for distribution to handicapped readers soon after issuance of the print book. With the exception of an experimental production of a braille book in 1969, it was the first time in the United States that compositor's tapes had been used to produce a book of this length—786 pages, or eight braille volumes. The book was produced in braille by this fastest possible method because of the high interest of readers in the subject on the occasion of the centennial celebration of Helen Keller's birth.

When the *National Geographic* project began, only about 20% of print books were produced using compositor's tapes. That number is expected to approach 80% some time in the 1980s. By then it is hoped that general braille production technology will be ready to use this new application for faster and more efficient production.

The process is not as simple as using the tape from one machine to drive another. At this stage of development, manual intervention is needed to remove print codes from the tapes, to recode for braille contractions, and to format the braille pages, although computer programs can be devised to automate these functions.

The rules for use of braille contractions and the formatting conventions of braille have made widespread automation difficult. These matters are being addressed by technical experts working with the Braille Authority of North America which sets and oversees the standards for various braille codes (Cylke, 1981, p. 63). Programs specific to different European languages have been developed to accommodate the specific braille contractions used in each language.

D. Optical Character Recognition

The optical scanning to transmit printed pages direct to computer storage is being examined by some braille producers, but its feasibility for recording the text in a braille production system has yet to be demonstrated (Foulke, 1981, p. 102). If, as Foulke, who is currently director of the Perceptual Alternatives Laboratory at the University of Louisville, Kentucky, points out, a page could be read by a device that scanned the page optically, recognized the characters printed on it, and sent the appropriate signals to the computer, another significant reduction in expensive human labor would be realized, and the results should be a further reduction in the cost of producing braille. Since optical character recognition (OCR) is rapidly approaching an advanced state of development, further consideration of this technology for use in large-scale production systems appears justified.

E. Tangible Graphic Displays

"Tangible graphic aids" refers to illustrations, tables of figures, and maps that are found in textbooks of concern to both blind and sighted students. In his recent article Foulke discusses the importance of these tangible graphic aids in the education of blind children (1981, pp. 101–108). It is his view that while they assume no less importance to the blind, their usefulness is limited. Some technological developments have contributed toward some improvement of the situation.

Blind children experience an insignificant number of tangible graphic displays in comparison to the number of visual graphic displays available to sighted children. Tactual maps, one form of tangible graphic display, are produced in a variety of media. Paper maps may be embossed or have images imposed through Virkotype printing or silk screening. Globes in relief are produced by the larger braille printing houses such as the American Printing House for the Blind. Desk or wall maps occasionally are carved of wood. Some of these can be dissected state by state or country by country. Such wooden maps serve as a master from which maps are moulded in papier mâché, plastic, or rubber. A variety of masters is used to produce maps in vacuum-formed plastic.

Books that present the subject matter of scientific disciplines abound in graphs and figures to communicate information and concepts, which must in turn be made available to the readers. Recording for the Blind, which specializes in recording textbooks for blind college students, has developed simple techniques and tools for use by their volunteer workers to produce graphs and tables on plastic sheets. (Foulke, 1981, p. 104)

A tactile graphics system acquired from Japan, which can produce raised line illustrations from standard print for touch reading, is a promising development. In the process, a photocopier reproduces images in black and white and shades of gray. A second copier uses chemically treated paper and heat to raise the images to differing heights. The amount of heat absorbed determines the height of the image. Darker areas absorb more heat and are in higher relief. White reproduces flat; black is at least the height of a braille dot, and grays are in between.

John Gill, director of the Warwick Research Unit for the Blind, Warwick University, Great Britain, in 1973, developed a system for producing a map layout using a computer-aided design (Gill, 1974, p. 64), and a machine tool for engraving a laminated plastic sheet. In this system, the topographical information is entered into a computer from a coordinate table. The visual display unit permits editing by inserting lines, moving the end points of lines, or changing the scale. A wide variety of line types—solid, dotted, or dashed—can be specified from the keyboard. The height of the symbols can be controlled by the operator on final copies. Alphanumeric text can be entered from the keyboard, and this text is automatically converted into Grade 1 (uncontracted) braille with a choice of four different cell sizes.

Output is requested when a satisfactory display is obtained. Further, the output can be on a digital plotter, magnetic tape, or punched paper tape. A map can be stored on tape and quickly modified at a later date. The engraving machine can either be controlled directly from the computer used in the design stage, or from a smaller computer with the data transferred on punched paper tape. The engraving machine, which is computer-controlled, makes a negative in the form of a mirror-imaged copy of the map on laminated plastic. Thermoplastic copies are produced from a male epoxy–resin master on a vacuum-forming machine.

Gill's prototype is no longer in existence. It was, however, operated long enough to provide convincing proof of the computer-aided design concept. Unfortunately, systems of this type are expensive and must be operated by trained personnel. Consequently, their implementation is feasible only in settings in which the volume of use justifies the installation and operating costs. (Foulke, 1981, p. 106)

F. Direct-Access Reading Aids

In presenting printed material to the blind and physically handicapped, sighted persons must now reduce it to a form, usually braille or recorded, understandable to blind or other physically handicapped readers. Direct-access reading aids offer the opportunity to eliminate the human intervention that stands between such handicapped persons and the material they wish to read.

Use of computer-assisted, electronic reading machines is being studied. A machine capable of scanning printed material and presenting it in an audible or tactile form understandable to blind and physically handicapped readers would permit independent reading of ordinary printed material and would be a valuable addition to present reading techniques.

In an important experimental effort, several manufacturers have improved the availability of braille reading material through cassette equipment that accepts, stores, and displays braille on a tactile board. These compact and portable machines include the Digicassette manufactured in France and the Braillocord manufactured in Germany.

Since with the use of these machines braille characters are never embossed on paper, these machines are called "paperless braille machines." These machines provide for a transitory display of braille characters by causing the tips of pins to protrude through holes in the display surface in patterns that form braille characters. Only one line of characters at a time is presented. At the end of the current line, a switch is pressed which causes it to disappear and to be ready for the next line. Conventional magnetic tape cassettes can be used to store the dot patterns. A keyboard is included that may be used by the reader to write on the cassette tape. Thus operators of these machines can both read and write.

The VersaBraille device developed by Telesensory Systems, Incorporated, of California, and the Digicassette developed by Oleg and Andree Tretiakoff, are self-contained writing, reading, and notetaking systems. They record braille in electronic impulses on cassette tape and displays it in braille on brief lines of electromechanical cells. To enhance communication, the systems can be attached to computers, typewriters, or teletypewriters.

The wide acceptance of "paperless braille" has implications in that the cost of preparing the cassettes reproduced on paperless braille machines will be very much less than the cost of preparing braille books. The contents of a full-length book, recorded on a single cassette, will reduce the problems relating to the distribution and storage of braille reading matter (Foulke, 1981, p. 102).

Displaying text a line at a time—a characteristic of paperless braille machines—may not be suitable for certain kinds of reading matter such as tables and complex mathematical expressions that require more than one line. One recently developed prototype machine displays a full page of braille, similar to normal paper braille page. Various indexing and search schemes help the reader find the desired point on the cassette.

G. Optacon

A method of touch reading for more than a decade, the Optacon (optical-to-tactile converter) has been used by a growing number of blind persons. To use this direct reading aid, the blind person moves a miniature camera across a line of ordinary print or diagrams on a page with one hand. The index finger of the other hand is placed on the Optacon's tactile screen, which is approximately one inch long and one-half inch wide. As the camera is moved across a letter, the image is simultaneously reproduced on the tactile screen. Vibrating reeds that are raised under the user's finger exactly duplicate the print symbol. Although reading with the Optacon is slow, it is useful for private reading and to studying complex material where speed is not a primary factor (Cylke, 1981, p. 65).

The Optacon is enabling many already-employed blind to be promoted beyond entry-level positions which frequently underutilize their talents. In addition to employment, the Optacon is important for a myriad of everyday tasks ranging from checking bank statements, paying bills, and looking up telephone numbers to following recipes and reading stories to children. The Optacon has even enabled the blind to vote independently, providing a truly secret ballot.

H. Braille Computer Terminals

The Braillink Terminal, a portable braille computer terminal to help in the employment of blind persons in industries using modern computer technology, has been designed by Clarke and Smith Industries, Ltd, England. It has a dual-purpose keyboard for standard typing and braille and a 48-cell braille display line. Two minicassette tape drives provide storing and editing capacity. The terminal can be used by blind and sighted operators.

Blind persons can store and obtain information from a computer by using special means of communication. Voice-response terminals are becoming available as are other mechanisms. For example, Lawrence Berkeley Laboratories has developed a computer terminal that blind persons can operate by sound and touch. Instead of displaying images on a screen, the system converts the signals into tactile impulses (vibrating rods) that permit the "reader" to find any place in the text by pressing an "editor" button. The terminal spells out the words in discernible speech. The Royal Institute of Technology in Swedan is testing a terminal system for two-way transmission of braille messages by deaf-blind persons. The braille can also be converted into print.

Such terminals are designed to provide blind persons access to the same computerized information available to their sighted colleagues. Business and industry have been using talking terminals for some time, and such use is encouraging insofar as employment opportunities for blind thus can be enhanced or expanded. One talking terminal, for example, is called dealer–audio response terminals. These units are linked by telephone and minicomputers to the company's computers at headquarters located in another city. They were introduced in 1979 to improve parts service for the John Deere Company's lines of agricultural and industrial equipment and consumer products. The ability of those terminals to respond verbally to dealers simplifies and speeds the order process. The "voice" of a computer at a terminal guides the dealer through a six-step procedure and tells him when parts will be shipped (see the article Talking Computer Terminal . . .).

I. Optical Scanners

While optical character readers are still under development for use in braille publishing, they are receiving increased attention in conjunction with direct information access by blind persons.

The development of the Kurzweil reading machines has stimulated interest in seeking new devices and unconventional methods for translating printed material into braille and other formats usable by blind readers. Kurzweil Computer Products, Inc. completed initial development of a high-performance reading machine featuring multifont character recognition. Designed specifically as an aid for blind people, the Kurzweil machine will "read" a wide variety of printed matter—books, magazines, typewritten letters—and yield output in the form of full-word, synthesized English speech. The speech rate may be varied by the user up to the normal speech rate of approximately 200 words per minute. The reading machine will also have an alternate "spelled speech" mode to allow a user to hear his material spelled out letter by letter. Work is in progress to develop a braille output capability. Kurzweil reading machines have been installed in libraries in nearly every state of the union. These devices give blind and physically handicapped readers direct access to the print collections similar as to that available to the general public.

Speech generated by mechanical and electronic hardware involves speaking devices based on impulses received from a computer system. These devices produce speech of two general types: performed words that are triggered by the computer and concatenation of basic speech sounds (phonemes) that are simulated by the driving system. The first type is represented by the "talking calculator," in which the user presses numeral and function buttons, causing stored words to be spoken. Educational devices of this type have appeared on the market to teach spelling, reading, and mathematics. Vocabulary is limited to a few hundred words stored in the device's "dictionary," but the device pronounces these words accurately (Cylke, 1981, p. 62).

The Speech Plus talking calculator verifies every keystroke and computation using synthetic speech. It has a 24-word vocabulary and comes in English, French, German, and Arabic models.

The Canon Communicator allows nonvocal, motor-impaired persons to communicate by entering messages on a keyboard letter by letter. The pocket-sized system then prints the messages on a paper tape. Powered by a rechargeable battery pack, it can be attached to limbs.

The quality of "talking terminals" and "talking computers" is improving rapidly. It is even possible to build in a limited ability to analyze the syntax of a sentence to permit some modulation of the voice tone, but the result is still far from the speech of a human reader.

J. Tone Output Reading Machines

Over the years, other ideas and designs for personal reading machines using sound, particularly tones and tonal combinations, have been proposed.

As long ago as 1912, Fournier d'Albe, then Lecturer in Physics in the University of Birmingham, invented an instrument, the Octophone, which he claimed would enable blind persons to discover lights and bright objects by ear. This was accomplished by using selenium, which has the property of varying its conductivity of electricity in accordance with the amount of light to which it is exposed.[3] Printed letters are translated into a "sound alphabet" that d'Albe believed could be easily learned.

After two years' further work, d'Albe produced an instrument which he called the "type-reading Optophone," by means of which blind persons were to read ordinary ink print. This first rough instrument was shown at the International Conference on the Blind at Westminister in 1914 and also

---

[3]If a telephone receiver (essentially an instrument sensitive to change in electrical currents) is connected in series with an electric battery and a porcelain tablet having on its surface two separate conducting lines of graphite connected together or bridged over by light-sensitive selenium, a current will pass through the telephone, and the current will vary as the lighting of the tablet is varied. The prepared tablet is called a "selenium bridge." Its purpose is to enable the blind to read ordinary printed matter—such as books or newspapers. This is accomplished by producing in a telephone receiver series of musical notes forming tunes or musical motifs, representing the various letters as these are passed over by the instrument in traversing a line of print.

at the Royal Society. By 1917, he had worked out another model, which he submitted to the National Institute for the Blind. In the course of a test, he read blindfold an unknown passage from *The Times,* but this experiment was not successful. The expense of the machine, its complexity, and the possibility of attaining a successful rate of reading speed within a reasonable time made its general acceptance impractical.

Among direct-access reading aids using tonal patterns is the "Visotoner" which scans printed letters and translates them into a musical code using nine tones, not unlike those found in a modern touch telephone. The Visotoner and its tactile version, the Visotactor, are the work of Mauch Laboratories, sponsored by the Veterans' Administration's Prosthetic and Sensory Aid Service.

A parallel but somewhat different investigation was conducted by Beddoes at the University of British Columbia. In both the Mauch Visotoner and Beddoes' Lexiphone, a narrow slit from the letter space images onto a one-dimensional array of photocells, 9 in the case of the Visotoner and 54 in the case of the Lexiphone. In the Visotoner, the photocell signals activate corresponding oscillators whose outputs are summed to produce chords played through an earphone. As in the original Optophone, the tones produced by the oscillator are arranged so that the bottom photocell corresponds to the lowest-frequency tone and the highest photocell corresponds to the highest-frequency tone (Mann, 1974, p. 263). As its optical probe is moved along a line of print, a 10-tone (10-channel) code is heard stereophonically in earphones. Each tone is heard at a different volume in each ear. High tones are heard louder in the right ear and softer in the left. With low tones, the situation is reversed. Severe limitations of the resolution and field of the Visotoner require precise manual tracking which is provided by a third component termed a "Colineator."

Reading rates up to 40 words per minute have been reported by the developers, but there is as yet no systematic body of experimental evidence nor any independent evaluation.

In 1972, Mauch reported a stereophonic version called the Stereotoner. In this instrument, 10 photosensors present essentially the same chordal range, but weighted to the left and right ears so that the lower parts of letters appear to originate from the user's left, the middle parts from the center, and the upper parts from the right. The Stereotoner incorporates a wide optical zooming range of 10 to 1, accommodating a field on the paper of from 75 to 750 mil, thus permitting headlines and titles to be read. Other new characteristics are a switch to permit reversed operation so as to read light letters on a dark background, a very small optical probe, and a compact lightweight control box suspended from the user's neck, thus freeing one of his hands (Mann, 1974, p. 263).

K. Phonograph—Talking Book Machine

Communication, especially receiving information, is a problem many handicapped persons face. Advances in technology in the past 50 years have provided devices to help handicapped persons overcome this communications barrier. For both blind and those physically handicapped persons unable to hold a book or turn its pages, the phonograph has proven to be such a device.

The potential use of the phonograph to provide recorded books for the blind was recognized as early as December 24, 1877, when Thomas A. Edison applied for a patent for his phonograph or "talking machine." But it was at the hands of Robert Irwin, American Foundation for the Blind, that the phonograph was conceived as a device for reading entire texts of books at a cost low enough to make their production and distribution to the blind feasible. Recording and sound reproducing equipment then available for home use was not appropriate because of the expense, handling problems, and fragility.

Irwin realized that to produce records in the small quantities required, (100 copies or so) at acceptable cost, more material was recorded on each disk by cutting the sound grooves closer together and making the record revolve at a much slower speed than on the ordinary commercial phonograph. Various speeds were considered, and 33 $\frac{1}{3}$ rpm was selected, partly because sound-reproducing equipment was available and had been used successfully for some years in commerical radio broadcasts. Phonograph records then in common use were cut with 90–100 grooves per inch; this was increased to 150 grooves per inch, which was found to produce acceptable recordings of speech.

The ordinary shellac record could not be used. No practical amount of packing was sufficient to protect the records against the jars to which they would be subjected. With the cooperation of the Radio Corporation of America, a record material composed largely of vinylite was perfected which was sufficiently resistant to wear and, at the same time, sufficiently flexible to withstand the treatment which library books received.

The best size for the records came under scrutiny. Originally, the 12-in. record was selected for recorded books, principally because pressing discs for this size were available and also because a 12–in. record seemed to be the largest which could be stored conveniently on shelves in common use.

Since fiscal year 1959, the records were changed to a more convenient size and recorded at slower speeds: $16\frac{2}{3}$ rpm, (for records produced from 1963); $8\frac{1}{3}$ rpm for magazines (1968); $8\frac{1}{3}$ rpm for books (1973). Thus twice as much material could be recorded on a disc, thereby enabling the Library of Congress to effect substantial savings, allowing for an increase in the number of copies of each title issued as well as lower shelf space requirements for each book.

The National Library Service for the Blind and Physically Handicapped, Library of Congress, began to use flexible discs in 1968 when a recorded version of the section in *Talking Book Topics* announcing talking book acquisitions was bound experimentally in the print edition. The format proved popular, and subsequently, national circulation magazines were recorded on flexible discs.

The flexible discs are cheaper, lighter to mail, and less bulky to store. Although flexible discs do not stand up for as many playings as do hard discs, they provide excellent service if their use is limited to situations where repeated playing is unlikely or where the user need not return them. Other advantages of the flexible discs are that they are resistant to damage and breakage and that the cost is sufficiently low to permit production in large quantities. Further, conversion of magazine circulation from a borrow-and-return basis to direct mailing from producer to reader—possible because of the low cost of the flexible discs—has resulted in savings realized by libraries in staff time and storage space and provided for more timely receipt by readers.

The flexible disc has proven to be a successful format for recording popular books. Recordings on the flexible discs can be produced quickly in large quantity and at relatively low cost, satisfying readers' demand for popular titles on a timely basis. For example, in 1976 flexible discs were used to produce for quick distribution a recorded version of by Alex Haley's *Roots*. It was available to the readers shortly after the television series based on this book was broadcast.

The new 8⅓ rpm flexible disc was used experimentally for a full-length book for the first time in fiscal year 1972 for recording *Wheels* by Arthur Hailey. This talking book consisted of two parts of five records each, produced on flexible discs that were spiral bound and could be played without removal of the binding and covers. Favorable readers' comments led to the production of other titles in the same format.

The first national circulation magazine to be produced in quantity on flexible discs was *U.S. News & World Report;* this was done in 1971 by the magazine publisher. The first national circulation magazine to be produced on a flexible discs by the Library of Congress was the popular weekly, *Sports Illustrated;* the first issue on flexible discs reached readers in the spring of 1972. As of 1981, 37 magazines were recorded on flexible discs under the talking book program. These magazines are sent by the producer directly to the reader. They are not returned but rather kept for personal use.

Over the years, the machines on which to play the records have progressed from large, heavy (30 pounds), one-speed tube-type players for records only to the present lightweight multispeed transistorized models designed for either cassettes or discs with optional accessories for greater ease of operation by physically handicapped persons lacking digital dexterity. Later models not only achieved greater ease of operation by physically handicapped persons but were modified to enhance aesthetic appeal.

Since 1971, containers in which the records are sent though the mail have been made of lightweight, high-impact plastic with snap locks to facilitate easier handling by handicapped individuals as well as by the Postal Service. Previously, containers were of black fiberboard with straps.

L. Cassette Technology

The most dramatic change in the Library of Congress program has been the development of cassette technology. The first cassette player was introduced into the program in 1969 with a speed of $1\frac{7}{8}$ in. per second. The Philips–Norelco-type tape cassette and cassette player were developed commercially, and by 1968, the tape cassette and player were widely available on the commercial market. The potential for using this system was quickly recognized. A pilot study to test commercially available tape cassettes and tape cassette players was begun in July 1968 to determine the suitability of this equipment for the talking book program. By 1974, books were in production at the slower speed of $\frac{15}{16}$ in. per second.

Recent improvements in recording technology and tape quality are making even slower speeds possible. The Library of Congress and several other agencies also record on four tracks across the $\frac{1}{4}$-in. wide tape; the slower speed and the use of four tracks instead of two for voice recording permits 6 hr of playing time on the common C–90 (90 min) cassette.

Cassettes have appreciably increased the quantity of available recorded titles. Cassettes, more portable than disc and braille format, have been of inestimable benefit to the mobile reader. Cassette recording has also encouraged wider participation by volunteers in the Library program for handicapped readers.

Especially in the small cassette form, tapes are more compact and lighter than records and provide the same playback time. They can be duplicated much more easily, and cassette players are smaller, cheaper, and more versatile than record players.

1. SPEECH COMPRESSION

The recent development of inexpensive electronic techniques for the time compression of recorded speech have made it possible to give to those who read by listening some control over the rate at which they read. The mean reading rate for trained oral readers is 175 words per minute (wpm). Research has shown that aural readers can listen at word rates up to 275 wpm without much loss in comprehension. Beyond this rate, the comprehension of unfamiliar reading matter begins to decline rapidly. However, within the range bounded at its upper end of 275 wpm, aural readers are now able to choose the word rates that suit their purposes, and to change those word rates as their purposes change (Foulke, 1981, p. 103). Cassette machines distributed in 1981 by the Library of Congress for the use of eligible persons provide the function of speech compression. By pushing a switch, operators of such machines can vary the word rate of the recorded speech without changing the pitch of the speaker's voice, and without seriously distorting the quality of the speech signal. This pitch-restoration device permits listening at speeds which range from normal to 0.8 times slower or 2.5 times faster than normal. In the 1970s, two books were produced with some high-quality speech compression applied to the master tape before duplication. Field tests with these books made it apparent that the reader, not the producer, should control the speed at which text is read.

Since 1971, the Library of Congress has provided cassette playback machines with a variable speed control. Many users read from 25% below normal to 100% above normal, despite sound distortion. Pitch correction now makes it possible for more people to enjoy reading recorded material at other than normal speed.

2. SOLAR POWER

Another example of how technology has been applied to meet the needs of patrons is modification of a cassette machine so that its battery can be recharged by solar power. This was accomplished by making a panel of small silicon solar cells linked together to operate the machine in direct sunlight or recharge batteries for use at other times. The standard cassette player was modified with a jack to accept the solar-powered source. Such equipment was provided to an American citizen living in a remote region of Brazil where there is no electricity and therefore no way to recharge batteries for disc and cassette players. While the feasibility of battery charging using solar power has been demonstrated, the cost of the solar cell discourages wide application and use of this technology at this time.

3. COMBINATION MACHINE AND EASY-TO-USE CASSETTE MACHINE

Currently under development to replace the two machines (cassette player and phonograph) now in use, the combination machine will play $1\frac{7}{8}$ and

$^{15}/_{16}$ ips cassettes as well as 33⅓, 16⅔, and 8⅓ rpm discs. It will have a built-in speed control so that readers will be able to skim or to listen at normal speeds.

Also in the planning stages of development is an easy-to-use cassette machine designed for patrons who require few controls and more automatic operation. The planning model has only two controls and includes several automatic features. The tape will rewind automatically when a cassette is first inserted into the tape deck and the cover closed. A beep signal will indicate "ready for play." A sliding switch is then used to start the tape and select the desired volume in one operation. There will be no need to turn the tape over; the machine changes sides automatically. Once the sliding switch is moved from the stop position, the machine can play a four-side cassette—6 hr of reading material—without requiring the reader to touch either the cassette or the controls.

M. Indexing

Lack of indexing has inhibited use of recorded materials by blind and physically handicapped readers. Solution of this problem is being addressed in the testing of a refined voice-indexing system compatible with the tape cassette players used in the Library of Congress reading program. The recording of index words by the National Library Service for the Blind and Physically Handicapped is superimposed over the recording of the narrated text at 16 times the speed of the text. The index words are heard and understood only when the cassette player is in the fast-forward mode. This technical innovation promises to solve the problem of indexing recorded materials and presages the introduction of recorded dictionaries and other reference materials into special collections for blind and physically handicapped readers.

Voice indexing of recorded materials was introduced in *Access National Parks: A Guide for Handicapped Visitors,* the first mass-produced fully voice-indexed book on cassette. Voice indexing is a technique that uses key words such as the names of the individual parks to help readers locate specific information.

The 55,000-entry *Concise Heritage Dictionary* is now being recorded, after testing to determine that such a lengthy and complex undertaking would succeed and determining which indexing procedures would be most useful to readers. Production of the dictionary will take about two years, with distribution on $^{15}/_{16}$ ips 40-side cassettes planned for 1983. The dictionary may be offered for sale, as well as being available on loan from network libraries.

Three voice-indexed books have been produced thus far by the Library of

Congress: *Access National Parks: A Guide for Handicapped Visitors,* in 1979; *Cooking for Myself,* in 1980; and *Everyone's Money Book,* in 1981.

N. Recorded Encyclopedia

The first recorded encyclopedia is now available at a cost of $1,176.00 from the American Printing House (APH), which created it with the aid of a grant from the Office of Special Education and Rehabilitative Services of the U.S. Department of Education. World Book–Childcraft International, Inc. donated the contents of the 1980 *World Book* for the effort.

The encyclopedia's 219 cassettes are housed in the covers of 19 books, which takes about 6 feet of shelf space. Each book contains indexing information in braille and large print where a reader can find the cassette number, track, and entry number for any subject on the cassettes the book houses. The reader then inserts the appropriate cassette into a special quick-search tape player provided with the encyclopedia, dials the track and entry number, and reads the article. Average look-up time is about a minute.

The cassette player is essential in using the encyclopedia. It is a 120-V, 60-Hz AC machine, but it can be successfully used with other voltages and line frequencies by means of a transformer.

O. Newspapers, Radio Reading

Local programs provide timely and currently useful information to blind and handicapped readers. For the last two years, the Essex Chapter of the American Red Cross, East Orange, New Jersey, has successfully provided the *Talking Newspaper,* a recorded edition of two local newspapers, for persons unable to see or handle a newspaper. Plans are to expand the service to include recordings of all eighteen papers in the district. Beginning in February 1981, blind persons in Muenster, West Germany, can hear a 6-min tape recording of news from the daily newspaper made available from the Westphalan Organization for the Blind and the telephone company. Each day, local journalists compile synopses of the news for a dial-in service. A Swedish editor reports that the output from compositor's tapes of his daily newspaper, *the Goetebergs–Posten,* is translated into electronic braille and transmitted to an FM radio station for broadcasting within a 130 km radius. A receiver unit at the subscriber's home would pick up the nightly transmission, usually between 1:00 and 2:00 p.m., and record it onto a disc or tape for later reading. Using a cassette braille reader terminal, the subscriber can easily find everything in the print edition, including the classified ads as well as radio and television programming. Technological cost breakthroughs are required to reduce the enormous cost of the reader terminal.

In some areas around the country, radio transmission of local newspapers is an important information source. Using both professionals and volunteers, these radio stations broadcast news, interpretive reports, and other topical material to handicapped persons with specially adapted radio receivers. Most use a public radio FM subchannel (SCA) to broadcast current and local information to blind and physically handicapped people in their communities. Specially tuned receivers separate the SCA signal from that of the main channel. Some of the services transmit on the main channel of an AM or FM station.

The first radio reading service was established in 1969 by C. Stanley Potter, the director of Services to the Blind and Visually Handicapped in Minnesota. Today there are more than 85 such stations in the United States and Canada. An organization, Radio Reading Services for the Blind and Other Visually Handicapped Persons, Inc., was incorporated in 1977 for the purpose of encouraging the establishment and operation of reading services and to share technical, fiscal, consumer relations, and program information. National Public Radio has organized a unit, Services for the Print-Handicapped, which is responsible for the production and distribution of programming for radio reading services.

A remote information access experiment, the Telebook, was conducted in 1977 by the Library of Congress and the Mitre Corporation which would give readers immediate access to reading materials by dialing a central, toll-free telephone number, and requesting that talking books or magazines be played via telephone or special FM radio receivers. A feature being tested was automatic indexing which allowed the operator to mark a spot when a reader wished to stop in the middle of a book or magazine and resume reading later. Reader responses are in the process of evaluation; the results are expected to have a significant effect on future planning.

P. Hearing Impairments

Advances in technology have resulted in new devices and adaptations of devices that enable severely hearing impaired to communicate. According to a 1977 National Health Survey published in February 1981 by the National Center for Health Statistics, 16.2 million persons were estimated to have hearing impairments, or a rate of 76.4 per 1000 persons. This figure includes tinnitus (ringing in the ears). Approximately one-half of hearing impairments involve only one ear. Overall, the rate of hearing impairments increases with age and ranges from 14.3 per 1000 for persons under 17 years of age to 385.5 per 1000 for persons 17 years and older. According to the National Health Survey, approximately 236,000 Americans are totally deaf, and an estimated 20,000,000 are partially deaf.

In both blindness and deafness, the impact of the handicap is directly related to the age at which the loss of sight or hearing occurs. In the deaf young person, potential barriers to language development are present, particularly in speech development. Deaf persons must accommodate themselves to speech as a primary communication medium even though many deaf persons may prefer to communicate with sign language and finger spelling. Those who develop engineered devices, therefore, are working to improve both speech production and reception for hearing impaired persons (Elliott, 1978, p. 296).

The hearing aid, perhaps the best known of speech reception aids for the hearing impaired, may be of little or no benefit. A variety of speech display systems have been available for some time and have been developed as adjuncts to lip reading. This is accomplished by complementing the information available on the lips of the talker in such a way as to make basic phoneme elements or symbols explicit. One such device, the Upton Speechreading Aid, is often referred to as the "Upton eyeglass." This speech-reading aid consists of tie clip microphone, which picks up speech sounds, and a computer-like analyzer, the size of a small transistor radio. As described by the inventor, Herbert W. Upton, the electronic analyzer extracts certain sounds that are difficult to distinguish on the lips of the talker. These sounds are shown on a six-bar light-emitting diode mounted on the right bow of the wearer's glasses. Mounted directly in front of the eye on the eyeglass lens is $1/25$-in. mirror, an optical element curved to cause the LED pattern to be in focus to the wearer; in fact, when the wearer looks at the speaker, the mirror reflects the light pattern and causes it to appear as if it were on the speaker's lips. The wearer uses the normal lip movements of the talker, supplemented by the light pattern to lip read. Bars of the light pattern light up according to the sounds being made—for example, S, SH sounds, or plosives like T, D, or K, as well as front, middle, or back vowels.

Since 1969, Gallaudet College has been working on the development of a speech-analyzing lipreading aid based on the principles of Cued Speech, called the Automatic Cuer or Autocuer. In Cued Speech, eight finger configurations for consonants and four hand positions for vowels (varying in proximity to the talker's face) are used in synchronization with speech to produce, with the hand and lips in combination, visually different patterns for each syllable of the spoken language. The inventor of Cued Speech, R. Orin Cornett, states that it is important to remember that not all sounds used in our spoken language are distinguishable from each other on the lips of the speaker; many syllables have "look alikes," such as "mee" (as in meet), "bee," and "pea." Cued Speech, based on the pronunciation and not the spelling of the words, was originated for the purpose of clarifying lipreading patterns that would otherwise be ambiguous to a deaf person.

The Autocuer is designed to provide to the deaf wearer the cues of manually cued speech, operating automatically from the sound of the speaker's voice. The Autocuer utilizes a microphone to generate a signal which is filtered, preshaped, and delivered to a small computer about the size of a small book. The resulting data is used to segment the speech string into phonemes, assign them to cue groups, and present the information as a visual pattern on an eyeglass lens. The cues are seen as a virtual image in the air approximately 4 ft in front of the wearer, and, like the Upton eyeglass, the wearer can, by positioning his head, place the cues on the face of the speaker near the lips. Research is currently underway to further miniaturize the device. It is anticipated that subsequent to field tests, the production model, microcomputer and all, can be placed within the bows of the wearer's glasses (Cornett, 1981).

Some advances in technology have provided deaf–blind persons with the means to participate in distant communication. For example, the Royal Institute of Technology in Sweden is testing a terminal system for two-way transmission of braille messages. The braille can also be converted into print. In England, John Gill of the Research Unit for the Blind at the University of Warwick, earlier in connection with tangible graphic aids, has developed a new system to provide braille output from the existing Prestel information system. Prestel, a system operated by British Telecom, transmits data over a telephone line for display on a modified TV monitor. Gill's system is designed for use by deaf–blind individuals and uses microcomputer technology to transfer data from the Prestel system, and then reformats and translates it into contracted braille as embossed data on paper.

IV. BIBLIOGRAPHIC CONTROL

Efforts now underway will ultimately provide a single source for locating single-copy volunteer-produced material scattered across the country. Through the use of computer technology, these bibliographic records can now be centralized and the books more expeditiously made available for handicapped persons who need them. The first edition of the computer–output–microfiche (COM) catalog, *Reading Material for the Blind and Physically Handicapped,* along with microfiche readers, was distributed by the Library of Congress to network libraries early in 1977. The database is maintained in machine-readable form which is easily edited and updated. The catalog now includes all titles mass-produced since the early 1960s and many titles produced by volunteers for the LC collections and individual libraries. Included, too, are entries of recorded textbook material produced by Recording for the Blind.

Following recent successful tests, permanent arrangements were made to have the catalog database available for online searching on a nationwide computer system. The database has been used to prepare bibliographies, locate books, and compile management information.

The computerized bibliographic system now being developed will, when completed, enable a librarian anywhere in the country to determine the availability of a title in a format usable by a handicapped reader. The system will also conserve the time and energy of volunteers by preventing inadvertent duplication of materials.

Automation is used also to link the four multistate service centers described earlier (p. 251). In 1979, the centers were linked by on-line computers to each other and to the National Library Service. This enables material requests to be addressed with greater ease and to achieve a faster turnaround time—the time between order and receipt of a book by a reader. A speed up in the turnaround time can be accomplished through machine-readable order forms.

V. INTERNATIONAL COOPERATION

Many countries are seeking closer contact through their public libraries for the blind with their counterparts in the United States. Until 1977, libraries serving blind readers had neither organized internationally nor entered into formal multinational agreements to exchange reading materials or to standardize original products or equipment so that exchange is possible. Frank Kurt Cylke, Director of the National Library Service, made a "Proposal for International Coordination of Library Service for Blind and Physically Handicapped Individuals" to the meeting of the Section on Libraries in Hospitals of the International Federation of Library Associations and Institutions (IFLA), held in September 1977 in Brussels. The proposal called for the development of common technical and service guidelines for materials in braille and recorded formats. According to the proposal, among five areas that required immediate attention was the need to develop a "coordinated application of existing and future technologies to production requirements" (Cylke, 1978, p. 70).

Standardization of audio technology was considered by IFLA along with policies to promote sharing and increased production of braille and sound recordings of books and magazines at a conference of the international professional community in Boston in June 1980 (held in conjunction with the Helen Keller Centennial Congress).

The work of IFLA assumes importance in that, in addition to present achievements, it also holds promise for future international agreements to solve problems posed by the lack of technical uniformity.

VI. CONCLUSION

While the printed medium remains the most important instrument in the present age of electronic information technology, advances continue to offer new ways for disabled persons to directly obtain access to information sources previously denied them.

Federal legislation enacted since 1973 encourages handicapped persons to function as independent, contributing citizens and focuses public awareness on the needs of these individuals for reading and information materials and other services.

Over the years, blind and handicapped persons have become more mobile, more integrated in community life and activity. The technological advances carry significant implications for this group, not only for information access, but to overcome or compensate for specific handicaps.

Research needs are relatively easy to identify, but solutions take time, Organizations, government agencies, business, industry, and private foundations have addressed the problem. Lois L. Elliott has observed that many of the major advances in information access and communication aids have been made by persons who have been motivated to seek improvements to assist a disabled member of their own family. An example is the work on the Optacon developed by a father to assist his blind daughter. On occasion, handicapped persons themselves have brought about important innovations. One such example is the Upton eyeglass, the work of a deaf engineer. Many such new developments in this area may be characterized by an intense desire to aid a handicapped person as contrasted to the approach that sets out to reach an objective, nonpersonal problem to develop a device that solves a problem, for example, in industrial plant processes (Elliott, 1978, p. 298).

An awareness of research and development, and knowledge of currently available resources, will aid librarians and others concerned with information to provide the best possible service to their handicapped patrons.

REFERENCES

American Foundation for the Blind (1980). "Reading With Print Limitations." 5 vols. American Foundation for the Blind, New York.
Berryman, J. (1981). Computerized braille production: A producer's viewpoint. *Journal of Visual Impairment and Blindness* 75, 261–264.
Clark, L., ed. (1963). "Proceedings of the International Congress on Technology and Blindness, New York City, 18–22 June 1962." 3 vols. American Foundation for the Blind, New York.
Cornett, R. (1981). "The Autocuer." Gallaudet College, Washington, D.C.
Cornett, R. (undated). "Cued Speech: What and Why." Gallaudet College, Washington, D.C.
Cylke, F. K. (1981). Library service for the blind and handicapped. *In* "American Library Association Yearbook, a Review of Library Events 1981" 6, pp. 84–87. Additional articles may be found in the following volumes: 1 (1976), 115–116; 2 (1977), 66; 3 (1978), 69–71; 4 (1979), 61–63; 5 (1980), 85–88.
Cylke, F. K., Deschere, A., Evensen, R., and Gibson, M. (1981). Research to develop information service aids and programs for handicapped individuals. *Drexel Library Quarterly* 16, 59–72.
Cylke, F. K., Wintle, M. J., and Hagle, A. D. (1980). Talking books. *In* "Encyclopedia of Library and Information Science" 30, 70–95. Marcel Dekker, New York.
"Dorland's Illustrated Medical Dictionary" (1974). 25th ed. W. B. Saunders, Philadelphia.
Dufton, R., ed. (1966). "Proceedings of the International Conference on Sensory Devices for the Blind, London, June 1966." St. Dunstan's, London.
Elliott, L. L. (1978). Development of communication aids for the deaf. *Human Factors* 20, 295–305.
Foulke, E. (1981). Impact of science and technology on the early years. *Journal of Visual Impairment and Blindness* 75, 101–108.
Gill, J. M. (1974). Tactual mapping. American Foundation for the Blind *(AFB) Research Bulletin* 28, 57–80.
Glaser, E. L. (1980). Modern technologies applied to communications for the blind. *In* "AAWB Annual 1978–1980," pp. 51–59. American Association of Workers for the Blind, Washington, D.C.
Lauer, H., and Mowinski, L. Communication aids for the blind. *In* "AAWB Annual 1979–1980," pp. 60–72. American Association of Workers for the Blind, Washington, D.C.
McCarroll, J. (1981). Innovative technology-improving access to information for disabled persons. *Drexel Library Quarterly* 16, 73–80.
Mann, R. W. (1974). Technology and human rehabilitation: Prostheses for sensory rehabilitation and/or sensory substitution. *In* "Advances in Biomedical Engineering" 4, pp. 209–353. Academic Press, New York.
Market Facts, Inc. (1981). "Readership characteristics and attitudes: Service to blind and physically handicapped users." Library of Congress, National Library Service for the Blind and Physically Handicapped, Washington, D.C.
National Society for the Prevention of Blindness (1980). Data analysis. *In* "Vision Problems in the U.S." 2, 4–5. National Society for the Prevention of Blindness, New York.
Strong, W. J. (1975). Speech aids for the profoundly/severely hearing impaired: Requirements, overview, and projections. *Volta Review* 77, 536–56.
Talking computer terminal promises deliveries! (1981). *Modern Materials Handling* 36 (6 October), 58–59.

Terrant, S. W. (1980). Computers in publishing. *Annual Review of Information Science and Technology* **15,** 191–219.
U.S. Bureau of the Census (1980). "Statistical Abstract of the United States." Government Printing Office, Washington, D.C.
U.S. Congress, House of Representatives, Committee on Science and Technology (1979). "Hearings on Research Programs to Aid the Handicapped, 22–23 September, 1976." Government Printing Office, Washington, D.C.
U.S. Library of Congress, National Library Service for the Blind and Physically Handicapped (1980). "Reading Machines for the Blind, a Bibliography." Reference Circular 80-3.
U.S. Library of Congress, National Library Service for the Blind and Physically Handicapped (1981). *News* **12,** Nos. 1–6.
U.S. National Center for Health Statistics (1981). "Prevalence of Selected Impairments 1977." DHHS Publication (PHS) 81-1562, National Health Survey, Series 10, No. 134. Government Printing Office, Washington, D.C.
Upton, H. W. (1974). Upton electronics aids to speech/hearing. *Bell Helicopter News* **22** (April), unpaged.

Beyond the Master's Program: Library Schools and Continuing Education of Library, Media, and Information Professionals

JOHN A. MCCROSSAN
University of South Florida

I.	Introduction	278
II.	Definitions	279
III.	Amount and Types of Continuing Education Opportunities Offered by Library Schools	280
	A. Introduction	280
	B. Activities Planned Specifically as Continuing Education for Professionals	280
	C. Sixth-Year Post-Master's Programs	282
	D. Doctoral Programs	283
	E. Traditional Library School Courses	284
IV.	The Relationship of Other Agencies to Library School Continuing Education Activities	285
	A. Introduction	285
	B. Responsibilities of Others for Continuing Education of Librarians	286
	C. Financial and Other Assistance to Library Schools for Continuing Education	287
	D. Coordinating Responsibilities Among Different Types of Agencies	289
V.	Priority for Continuing Education	289
VI.	Conclusions	291
	References	291

I. INTRODUCTION

Historically, library schools have been involved mainly—many times almost exclusively—in preservice education rather than in continuing education of professionals. This situation is beginning to change, and may change substantially in the future. As the job market for beginning librarians has tightened, enrollment of students in the accepted entry-level training program—the Master's degree program—has dropped. It seems likely that this trend will continue or at least that there will be no significant increases in Master's degree enrollment in the foreseeable future. Therefore, library schools will need to redeploy their resources from training beginning librarians to other activities, such as continuing education of those who already have professional positions.

Even more important, as librarians' work changes and becomes more and more complex, continuing education opportunities will be more essential. There may have been a time when a Master's degree was a terminal degree for librarians, and perhaps they could function fairly well in their positions throughout their professional lives with only a minimum of additional education or training. That time, however, has long since passed. Rapid changes in library and information science require the average professional to continue education throughout life. The development of automated data bases and their increasing use in libraries illustrates only one area in which professional librarians need to be trained since knowledge gained in their Master's program rapidly becomes obsolescent.

It is true that library schools are not the only agency currently providing continuing education for library professionals. Other agencies include state library agencies and library associations. However, library schools play a unique role in that they are generally the only organizations that offer work leading to the awarding of academic credits and degrees for the study of librarianship. Librarians do not always want or need such credentials, but many times they do. Moreover, library schools, unlike other library-related agencies, are dedicated mainly to instruction. Each school employs a number of faculty who are specialists in various aspects of librarianship and spend much of their lives teaching students about those specialties. Being very experienced professional educators, they are expert in developing educational programs—their goals, objectives, and methods of evaluation. Therefore, it seems logical that the library schools should play a major role in efforts to upgrade continuing education of librarians.

This chapter explores the role of library schools in the continuing education of library, media, and information professionals. It deals with such matters as the type and quantity of continuing education efforts of library schools, the relationship of other agencies to library school continuing education programs, priorities the schools give to these programs, and some suggestions for change.

II. DEFINITIONS

Sometimes, when continuing education in general or specifically the continuing education of library professionals is discussed, problems of definition arise and much time and effort is spent in attempting to devise a definition acceptable to all. One of the problems is concerned with distinguishing continuing education from related activities, such as preservice education, in-service training, and staff development. Another problem relates to the breadth of definition of continuing education; some would say that the term should not include formal education leading to an advanced degree, while others would favor a broader definition.

However fruitless an attempt at a universally acceptable definition may be, it is important to explain how the term is used for a particular purpose. In this paper, continuing education is defined to include all education which librarians acquire from library schools after they have received the Master's degree in librarianship. The Master's degree program is excluded since that degree is considered to be preservice education necessary for entrance into the filed, the large majority of beginning professional positions requiring the Master's. Programs which library schools offer primarily as continuing education for professionals are included: special workshops, seminars, and institutes. Regular credit courses taken by professionals and advanced degree programs are also included. The reason for using such a broad definition is that it is the purpose of this paper to explore the role and contribution of library schools to continuing education of professionals and not simply to discuss certain types of activities which are usually labeled "continuing education." Since credit courses and advanced degree programs have potential to contribute substantially to the continuing education of professionals, it is essential to include discussion of them.

The term "library school" is used here to refer to graduate schools offering programs in library–information science. As of October 1981, there were 69 such programs in the United States and Canada accredited by the American Library Association. In addition to these programs in schools which are full members of the Association of American Library Schools, there are a number of other programs, of which 34 hold associate membership in the Association (Association of American Library Schools, 1981b). Except as noted otherwise, this paper focuses on the accredited programs.

Throughout this paper, the term "library" or one of its derivatives is used to refer to the variety of library, media, and information specialties for which library schools prepare students. It is also assumed that the term "librarian" refers to the professional library, media, or information specialist, not to support or clerical staff. The continuing education and training needs of the latter types of personnel are extremely important, but it is the purpose of this report to deal only with professionals. In any case, library schools rarely only would provide continuing education programs for support or clerical staff.

III. AMOUNT AND TYPES OF CONTINUING EDUCATION OPPORTUNITIES OFFERED BY LIBRARY SCHOOLS

A. Introduction

Library school continuing education activities can be divided into two major types. One type consists of programs planned specifically as continuing education for library professionals: workshops, conferences, and institutes. The other type is made up of programs not specifically planned as continuing education but which librarians can and frequently do use in their continuing education—sixth-year post-Master's programs, doctoral programs, and traditional degree program courses taken as nondegree-seeking students.

B. Activities Planned Specifically as Continuing Education for Professionals

Programs which library schools offer especially as continuing education for library professionals have been categorized as workshops, institutes, seminars, conferences, forums, colloquia, and short courses in the annual statistical report dealing with library education Association of American Library Schools (AALS) (1981c).

Sometimes these programs are open to students in a degree program, but more often they are aimed mainly at professionals and do not result in the receipt of academic credit or a degree. Increasingly, however, continuing education units (CEU's) are offered for such educational experiences, one CEU being awarded for each 10 contact hours of participation in a continuing education activity under qualified instruction.

A review of the annual AALS statistical report reveals extensive continuing education activities in library schools. The 1981 report, which includes statistics for 1979–1980, indicates that 56 of the 69 library schools accredited by the American Library Association offered a total of 502 continuing education opportunities with a total enrollment of 20,611, an average of 9 offerings and 368 students per school. Workshops were by far the most popular type of program, accounting for 170 events or 34% of the total. Colloquia were the next most popular type, with 83 colloquia offered by the responding schools. Almost twice as many schools offered workshops as any other type of activity (Table 1).

There was a wide variation in the number of offerings of the different library schools, ranging from one offering in three schools to 33 in one school. A large majority of offerings—359—were given on campus. Twenty were offered off campus at a university facility, 106 took place off campus at another location, and 17 used other modes of delivery, such as teleconferences.

Few schools targeted their continuing education programs to particular groups of librarians or had subject emphasis priorities. Seventy-eight percent of the schools indicated no priority group beyond professionals in general. Sixty-seven percent indicated they had no subject emphasis priority, and a wide variation in subject emphasis was noted by the 33% which had such a priority. Seventeen priority topics were listed by one or more of those schools. These topics were widely varied, including automation, children's literature and services, management, mainstreaming, networking, and statistics. Of the 63 schools responding to the question, 50 indicated that institutional CEU's were available for at least part of the continuing education program.

TABLE 1
Type of Continuing Education Opportunities Provided by Library Schools

	Number of schools reporting	Number of events held	Total enrollment	Mean number per institution
Institutes	23	45	2720	1.95
Seminars	19	3	1161	1.74
Workshops	41	170	6688	4.15
Conferences	19	29	2964	1.52
Forums	6	43	1235	7.16
Colloquia	19	83	3032	4.37
Short courses	19	68	1010	3.58
Other	5	31	1810	6.2
		502	20,611	

In addition to the full members of the AALS, 13 of the 31 associate members responded to the questions on continuing education, with eight reporting 28 events with a total enrollment of 996 students. The primary target groups of their continuing education efforts were reported to be school library media personnel and public librarians. This is not surprising since such programs usually emphasize preparation of school media specialists and sometimes train librarians for small public libraries. There was no consistent pattern of subject specialization among the programs. Young adult literature was the only subject emphasis listed by more than one of them.

C. Sixth-Year Post-Master's Programs

Thirty-nine of the 70 ALA-accredited library schools offer sixth-year post-Master's programs leading to a degree, certificate, or diploma (American Library Association, 1982). The programs, about one year in length, are typically designed for practitioners who want to improve professional competencies.

For many years, the only advanced degree program in librarianship was the doctoral program, which was offered at a very few institutions. As of 1948, only Illinois, Chicago, and Michigan offered a doctoral program in librarianship (Asheim, 1975). Thus, very few librarians had an opportunity to take advanced degree work. Moreover, pursuing a doctorate was not nearly so essential or even desirable as it has become since. The scarcity of librarians made it much less compelling to secure a doctoral degree in order to be able to enter the field of library education or to obtain a top-level library administrative position. Also, since doctoral work is generally heavily theoretical and research-oriented, it did not meet the needs of many practitioners who wanted continuing education to improve their job-related competencies.

The first post-Master's program was initiated at Columbia University in 1961, and the number increased dramatically to a total of 23 by 1974 (Rogers, 1975). As noted, the number increased to 39 by 1981. In the early years, many library educators and librarians thought that the sixth-year program would become the major type of continuing education offered by library schools. Some felt it would be ideal for the many librarians who presumably wanted to pursue advanced study but did not want to enter a doctoral program (Harrison, 1968; Danton, 1970; Kortendick and Stone, 1971). Kortendick and Stone recommended that the post-Master's program be the primary method for librarians to upgrade their skills to meet the changing information needs of society. They discovered that a relatively small percentage of respondents had taken courses in librarianship since the receipt of the Master's degree, but a large proportion indicated that they planned to take such work in the future. Fifteen percent had taken six or more credit hours since receiving the Master's degree, but 51% indicated they would enroll in a course in the future; 33% said they were interested in a one-year post-Master's program.

Since then, the sixth-year program has met with mixed success. Some librarians who have pursued it indicate that they have learned a great deal that is useful in their continuing education. In terms of numbers enrolled, however, it would generally not be considered successful. In one study, it was discovered that the enrollment in each school ranged from 1 to 16 and that a total of only 125 students were enrolled in all 19 schools responding (Rogers, 1975). A 1979 survey found that each program had an average of only 5–15 students and that full-time students were a rarity (Burgess, 1979).

The typical sixth-year post-Master's program consists of about 24–36 semester hours of work, usually with about 10–12 hours devoted to independent study, so that the student, who is usually quite experienced, can do in-depth study of a topic of particular interest. Many of the programs require specialization in an area such as administration, automation, service to special groups, and other topics of value to practitioners. This does not mean that theoretical issues are excluded from the programs, because they certainly constitute a very important part of them. However, there is generally much emphasis on practical matters related to day-to-day library and information work.

Why does a program with such great potential attract so few students? Undoubtedly, one of the major reasons is that the reward system in most libraries does not take into account a staff member's pursuing a sixth-year program. School systems offer salary and other incentives to teachers and librarians who take work beyond a Master's degree, but few public, academic, or special libraries do so because of limited budgets and (perhaps) lack of understanding of the value of such a program on the part of library administrators. Since a librarian must spend a great deal of time, money, and effort on such a program, it would seem that libraries should give full consideration to giving employees tangible rewards for doing so. This, of course, assumes that a given employee pursues studies that administrators believe would assist in job performance.

D. Doctoral Programs

Although doctoral programs are not generally referred to as continuing education, they do provide much of continuing education value to library professionals. In some cases, a doctoral program may be considered both entry level and continuing education for the same person. For example, an experienced reference librarian on sabbatical may be greatly increasing knowledge of reference service and related areas during doctoral study and, at the same time, may be developing new skills with the thought of possibly becoming a library school faculty member after receiving the doctorate.

Like sixth-year programs, doctoral programs in librarianship are quite small in number. As of October 1981, 22 accredited library schools offered work leading towards a doctorate (American Library Association, 1982). The programs have very small enrollments, with the average university awarding no more than two or three doctoral degrees a year. In 1980, the latest year for which statistics are available, the total enrollment of doctoral students in American and Canadian library schools was only 515 and only 66 degrees were awarded during that year (AALS, 1981c).

One unresolved problem is that of financial incentives for practicing librarians who have acquired a doctorate to remain in work with the public or in technical services. Most librarians who obtain doctorates become library administrators or library school faculty members, thus depriving the public and technical service areas of highly motivated and highly qualified people.

E. Traditional Library School Courses

Practicing librarians who have a Master's degree in librarianship and are not enrolled in an advanced degree program may take regular Master's or advanced graduate library school courses as continuing education. Although there is little statistical evidence of how often this occurs, it is apparently quite frequent. Library school faculty members report it is not at all unusual to have one or more such librarians enrolled in a regular class. As noted above, in one study 15% of the professionals responding indicated they had taken 6 or more credit hours since receiving the Master's degree, and 51% said they planned to take a course in the future (Kortendick and Stone, 1971).

It is not difficult to understand the value of such regular courses as continuing education for practicing professionals, especially courses which given professionals have not had before or courses covering areas in which there has been much recent change. For example, most professionals have not had a course in automated information services. A cataloging course which covers the revised Anglo–American cataloging rules may be very beneficial to librarians who had the same course before the publication of the rules.

The normal frequency of class meetings—two or three times a week during normal working hours—may present serious problems to the working professional. Library schools have sought to meet this problem in a variety of ways: offerings at night, on weekends, and in a collapsed time frame (two full days weekly for several weeks).

Library schools are also giving more courses off campus in locations convenient to groups of students. Many universities have considerably simplified their registration procedures so that students in off-campus settings can register for a particular course during the first class meeting.

Library schools are attempting to facilitate participation by practicing professionals in continuing education. The AALS strongly encourages library schools to do all they can in this regard. The statement on continuing education adopted by the AALS Board in 1981 strongly recommends that library schools offer both short educational programs, such as workshops and conferences, and also regular courses at times and places which are convenient to prospective continuing education participants (AALS, 1981a).

IV. THE RELATIONSHIP OF OTHER AGENCIES TO LIBRARY SCHOOL CONTINUING EDUCATION ACTIVITIES

A. Introduction

A number of agencies, in addition to library schools, have responsibility for continuing education of librarians. Responsibilities of the various organizations are discussed in a number of reports (Hiatt, 1971; Warncke, 1973; Stone, 1974; Taylor, 1978).

While it is not the purpose of this report to review in any detail the role of other continuing education providers, it is important that their activities be noted in order to consider the library-school role in its proper perspective. Moreover, some agencies provide significant assistance to library schools to help them in their continuing education efforts. Sometimes this assistance is in the form of financial support such as that given by the federal government. At other times, it may consist of less tangible but equally important aid. Library associations, for example, provide library schools with an excellent communication link with the profession and also sometimes collect information on the types of continuing education needed or assist library science faculty in planning or delivering such programs. Because there are a number of different types of providers of continuing education for librarians, the question sometimes arises as to whether responsibility for different types of programs should be assigned to different types of providers. This question has a number of ramifications and needs to be explored in some depth.

B. Responsibilities of Others for Continuing Education of Librarians

Other organizations which provide continuing education opportunities for librarians include the following:

1. library associations—national, regional, state, and local
2. the federal government
3. state library agencies
4. libraries, library systems, and other organizations which employ librarians
5. units of academic institutions other than library schools

Regular association conferences and conventions often have continuing education value for librarians, especially parts of those meetings which deal in depth with some topic of interest. Moreover, some associations also organize workshop-type programs of varying length up to three or four days. The most significant federal role—providing grant funds to be used by library schools for continuing education—is discussed in Section IV C.

State library agency continuing education programs have a long history. Workshops developed by state library consultants have traditionally been aimed mainly at public library personnel and, more recently, at the staffs of both public libraries and state institution libraries. The education program provides one method for state agencies to fulfill their role of developing and improving library services throughout the states. Both those librarians who have Master's degrees in library science and those who have less training participate in these activities because of the wide range of educational background of public and institutional librarians.

Employers play two different kinds of very critical roles in the continuing education and development of librarians on their staffs. First, employers can provide incentives to participate, such as released time to attend classes and credit for such participation on performance ratings. Second, many libraries organize educational in-service training programs of their own for their staff members.

A number of units of academic institutions, in addition to library schools, have various types of continuing education useful to library professionals. These include departments which offer courses in business, adult education, public administration, guidance, and computer science. Occasionally, such a department will produce a workshop or a course especially for librarians; much more frequently, however, librarians will take a course or workshop in the subject area of the department.

C. Financial and Other Assistance to Library Schools for Continuing Education

Library School offerings of continuing education programs are limited by funding problems. Because universities seldom have major funds available for non-credit programs, it is usually necessary to seek support from outside funding agencies. For a number of years, this situation has been alleviated by grants from the federal government and, to a considerably lesser extent, from other sources, especially state library agencies. Such funding is discussed in a number of places (Stone, *et al.*, 1974; McCrossan, 1978; Mounce, 1978; Taylor, 1978; Conroy, 1980).

The major federal government program which has assisted library schools is the Higher Education Act Title II B. While modest in size, Title II B funds have been invaluable to library school continuing education efforts since grants were first made in 1968. The program supports both fellowships and institutes. Fellowships are awarded for full-time study in degree programs. Institute grants cover costs of programs ranging from a week or so to more than a year. Typically, each institute is devoted to study of a topic of interest to a group of practicing librarians and is designed to improve their professional competencies. In the early years, funding was relatively generous, and a sizable proportion of library schools received grants. In recent years, funding has dropped dramatically, especially funding for institutes, according to annual summaries of the program (*Bowker Annual*, 1969–1981 editions). In 1968, 66 institutes were funded; in 1971, the number had dropped to 38; 24 were funded in 1979 and none in 1980.

A number of state library agencies have allocated Library Services and Construction Act (LSCA) funds for support of continuing education activities within given states (Taylor, 1978). Library schools receiving such support have produced workshops and short courses covering priority areas such as services for minorities, services for the handicapped, and improvement of library administrative practices. Since LSCA has traditionally listed public libraries as its first priority, and more recently state institutional libraries as well, activities funded with LSCA money are usually directed primarily at public or institutional libraries and librarians. Unfortunately, the amount of LSCA funds has remained about the same for a number of years. As costs of programs and demands for funds have increased greatly, a larger portion of money is used to support library services of local libraries or library systems. Therefore, the amount available for other activities, such as continuing education, has had to be allocated in competition with other strong demands.

The major contribution of library associations—national, regional, state, and local—to library schools in continuing education is the provision of communication links to the profession and the assistance of members in the planning of programs. The 1982 Florida Library Association conference was planned to involve a unique type of cooperation between library schools and a state library association (Seltzer, 1981) with the provision of CEU's and a certificate to participants in certain educational programs at the conference. The CEU's will be administered under the auspices of the library school of the University of South Florida. For a small charge, the University of South Florida will issue a certificate to each participant indicating how many CEU's have been earned. A permanent record will be maintained at the university so the participant can request a copy of it at a later date. Both of the two Florida library schools accredited by the American Library Association—at the University of South Florida and at Florida State University—will present major programs at the conference for which CEU's can be earned by participants.

The major professional organization of library educators—the AALS—provides important leadership on continuing education as well as other library school activities. Association conferences regularly have meetings dealing with continuing education, and the association has adopted important policy statements on the matter. The statement of 1981 is very strong and specific in content (AALS, 1981a). It indicates that the library schools and the association must take a leadership role in continuing education for the entire profession. Among other recommendations, the statement specifies that each library school should

1. Develop continuing education goals and objectives and design a total continuing education program of regular courses and special short continuing education offerings
2. Set priorities in continuing education
3. Assign responsibility for coordination of continuing education
4. Incorporate practitioner input into continuing education decisions

The Continuing Library Education Network and Exchange (CLENE) has stimulated development of activities by various providers, including library schools. A good summary of its activities is that of Stone (1978). Dating from 1975, CLENE is a national organization devoted to promotion of continuing education of library and information personnel, with activities that include

1. Sponsoring special conferences and regular meetings on continuing education
2. Issuing a newsletter
3. Producing a regular list of continuing education opportunities available
4. Sponsoring studies of continuing education
5. Developing a national recognition system for continuing education which will provide a systematic method to award and keep records of student participation in noncredit continuing education offerings

D. Coordinating Responsibilities Among Different Types of Agencies

The question of assigning responsibilities for different kinds of continuing education to different agencies has been discussed in a number of sources including Warncke (1973) and Stone (1978). Should one agency concentrate on certain kinds of activities leaving other types to other agencies? For example, should library associations concentrate on workshop-type activities on practical aspects of librarianship and leave the more scholarly, theoretical programs to library schools? Should one agency concentrate on one subject area leaving other areas to other agencies? Since a library school is generally the only kind of agency which can offer continuing education activities which may lead to the receipt of credits and degrees for study of librarianship, should the school therefore concentrate on those types of programs and leave non-credit activities to other agencies?

To summarize, the consensus of the profession at this point seems to be that library schools, like other continuing education agencies, should provide a variety of types of continuing education offerings in whatever formats are needed to suit their particular area and clientele. This assumes that the library schools do not neglect to have types of programs for which they are uniquely qualified: those that offer university credits or degrees and those which are theoretical in nature and thus seem quite appropriate to a university setting.

V. PRIORITY FOR CONTINUING EDUCATION

A number of authors have indicated that library schools could give a higher priority to continuing education than they do (Smith, 1977; Bell, 1980; Conant, 1980; Durrance, 1980). However, these same authors indicate that the low priority is probably due, at least to some extent, to factors beyond the library school's control, such as university priorities which favor such traditional activities as the Master's program and faculty research.

A survey of the membership of the AALS dealing with opinions of library school faculty and deans toward a proposed legislative program for library education sheds some light on this topic (Durrance, 1980). Responses to the continuing education question on the survey were positive in that 69% of the respondents indicated their belief that comprehensive continuing education programs for librarians are essential in order for them to develop the expertise recognized as necessary by the White House Conference on Library and Information Services. On the other hand, only 20% assigned continuing education first priority when compared with four other items in the proposed legislative program.

A follow-up analysis (Bell, 1980) of attitudes of library educators to different kinds of continuing education showed that at least 60% of those studied agreed that all of the listed types of activities were appropriate for continuing education in a library school:

1. workshops
2. institutes
3. invited conferences
4. short, intensive, non-credit courses
5. short intensive courses for credit
6. full-length courses designed especially for practitioners
7. regular degree program courses on new technologies
8. regular degree program courses in other areas
9. individualized short-term study projects

A large majority—over 90% of the respondents—approved of workshops and institutes as appropriate for library school continuing education opportunities. A smaller majority approved of the others, but at least 60% approved of all the other types of activities listed above.

Bell (1980) notes that while the attitudes of library school faculty toward continuing education are positive, they are not really very strong. She also argues that in order to determine whether those attitudes are strong enough to affect decision making on continuing education, one also would have to study attitudes toward other programs carried out by library schools.

It it is true that library educators as a group do not give high priority to continuing education, this attitude should not be entirely surprising. As noted, funding for non-traditional types of continuing education activities is usually quite difficult to obtain. Moreover, library schools have many responsibilities, and continuing education is only one. Universities are generally very traditional and change slowly. They are beginning to recognize the value of nontraditional kinds of programs, such as continuing education, but until faculty effort in these areas is sufficiently rewarded, progress will be slow.

VI. CONCLUSIONS

The growing need for continuing education for library professionals and the changing job market indicate that library schools will need to become more involved in continuing education in the future. Since library and information science are rapidly developing and changing, much of the education which professionals receive in the entry-level Master's degree program becomes outdated within a few years and must be supplemented by programs of continuing education. Such education takes a variety of forms and can be pursued in a number of different ways. However, since library schools are the major academic unit which provides education for librarians, they will need to play a very important role in this process.

Economic necessity will also lead library schools to become more involved in continuing education. Up to the present time, the schools have concentrated their efforts mainly on preservice education. However, as the economy has changed, the number of students enrolled in Masters' programs has dropped. For example, in 1973, 6515 Master's degrees were awarded by accredited library schools. By 1979, this figure had dropped to 5139 ("Placements and Salaries" 1969–1981). Of necessity, it seems that library schools will turn to various post-Master's courses, workshops, and programs. Undoubtedly, the Master's program will be an extremely important offering of library schools for many years to come. Continuing education of various kinds, however, will continue to grow in importance in the schools and in the profession.

REFERENCES

American Library Association (1981). "ALA Handbook of Organization, 1981–82." American Library Association, Chicago.
American Library Association (1982). "Graduate Library Education Programs March 1982." American Library Association, Chicago.
Asheim, L. (1975). Trends in library education—United States. In "Advances in Librarianship" 5 (M. J. Voigt, ed.), pp. 147–201. Academic Press, New York.
Association of American Library Schools (1978). AALS/Continuing Education Committee resolution. *College and Research Libraries News* **39**, 236–237.

Association of American Library Schools (1981a). AALS policy statement on continuing library and information science education. *Journal of Education for Librarianship* 21, 351–52.
Association of American Library Schools (1981b). "Directory of the Association of American Library Schools, 1981." Association of American Library Schools, State College, Pennsylvania.
Association of American Library Schools (1981c). "Library Education Statistical Report." Association of American Library Schools, State College, Pennsylvania.
Bell, J. A. (1980). Continuing education attitudes and opinions. *Journal of Education for Librarianship* 40, 81–86.
"Bowker Annual of Library and Book Trade Information" (1969–1981 issues). R. R. Bowker, New York.
Burgess, R. S. (1979). Continuing education. *College and Research Libraries News* 40, 272.
Conant, R. W. (1980). "The Conant Report: A Study of Education for Librarians." MIT Press, Cambridge.
Conroy, B. (1978). "Library Staff Development and Continuing Education: Principles and Practices." Libraries Unlimited, Littleton, Colorado.
Conroy, B., and the Continuing Education Steering Committee (1980). "A Statewide Plan for Continuing Education for Florida Library and Media Personnel." Florida Department of State, Tallahassee, Florida.
Danton, J. P. (1970). "Between M.L.S. and Ph.D.: A Study of Sixth-Year Specialist Programs in Accredited Library Schools." American Library Association, Chicago.
Durrance, J. C., ed. (1980). Continuing education. *Journal of Education for Librarianship* 21, 81.
Galvin, T. J. (1976). Change in education for librarianship. *Library Journal* 101, 273–277.
Hiatt, P. (1971). The educational third dimension, III: Toward the development of a national program for continuing education for library personnel. *Library Trends* 20, 169–183.
Harrison, J. C. (1968). Advanced study; a midatlantic point of view. *In* "Library Education: An International Survey," (L. E. Bone, ed.). Univ. of Illinois Graduate School of Library Science, Urbana, Illinois, pp. 329–336.
Kortendick, J. J., and Stone, E. W. (1971). "Job Dimensions and Educational Needs in Librarianship." American Library Association, Chicago.
McCrossan, J. A. (1967). Education of librarians employed in small public libraries. *Journal of Education for Librarianship* 7, 237–44.
McCrossan, J. A. (1978). Planning and evaluation of library programs throughout the states. *Library Trends* 27, 127–143.
Mounce, M. W. (1978). The education of library development personnel. *Library Trends* 27, 197–208.
National Commission on Libraries and Information Science (1975). "Toward a National Program for Library and Information Services: Goals and for Action." National Commission on Libraries and Information Science, Washington, D.C.
Nelson, J. (1976). Kentucky model for continuing education. *Journal of Education for Librarianship* 16, 129–138.
Placements and salaries (1969–1981). "Bowker Annual of Library and Book Trade Information." R. R. Bowker, New York.
Rogers, A. R. (1975). Report on sixth-year programs in the United States. *Journal of Education for Librarianship* 16, 67–74.
Seltzer, A. M. (1981). Memo from the president. *Forida Libraries* 31, 4.
Smith, B. J. (1977). Status of continuing education for librarians. *Adult Leadership* 25, 293–294.

Stone, E. W. (1974). "Continuing Library Education as Viewed in Relation to Other Continuing Professional Education Movements." American Society for Information Science, Washington, D.C.

Stone, E. W. (1978). Continuing education for librarians in the United States. *In* "Advances in Librarianship" 8 (M. H. Harris, ed.), pp. 241–331. Academic Press, New York.

Stone, E. W. (1980). Continuing professional education. *In* "ALA World Encyclopedia of Library and Information Services." American Library Association, Chicago.

Stone, E. W., Patrick, R. J., and Conroy, B. (1974). "Continuing Library and Information Science Education Final Report to the National Commission on Libraries and Information Science." U.S. Government Printing Office, Washington, D.C. and American Society for Information Science, Washington, D.C.

Taylor, N. B. (1978). The role of state library agencies in continuing education. *Library Trends* **27**, 189–196.

Warncke, R. (1973). Continuing education: whose responsibility? *Minnesota Libraries* **24**, 59–65.

Subject Index

A

Abbreviations, in corporate catalog entries, 165–166
Abstracting services, for librarianship journals, 146–147
Academic libraries
 job analysis and, 56–72
  classification and compensation plans and, 58–60
  interviews and, 63–64
  job descriptions and, 61–62
  job observation or audit and, 64–65
  personnel utilization and job redesign and, 58
  questionnaires and, 62–63
  recruitment and selection and, 56–57
  task analysis and, 65–69
  training and development and, 57–58
 job evaluation in, 73–91
  classification system and, 77
  evaluator-related problems in, 74–75
  factor-comparison system and, 77–78
  factor-related problems and, 73–74
  job factors and, 79–81
  point system and, 78–79
  ranking system and, 76
 personnel planning and utilization in, 48–56
  budget information and, 53
  employee information and, 53–54
  library programs and, 52
  need for, 48–51
  new library programs and, 52–53
  recruitment data and, 51–52
  turnover rates and, 51
 status of librarians in, 26–30
 West African, 201–207
Administration
 in colonial era, 183–185
 after decolonization, 231–233
American Association of Law Libraries, membership of, 21–24
American Library Association, membership of, 13–16
American Society for Information Science, membership of, 16–18
Association for Educational Technology and Communications, membership of, 25–26
Author(s)
 choice of catalog entry for, 153–162

Author(s) *(cont.)*
   corporate, 159–162
   multiple, 154
   single, 153
   of librarianship journals, 134–137, 140–143
     copyright and, 143
     review of manuscript and, 141–142
     time lags in publishing and, 142–143

B

Bibliographic citations, in main-entry catalogs, 152–153
Bibliographic control, for handicapped persons, 271–272
Blindness, *see* Handicapped persons
Book reviewing, for librarianship journals, 145–146
Braille
   computer terminals and, 259–260
   production of, 252–255
Budget, of academic libraries, 53

C

Cassette technology, 265–267
   combination machine and easy-to-use machine, 266–267
   solar power and, 266
   speech compression and, 265–266
Catalog(s), main-entry, 151–172
   bibliographic citations and, 152–153
   catalogs and catalog codes and, 151–152
   choice of entry and, 153–162
   conference publications and, 169–171
   form of entry and, 162–168
   serials and, 168–169
Catalog codes, 151–152
Classification
   job analysis and, 58–60
   job evaluation and, 77
Codes, for main-entry catalog, 151–152
Commentators, choice of catalog entry for monograph and, 157
Compensation plans, job analysis and, 58–60
Compilers, choice of catalog entry for, 154–155
Compositor's tapes for braille, 255
Computer terminals, braille, 259–260
Conference publications, in main-entry catalog, 169–171
Continuing education, 277–293
   amount and types offered, 280–285
     doctoral programs, 283–284
     planned specifically as continuing education for professionals, 280–282
     sixth-year post-master's program, 282–283
     traditional library school courses, 284–285
   definitions and, 279–280
   priority for, 289–291
   relationship of other agencies to library schools, 285–289
     coordinating responsibilities and, 289
     financial and other assistance to library schools and, 287–289
     responsibilities of others, 286–287
Contributors to preexisting works, choice of catalog entry for, 157–158
Copyright, journal articles and, 143
Corporate bodies, in catalog entry
   choice of entry, 159–162
   form of name, 164–168
Culture, West African libraries and, 176–180, 236–238

D

Direct access reading aids, 257–258
Doctoral programs, 283–284

E

Economy, West African libraries and, 234–236
Editor(s) choice of catalog entry for, 155–156
   of librarianship journals, 140–143
     copyright and, 143
     review of manuscripts and, 141–142
     time lags in publishing and, 142–143
Education, *see also* Continuing education
   West African libraries and
     in Colonial era, 190–197
     decolonization and, 201–207, 211–219

Employee information, academic libraries
and, 53–54
Entry(ies), in main-entry catalogs
choice of, 153–162
conference publications and, 169–171
form of, 162–168
serials and, 168–169

F

Factor-comparison system, in job evaluation, 77–78
Financial assistance, for library schools, 287–289

G

Gold Coast Library Board, 211–213
Governmental planning, 99–126
deliberated documents, 119–125
bibliographic chain of, 120–125
deliberative activities, 100–106
executive agencies, 105–106
in general, 100–105
Health Planning and Resources Development, 106–119
authority and charge and, 107–110
plan and, 118–119
process and, 110–118
Guides, to librarianship journals, 129–130

H

Handicapped persons, 247–275
bibliographic control and, 271–272
definition of impairment and, 248–250
international cooperation and, 272–273
resources and services for, 250–271
braille computer terminals, 259–260
braille production and tactile technology, 252–255
cassettes, 265–267
compositor's tapes, 255
direct access reading aids, 257–258
hearing impairments and, 269–271
indexing, 267–268
National Library Service, 250–252
newspapers read on radio, 268–269
Optacon, 259
optical character recognition, 256
optical scanners, 260–261
phonograph-talking book machine, 263–265
recorded encyclopedia, 268
tangible graphic displays, 256–257
tone output reading machines, 261–262
Health Planning and Resources Development (Public Law 96–79), 106–119
authority and charge and, 107–110
plan and, 118–119
process and, 110–118
Hearing impairment, resources and services for, 269–271

I

Indexing, for handicapped persons, 267–268
Indexing services, for librarianship journals, 146–147
Initials, in corporate catalog entries, 165–166
Interviews, in job analysis, 63–64

J

Job analysis
methodology for, 60–72
interviews, 63–64
job descriptions, 61–62
job observation or audit, 64–65
other considerations in, 69–72
questionnaires, 62–63
task analysis, 65–69
personnel functions dependent on, 56–60
classification and compensation plans, 58–60
personnel utilization and job redesign, 58
recruitment and selection, 56–57
training and development, 57–58
Job audit, in job analysis, 64–65
Job descriptions, in job analysis, 61–62
Job evaluation
job factors in, 79–81
in libraries, 81–91

Job evaluation (cont.)
  methodology for, 75–79
    classification system, 77
    factor-comparison system, 77–78
    point system, 78–79
    ranking system, 76
  process of, 73–75
    evaluator-related problems in, 74–75
    factor-related problems in, 73–74
Job factors, in job evaluation, 79–81
Job observation, in job analysis, 64–65
Job redesign, 58
Journals of librarianship, 127–150
  authorship and, 134–137
  book reviewing and, 145–146
  critical reception of, 138–140
  editor and author and, 140–143
    copyright and, 143
    review of manuscripts and, 141–142
    time lags in publishing and, 142–143
  indexing and abstracting services for, 146–147
  interest of profession in writing and, 143–145
  journals, 128–132
    guides to, 129–130
    number of, 128–129
    varieties of, 130–131
  subjects and methodologies of, 132–134

L

Librarians, demographic and economic status of, see Status of librarians
Library of Congress, status of librarians in, 36–37
Library programs, in academic libraries, 52–53
Library science faculty, status of, 37–39
Library work, definitions of, 2–4
Literacy, West African libraries and, 180–183

M

Main-entry catalogs, guide for searching in, 151–172
  bibliographic citations and, 152–153
  catalogs and catalog codes and, 151–152
  choice of entry and, 153–162
    conference publications and, 169–171
    form of entry and, 162–168
    serials and, 168–169
Manuscript review, for journals of librarianship, 141–142
Medical libraries, status of librarians in, 39–40
Monographs, choice of catalog entry for, 153–162
Music Library Association, membership of, 24–25

N

Names, personal, in catalog entry, 163–164
National Library Service, 250–252
Newspapers, read on radio, for handicapped persons, 268–269

O

Optacon, 259
Optical character recognition, 256
Optical scanners, 260–261

P

Personal names, in catalog entry, 163–164
Personnel planning and utilization
  information for, 51–56
    budget information, 53
    employee information, 53–54
    library programs and, 52
    new library programs and, 52–53
    recruitment data, 51–52
    turnover rates, 51
  job analysis and, 58
  need for, 48–51
Phonograph, for handicapped persons, 263–265
Place, corporate catalog entry under, 164–165
Planning, see also Personnel planning and utilization
  governmental, 99–126
    deliberated documents and, 119–125
    deliberative activities in, 100–106
    Health Planning and Resources Development and, 106–119

Subject Index 299

Point system, in job evaluation, 78–79
Post-master's education, 282–283
Public libraries
　status of librarians in, 30–34
　West African, 211–219

Q

Questionnaires, in job analysis, 62–63

R

Radio reading, for handicapped persons, 268–269
Ranking system, in job evaluation, 76
Recorded encyclopedia, 268
Recruitment
　by academic libraries, 51–52
　job analysis and, 56–57
Research needs, West African libraries and
　in Colonial era, 185–190
　decolonization and, 207–211

S

School libraries, status of librarians in, 34–36
Selection of personnel, job analysis and, 56–57
Serials, in main-entry catalog, 168–169
Sixth-year post-master's program, 282–283
Social agencies, West African libraries and, 233–234
Society of American Archivists, membership of, 19–21
Solar powered cassette machines, 266
Special Libraries Association, membership of, 18–19
Speech compression, 265–266
State libraries and agencies, status of librarians in, 36
Status of librarians, 1–45
　association surveys and, 13–26
　　American Association of Law Libraries, 21–24
　　American Library Association, 13–16
　　American Society for Information Science, 16–18
　　Association for Educational Technology and Communications, 25–26
　　Music Library Association, 24–25
　　Society of American Archivists, 19–21
　　Special Libraries Association, 18–19
　definitions of library work and, 2–4
　in institutions, 26–40
　　academic libraries, 26–30
　　Library of Congress, 36–37
　　library science faculty, 37–39
　　medical libraries, 39–40
　　public libraries, 30–34
　　school libraries, 34–36
　　state libraries and agencies, 36
　library work universe and, 4–13
　　comprehensive census analyses and, 4–5
　　new graduates and, 5–13
　　surveys of information professionals and, 40–42

T

Tactile technology, 252–255
Talking book machine, 263–265
Tangible graphic displays, 256–257
Task analysis, in job analysis, 65–69
Time lags, in publishing journal articles, 142–143
Tone output reading machines, 261–262
Training, job analysis and, 57–58
Translator, choice of catalog entry for, 156–157
Turnover rates, in academic libraries, 51

W

West African libraries, 173–245
　colonial era, 183–199
　　colonial context and, 197–199
　　European education and general libraries, 190–197
　　research needs and development and, 185–190
　comparative analysis of, 174–176, 231–240
　　adaptation and innovation and, 238–240
　　administrative organization and, 231–233
　　cultural legacy and, 236–238

West African libraries (*cont.*)
   economic infrastructure and, 234–236
   social agencies and, 233–234
  decolonization and, 199–231
   European library traditions and, 226–231
   higher education and academic libraries, 201–207
   library profession, 219–226
   popular education and public libraries, 211–219
   in postwar period, 199–201
   research needs and library development, 207–211
  geographical and cultural setting of, 176–180
  pre-Colonial era, 180–183
West African Library Association, 223–226
Writing, interest of profession in, 143–145